BIRTHS, DEATHS, & MARRIAGES
FROM EL PASO NEWSPAPERS THROUGH 1885

for
Arizona, Texas, New Mexico,
Oklahoma and Indian Territory

Published for El Paso's
Quadricentennial Celebration
1581–1981

Compiled by the El Paso Genealogical Society
Mrs. Jane Beard

Southern Historical Press, Inc.
Greenville, South Carolina

Copyright 1982
By: The Rev. Silas Emmett Lucas, Jr.

Please direct all correspondence and orders to:

www.southernhistoricalpress.com
or
**SOUTHERN HISTORICAL PRESS, Inc.
PO BOX 1267
375 West Broad Street
Greenville, SC 29601
southernhistoricalpress@gmail.com**

ISBN #0-89308-171-X

Printed in the United States of America

CONTENTS

ACKNOWLEDGEMENTS

Without the help of many people this book could never have been produced. The hours of effort in reading the many reels of microfilm, typing, proof-reading and indexing were a monumental task.

Special thanks and recognition must be extended to the El Paso Public Library, particularly Julienne Sears, current head reference librarian, and Kenneth Wayne Daniel, former head of the department, who have been so cooperative in our research. Also, to the El Paso Branch of the Mormon Genealogical Library and librarian, Mrs. Lovell Lovett for the help we received.

The Sun Publishing Company of El Paso for their donation of supplies and UTEP Library for their cooperation, we wish to express our appreciation.

El Paso Genealogical Society

Mrs. Jane A. Beard, Chairman

FOREWORD

When we started this project we had no
idea what a tremendous job it would become. However, our idea was to try to
bridge the twenty year gap from 1880 -
1900 with as much information as we
could.

Many people came to the Southwest in
search of health - some found it - most
did not. So, many died in this area who
came from all over the United States and
some foreign countries. So we have tried
to list all births, deaths and marriages,
wherever they occurred, that had a Southwestern connection.

There is one major problem in working
from old newspapers - spelling- and here
in the Southwest it is compounded with
Spanish names. The old hand set type
was often mis-sorted so that VELARDE
might come out UELARDE, UFLARDE, or any
other variation of letters and CRUMMING
might be DRUMMING. In addition many
Spanish names were spelled phonetically.

Also, it is important to remember that
there were many towns of the same name
in more than one state or Territory. We
have tried to designate which state
where it could be determined, but some-
times there was nothing to indicate.
Some of these were:
Georgetown, N. M. or Texas
Hillsboro, N. M. or Texas
San Antonio, N. M. or Texas
Socorro, N. M. or Texas
Eddy, N. M. or Texas
Las Vegas, N. M. or Nevada
There were probably others, also.
We have only brought this book through
1885. We hope to bring out future books
in series 1890, 1895, 1900.

NEWSPAPER ABBREVIATIONS

BU	The Bullion
EPDH	El Paso Daily Herald
EPDS	El Paso Daily Star
EPIR	El Paso Evening Inter-Republic
EPMS	El Paso Morning Star
EPT	El Paso Times
LS	Lone Star
MT	Mesilla Times
NTF	Newman's Thirty Four Semi-Weekly
RGR	Rio Grande Republican
SH	El Paso Sunday Herald
TB	The Borderer
TR	The Two Republics

OTHER ABBREVIATIONS

aka	also known as or alias
b	born
bro.	brother
bur.	buried
ch.	child or children
d	died
dau.	daughter
dty.	deputy
fa.	father
hus.	husband
m.	married
M/M	Mr. and Mrs.
mo.	mother
par.	parents
Sher.	Sheriff
sis.	sister
surv.	survivors

THE NAME OF TEXAS

In a recent article published in the North
American Review, Governor Ireland, of Texas, asserts that the word "Texas" means
"welcome", and that on the landing of the
first white men on the coast of Texas, the
Indians greeted them with the exclamation
of "Texas" or "Welcome".

This theory, according to a correspondent
in the Texas Vermerio, is not correct. In
the ancient Spanish archives, stored away
in the land office at Austin, it appears
that certain lands were situated 'en el
pais de los Tejas', or in the county of the
Texas, or Tejas Indians, "x" and "j" being
pronounced alike.

It is well known that the Texas or Tejas
were a tribe of Indians living in the valley of the Rio Grande, who were extermi-
nated or driven off by a more savage tribe.
The word Texas or Tejas is the root of names
of all the Indian tribes in Texas and Mexico. The prefix indicated the locality of
the tribes.

The As-Tejas or Astecs dwelt on the high
lands of Anahuac. Tol-Tejas or Toltecs
lived as far south as Yucatan. The Huas-
Tejas lived on the Gulf coast between Matamoras and Vera Cruz and the Tial-Tejas
were located in the state of Coahuila.

ORIGIN OF THE "LONE STAR"

The Lone Star - 19 Sept. 1885:

In 1849, a gentleman of the long ago, met
at the home of Mr. POLLEY in Bailey's
Prairie, Brazos county, old Governor HENRY
SMITH, provisional governor of the embryo
republic of Texas. In conversation about
the Texas emblem - the five-pointed star -
he gave its Texas origin. He stated that
while provisional governor, it became necessary to send some official documents to
New Orleans. The gentleman who was to take
the documents insisted that they should
have some sort of seal. The provisional
governor had adopted none. Just then someone observed a five-pointed brass button
on the governor's overcoat. It was cut
off immediately and used as a state seal.
Arrived at New Orleans, the newspaper re-
porters, seeing the impression of the five-
pointed brass button in the wax, made it
an emblem for the Lone Star.

El Paso Times - Dec. 10, 1885:

GERONIMO

A Sketch of the Notorious Chief

The great war chief of the Chiriculhuas is not, as supposed, an Apache, but a full-blooded Mexican, born at La Joya on the Rio Grande, fifty miles below Albuquerque. His father, Jose Louis Lobato, was a famous violinist, generally known and referred to as Jose Louis el Musico.

Geronimo was one of a family of five children and the oldest of the boys. Jose Louis, wife and children, resided at Manzano, sixty miles east of Albuquerque, for several years. In the spring of 1858 we had a large wood contract with the government at Albuquerque, and quite vividly remember one morning, just about sunrise, at Coyote Springs, fourteen miles east of Albuquerque, of discovering eighteen Navajo Indians near camp, with 200 mules belonging to Juan Cristobal Armijo, Manuel Barrella and other citizens of the Rio Grande in the act of confiscating our animals. Our mulero succeeded in catching the bell mare, and, mounting her, made camp, all the mules belonging to us except ten following. The Indians, foiled in securing 100 more additional animals, proceeded in a southerly direction, keeping upon the plain.

News went to the military at Albuquerque and three companies of Cavalry, headed by Blas Lucero, who still lives in Albuquerque, as guide, proceeded to cut off the Navajoes, prevent them from crossing the Rio Grande to the west into their own country, and recapture the stolen stock. The troops followed the Rio Grande River down as far as El Sierita, where the road passes from Manzano and Abo Pass to La Joya. The Indians from this point discovered a Mexican carrette coming towards them, driven by two Mexicans, containing two women and five children. Several of the Indians went out to capture the concern, but the men driving made a hard fight for liberty, and a running battle for a distance of three miles was the result. The ammunition of the two men having been exhausted, the Indians closed in and killed them with lances. The oxen were killed for food and the two women - mother and grandmother to Geronimo - himself and four brothers and sisters made captives.

The Navajoes from their lookout position had discovered the long line of brass buttoned soldiery with glittering sabers, and knew exactly where they were. In the night, between the hours of ten and twelve o'clock, the Navajoes made for the river, and at daylight in the morning, when the trail was discovered, they were no doubt thirty or forty miles west, making for their stronghold in the mountains near old Fort Defiance. Where they crossed the Rio Grande the troops found the old woman dead, having been pierced through with a lance, because, it was afterwards ascertained, she made a noise with a view of apprising the troops. The troops followed the trail in hot pursuit, galloping and running their horses for forty miles, when they were "pretty well played", resulting in their return to the Rio Grande without any dead Indians or captured animals.

Mrs. Lobato and the children were among the Indians for about two years, before being rescued by the United States government, and then only the mother and three children succeeded in gaining their freedom, Geronimo and a sister two years his senior having been traded to the Apaches and were never recovered.

We believe it was in 1859 or 1860 that Colonel Chavez, with his New Mexico volunteers, captured several Navajoes and made an exchange for the Mexican prisoners. Both mother and daughter were wedded to Indians, and in addition to two children by her husband, Mrs. Lobato left a babe behind, the off-spring of her Indian liege and lord - the tribe claiming the child as a genuine Navajo, and not transferable, notwithstanding the fact that the child was but one day old.

Geronimo is now about thirty-eight years of age and one of the best-known Indian commanders in the United States. He is noted for his cunning and ferocity, added to his extraordinary skill as a trailer and dexterity in the use of arms, and his great influence among the people of his adoption. He speaks English, Spanish and several Indian dialects and combines many of the detestable traits of the Indians with all the vilest distribution of the superior race. We believe his mother, brother, sister and aunts still reside at La Joya, on the Rio Grande, while his father, Jose Louis, the Mexican Ole Bull of his time, has gone beyond the reach of Indian or civilized foe.

1

The vindictive and irreclaimable bad character of Geronimo leaves but little doubt that he will never cease from attempting to block the progress of civilization or become reconciled to the monotony of a peaceful existence as a government pet, unless thoroughly converted by cold lead into such a condition as would make him good aboriginal anatomical subject for some medical museum. Of the renegades who two years ago consented to return to their reservations, he was the last to put in an appearance, and that his good treatment by the authorities during his stay on the reservation was worse than thrown away, is simply demonstrated by the thirty-six victims whose lives were brutally sacrificed by his savage wantonness.

EPH - Jan. 1883:

Original words to "DIXIE" by Dan Emmett from his own manuscript:

> I wish I was in the land of cotton,
> Old times dar am not forgotten,
> In Dixieland whar I was bawn in,
> Arly on a frosty mawnin'.
>
> Ole Missus marry Will de weaber,
> Will he was a gay deceaber,
> When he put his arm around her,
> He looked as fierce as a forty-pounder.
>
> His face was sharp as a butcher's cleaber,
> But dat didn't seem a bit to greab'er,
> Will run away, missus took a decline,
> Jer face was de color ob de bacon rine.
>
> While Missus libbed, she libbed in clober,
> When she died, she died all ober,
> How could she act de foolish part
> And marry the man who broke her heart?
>
> Buckwheat cakes and cawn meal batter
> Make you far or a little fatter,
> Here's a health to the nex' ole missus,
> An' all de gals as wants to kiss us.
>
> Now if you want to dribe away sorrow,
> Come and hear dis song tomorrow,
> Den hoe it down an' scratch de grabble,
> To Dixie's land I'm bound to trabble.
>
> Chorus:
> I wish I was in Dixie hooray, hooray?
>   In Dixie land
>   We'll take our stand
> To lib an' die in Dixie
> Away, Away, Away, down souf in Dixie!
> Away, Away, Away down souf in Dixie!

_____ - Probable fatal illness - dau. of S. A. RUSSELL of N. M.,
bro. J. H. of Springfield, Ill., bro. CHARLES of Manhattan, Kans.,
sis. Mrs. SPILMAN.
Paper & date: BU Oct. 10, 1885
Date & place of death: Des Moines, Iowa

_____, MARY R. - Parents: FLETCHER & _____ _____
Paper & date: LS Mar. 24, 1883
Date & place of death: Mar. 9, 1883, Las Cruces, N. M.

(father) - Murdered by son-in-law, JIM CRESSWELL, dau. Mrs. JIM CRESS-
WELL.
Paper & date: LS Dec. 16, 1882 & Feb. 28, 1883
Date & place of death: 1869, Ft. Worth, Texas

ABBOTT, _____
Paper & date: LS June 27, 1883
Date & place of death: June 24, 1883, San Marcial, N. M.

ABERNATHY, MRS. J. I. of Kansas City - bro. Dr. J. S. MARTIN, Socorro, N.
M., nephews, Dr. T. A. DAVIS and CHARLES DAVIS, Socorro, N. M.
Paper & date: BU Aug. 22, 1885
Date & place of death: On European tour.

ABERS, BEN - Hit by chair by _____ ALLEN
Paper & date: LS Aug. 4, 1883
Date & place of death: Graball, Texas

ABEYTIA, ANTONIO y A., age 48 - Family & wife, Mrs. RUFINA VIGIL de ABEY-
TIA
Paper & date: LS Dec. 23, 1885; BU Dec. 19, 1885; BU May 1, 1886
Date & place of death: Dec. 18, 1885, Socorro, N. M.

ABEYTIA, DOMINGO - Crushed by a tree. La Luz Canyon near COGHLAN's Mill
in N. M.
Paper & date: RGR Mar. 8, 1884
Date & place of death: a week ago

ABEYTIA, Sr. JUAN DIONICIO - Shot by husband - convicted Apr. Court of
Mora, N. M. 1883
Paper & date: LS Apr. 12, 1884
Date & place of death:.....

ABEITA, JULIAN - Was serving term in penitentiary - stabbed JUAN JOSE
GALLEGOS last spring.
Paper & date: BU Oct. 10, 1885
Date & place of death: this week, Santa Fe, N. M.

ABRAHAMS, DR._____ - Shot by _____ CLARK, negro, probably fatal. Survived
by wife.
Paper & date: EPT Aug. 23, 1883
Date & place of death: Houston, Texas

ABRAHAMS, Mr. HENRY - Killed by Indians "last week" - had been carrying
mail between Mimbres & Apache Pass - about May 8, 1872.
Paper & date: TB May 15, 1872
Date & place of death:......

ACHUGA, A., of Arizona - Murdered by Apaches
Paper & date: RGR Jun. 27, 1885
Date & place of death: Recently

ACOSTA, NICOLAS - Shot, killed by crazy Indian CARPIO MONTE, brother of
Chief ROWAN CHIQUITO - cattle herder on P. COGHLAN's ranch at Three
Rivers near Mescalero Agency.
Paper & date: LS Sep. 9, 1882; LS Apr. 14, 1883; EPT Apr. 16, 1883
Date & place of death: Aug. 1882, Three Rivers, N.M.

ADAIR, JOHN G. - b. in Rathdaire, Ireland, formed partnership 8 or 9 yrs. ago with CHARLES GOODNIGHT - large spread in Texas Panhandle.
Paper & date: LS Jun. 17, 1885
Date & place of death: Jun. 14, 1885, St. Louis, Mo.

ADAIR, JOSEPH D. - Shot by Dty. Sher. WAYNE PARKS in self defense.
Paper & date: LS Feb. 7, 1885
Date & place of death: Feb. 4, 1885, Colorado City, Texas

ADAMS, ____ - Yellow fever
Paper & date: EPT Oct. 3, 1883
Date & place of death: Before Sept. 27, 1883, Hermosillo, Mexico.

ADAMS, " OLD MAN" - Missing - believed killed by Indians.
Paper & date: LS Jun. 6, 1885
Date & place of death: New Mexico

ADAMS, _____ - To hang at Eagle Pass, Texas
Paper & date: LS Nov. 11, 1885
Date & place of death: Texas

ADAMS, CALEB of Dallas - Killed by ____ WOODALL
Paper & date: LS Dec. 9, 1884
Date & place of death: Dec. 3, 1884, Grand Sabine, Texas

ADAMS, DWIGHT - Killed by BENNETT HOWELL, shot - justifiable (self-defense)
Paper & date: LS Aug. 16, 1884
Date & place of death: CHISM's Ranch 6 miles from Roswell.

ADAMS, FRANK - Boy killed by Indians probably May 23, 1885
Paper & date: EPT May 28, 1885; BU Aug. 16, 1892
Date & place of death: Near Grafton, N. M.

ADAMS, HORACE, Mechanical Engr. of San Francisco, Calif. - yellow fever
Paper & date: EPT Oct. 6, 1883
Date & place of death: Mazatlan, Mexico.

ADAMS, JOHN (Negro) - drowned
Paper & date: EPT June 23, 1884
Date & place of death: June 22, 1884, El Paso, Texas

ADLER, GEORGE - Shot himself
Paper & date: LS July 11, 1883
Date & place of death: San Antonio, Texas

AGUERO, Mrs. _____ - Beaten and kicked by husband.
Paper & date: LS June 6, 1885; RGR May 30, 1885
Date & place of death: May 23, 1885, Tularosa, N. M.

AGURS, JOHN - Shot by DICK HIGGINS & J. M. TROSPER, trials Carthage, Tex. and Bethany, La.
Paper & date: EPT May 5, 1884
Date & place of death: On Texas side of line, Panola Co., Texas

AH JIM (Chinaman) - Knocked in head
Paper & date: EPMS Dec. 4, 1884
Date & place of death: Ft. Worth, Texas

AIKEN, _____ - Murdered for stepping on someone's toes in a saloon.
Paper & date: LS Feb. 21, 1883
Date & place of death: Weatherford, Texas

AIKEN, J. W. and son, JOSEPH - Battle with Sher. and posse
Paper & date: EPDT Nov. 24, 1884
Date & place of death: Nov. 22, 1884, Sherman, Texas

"ALAMO BILL" - Shot by ED SCOTTEN
Paper & date: EPDH Dec. 28, 1881
Date & place of death: Apr. 1, 1881, El Paso, Texas

ALARID, JUAN of Socorro, N. M.. - Lynched
    Paper & date: LS Aug. 19, 1882
    Date & place of death: Aug. 16, 1882

ALBILLAR, DONA MANUELA of Las Cruces, N. M. - "old washerwoman"
    Paper & date: LS Nov. 2, 1881
    Date & place of death: Oct. 26, 1881

ALDATE, NICOLAS - Burned
    Paper & date: EPT June 24, 1884
    Date & place of death: May 29, 1884, Pinos Altos, N. M.

ALDERA, CIPRIANO - To be hung for murder
    Paper & date: EPT Aug. 13, 1885
    Date & place of death: Aug. 14, 1885, Laredo, Texas

ALEXANDER, Mrs. _____ - Shot by husband
    Paper & date: LS Aug. 25, 1883
    Date & place of death: Elma, Texas

ALEXANDER, GEORGE - Sunstroke
    Paper & date: LS Aug. 13, 1884
    Date & place of death: San Antonio, Texas

ALEXANDER, JIMMY - (17 years) - Shot by brother, REESE ALEXANDER -acci-
    dent. Surv.: fa. J. B. ALEXANDER, bros. REESE - age 11 & JOHN
    Paper & date: LS Feb. 27, 1884
    Date & place of death: Few days ago, Robinson, N. M.

ALEXANDER, W. of Austin, Texas - ex-Attorney General of Texas during Gov.
    DAVIS's regime.
    Paper & date: LS Feb. 22, 1882
    Date & place of death: Feb. 16, 1882

ALFRED, LOUIS (Negro) - Shot by white man _____ McBRIDE.
    Paper & date: LS July 5, 1884
    Date & place of death: June 30, 1884, Texarkana, Texas

ALLEN, _____ (an old Negro) - Beaten and shot by mob
    Paper & date: LS Aug. 4, 1883
    Date & place of death: Alexander, Texas

ALLEN, _____ - Murder. Old man, sub-contractor on Sunset Road R. R.
    Paper & date: LS Feb. 18, 1882
    Date & place of death: Feb. 2, 1882, between Villa & Los Campos, Tex.

ALLEN, HENRY of Arkansas - Fight with WOODALL bros.
    Paper & date: LS Aug. 9, 1884; EPT Aug. 12, 1884
    Date & place of death: Aug. 5, 1884, Fredonia, Texas

ALLEN, Mrs. MAY G. - Pelvic peritonitis. Buried in Chicago, her former
    home. Survivors: hus. S. M. ALLEN, 3 children.
    Paper & date: LS Apr. 22, 1885; EPT Apr. 19, 1885
    Date & place of death: Apr. 18, 1885, El Paso, Texas

ALLEN PETER - Waylaid and killed by unknown.
    Paper & date: LS July 19, 1884; EPT July 17, 1884
    Date & place of death: July 15, 1884, near Blue Ranch, Lee Co., Texas

ALLEN, SIM (Negro porter on R. R.)-accidentally shot by conductor, _____
    MARLEY.
    Paper & date: EPDH June 21, 1882
    Date & place of death: Between El Paso & Sierra Blanca, Texas

ALLISON, Dr. ___ of Brownwood, Texas - Paralysis
    Paper & date: LS Apr. 5, 1882
    Date & place of death: Last week

ALLISON, COKE SELDEN-age 1 yr. 5 mo.8 dys. youngest son of W.H.H. & MAE
    A. ALLISON   (cont'd next page)

ALLISON cont'd:
   Paper & date: BU Aug. 1, 1884
   Date & place of death: June 28, 1884, Socorro, N. M.

ALLISON, Dr. T. H. - Assassinated by JIM FETHERBY
   Paper & date: EPT Nov. 14, 1884
   Date & place of death: Nov. 12, 1884, Longview, Texas

ALMY, Lt. ____ - Killed by Apache "JOHN DALAY"
   Paper & date: TB July 11, 1874
   Date & place of death: San Carlos, Ariz.

ALVARIO, JUAN - Hung by mob for rape of 8 year old EDNA WELDRED, dau. of
   JOHN WELDRED
   Paper & date: EPDH Aug. 23, 1882
   Date & place of death: Aug. 16, 1882, Socorro, N. M.

ALZAS, MATIAS - Yellow fever
   Paper & date: EPT Sept. 20, 1883
   Date & place of death: Guaymas, Mexico

ALZATA, - an Indian shot by troops
   Paper & date: EPDH July 19, 1882
   Date & place of death: Few months ago, Presidio del Norte, Mex.

AMADOR, ____ - infant - Surv. Fa.: MARTIN AMADOR
   Paper & date: RGR Apr. 18, 1885
   Date & place of death: Apr. 16, 1885

AMADOR, JOSE MA.-Surv. wife and family- Fell dead in the street near his
   house - known to have heart disease.
   Paper & date: TB Apr. 24, 1872
   Date & place of death: Apr. 17, 1872, Las Cruces, N. M.

AMADOR, JOSE MARIA, infant - Surv. Fa: MARTIN AMADOR
   Paper & date: TB Sept. 28, 1872
   Date & place of death: Aug. 28, 1872

AMES, Mrs. P. A.-Surv. Hus.-Dr. P. A. AMES
   Paper & date: LS Jan. 14, 1882
   Date & place of death: Jan. 10, 1882, Las Vegas, N. M.

AMITE, HENRY - Surv. Mo. who lives on Railroad Dr., Las Cruces, N. M.
   Paper & date: RGR Nov. 15, 1884
   Date & place of death: Nov. 9, 1884, Las Cruces, N. M.

AMSLER, SAM - Accidentally shot by a Negro
   Paper & date: LS Nov. 21, 1885
   Date & place of death: Sealy, Texas

AN GEE (Chinaman) Typho-malarial fever
   Paper & date: LS Aug. 22, 1883
   Date & place of death: Aug. 21, 1883, El Paso, Texas

ANASTACIO, ____ (desperado) - Killed while resisting arrest by Consta-
   ble TIBURCIO DURAN
   Paper & date: LS Nov. 21, 1885
   Date & place of death: Nov. 18, 1885, Tularosa, N. M.

ANAVE, ____ - boy- crushed by falling wall. Surv. fa. RUMALDO ANAVE
   Paper & date: LS Jan. 31, 1885
   Date & place of death: Santa Fe, N. M.

ANDALESIA (Last name unknown)-half-crazy boy who ran away with the cir-
   cus (Mexican) fell off a camel he was riding and was killed.
   Paper & date: RGR June 2, 1883
   Date & place of death: Silver City, N. M.

ANDERSON, Mrs. ____ -Baptist preacher of El Paso preached her funeral
   Paper & date: EPT Feb. 27, 1885/ Date & place of death: Murphysville,Tx

ANDERSON, FRED, formerly of Lordsburg, N. M. - murdered
     Paper & date: LS Mar. 5, 1884
     Date & place of death: Feb. 28, 1884, San Simon Valley, N. M.

ANDERSON, G. B. - Killed by SIDNEY LEWIS
     Paper & date: LS Aug. 12, 1885
     Date & place of death: Limestone Co., Texas

ANDERSON, GEORGE- believed to be from Penn. - his friend, DONALD McRAE,
     also ill but recovered.
     Paper & date: RGR Oct. 4, 1884
     Date & place of death: Sept. 12, 1884, BOWMAN's Camp, San Augustin,
     N. M.

ANDERSON, JAMES - Frozen to death
     Paper & date: LS Jan. 12, 1884
     Date & place of death: Jan. 5, 1884, Chickasaw Nation, Okla.

ANDERSON, JAMES A.-First editor of Ruby, Az. "News"- killed
     Paper & date: EPDH June 24, 1883
     Date & place of death: Nov., 1882

ANDERSON, JOE (negro) - Lynched
     Paper & date: LS June 16, 1883
     Date & place of death: La Salle Co., Texas

ANDERSON, JOSEPH N. of Cold Springs, Texas - Suicide by morphine.
     Paper & date: LS Nov. 3, 1883
     Date & place of death: Oct. 29, 1883, Chihuahua, Mexico

ANDERSON, LOUIS - of Middle Gila, N. M.- shot self accidentally
     Paper & date: LS Aug. 13, 1884
     Date & place of death: Recently

ANDERSON, MITHCELL, Choctaw Indian 17 years- condemned for murder of
     _____WINCHESTER, blamed father.
     Paper & date: EPT May 8, 1885
     Date & place of death: May 6, 1885, Marhala Tubbee Dist., Indian Ter-
     ritory

ANDERSON, PETER - Killed by GERONIMO and his Apaches
     Paper & date: LS May 27, 1885
     Date & place of death: Alma, N. M. vicinity

ANDERSON, SAM - Shot by LYMAN S. ALLEN during a spree.
     Paper & date: LS May 30, 1885
     Date & place of death: Lincoln, N. M.

ANDERSON, Rev. T. M. -Lingering illness. Baptist - Mason. b. So. Carolina
     to Texas 1849
     Paper & date: EPT May 7, 1884
     Date & place of death: May 3, 1884, Cameron, Texas

ANDLER, K. - Jumped overboard and drowned. He was booked from New Orleans
     to Rockport, Texas
     Paper & date: LS Aug. 25, 1883
     Date & place of death: Near Caballo Pass in the Gulf.

ANDREWS, A. G. - Killed by S. C. LEWIS - trial in Mexia, Texas
     Paper & date: LS Aug. 15, 1885
     Date & place of death: Texas

ANDREWS, ALEXANDER - Cave in. Age 34, native of Wisconsin, Scotch descent,
     unmarried.
     Paper & date: EPMS Dec. 13, 1884
     Date & place of death: Last week Kingston, Az.

ANDREWS, Col. JOHN B. -Pioneer citizen in Houston.
     Paper & date: LS Sept. 13, 1882
     Date & place of death: Recently in Houston, Texas

ANDREWS, Capt. SAMUEL - Old soldier, broke his neck in a fall.
Paper & date: LS Sept. 16, 1885
Date & place of death: Corsicana, Texas

ANDRO, Mrs. M. - Killed by hus. Surv. hus. M. ANDRO
Paper & date: LS Mar. 31, 1883
Date & place of death: Mar. 23, 1883, Bracketsville, Tex.

ANGLIN, _____ - Knifed by _____ YOUNG, not expected to live.
Paper & date: LS July 7, 1883
Date & place of death: Near Weatherford, Tex.

ANTHONY, JOHN - Killed by falling rock
Paper & date: LS July 12, 1884
Date & place of death: July 5, 1884, San Antonio, N. Mex.

ANTHONY, W. B. - Run over by train
Paper & date: LS Mar. 7, 1883
Date & place of death: Mar. 2, 1883, Dallas, Texas

ANTIANA, GUS (an Italian) - Suicide by strychinine, buried Dec. 22, 1884
Paper & date: LS Dec. 23, 1884
Date & place of death: Dec. 21, 1884, El Paso, Texas

APODACA, JOSE R. - Murdered by CANDIDO & JUAN CASTILLO
Paper & date: LS Aug. 26, 1882
Date & place of death: About 3 weeks ago, Sabinal,Valenica co., N. M.

APODACA, JUAN - Run over by train
Paper & date: LS Apr. 28, 1883
Date & place of death: Near Albuquerque, N. M.

APODACA, MAXIMO of Dona Ana co., N. M. - Jumped to his death - given life
for murder of NESMITH family.
Paper & date: LS Nov. 4, 1885; RGR Nov. 7, 1885
Date & place of death: Santa Fe, N. M.

AQUAILANE, DOMINIC, Italian - shoemaker - Drowned himself in a cistern.
Paper & date: LS Aug. 5, 1885
Date & place of death: Wills Point, Texas

AQUAILANE, Mrs. DOMINIC - Drowned herself in a cistern.
Paper & date: LS Aug. 5, 1885
Date & place of death: Few days ago Wills Point, Tex.

ARAGON, Don MACEDONIO - Fight with cowboys
Paper & date: LS Sept. 26, 1883
Date & place of death: Sept. 21, 1883, Ute Creek, N. M.

ARANDA, ANTONIO JOSE - Killed by Texas cow driver
Paper & date: LS Jun. 24, 1885
Date & place of death: Zuni Mtns., N. M.

ARANDA, FELIPE - Aged nearly 60
Paper & date: RGR Mar. 14, 1885
Date & place of death: Mar. 7, 1885, La Mesa, N. M.

ARCHULETA, DIEGO of Rio Arriba Co., N. M. - Sick for sometime.
Paper & date: LS Mar. 26, 1884
Date & place of death: Mar. 22, 1884, Santa Fe, N. M.

ARCHULETA, GUADALUPE - Lynched for shooting JOHN BLANCETTE, brother of
sher. of Rio Arriba Co.
Paper & date: LS Nov. 4, 1882
Date & place of death: A few days ago, Bloomfield, N. M.

ARMINTO, LASARO (LORAZA?) - Will die, shot while returning to El Paso,
Texas from Paso del Norte, Mex. by LOUIS MESA
Paper & date: EPDH Sept. 21, 1881
Date & place of death: ....

ARMENTA, LUIS - Age 18 - Fell from hay wagon, injured his spine.
Paper & date: LS Nov. 17, 1883; RGR Nov. 17, 1883
Date & place of death: Nov. 14, 1883, Las Cruces, N. M.

ARMIJO, _____ - Murdered by ASTREA, an Indian. Son JACINTO ARMIJO.
Paper & date: TB May 29, 1872
Date & place of death: Few years ago

ARMIJO, CARLOS, age 9 mo. - Par. CARLOS H. & BEATRIZ OTERO ARMIJO of Las
Cruces, New Mexico.
Paper & date: RGR Sept. 8, 1883
Date & place of death: Las Cruces, N. M.

ARMIJO, JUAN CRISTOBAL - "One of the leading Mexicans in our territory
in points of wealth and intelligence." Sons NESTOR ARMIJO of Las
Cruces, N. M., NICHOLAS of Bernalillo, JUSTO of Bernalillo. Bro. -
AMBROSIO ARMIJO died 3 years ago. JUAN lived in Albuquerque, N. M.
Paper & date: RGR Jan. 3, 1885
Date & place of death: Dec. 27, 1884, Bernalillo Co., N. M.

ARMOUR, JAMES D. - Took cramps while swimming and drowned.
Paper & date: LS Sept. 13, 1884; LS Sept. 20, 1884
Date & place of death: 12 mi. No. of Mount Calm, Tex. near Dawson.

ARMSTRONG, Dr. W. H. - Thrown from buggy.
Paper & date: LS July 30, 1884
Date & place of death: July 24, 1884, Dallas, Tex.

ARNOLD, ELLA - actress - delirium tremens
Paper & date: EPT May 1, 1883
Date & place of death: Waco, Texas

ARNOLD, SABINA of Corpus Christi, Tex.
Paper & date: LS Nov. 23, 1881
Date & place of death: Nov. 13, 1881

ASHBY, JEFF - shot by GILLETT RAGINS
Paper & date: LS Nov. 15, 1884
Date & place of death: Nov. 8, 1884, Clarksville, Tex.

ASKEW, Capt. MILTON, conductor on Santa Fe R. R.
Paper & date: LS Aug. 8, 1885; EPT Aug. 6, 1885
Date & place of death: Aug. 5, 1885, Las Vegas, N. M.

ASTREA - Fight among Indians to name their chief, ASTREA was killed. He
is the same Indian who, a few years back, murdered the father of JA-
CINTO ARMIJO.
Paper & date: TB May 29, 1872
Date & place of death:.....

ATKINSON, ED. - drowned. Fa. Capt. J. J. ATKINSON, Houston, Texas
Paper & date: LS June 4, 1884
Date & place of death: Trinity River in Texas.

ATKINSON, FRANK - Train accident at Algodones, N. M., scalded. Bur. Kir-
win, Kans. Relatives in Kirwin, Kansas.
Paper & date: LS July 22, 1885; EPT July 21, 1885
Date & place of death: July 19, 1885 near Wallace, N. M.

ATTAWAY, Capt. L. L. - Shot by CRAWFORD BLACK
Paper & date: LS July 30, 1884
Date & place of death: At Caledonia, Tex.

AUDA, PEDRO DE - Shot by soldiers. Article dateline - Monterrey, Mex.
July 31
Paper & date: EPT Aug. 1, 1884
Date & place of death: near Jalisco, Mex.

AUGUR, Miss ____ - Malarious fever. Fa.-Gen. C. C. AUGUR; bro. FERD or
FRED. (cont'd next page)

9

AUGUR cont'd:
    Paper & date: EPT June 3, 1883
    Date & place of death: May 30, 1883, San Antonio, Tex.

AUSTIN, _____ - infant. Fa.-W. H. AUSTIN.
    Paper & date: EPDH Oct. 11, 1882
    Date & place of death: Oct. 10, 1882, El Paso, Texas

AUSTIN, Col. JOHN
    Paper & date: EPT June 29, 1883
    Date & place of death: Aug. 18   Tex.

AWELINE, BOB - Indian massacre by COCHISE.   See MILLS, _____bro. of Maj.
    MILLS.
    Paper & date: EPT Jan. 20, 1887
    Date & place of death: June, 1860 Cook's Peak, Grant co., N. M.

AVERETT, GEORGE - age 25 - Suicide
    Paper & date: EPMS Dec. 16, 1884
    Date & place of death: (Tues.) last week near Lebanon, Collin co., Tex.

AXTEL, O. K. - Thrown from horse under wheels of train.   Nephew of Judge
    AXTEL.
    Paper & date: LS Nov. 26, 1884
    Date & place of death: Nov. 25, 1884 Las Vegas, N. M.

AYETON, Pvt. Tex. Ranger - Shot by PILANUS GONZALES and son, age 13.
    Paper & date: EPT June 4, 1885
    Date & place of death: Few days ago, near Laredo, Tex.

BABB, BILL - Killed by own son, "a desparate character".
    Paper & date: LS Oct. 29, 1881
    Date & place of death: Texas, away from El Paso

BACA, ALTAGRACIA - Par.: Don and Dona SEVERO A. BACA.
    Paper & date: BU July 4, 1885
    Date & place of death: 29 Jun. 1885, Socorro, N. M.

BACA, ANDREA - Accidentally shot
    Paper & date: LS Nov. 18, 1885
    Date & place of death: Cienga, N. M.

BACA, EUNOFRIO - Lynched for murdering A. M. CONKLIN; bro. ABRAM; uncle-
    probate Judge of El Paso _____ BACA
    Paper & date: SH Dec. 14, 1884
    Date & place of death: 1818, Socorro, N. M.

BACA. TERESITA, only dau.- suicide by drowning, possible accident.   Par.
    M/M FELIPE BACA
    Paper & date: LS May 23, 1883; EPT May 23, 1883; BU Jun. 1, 1883
    Date & place of death: 21 May 1883, Socorro, N. M.

BACKER, JAMES - Boiler explosion at cotton gin.
    Paper & date: LS Oct. 8, 1884
    Date & place of death: Near Fredricksburg, Tx.

BADEN, MAT - Shot by WILL JONES; surv. - wife
    Paper & date: EPT Sep. 20, 1885
    Date & place of death: Sep. 18, 1885, Caddo, Ind. Terr.

BAILEY, ASA - Killed in a fight
    Paper & date: LS Jan. 2, 1884
    Date & place of death: Dec. 26, 1883, McDade, Tx.

BAILEY, CHARLES (young man) - Struck over the head.
    Paper & date: LS Sep. 26, 1885
    Date & place of death: Near Rosenburg, TX

10

BAILEY, D. - Hung by mob for murder of BOSS GREEN.
Paper & date: LS Nov. 21, 1883
Date & place of death: Few nights ago, Comanche, TX

BAILEY, (BAYLEY), JACK - Killed in a fight.
Paper & date: LS Jan. 2, 1884
Date & place of death: Dec. 26, 1883, McDade, Texas

BAILEY, JACOB of Barnsfield, Ohio - Consumption
Paper & date: LS Oct. 31, 1883
Date & place of death: Oct. 30, 1883, El Paso, Texas

BAILEY, JIM - Hung by mob for murder of BOSS GREEN
Paper & date: LS Nov. 21, 1883
Date & place of death: Few nights ago, Comanche, Texas

BAIN, PATRICK - Railroad accident
Paper & date: LS Jun. 2, 1883
Date & place of death: Marshall, Texas

BAINES, Rev. GEORGE W. of Belton, Texas well - known Baptist minister;
son: Rev. G. W. BAINES, Jr., of El Paso, Texas; son-JOSEPH W. BAINES
of McKinney, Texas
Paper & date: LS Jan. 10, 1883; EPDH Jan. 3, 1883; EPDH Jan. 17, 1883
Date & place of death: Dec. 28, 1882, Belton, Texas; buried Salado,
Texas his old home.

BAIRD, SPRUCE - Heirs sued by RICHARD PAGE for land near Albuquerque,
N. M.
Paper & date: LS July 22, 1885
Date & place of death:........

BAIRD, W. A. (BILLY) - Conductor, run over by Mex. National R. R. train.
Worked out of El Paso, Texas buried American Cemetery, Mexico City,
Mexico. bro.- in Ft. Worth, Texas.
Paper & date: LS Jan. 19, 1884; EPDH Jan. 20, 1884
Date & place of death: Dec. 12, 1883, near Toluca, Mexico.

BAIRD, WILLIAM - age 86
Paper & date: LS Apr. 18, 1883
Date & place of death: Apr. 13, 1883, Cleburne, Texas

BAJUEDATACHI - Killed by Indians
Paper & date: EPT Jul. 12, 1883
Date & place of death: Jun. 17, 1883, Sonora State, Mexico

BAKER, _____ - Stabbed
Paper & date: LS Mar. 22, 1884
Date & place of death: Mar. 19, 1884, Chihuahua, Mexico

BAKER, JEFF (Negro) - Run over by train
Paper & date: LS Aug. 11, 1883
Date & place of death: McKinney, Texas

BAKER, JOAB - Fell from wagon and was run over.
Paper & date: LS Feb. 4, 1885
Date & place of death: Monero, N. M.

BALDRIDGE, W. J. - Died at pest house of small pox, owner of American
Restaurant, estate to be settled Sep. 1884 in El Paso, Texas
Paper & date: EPT Aug. 7, 1884; EPDH Mar. 15, 1882
Date & place of death: Mar. 15, 1882, El Paso, Texas

BALDWIN, _____ - "Fatally murdered"
Paper & date: LS Sep. 3, 1884
Date & place of death: Last week, Gordon, Texas

BALDWIN, GRANVILLE - To be hanged for rape
Paper & date: LS Jun. 27, 1883
Date & place of death: Grimes co., Texas

BALISAN, MASADONIO - While hunting was leaning on his gun, loaded with
   bird-shot, riddled flesh, destroyed right eye and left bones exposed.
   Probably fatal.
   Paper & date: RGR Apr. 18, 1885
   Date & place of death:.....

BALL, HARRY - Killed by JAMES RILEY - sentenced at Ft. Worth, Texas
   Paper & date: LS Jun. 10, 1885
   Date & place of death: Last Aug., Texas

BALLARD, _____ - Shot by HANK WILLIAMS
   Paper & date: LS Jan. 31, 1885
   Date & place of death: Ash Forks, N. M.

BALLARD, GEORGE - Shot by J. M. TAYLOR
   Paper & date: LS Mar. 25, 1885
   Date & place of death: Mar. 23, 1884, Bell co., Texas

BALLEJOS, JOSEFA - Burned
   Paper & date: LS Nov. 10, 1883
   Date & place of death: Nov. 8, 1883, Las Cruces, N. M.

BALLINGER, L. H., of Galveston, Texas; prominent politician; tetanus
   caused by vaccination.
   Paper & date: LS Apr. 5, 1882
   Date & place of death: Last Friday

BANKS, WYATT (Negro) - Hanged for murder killing ADDISON WISE (or WISER)
   May 1882
   Paper & date: LS Apr. 25, 1883; EPT Apr. 27, 1883
   Date & place of death: Apr. 24, 1883, Franklin, Texas

BAREFIELD, H. L. - Run over by train.
   Paper & date: LS Oct. 18, 1884
   Date & place of death: Oct. 9, 1884, near Liberty, Texas

BARELA, FERMIN - Killed by ANTONIO GIRON
   Paper & date: LS Apr. 11, 1883
   Date & place of death: Dona Ana, N. M.

BARELA, FRANCISCO - age 22 - Accident - shot by RAFAEL VELARDE
   Paper & date: LS May 24, 1884
   Date & place of death: May 22, 1884, PROVENCIO;s Store, El Paso, Tx.

BARELA, Mrs. JOSE - Fainted and died; hus.- JOSE BARELA
   Paper & date: LS Aug. 12, 1885; RGR Aug. 1, 1885
   Date & place of death: Jul. 28, 1885, Las Cruces, N. M.

BARELA, MARCELINA - Murdered in her bed; Mexican woman; assailant unknown
   Paper & date: LS Oct. 29, 1881
   Date & place of death: A few days ago, near Silver City, N. M.

BARELA, NICJOLAS - age 67 - sis. Mrs. BLASA RUELAS; niece Mrs. A. J.
   BUCHOZ
   Paper & date: RGR Nov. 3, 1883
   Date & place of death: Oct. 25, 1883, Mesilla, N. M.

BARELA, SANTOS - Legally hanged for murder committed in Colorado, N. M.
   Paper & date: RGR Apr. 11, 1885
   Date & place of death: May 20, 1881, Mesilla, N. M.

BARLOW, H. P.
   Paper & date: LS Mar. 12, 1884
   Date & place of death: Mar. 7, 1884, Albuquerque, N. M.

BARMAN, JOSEPH of St. Louis, Mo. - committed suicide
   Paper & date: LS Oct. 28, 1885
   Date & place of death: Oct. 23, 1885, Dallas, Texas

BARNES, J. of San Antonio, Texas - drowned
    Paper & date: LS Sep. 27, 1884
    Date & place of death: Last week, Pecos River, Texas

BARNES, RICHARD - Killed by COCHISE
    Paper & date: TB Nov. 8, 1871
    Date & place of death: Oct. 21, 1871, San Simon Cienga

BARNES, SALLY
    Paper & date: LS Aug. 8, 1885
    Date & place of death: Las 'Vegas, N. M.

BARNEY, J. G. of Alma, N. M. - Missing several months, body identified
    near Savoya. Killed by white men. Wife (later married JOE SHERIDAN
    of Mineral Creek, Mogollon Range, N. M., lives at Cooney)
    Paper & date: BU May 1, 1884; BU Oct. 3, 1885
    Date & place of death: 1883-1884, Mogollon Mts., Ariz.

BARRADALL, Dr. O. W. - Shot by CHARLES HERRING (HERREN). Born in Va. By
    way of Memphis, Tenn. to Fort Worth about 5 years ago. Surv.-wife
    Paper & date: LS Jul. 2, 1884; EPT Jun. 30, 1884
    Date & place of death: Jun. 25, 1884, Ft. Worth, Texas

BARRERO, FRANCISCO
    Paper & date: EPDH Oct. 4, 1882
    Date & place of death: Maverick co., Texas

BARRETT, E. I. from Ky. - Train accident
    Paper & date: LS Mar. 14, 1883
    Date & place of death: Last week, Ft. Worth, Texas

BARRETT, J. J. - Jumped from moving train
    Paper & date: LS Apr. 4, 1883
    Date & place of death: Mar. 29, 1883, near Binm Sta., Texas

BARRIO, FRANCISCO (old resident) - Pneumonia
    Paper & date: LS Mar. 5, 1884; RGR Mar. 1, 1884
    Date & place of death: Feb. 26 or 29, 1884, Mesilla, N. M.

BARRINGTON, J. P. of Gainesville, Texas - Killed by wife JENNIE with an
    overdose of morphine.
    Paper & date: LS Aug. 26, 1885; SH Jul. 26, 1885
    Date & place of death: Mid-July 1885, Indian Territory

BARRY, Capt. Wm. M. of San Antonio - Murdered by bandits. Buried in San
    Antonio, Texas. Surv.- Wife
    Paper & date: LS Jan. 24, 1885
    Date & place of death: Jan. 18, 1885, road from Jimulco, Mex. to state
    of Durango, Mex.

BARTH, MORRIS, about 30, single, of Holbrook, Ariz. - Train collision on
    Feb. 19, 1885, died at Albuquerque; bro.- SOL BARTH of St. John's,
    Ariz.
    Paper & date: LS Feb. 21, 1885
    Date & place of death: Bluewater Sta., N. M.

BARTLESON, Dr. M. A. - Suicide. County Commissioner of Dona Ana from
    Hillsboro before Sierra Co. was formed.
    Paper & date: RGR Mar. 28, 1885
    Date & place of death: A few days ago, Colorado.

BARTLETT, JAMES - aged 20 yrs.- Killed by Sher. ANGUIA and posse. Alias
    "KID" LEWIS. Had killed 4 men.
    Paper & date: LS Oct. 3, 1883
    Date & place of death: Sep. 24, 1883, Clifton, Ariz.

BARTLETT, NELLIE - Pianist - called Mrs. DOC CAIN
    Paper & date: EPT Sep. 18, 1883
    Date & place of death: Sep. 11, 1883, Silver City, N. M.

BARTLOW, Mrs. JOHN L. - Pneumonia - hus.: Editor of "New Mexican", Col.
JOHN (I. or L. BARTLOW (or BERTOW)
Paper & date: EPT Jun. 17, 1883; EPT Jun. 24, 1883
Date & place of death: Jun. 14, 1883, Santa Fe, N. M.

BARTOW, Maj. CHARLES A. - Prominent railroad man
Paper & date: EPMS Nov. 27, 1884
Date & place of death: Nov. 20, 1884, Houston, Texas

BARTOW, HENRY - Dty. Sher.- Shot by WILLIAM MARMADUKE
Paper & date: LS Feb. 16, 1884; LS Feb. 23, 1884
Date & place of death: Feb. 10, 1884, Pinos Altos, N. M.

BASHAW, HENRY - Shot in feud with SAULS family; Surv.: W. R. BASHAW: HEN-
RY HARRIS
Paper & date: LS Dec. 5, 1884
Date & place of death: Dec. 5, 1884, Gatesville, Texas

BASS, BILL - To be hanged Oct. 31, 1884
Paper & date: LS Oct. 8, 1884; EPT Oct. 4, 1884
Date & place of death: Paris, Texas

BASS, WILLIE - age 14 - Arm torn off - will die.
Paper & date: LS Oct. 25, 1882
Date & place of death: Belton, Texas

BASSETT, JEFFERSON (German)
Paper & date: LS Jun. 20, 1885
Date & place of death: Brenham, Texas

BASSETT, "KID" - Lynched
Paper & date: LS Feb. 16, 1884
Date & place of death: Near Sioux City, N. M. (?)

BASSETT, Mrs. O. T. of El Paso; hus.: O. T. BASSETT, lumber merchant;
bro.: H. A. NEBEKER of In.; son: 18 months old
Paper & date: LS Sep. 27, 1882
Date & place of death: Sep. 26, 1882, Clinton, In., her old home.

BASSINI, EMILIO (Italian from Mex.) - Heart disease
Paper & date: LS Aug. 6, 1884
Date & place of death: Aug. 2, 1884, El Paso, Texas

BATEMAN, _____ - (15 year old boy) - Stabbed by 8 year old bro., TOM
BATEMAN.
Paper & date: LS Nov. 11, 1885
Date & place of death: Elmo, Texas

BATTLE, JAMES - Run over by yard engine
Paper & date: LS Jul. 25, 1883
Date & place of death: Marshall, Texas

BAXTER, ALLEN - Train collision
Paper & date: LS Sep. 27, 1884
Date & place of death: Sep. 20, 1884, near A & P Junction, El Paso,
Texas

BAXTER, DANIEL - Stabbed by FRANK THURMOND a few nights ago.
Paper & date: EPT Aug. 28, 1884
Date & place of death: Aug. 27, 1884, Deming, N. M.

BAXTER, J. J. _ Killed by Indians.
Paper & date: LS May 27, 1885; RGR Jun. 20, 1885; RGR Jun. 27, 1885
Date & place of death: On the Gila West Fork near Pinos Altos, N. M.

BAXTER, JOHN - Age 18 - Murdered by Mexicans - beaten to death.
Paper & date: LS Jan. 21, 1885
Date & place of death: Jan. 18, 1885, Springer, N. M.

BEALL, Mrs. - age 70 - son: Capt. THOMAS J. BEALL of El Paso, Texas; son:
Dr. ELIAS BEALL of Ft. Worth, Texas
Paper & date: EPDH Mar. 4, 1883; EPDH Sep. 23, 1883
Date & place of death: Feb. 27, 1883

BEALL, ED M. - of San Antonio - aftermath of accidental self-inflicted
shot in leg; leg amputated with bowie knife and carpenter's saw; man
died.
Paper & date: LS Oct. 12, 1881
Date & place of death: Oct. 8, 1881

BEALL, Col. GEORGE T., JR., Judge - died suddenly; wife of Baltimore is
fatally ill.
Paper & date: LS Sep. 9, 1885; RGR Sep. 12, 1885
Date & place of death: Sep. 4, 1885, Lincoln, N. M.

BEALL, HENRY S. - young man - shot himself in the head, wife and family
in Cameron, Ohio; Uncle in Mt. Carmel, Ill.
Paper & date: LS Dec. 29, 1883; EPDH Dec. 30, 1883
Date & place of death: Dec. 27, 1883, El Paso, Texas

BEAL, W. H. - Shot by friend J. STRANGE
Paper & date: EPT Jul. 17, 1884
Date & place of death: Jul. 13, 1884, Dallas, Texas

BEAN, JAMES in Wellington, Kans. - 12 shots in body and two Winchester
bullets. Desperado from near Ft. Worth, Texas
Paper & date: LS Nov. 15, 1882
Date & place of death: Recently

BEAR, EDWARD - Placed on train for Caldwell, Kans., will die. He and his
bro. JAMES were murderers.
Paper & date: EPDH Nov. 1, 1882
Date & place of death: 1882, shot in Sunset, Wise co., Texas.

BEAR, JAMES - Shot. Bro.: EDWARD BEAR, both were murderers.
Paper & date: EPDH Nov. 1, 1882
Date & place of death: Oct. 11, 1882, Sunset, Wise co., Texas

BEATON, N. B. - Rattlesnake bite
Paper & date: IS Sep. 3, 1884
Date & place of death: Aug. 27, 1884, Colorado, Texas

BEATTIE, AL of Chicago - jumped from train.
Paper & date: EPMS Nov. 29, 1884
Date & place of death: Near Houston, Texas

BECK, ADDISON - U. S. Marshal - shot by whiskey peddlers JOHN BANK (or
BURKE) and JOHN M. JACKS, Cherokee Indians.
Paper & date: EPT Sep. 29, 1883
Date & place of death: Sep. 27, 1883, between Childress Sta. and Webb
Falls, Ind. Terr.

BECK, HERMAN - Shot by MARTIN NELSON
Paper & date: EPT May 7, 1885
Date & place of death: May 5, 1885, Bonito, N. M.

BECKWITH, _____ - 1 yr. old boy - burned; mo.: Mrs. MARY E. BECKWITH....
charged.
Paper & date: LS Dec. 12, 1885
Date & place of death: Cerrillos, N. M.

BEECHER, JAMES - Shot by "BUCK" WILSON, Pvt., Co. G, 4th Cav. in defense
of an old man and himself (DANIEL WILSON)
Paper & date: LS Mar. 11, 1885
Date & place of death: Central City, N. M.

BEESON, Rev. Dr. W. E. - Pres. of Trinity College at Tehuacana, Texas
Paper & date: LS Sep. 13, 1882
Date & place of death: Sep. 5, 1882

BEHRANS, ROBERT - S.P.R.R. employee, fell under the engine.
Paper & date: EPDH Sep. 21, 1881
Date & place of death: Sep. 15, 1881, Deming, N. M.

BELARDE, ANASTACIO of Las Cruces - Murder by JUAN BARELA
Paper & date: LS Nov. 30, 1881
Date & place of death: Thurs. previous

BELARDE, BENIGNE - Struck by lightening, July 18, 1885, will probably die.
Paper & date: LS July 25, 1885
Date & place of death: Santa Fe, N. M.

BELL, JOHN - Killed by Indians. Relations at Harrisville, St. Clair co.,
Missouri
Paper & date: LS Nov. 9, 1881
Date & place of death: After Oct. 24, 1881, near Lucero, Chihuahua.

BELL, Mrs. JOHN (negro) - Shot by hus. because he had nothing else to do.
Hus.:JOHN BELL (negro)
Paper & date: LS Jun. 10, 1885
Date & place of death: Eagle Pass, Texas

BELLHOUSE, _____ - Murdered by Indians between Casas Grandes and Gavi-
lan on way to Silver City, N. M.
Paper & date: TB Mar. 28, 1871
Date & place of death: ...

BENAVIDES, Mrs. THOMAS GAMEROS DE - age 76. Member of prominent Bena-
vides family.
Paper & date: LS Mar. 7, 1885
Date & place of death: The other day, Laredo, Texas

BENEDICT, _____ - Dying of consumption, sent to his family in Dallas, Tx
Paper & date: LS Oct. 21, 1885
Date & place of death: ....

BENNETT, F. J. - Lawyer formerly of New York. Shot himself --suicide.
Paper & date: LS Nov. 22, 1884
Date & place of death: Nov. 16, 1884, Dallas, Texas

BENSON, WILSON - Shot by bro.-in-law, ARCHIE BOLAN
Paper & date: LS Jun. 30, 1883
Date & place of death: Near Mount Pleasant, Texas

BENTON, ROBERT - old man of Blue Creek, Ariz. GERONIMO and his Apaches.
Paper & date: LS May 27, 1885; RGR Jun. 27, 1885
Date & place of death: Alma, N. M. vicinity

BERGERON, ISIDORE (or A.) - Suicide, shot himself; bro.: L. A. BERGERON
of Calvert, Texas; bro. in Galveston, Texas; bro. in Louisiana; wife
(seperated)
Paper & date: LS Mar. 15, 1882; LS Mar. 8, 1882; EPDH Mar. 8, 1882
Date & place of death: Mar. 5, 1882, Sunday - El Paso, Texas

BERGMANN, ADAM - Shot by unknown in his home.
Paper & date: LS Jul. 18, 1883
Date & place of death: Dallas, Texas

BERLINER, REMA - 4 mo. 8 days; par.: GEORGE & MARIE BERLINER
Paper & date: EPDH Sep. 9, 1883
Date & place of death: Sep. 6, 1883, El Paso, Texas

BERNARD, FATHER of Socorro, N. M.
Paper & date: LS Sep. 16, 1882
Date & place of death: Recently

BERNARD, SISTER MARY (Mo. Superior) - MARIA BERNARDA
Paper & date: LS Apr. 18, 1883
Date & place of death: Apr. 15, 1883, convent in Mesilla, N. M.

16

BERRY, LANGFORD G. - General debility; ticket agent of S.P.R.R.; home
   in Oakland Calif.
   Paper & date: LS Nov. 22, 1882
   Date & place of death: last Sunday night, El Paso, Texas

BERRY, MIKE of Texarkana, Texas; shot and killed by W. H. RUSSELL
   Paper & date: LS Oct. 26, 1881
   Date & place of death: Oct. 19, 1881

BEST, TYRE - Young man of Kentucky; suicide by morphine
   Paper & date: LS Oct. 18, 1884
   Date & place of death: Oct. 12, 1884, Pickwick Hotel, Ft. Worth, Tx.

BEXTELL, JOHN - Murdered by TOM STEVENS
   Paper & date: EPT Oct. 30, 1896
   Date & place of death: 1881, Grayson co., Texas

BICKLEY, J. J. - in Bell co., Texas; runaway team
   Paper & date: LS Oct. 25, 1882
   Date & place of death: a few days ago.

BIGGS, JAMES - Killed by Indians in Chocolate Pass, Mex. (18 Mexicans
   were also killed). A Grant co., N. M. mier (account on 12/15/82 by
   F. JOSSELYN, "DEAF SANDY" of Silver City, N. M.)
   Paper & date: LS Dec. 9, 1882; LS Dec. 15, 1882
   Date & place of death: recently in Mex.

BILES, Dr. J. H. - Suicide - cause domestic infidelity.
   Paper & date: LS Dec. 5, 1885
   Date & place of death: Pittsburg, Texas

BILLINGS, JOHN "JOSH" - Miner and prospector; affection of liver and di-
   gestive organs.
   Paper & date: LS May 30, 1885
   Date & place of death: St. Vincent Hospital, Santa Fe, N. M.

BISHOP, ANNETTA - Strychnine taken for bromide - accident
   Paper & date: LS Feb. 18, 1885
   Date & place of death: Ft. Concho, Texas

BISSELL, DOCK - Pneumonia and hemorrhage.
   Paper & date: LS Jan. 30, 1884
   Date & place of death: Jan. 27, 1884, Las Cruces, N. M.

BLACK, B. G., sher. elect - Shot at his door by NEWTON T. HARRIS and G.
   MACK CROOK and Dty. Shers. _____ HOLMAN and _____ YATE.
   Paper & date: LS Nov. 19, 1884; EPT Aug. 2, 1885
   Date & place of death: Nov. 16, 1884, Fannin co., Texas

BLACK, H. - Suicide by morphine; from Woodcock, Penn.
   Paper & date: LS Mar. 1, 1882
   Date & place of death: Feb. 22, 1882, Austin, Texas

BLACK, JOE M. - Killed by Indians; bro.: C. M. BLACK; bro.: C. C. BLACK
   of Turnersville, Coryell co., Texas; mo.; 2 sis. and bro. in Colorado
   City, Texas.
   Paper & date: EPDH Nov. 9, 1881; LS Nov. 9, 1881
   Date & place of death: after Oct. 24, 1881, near Lucero, Chihuahua

BLACK, POPE - Shot and killed by Dty. U.S. Marshal LOUIS C. KENNON
   Paper & date: LS Dec. 20, 1882; LS Apr. 14, 1883
   Date & place of death: Dec. 15, 1882, Florida near Deming, N. M.

BLACK, ROBERT (or WILLIAM) - Shot by SUSAN YONKES (or YONKER/YOUNKER)..
   self defense, both parties from Lincoln co., N. M. She left town after
   acquittal with a negro of bad odor.
   Paper & date: EPT Aug. 28, 1884; EPT Sep. 3, 1884
   Date & place of death: Aug. 24, 1884, Socorro, N. M.

BLAKE, FRANCIS - age 40- b. Dorchester, N. H.,to N. M. in 1860; Masonic
   and Episcopalian services; widow and loving children.
   Paper & date: TB Jan. 24, 1872
   Date & place of death: Mon., Jan. 22, 1872, Las Cruces, N. M.

BLAKE, GEORGE E. - infant; par.: ROCKWOOD H. and GUADALUPE BLAKE.
Paper & date: TB Dec. 28, 1872
Date & place of death: Dec. 22, 1872

BLAKE, J. HUBERT (Irish barrister) - died of drink
Paper & date: LS Oct. 31, 1885
Date & place of death: San Antonio, Texas

BLANCETTE, JOHN - Wounded by a Mexican, GUADALUPE ARCHULETA; bro.: Sher.
of Rio Arriba co., N. M.
Paper & date: LS Nov. 1, 1882
Date & place of death: a day or 2 ago, Bloomfield, Rio Arriba co,N.M.

BLANCHARD, CHARLES, SR. - age 83 - a number of children including Hon.
CHARLES BLANCHARD ot Las Vegas, N. M. and HERMAS BLANCHARD of Socorro,
N. M.
Paper & date: BU Jun. 1, 1883
Date & place of death: May 26, 1883, ___ot Mare, near Quebec, Canada

BLANCHARD, J. B. - Killed by Indians; an old resident in Tubac le Vendee;
believed to be from eastern or middle states.
Paper & date: TB Jun. 8, 1871
Date & place of death: Jun. 1, 1871, Calabasas

BLANCHARD, LAURA A. - age 15 mos.; par.: WARD B. and ISABEL BLANCHARD;
sis.: ISABEL
Paper & date: LS Oct. 13, 1883; EPT Sep. 2, 1884
Date & place of death: Oct. 10, 1883, Ysleta, Texas

BLANCHARD, WARD B. - Congestion of the stomach; funeral Apr. 6, 1884;
Ysleta, Texas; wife: ISABEL; dau.: ISABEL; family of El Paso, Texas;
son: CHARLES A. BLANCHARD; b. in Penn. where relatives are.
Paper & date: LS Apr. 5, 1884; EPDH Apr. 6, 1884; EPDH Apr. 13, 1884;
EPDH Jun. 24, 1890; EPT Sep. 2, 1884
Date & place of death: Apr. 5, 1884, Ysleta, Texas

BLANCO, JESUS - Struck by lightning; uncle: JUAN LUNAS
Paper & date: LS Jul. 1, 1885
Date & place of death: Las Lunas, N. M.

BLASHEK, _____ - 4 yr. old boy drowned in mill race
Paper & date: LS May 9, 1885
Date & place of death: Roswell, N. M.

BLEWITT, Rev. G. L. - heart attack
Paper & date: LS Sep. 3, 1884
Date & place of death: Aug. 29, 1884, Dallas, Texas

BLITHE, ERNEST - suicide
Paper & date: LS Aug. 1, 1883
Date & place of death: near Texarkana, Texas

BLUFORD, PINK - gambler of Colo.; flux
Paper & date: EPT Jul. 25, 1883
Date & place of death: Jul. 24, 1883, Silver City, N. M.

BLYTHE, THOMAS A. - of San Francisco, Calif. - heir: Miss DICKSON, for-
merly of Prescott, Ariz.
Paper & date: LS Apr. 18, 1883
Date & place of death: recently, San Francisco, Calif.

BOARD, DAVID M. - brakeman; run over by train; buried Concordia Cemetery,
El Paso, Texas, Oct. 7, 1883; native of Mercer co., Ky; came to El
Paso 16 mos. ago from Las Vegas, N. M.; family in Ky.
Paper & date: LS Oct. 6, 1883; LS Oct. 10, 1883; LS Oct. 7, 1883;
EPT Oct. 7, 1883
Date & place of death: Oct. 4, 1883, El Paso, Texas

BOATMAN, _____ (Negro) - dropped dead
Paper & date: LS Sep. 13, 1884
Date & place of death: Sep. 7, 1884, San Antonio, Texas

BOETTCHER, CHARLES - Thrown from wagon, wheel passed over his head
    Paper & date: LS May 23, 1885
    Date & place of death: May 16, 1885, near Weimar, Texas

BOGGETT, PADDY - Shot by DOC PARGOOD - probably fatal.
    Paper & date: LS Jan. 31, 1885
    Date & place of death: Williams, Ariz.

BOHEN, A. - found dead
    Paper & date: LS Oct. 28, 1885
    Date & place of death: near Jefferson, Texas

BOISSELIER, ADELA - age 12 - fa.: JULIUS BOISSELIER
    Paper & date: LS Dec. 8, 1883
    Date & place of death: Dec. 6, 1883, Paso del Norte, Mexico

BOLADA, MANUEL - Shot ten years ago by ____ ROSALES
    Paper & date: EPDH Mar. 16, 1884
    Date & place of death: Feb. 26, 1874, Mexico City

BOLTON, Mrs. ELEANOR
    Paper & date: LS Apr. 4, 1885
    Date & place of death: White Oaks, N. M.

BOLTON, JOHN T. - One of a RAYMOND excursion party from U. S.
    Paper & date: EPT Apr. 28, 1885
    Date & place of death: short time ago, Mexico City

BOMBREY, WILLIAM - Railroad cars; colored; a drayman; caught by Inter-
    national R. R. line
    Paper & date: LS Sep. 23, 1882
    Date & place of death: Sep. 19, 1882, San Antonio, Texas

BOND, ____ - Killed by GEORGE DAVIS in self-defense
    Paper & date: LS Dec. 31, 1881
    Date & place of death: Dec. 21, 1881, Johnson co., Texas

BOND, ____ - Shot by ____ TUCKER, sher.; had stolen El Paso Mayor
    MAGOFFIN's grey horses; BOND's partner, ____ PEVELY, claimed the
    horses after the shooting.
    Paper & date: LS Nov. 23, 1881; EPDH Oct. 12, 1881
    Date & place of death: last week, Deming, N. M.

BOND, ____ - Shot and killed by guards from train; convicted horse thief
    Paper & date: LS Mar. 22, 1882
    Date & place of death: Mar. 17, 1882, near San Antonio, Texas

BOND, JOHN T. - train wreck
    Paper & date: EPT May 1, 1883
    Date & place of death: on T & P R. R. near Ft. Worth, Texas

BOND, WILLIAM - age 74 years - services by Rev. M. MATTHIESON at house
    of Mrs. E. C. MARTIN; bur. Masonic Cemetery, Las Cruces, N. M.; b.
    Richmond, Wayne co., In., 1810; par.: Quakers; m. MARY HITCHCOCK;
    lived on shore of Lake Michigan, St. Louis, Shreveport, East Texas and
    back to St. Louis because of wife's health; to Calif. 1849; made and
    lost three fortunes; Harbor Master at St. Louis 1871; wife d. Mont-
    gomery co., Kan.; bought ranch near Deming, N. M.; children: (1) WM.
    H. BOND, ex-sher. and ex-state senator, Leavenworth co., Kan.; (2)
    IRA M. BOND, Edit. and Prop. Mesilla News; (3) THOS. L. BOND, ex-
    register of U. S. Land Office, Salina, Kan. and ex-state senator; (4)
    PHILIP Q. BOND, ex-merchant of Salina, Kan; (5) FANNIE BOND, d. aged
    12.
    Paper & date: RGR Jul. 5, 1884
    Date & place of death: June 30, 1884

BONNER, ROBERT - age 6 yrs. - son of master mechanic of S.P.R.R. ROBERT
    BONNER.
    Paper & date: EPDH May 31, 1882; EPDH Jan. 3, 1883
    Date & place of death: May 29, 1882, El Paso, Texas

BONNEY, WILLIAM (BILLY THE KID), alias McCARTHY, _____ - Buried Jul.
16, 1881, Sumner, N. M., in neglected military cemetery.
Paper & date: EPDH Sep. 21, 1881
Date & place of death: Jul. 14, 1881, Ft. Sumner, N. M.

BOOKOUT, _____ - Murder in "cold blood" by W. W. PARKS and his son,
THEODORE.
Paper & date: LS Apr. 1, 1882
Date & place of death: Last week, Archer co., Texas

BOONE, _____ - Shot and killed by WM. VAUGHN; two brothers killed were
gr-grandsons of DANIEL BOONE.
Paper & date: LS Dec. 30, 1882
Date & place of death: Last Monday, Ladonia, Texas

BOOTH, EVERETT - Negro - Shot by JOHN MOORE.
Paper & date: EPT May 1, 1883
Date & place of death: Apr. 29, 1883, Boulder, near Waco, Texas

BORNGASSER, GEORGE F. - Murdered; BENIGNO GONZALES, MANUEL GONZALES,
JOSE ALCARIO MONTOYA have been arrested.
Paper & date: TB Feb. 28, 1872
Date & place of death: La Bajada

BORUNDA, RAMON - Drowned swimming the Rio Grande with a telephone pole.
Paper & date: EPT Aug. 2, 1884
Date & place of death: Aug. 1, 1884, El Paso, Texas

BOSTON, CHARLES - Accidentally shot by VICTOR GABRILLE
Paper & date: LS Mar. 26, 1884
Date & place of death: Last week, Lordsburg, N. M.

BOSWELL, JOHN - Throat cut by JOE GRAHAM, negro, will not recover.
Paper & date: EPT Aug. 5, 1884
Date & place of death: Rice, Texas

BOSWELL, JOHN B. - Murder by HARRIS NORTON who was arrested near Honey
Grove.
Paper & date: LS Nov. 11, 1882
Date & place of death: A few days ago, Blossom Prairie, Texas

BOTHAMLY, _____ - Englishman shot; NELLIE C. BAILEY tried and acquitted;
maintained he shot himself; she has been married 3 times; was traveling with deceased at time of his death.
Paper & date: EPT Jan. 21, 1884
Date & place of death: About year ago, Indian Terr.

BOTTS, Maj. BENJAMIN A. - an old Texas Ranger
Paper & date: LS Sep. 26, 1885
Date & place of death: Houston, Texas

BOTTSFORD, Lt. CHARLES E. - Shot himself - suicide; bur. Nov. 30, 1884;
military funeral; unmarried, age about 50; family in N. Y.; entered
army in 1863 in N. Y.
Paper & date: EPMS Nov. 30, 1884; EPMS Dec. 2, 1884; LS Dec. 2, 1884;
EPDH Nov. 30, 1884; EPT Nov. 30, 1884
Date & place of death: Nov. 29, 1884, Ft. Bliss, Texas

BOUDINOT, ELIAS - Killed in feud.
Paper & date: EPT Jun. 26, 1883
Date & place of death: Jun. 23, 1883, home in Ind. Terr.

BOW, PATROSIMO- Wounded with axe by Justice of Peace RICARDO BOCA, Apr.
2, 1883
Paper & date: EPT Apr. 11, 1883
Date & place of death: Apr. 9, 1883, San Antonio, N. M.

BOWEN, _____ - Killed by JESSE W. JONES, an alias, a stage robber.
Paper & date: EPT Oct. 7, 1885
Date & place of death: Wichita Falls, Texas

BOWEN, SID - Poisoned; not a temperance man.
    Paper & date: LS Apr. 22, 1885
    Date & place of death: Albuquerque, N. M.

BOWERS, CHARLES - Murder
    Paper & date: LS Feb. 18, 1882
    Date & place of death: Feb. 2, 1882, between Villa and Los Campos,Tx.

BOWERS, CHARLES of Brady City, Texas; suicide by cutting throat.
    Paper & date: LS Jan. 21, 1885
    Date & place of death: Menardville, Texas

BOWMAN, ERNEST R. - 18 yrs. - Pneumonia; youngest son of M./M. GEORGE
    D. BOWMAN.
    Paper & date: LS Jan. 19, 1884; RGR Jan. 19, 1884
    Date & place of death: Jan. 13, 1884, Mesilla, N. M.

BOWMAN, MASON T. - sheriff
    Paper & date: LS Jun. 13, 1883
    Date & place of death: Colfax co., N. M.

BOX, STEPHEN - Suit of heirs claim Mrs. BOX sold land in Palestine, Tex.
    without being appointed executrix.
    Paper & date: LS Oct. 24, 1883
    Date & place of death: ....

BOYCE, JAMES - Killed by H. D. BOYCE.
    Paper & date: LS Mar. 4, 1885
    Date & place of death: Last week, DeKalb, Texas.

BOYD, CLARA PEARL - infant - Inflammation of the bowels; Par.: M. A. &
    CLARA A. BOYD.
    Paper & date: LS Jun. 23, 1883
    Date & place of death: Jun. 20, 1883, El Paso, Texas

BOYD, JOHN of Eagle Pass, Texas - Murder; GEORGE HAMMER charged with his
    murder, trial at Castroville, Texas
    Paper & date: LS Jan. 11, 1882
    Date & place of death:.........

BOYD, Capt. O. B. - Tr. K, 8th Cav.- age 41; b. Batavia, N. Y.; grad.-
    West Point; bur. Fairview, N. M.; wife and 3 children at Ft. Clark,
    Texas; dysentary.
    Paper & date: EPT Jul. 29, 1885
    Date & place of death: Jul. 23, 1885, near Grafton, N. M.

BOYLE, DANIEL - Pneumonia; age ca. 50 yrs., a cripple; native of Penn.
    Paper & date: LS Jan. 31, 1883
    Date & place of death: Jan. 31, 1883, El Paso, Texas

BOYLE, JAMES - Murdered
    Paper & date: LS Jun. 16, 1883
    Date & place of death: Feb. 1883, Mora co., N. M.

BOYLSTON, JESSE - Gunsmith - suicide
    Paper & date: LS Mar. 28, 1883
    Date & place of death: Mar. 22, 1883, Jefferson, Texas

BRACENTIGAN, J. W. - Assassinated
    Paper & date: LS Sep. 10, 1884
    Date & place of death: Sep. 3, 1884, Fredricksburg, Texas

BRACKEN, A. J. - Suicide by morphine
    Paper & date: LS Jun. 16, 1883
    Date & place of death: San Antonio, Texas

BRADFORD, FRANK - Put shotgun in mouth and blew top of his head off.
    Paper & date: LS Jan. 21, 1885
    Date & place of death: Wilson co., Texas

BRADLEY, MARTIN - Negro - lynched for rape.
      Paper & date: LS Aug. 22, 1883; EPT Aug. 18, 1883
      Date & place of death: Aug. 17, 1883, Terrell, Texas

BRADSHAW, _____ Officer; shoot out with negro mob.
      Paper & date: EPT May 1, 1883
      Date & place of death: Apr. 30, 1883, Marshall, Texas

BRADY, JOSEPH - To be hanged May 14, 1883; guilty of murdering.
      Paper & date: LS Apr. 18, 1883
      Date & place of death: ....

BRAGG, Miss _____ - Suicide over ill health; burned to death.
      Paper & date: LS May 19, 1883
      Date & place of death: Conham (Bonham?), Texas

BRAGG, BRAXTON - Pneumonia; nephew of Gen. BRAXTON BRAGG.
      Paper & date: EPMS Nov. 27, 1884
      Date & place of death: Few nights ago, Waco, Texas

BRAGG, CHARLES H. (A.) - Murdered by GREEN McCULLOCH (McCULLOUGH); shot.
      Paper & date: LS Aug. 16, 1884; EPT Aug. 15, 1884
      Date & place of death: Aug. 12, 1884, Cotulla, Texas

BRAHAM, _____ - age 1 mo. 2 days - dau.; Par.: M./M. B. BRAHAM.
      Paper & date: LS Mar. 21, 1883
      Date & place of death: Mar. 18, 1883, El Paso, Texas

BRANFORD, SAM - Negro - Shot by HAIL JONES of Burton, Texas
      Paper & date: LS Nov. 22, 1884
      Date & place of death: Nov. 15, 1884, Round Top, Texas

BRANNAN, JOE - Texas desperado; shot while resisting arrest at his mo's
      home; surv. by mo.
      Paper & date: LS Feb. 21, 1885
      Date & place of death: Near Springfield, Mo.

BRANT, THOMAS - Killed by _____ JOHNSON
      Paper & date: LS Dec. 5, 1883
      Date & place of death: Nov. 30, 1883, Coolidge, Texas

BRAZELL, _____ - Murder; W. W. COX and J. J. RYAN, two defendants, re-
      leased from Cuero, Texas jail on bond.
      Paper & date: LS Mar. 14, 1883
      Date & place of death: Over 4 years ago.

BRECK, HERMAN - Shot by MARTIN NELSON.
      Paper & date: LS May 9, 1885
      Date & place of death: May 5, 1885, Bonito, N. M.

BREED, JOHN, JR. (FRED A.) - Train accident; age ca 30, single, of Hol-
      brook, Ariz.; nephew of JOHN BREED of Flagstaff, Ariz.
      Paper & date: LS Feb. 21, 1885; LS Mar. 4, 1885
      Date & place of death: Feb. 19, 1885, Blue Water Sta., N. M.

BREEDING, PROSE in Abilene, Texas; shot and killed by ZENO HEMPHILL.
      Paper & date: LS Jan. 24, 1883
      Date & place of death: Jan. 20, 1883

BREMER, _____ of Murphysville, Texas; murdered for money.
      Paper & date: EPT Jul. 22, 1885
      Date & place of death: Near San Pedro Springs, Texas

BREMOND, PAUL - age 74, Texas R. R. builder; acute peritonitis; will
      bequests: Mrs. BREMOND, ED BREMOND, 5 daus.
      Paper & date: EPT May 10, 1885; EPT Jul. 24, 1885
      Date & place of death: Galveston, Texas

BREWER, ED - ca 24, of Georgia; consumption; bur. El Paso, Texas
      (cont'd on next page)

22

BREWER (cont'd):
    Paper & date: EPT May 27, 1885
    Date & place of death: May 26, 1885, El Paso, Texas

BREWSTER, Col. H. P. (Judge) - Bur.: at sea from Galveston by his wish,
    old settler.
    Paper & date: EPMS Jan. 3, 1885; EPT Dec. 30, 1884
    Date & place of death: Dec. 28, 1884, Austin, Texas

BREWSTER, OTTO - Shot by PETER MARCELIZ
    Paper & date: LS Jun. 24, 1885
    Date & place of death: other day, Star co., Texas

BRICE, JAMES - Steam boiler exploded.
    Paper & date: LS Jul. 28, 1883
    Date & place of death: Dallas, Texas

BRIGGS, J. - Overdose of morphine.
    Paper & date: LS Sep. 13, 1884
    Date & place of death: will die; Dallas, Texas

BRILL, Mrs. _____ - 4 ch.: 3 boys and 1 girl, all young; Mrs. COMSTOCK
    to adopt girl, other 3 need care.
    Paper & date: EPT Oct. 20, 1885
    Date & place of death: last week, El Paso, Texas

BRINK, _____ - baby, 5 wks old; erysipelas; par.: M/M W. C. BRINK
    Paper & date: LS Sept. 12, 1883
    Date & place of death: Sept. 12, 1883, El Paso, Texas

BRINSTER, JOSEPH - Hanged for rape; description: age 33, 5'8½" tall, 150
    lbs; a dau. 10 yrs old with his bro. in Ohio; wife died in child-
    birth; has bro., step-bro. & step-sis.; BRINSTER is his army name ...
    will not give his real name. Claims he's innocent but can't prove it;
    lived in Columbus, Ohio in 1874; convicted of raping Mrs. MATTIE McT.
    DAVIS, Ft. Davis, Texas year and half ago; b. Alsace, Germany; ca 34;
    m. in Iowa.
    Paper & date: LS Jun. 6, 1883; LS Jun. 9, 1883; LS Jul. 4,1883; LS
    Jul. 7, 1883; EPDH Jul. 8, 1883
    Date & place of death: Jul. 5, 1883, Yselta, Texas

BRISTOL, _____ (son) - horse fell on him; fa.: Capt. W. H. BRISTOL
    Paper & date: LS Nov. 8, 1884
    Date & place of death: Nov. 1, 1884, McKinney, Texas

BROCKSMIT, W. A. - in Colfax co., N. M. - murdered on ranch; fa.: is audi-
    tor for Cedar Rapids, Burlington & Northern R. R.
    Paper & date: LS Jan. 21, 1882
    Date & place of death: Jan. 16, 1882, Sweet Water, Colfax co., N. M.

BROCKSWIT, PETER - suicide; his son is said to have been killed and
    scalped by Indians in Texas(?) 2 weeks ago.
    Paper & date: LS Nov. 7, 1883
    Date & place of death: Nov. 5, 1883, Brooklyn, N. Y.

BRONCO BILL - Shot by _____ CASEY's men
    Paper & date: LS Jun. 9, 1883
    Date & place of death: Socorro, N. M.

BROOKS, _____ - Young man - accidentally shot himself while getting on
    his horse.
    Paper & date: EPT May 24, 1884
    Date & place of death: other day, Bastrop, Texas

BROOKS, Mrs. _____ - Long illness; husband: Mr. BROOKS of BROOKS & HOPE-
    WELL, Palomas, Mex.? N. M.?
    Paper & date: RGR May 22, 1884
    Date & place of death: recently, Colorado

BROOKS, W. CLARENCE - sher. - shot by H. GIBBS; bro.: CLIFF, El Paso, Tx.,
    EUGENE N., Wharton co., Texas
    Paper & date: LS Jul. 2, 1884; EPT Jul. 2, 1884
    Date & place of death: Jun. 30, 1884, Wharton co., Texas

BROOKS, LETTIE - Took poison.
    Paper & date: LS Jun. 6, 1883
    Date & place of death: Lordsburg, N. M.

BROPHY, JOHN - Shooting fray with WILLIAM JOHNSON, neither expected to
    live.
    Paper & date: LS Dec. 23, 1885
    Date & place of death: Liberty, N. M.

BROSVELOS, JOSE - Stabbed by PETRONILIO RIVERA; death was instantaneous
    at a dance; wife and 4 small children.
    Paper & date: RGR Nov. 1, 1884
    Date & place of death: Oct. 23, 1884, Tularosa, N. M.

BROUGH, F. D. - Prospector & mining engineer; missing, presumed killed
    by Indians.
    Paper & date: SH Nov. 23, 1884
    Date & place of death: Near Pena Colorado, Texas

BROWN, BELLE - Took poison.
    Paper & date: LS Sep. 5, 1885
    Date & place of death: Sep. 1, 1885, Austin, Texas

BROWN, DAVID - Sheer neglect and starvation in tent at rear of American
    Restaurant; Dr. MANNING attended him at 11th hour.
    Paper & date: LS Feb. 4, 1882
    Date & place of death: Feb. 3, 1882, El Paso, Texas

BROWN, ELIZA - Negro - age 115.
    Paper & date: LS Feb. 4, 1885
    Date & place of death: Last week, Marshall, Texas

BROWN, FIELDING C. - Threw himself out the window; interests in Tomb-
    stone, Ariz.
    Paper & date: EPMS Dec. 10, 1884
    Date & place of death: New York

BROWN, HEISE - Shot and killed by J. M. PHILLIPS, Justice of Peace.
    Paper & date: LS Jan. 6, 1883
    Date & place of death: Jan. 3, 1883, Coolidge, N. M.

BROWN, Capt. HENRY S.
    Paper & date: EPT Jun. 29, 1883
    Date & place of death: Jul. 26, 1834, Texas

BROWN, Mrs. J. - Negro - Killed by her hus. J. BROWN with a razor.
    Paper & date: LS Oct. 28, 1885
    Date & place of death: Corsicana, Texas

BROWN, J. L. of Elmira, N. Y. - Inflammation of the stomach; Masonic
    Lodge, bur. in Masonic Cemetery, El Paso, Texas; family in Elmira,
    N. Y.
    Paper & date: LS Jul. 16, 1884; EPT Jul. 16, 1884
    Date & place of death: Jul. 10, 1884, Parral, Mex.

BROWN, JACK - Shot by horse thieves
    Paper & date: LS Nov. 19, 1884
    Date & place of death: Last week, near Fleming, N. M.

BROWN, Mrs. JERUSHA of San Saba, Texas - 90 yrs. old, result of fall
    which broke her arm.
    Paper & date: LS Oct. 26, 1881
    Date & place of death: Oct. 17, 1881

BROWN, R. H. - wife: S. A. BROWN - later married G. McELROY.
    Paper & date: EPT Dec. 4, 1885
    Date & place of death: El Paso, Texas

BROWN, ROBERT - bur. Mar. 13, 1885 in El Paso, Texas
    (cont'd next page)

24

BROWN (cont'd):
    Paper & date: EPT Mar. 15, 1885
    Date & place of death: Aguas Calientes, Mexico

BROWN, TOM - Lynched for murder of _____ MARTIN.
    Paper & date: LS Jan. 26, 1884
    Date & place of death: Jan. 20, 1884, Lockwood, Texas

BRUNNER, _____ - Poisoned; Mrs. CHRISTIAN charged and released.
    Paper & date: LS Jan. 16, 1884
    Date & place of death: San Antonio, Texas

BRURFORD, WILLARD - Thrown from horse.
    Paper & date: LS Aug. 22, 1883
    Date & place of death: Ft. Worth, Texas

BRYAN, JOHN - Brakeman; shot himself, remorse over carelessness result-
    ing in 2 men dead in train accident.
    Paper & date: LS Mar. 14, 1883
    Date & place of death: Mar. 7, 1883, Fort Worth, Texas

BUCHANAN, _____ - age 20; shot - will die; fa.: Co. Comm. _____ BUCHANAN.
    Paper & date: EPT Aug. 1, 1884
    Date & place of death: Kaufman co., Texas

BUCHANAN, Dty. Sher., Fannin co. - Shot while arresting SAM and ELI DYER
    Paper & date: LS May 27, 1885; EPT Jun. 10, 1885
    Date & place of death: Mar. 11, 1885, Dallas, Texas

BUCHANAN, ELLA - age 20; par.: M/M S. H. BUCHANAN.
    Paper & date: EPDH May 17, 1882
    Date & place of death: May 17, 1882, El Paso, Texas

BUCHANAN, JAMES - age 80; b.- Newburg, N. Y.; on the border and Mexico
    50 years.
    Paper & date: EPT Jul. 10, 1884
    Date & place of death: Jul. 9, 1884, Paso del Norte, Mexico

BUCHEE, ROBERT - Shooting affray with CARTER HARRIS; surv.: WILLIS BUCHEE
    Paper & date: LS Oct. 6, 1883
    Date & place of death: Sep. 30, 1883, Snipe Springs, near Carbon, Tx.

BUCHOZ, MARGARET B. - Infant aged 4 mos. 8 days; par.: A. J. and M. R.
    BUCHOZ.
    Paper & date: RGR Apr. 11, 1885
    Date & place ot death: Apr. 8, 1885, Las Cruces, N. M.

BUCKINGHAM, JOHN - Struck over head with pitcher by JESSE THOMPSON, alias
    _____ MORRIS.
    Paper & date: LS Sep. 27, 1884
    Date & place of death: Sep. 22, 1884, San Antonio, Texas

BUCKLEY, JAMES - Shot ca. Oct. 31, 1871 by confederates in a robbery.
    Paper & date: TB Nov. 15, 1871
    Date & place of death: .....

BUDWIG, _____ of Lavaca co., Texas
    Paper & date: LS Jul. 16, 1884
    Date & place of death: Jul. 7, 1884, Austin, Texas

BUENAVIDES, _____ (?) - Young man; accidental discharge of his gun.
    Paper & date: LS Jun. 23, 1883
    Date & place ot death: El Rio, N. M.

BUIN, BARNEY - Sunstroke
    Paper & date: LS Aug. 1, 1883
    Date & place of death: Denison, Texas

BULGER, JAMES - of Canada, brakeman; fell under train, body returned to
El Paso, Texas; sweetheart in San Francisco, Calif.
Paper & date: LS Jul. 4, 1883; EPT Jul. 3, 1883
Date & place of death: Jul. 1, 1883, 135 mi. east of El Paso, Texas

BULL, Mrs. CLARA - Hus.: ALEXANDER BULL; sis.: Mrs. A. J. BUCHOZ; fa.:
RAFAEL RUELAS, family of young children.
Paper & date: LS Nov. 26, 1884; RGR Nov. 15, 1884
Date & place of death: Nov. 8, 1884, Mesilla, N. M.

BULLARD, _____ - Boy, age 4, drank a swallow of carbolic acid (kept in
house as a preventative of small pox.); Fa.: JAMES BULLARD.
Paper & date: RGR Jan. 19, 1884
Date & place of death: 20 mi. out of Lake Valley, N. M.

BULLARD, Capt. JOHN M. - Murdered by Apaches; shot in breast and died
"without a groin" (groan?); native of Missouri; survived by a bro.
of Silver City, N. M.; bur. at Ft. Bayard with full military honors.
Paper & date: TB Mar. 16, 1871
Date & place of death: Feb. 23, 1871, near Pinos Altos, N. M.

BUNCH, ADOLPHUS - Negro - Shot while trying to escape by officer LEWIS
WILLIAMS.
Paper & date: LS Jul. 18, 1883; LS Jul. 21, 1883
Date & place of death: Houston, Texas

BUNTING, _____ - Murdered by Apaches; of west fork of Gila River.
Paper & date: RGR Jun. 27, 1885
Date & place of death: Recently

BURGOS, JUAN DE DIOS (DIAZ), Judge; sudden; wife and 7 young children.
m. in Chihuahua, Mexico.
Paper & date: EPT Mar. 14, 1885
Date & place of death: Mar. 14, 1885, El Paso, Texas

BURHAM, Mr. and Son - Murdered by Indians.
Paper & date: TB Mar. 28, 1871
Date & place of death: Between Casas Grandes and Gavilan on the way
to Silver City, N. M.

BURKE, _____ - Gunsmith; heart disease; wife and 3 small children.
Paper & date: LS Jan. 3, 1883
Date & place of death: Yesterday, El Paso, Texas

BURKE, C. H. - age 26, of Chicago, Ill.; consumption; Prof. of Greek
in an Indiana College; wife age 21: IDA M. PIERCE BURKE.
Paper & date: LS Mar. 15, 1882
Date & place of death: Mar. 8, 1882, San Antonio, Texas

BURKE, JOHN - Shot by HENRY TACKETT
Paper & date: EPT Dec. 9, 1883
Date & place of death: Dec. 8, 1883, Flagstaff, Arizona

BURKHART, Mrs. - Negro; shot by husband.
Paper & date: LS Apr. 18, 1885
Date & place of death: San Antonio, Texas

BURLESON, BURL - Negro of Wellborn, Texas; shot during arrest; struggle
with R. R. agent.
Paper & date: LS Jan. 27, 1883
Date & place of death: Jan. 15, 1883, Brazos co., Texas

BURN, _____ - Run over by T & P; Mo.: MARY BURN got a verdict of $5000
Paper & date: LS Sep. 20, 1882
Date & place of death: Four months ago, near Baird, Texas

BURNS, _____ - Rattlesnake bite
Paper & date: LS Apr. 11, 1883
Date & place of death: Apr. 5, 1883, San Antonio, Texas

BURNS, JAMES - Run over by train.
    Paper & date: LS Jun. 30, 1883
    Date & place of death: Toyah, Texas

BURNS, JIM - Bit the dust; a desperado; arrest of three officers MOORE,
    DAN TUCKER and McCLELLAN in Grant co., N. M.; indictment.
    Paper & date: LS Aug. 30, 1882; LS Sep. 9, 1882
    Date & place of death: Aug. 25, 1882, Silver City, N. M.

BURNS, MICKY of Deming, N. M.; murder for his money.
    Paper & date: LS Nov. 30, 1881
    Date & place of death: ....

BURNS, MIKE - Murdered; WILLIS ADAMS, bro. of SAMUEL J. ADAMS, charged
    in Dallas, Texas.
    Paper & date: LS Nov. 26, 1884
    Date & place of death: .....

BURR, SHIELDS - Yellow fever.
    Paper & date: EPT Oct. 3, 1883; EPT Nov. 18, 1883
    Date & place of death: Sep. 7, 1883, at sea off Mex. coast.

BURR, WM. - Murder by "SANTA CRUZ" SMITH at SHEDD Ranch.
    Paper & date: LS Jan. 3, 1883
    Date & place of death: Dec. 26, 1882, San Augustin, N. M.

BURSLEY, Capt. - Suicide; surv.: wife and daughter
    Paper & date: EPDH Oct. 4, 1882
    Date & place of death: Before 1881, San Antonio, Texas

BURT, Dr. EDWIN of Las Cruces, N. M.; pneumonia, age 51; mining re-
    sources at Organ, N. M., lumber interests in Michigan, and had been
    located in Brooklyn, N. Y.; surv.: wife, 2 daughters and 1 son.
    Paper & date: LS Oct. 10, 1885; RGR Oct. 10, 1885
    Date & place of death: Oct. 4, 1885, Mesilla, N. M.

BURTON, FANNIE - Negro - Gorging on watermelon and grapes; formerly of
    Bryan, Texas
    Paper & date: LS Aug. 16, 1884; EPT Aug. 15, 1884
    Date & place of death: Aug. 15, 1884, El Paso, Texas

BURTON, HANNAH - age 12; raped and murdered by WEB HELTON, ex-convict.
    Paper & date: EPT Jul. 21, 1884
    Date & place of death: Jul. 19, 1884, Galveston, Texas

BUSBY, CHARLES - Killed by R. R. cars
    Paper & date: LS Feb. 25, 1882
    Date & place of death: Last week, Ft. Worth, Texas

BUSCHER, FRITZ - Murdered
    Paper & date: TB Dec. 28, 1872
    Date & place of death: Dec. 16, 1872, Cherry Valley, below La Junta.

BUSH, Mrs. WM. and 3 children- Taking morphine for quinine; hus.: WIL-
    LIAM BUSH.
    Paper & date: LS Mar. 3, 1883
    Date & place of death: Near Corsicana, Texas

BUTCHER, ROBERT - Shot by ____ HARRIS; bro.: WILLIAM BUTCHER.
    Paper & date: EPT Oct. 3, 1883
    Date & place of death: Sep. 30, 1883, Comanche, Texas

BUTLER (?), _____ - Fight with Indians in Stein's Peak range.
    Paper & date: LS Oct. 19, 1881
    Date & place of death: Oct. 13, 1881, near Lordsburg, N. M.

BUTLER, EMMET - Killed after he killed Sher. TERRY of Llano co., Texas.
    Paper & date: EPT Dec. 30, 1884; LS Dec. 30, 1884
    Date & place of death: Dec. 28, 1884, Galveston, Tx (or Llano co,Tx?)

BUTLER, GEORGE - Brakeman; killed in train accident.
Paper & date: LS Dec. 26, 1885
Date & place of death: Manuelito, N. M.

BUTTER, _____
Paper & date: LS Sep. 19, 1883
Date & place of death: Sep. 14, 1883, Henrietta, Texas

BUTZ, THEODORE - Suicide
Paper & date: LS Jul. 28, 1883
Date & place of death: Galveston, Texas

BYERS, Mrs. ____ - Struck by lightening, not expected to recover.
Paper & date: LS Apr. 22, 1885
Date & place of death: Johnson co., Texas

BYERS, JOHN - Murder; suspects: HENRY HODGE and E. H. DWINNELLS
Paper & date: LS Mar. 29, 1882
Date & place of death: Raton, N. M.

BYERS, JOHN - Smallpox
Paper & date: LS Aug. 26, 1882 (Sat.)
Date & place of death: Few days ago, Albuquerque, N. M.

BYRNE, Gen. J. J. of Galveston, Texas; killed by Indians; surv.: wife
and dau. (wife later Mrs. MAX ELSER)
Paper & date: LS Nov. 10, 1883; EPDH Nov. 22 1882; EPDH Feb. 4,1883
Date & place of death: Mid-Aug. 1880, near Ft. Quitman, Texas

BYTHEWOOD, _____ - Sher. of Wharton. JAMES WATTESON sentenced in Hous-
ton to 5 yrs. for murder.
Paper & date: LS Nov. 5, 1884
Date & place of death: Last spring, Wharton, Texas

CADETTE - Chief of Mescalero Apaches and interpreter. Suspician points
to his son-in-law, SANTANA. (Cadette had killed one son-in-law.)
Paper & date: TB Nov. 23, 1872
Date & place of death: .....

CAHILL, BEN - Murder; a miner in Mexico
Paper & date: LS Jul. 26, 1882
Date & place of death: San Antonio, Sonora, Mexico recently

CAJEME (CAJOME) - Yaqui chief; murdered by authorities
Paper & date: EPT Jul. 12, 1883; BU June 18, 1887
Date & place of death: 2nd day of Feast of St. John, Guaymas, Mexico

CALABASA - aged Indian; Ex-Governor of the Pueblo of San Diego. Run
over by train near Wallace, N. M.
Paper & date: LS Feb. 3, 1883
Date & place of death: Jan. 29, 1883

CALDWELL, EDWARD - Killed after murdering R. H. MORRISON.
Paper & date: RGR May 26, 1883; LS May 23, 1883
Date & place of death: San Augustin, N. M.

CALDWELL, SHOCK - Executed for murder of W. R. NORVELL. Had fled to
Clinton, Mo. about 40 miles from Sedalia, Mo.
Paper & date: LS Aug. 23, 1882
Date & place of death: Aug. 18, 1882, McKinney, Texas

CALE, J. F. - Eleventh man killed by JOEL FOWLER (stabbed)
Paper & date: LS Nov. 14, 1883
Date & place of death: Socorro, N. M.

CALHOUN, HAYWOOD (Negro) - Bur. Nov. 27, 1884
Paper & date: EPMS Dec. 4, 1884
Date & place of death: Brazos county, Texas

CALL, _____ - of Hidalgo co., Texas.   Shot attempting escape.
   Paper & date: EPT Mar. 22, 1885
   Date & place of death: Grimes co., Texas

CALLAHAN, JOHN J. - Died natural death. Gambler formerly of El Paso, Tx.
   Paper & date: LS June 6, 1883; LS June 9, 1883
   Date & place of death: June 4, 1883 Silver City, N. M.

CALLAWAY, Mrs. TABITHA B.
   Paper & date: LS Nov. 22, 1884
   Date & place of death: Nov. 17, 1884, Albuquerque, N. M. at home.

CALVIN (Negro) - Killed by CHANCE McCAMPBELL, negro
   Paper & date: EPT May 28, 1896
   Date & place of death: 15 years ago near Floresville, Texas

CAMPBELL, _____ - Murder by MILT YARBERRY.
   Paper & date: LS Sept. 13, 1882
   Date & place of death: N. M.

CAMPBELL, GEO. - Shootout - DALLAS STOUDENMIRE - "two of the roughs".
   Paper & date: EPDH Dec. 28, 1881; NTF Apr. 20, 1881
   Date & place of death: Apr. 17, 1881

CAMPBELL, GRACE - Bur. Aug. 4, 1885; Par.: M./M. ROBERT F.(& IRENE) CAMP-
   BELL. Bros. and sisters. b. Bastrop co., Texas, -18 years ago.
   Paper & date: LS Aug. 5, 1885; EPT Aug. 5 & 9, 1885
   Date & place of death: Aug. 3, 1885, El Paso, Texas

CAMPBELL, HENRY - Negro - to be hanged for murder of policeman --------
   SNOW?
   Paper & date: EPT June 25, 1884
   Date & place of death: Aug. 11, 1884, Houston, Texas

CAMPBELL, R. - Estate sales, El Paso, Texas
   Paper & date: EPDH Oct. 5, 1881
   Date & place of death:.....

CAMPBELL, W. C. - Shot by GEORGE McALLISTER
   Paper & date: LS Aug. 20, 1884
   Date & place of death: Last week, Point Rock, Texas

CANDELARIA, SERAFIN - Murdered by JOSE ANGEL PEREA and his 3 daus. -
   oldest named JULIANA.
   Paper & date: LS Nov. 28, 1883
   Date & place of death: Albuquerque, N. M.

CANNON, Col. LEANDER
   Paper & date: LS Apr. 1, 1882
   Date & place of death: Mar. 25, 1882, Galveston, Texas

CANTRELL, Dr. _____ and his son - murdered by JOE COX
   Paper & date: LS Oct. 8, 1884
   Date & place of death: 3 years ago, Weatherford, Texas

CARBO, Gen. JOSE GUILLERMO - Cerebral disorder.
   Paper & date: EPT Oct. 31, 1885
   Date & place of death: Oct. 29, 1885, Hermosillo, Sonora, Mexico

CARDALE, ALFRED
   Paper & date: LS Feb. 27, 1884
   Date & place of death: Feb. 25, 1884, Albuquerque, N. M.

CARLETON, GEORGE
   Paper & date: LS July 1, 1885
   Date & place of death: Albuquerque, N. M.

CARLTON, _____ - fa. awarded $2500 from T & P R.R. for killing of his son.
   fa.: J. CARLTON
   Paper & date: LS Jun. 16, 1883/ Date & place: Kauffman, Texas

CARLTON, JOHN from Las Vegas, N. M.; smallpox; bro. in Bernal, N. M.
Paper & date: LS Apr. 7, 1883
Date & place of death: April 6, 1883, El Paso, Texas

CARMELO, DEMITRIO - Killed by Indians
Paper & date: EPDH Oct. 5, 1881
Date & place of death: Between Wilcox and San Carlos, Ariz.

CARNEY, JOHN - Shot by THOMAS GRADY
Paper & date: BU Dec. 19, 1885
Date & place of death: Dec. 14, 1885, Lake Valley, N. M.

CARR, Mrs. _____ - Killed by Indians; formerly of Santa Rita, had been
accused of having poisoned her husband and had been in jail in Silver
City, N. M.
Paper & date: LS Jan. 25, 1882
Date & place of death: ca Jan. 23, 1882, near Clifton, Ariz. Terr.

CARR, FRANK - Killed by wife ANNA CARR who has been acquitted.
Paper & date: LS May 26, 1883; LS May 30, 1883
Date & place of death: Few weeks ago, Las Vegas, N. M.

CARRILLO, MARIANO - Thrown from a horse.
Paper & date: LS July 7, 1883
Date & place of death: Silver City, N. M.

CARROLL, E. B. of Va.; probably by Apaches.
Paper & date: EPT Sept. 29, 1884
Date & place of death: Recently; mtns 300 mi. beyond Chihuahua, Mex.

CARRUTHER, JAMES - Stockman; train accident
Paper & date: EPT Sept. 6, 1883
Date & place of death: Sept. 4, 1883, near Ross, Texas

CARSON, JOHN ot Biloxi, Miss., engineer; train wrecked by washout near
Calera, Mexico.
Paper & date: LS Sept. 13, 1884; EPDH Sept. 14, 1884
Date & place of death: Sept. 9, 1884 700 mi. s. E. P. on Mex. Cen-
tral R. R.

CARSON, WILLIAM - about 25 yrs. Shot by S. P. (or E. S.) WRIGHT. Claimed to be oldest son of KIT CARSON and 2nd wife - Mex. woman. No relative of Carson - he was young man from Boston who had another name
before he came west. Kit Carson and Mex. woman had 4 children: 1 boy
in Springer, N. M., dau. at school in Trinidad, Colo., Kit, Jr. employed by Sen. DORSEY in Palo Blanco, N. M.
Paper & date: LS Jan. 23, 1884; LS Jan. 26, 1884; EPDH Feb. 10,1884
Date & place of death: Jan. 18, 1884, near Watrous, N. M.

CARTER, DON - Suicide by morphine over death of his young wife.
Paper & date: LS Oct. 18, 1884
Date & place of death: Oct. 12, 1884, Longview, Texas

CARTER, W. P. - of Blue Ridge, Falls co., Texas; suicide by morphine.
Paper & date: LS May 20, 1885
Date & place of death: May 14, 1885, Waco, Texas

CARTER, WILLIE E. - age 7 mos. - enterocolitis; Par.: M./M. W. H. CAR-
TER
Paper & date: EPT May 19, 1885
Date & place of death: May 17, 1885, El Paso, Texas

CARTMELL, Judge N. B. - One of the oldest citizens; wife and 3 children
Paper & date: BU May 1, 1884
Date & place of death: April 6, 1884, Socorro, N. M.

CARUTHERS, JAMES - Train wreck; suit by rel. against Central RR filed in
Waco, Texas
Paper & date: LS Nov. 14, 1883
Date & place of death: ....

CASAD, THOMAS of Mesilla, N. M.; failing health but had family take him
to his favorite hunting grounds - 30 mi. from Mesilla, where he died
of pneumonia, age 69. b. Ohio, 1819; to Ill. to Los Angeles; 1874
to Mesilla. 1877 was editor of "Mesa Independent". Was a principal
owner of Brazito Land Grant. Leaves wife - SARAH V. CASAD and large
family.
Paper & date: LS Oct. 10, 1885; RGR Oct. 10, 1885; RGR Oct. 17, 1885;
RGR Oct. 2, 1886
Date & place of death: Oct. 7, 1885, Mesilla, N. M.

CASE, F. P. of Vinita, Ind. Terr.; murdered; white citizen of Cherokee
Nation; m. an Indian.
Paper & date: EPT Aug. 25, 1885
Date & place of death: Aug. 20, 1885, near Sacs and Foxes Agency,
Indian Terr.

CASEY, JOSEPH - Sentenced to hang for murder of Jailer ___ HOLBROOK.
Paper & date: LS June 23, 1883
Date & place of death: July 27, 1883, Tucson, Ariz.

CASPER, S. of Birmingham, Ala.; found dead.
Paper & date: EPT Oct. 30, 1884
Date & place of death: Oct. 27, 1884, near Longview, Texas

CASSEL, EMIL of Mesilla, N. M.
Paper & date: RGR Oct. 4, 1884
Date & place of death: Sept. 19, 1884

CASSIDY, THOMAS - Destitute
Paper & date: LS Nov. 11, 1885
Date & place of death: Waco, Texas

CASTANEDA, A. A. - Shot by BEN DOWD
Paper & date: LS Jan. 25, 1884; LS Dec. 12, 1883
Date & place of death: Dec. 10, 1883, Bisbee, Ariz.

CASTANEDA, MAXIMO - Suddenly
Paper & date: LS Dec. 12, 1883
Date & place of death: Dec. 11. 1883, Chamberino, N. M.

CASTILLO, JUAN - Hanging for rape.
Paper & date: LS Aug. 9, 1884
Date & place of death: Aug. 8, 1884, Raton, N. M.

CASTILLO, W. H. - Shot by unknown while asleep. Mother.
Paper & date: EPT Oct. 14, 1884
Date & place of death: Oct. 11, 1884, near Antioch, Lavaca co., Tex.

CASTRO, ANDRES - Suicide - did not love girl his fa. wished him to marry;
Father.
Paper & date: LS May 2, 1883
Date & place of death: Laredo, Texas

CATO, MALDONADO - Murdered.
Paper & date: EPT July 28, 1885; EPT July 30, 1885
Date & place of death: Whetstone Mtns. near Fairbanks, Ariz.

CAULEY, Mrs. ____ - Murdered by her only son RICHARD CAULEY, who had
spells of insanity.
Paper & date: EPDH Apr. 1, 1883
Date & place of death: Mar. 17, 1883, San Antonio, Texas

CAVALLOS, PEDRO - Thrown from horse.
Paper & date: LS Nov. 19, 1884
Date & place of death: Few days ago, San Antonio, Texas

CAYCE, S. - Texas Veteran.
Paper & date: EPT July 7, 1884
Date & place of death: July 3, 1884, San Antonio, Texas

CAZAR, LUKE - about 35; premature explosion;supposed to be from Va.
Paper & date: EPDH Oct. 26, 1881
Date & place of death: Oct. 19, 1881, 62 mi. East of E. P. on R. R.

CEARES,(?), CARNES (?), Dr. ISAAC T. - Suicide overdose of morphine.
(bad film)
Paper & date: LS June 27, 1883
Date & place of death: Socorro, N. M.

CHAMBERLAIN, FRANK - Suicide; laudanum
Paper & date: LS Dec. 9, 1885
Date & place of death: Ft. Bayard, N. M.

CHAMBERS, _____ (little daughter); fence pole fell on her.
Paper & date: LS Oct. 11, 1884
Date & place of death: Hico, Texas

CHAMBERS, LEWIS - Killed by Indians.
Paper & date: LS Nov. 9, 1881
Date & place of death: After Oct. 24 and before Nov. 9, 1881, near
Lucero, Chih., Mex.

CHAPIN (CHAPIFF), ____ - Murdered by Indians.
Paper & date: TB May 4, 1871
Date & place of death: Apr. 13, 1871, San Pedro Valley

CHAPMAN, ____ - Waxahachie R. R.; wife: CYNTHIA CHAPMAN obtained a
$10,000 judgement in Dallas U. S. Court against the R. R.
Paper & date: LS Jan. 6, 1883
Date & place of death: About a year ago.

CHAPMAN, ____ - Son-in-law C. L. MIXER, El Paso
Paper & date: EPDS Jan. 7, 1885
Date & place of death: Over a week ago, Kansas City.

CHAPMAN, ____ - Suicide
Paper & date: LS Mar. 10, 1883
Date & place of death: Mar. 5, 1883, Springer, N. M.

CHAPMAN, Dr. P. L. - Scarlatina typhoid; Grad. Ann Arbor Medical Center;
spent short time in Mesilla, N. M.; details of life not known.
Paper & date: RGR Jan. 26, 1884
Date & place of death: Jan. 23, 1884

CHAPPELL, COLEMAN of Stockton
Paper & date: EPT May 19, 1884
Date & place of death: May 18, 1884, Grass Valley, (N. M. or Calif.?)

CHAPPELL, SARAH (negro) name given as SARAH CHAPIN also; murdered by
JIM TAYLOR, Negro who was hanged in Galveston, Texas Dec. 21, 1883
Paper & date: Ls Dec. 29, 1883; EPT Nov. 18, 1883
Date & place of death: Giddings, Texas

CHARLES, ____ - Fight with Indians.
Paper & date: EPDH Oct. 26, 1881
Date & place of death: Oct. 13, 1881, near Stein's Peak range, N. M.

CHARLEY - a Chinaman; shot
Paper & date: EPT June 1, 1883
Date & place of death: May 29, 1883, El Paso, Texas

CHASE, Mr. and Mrs. and 2 children: Killed by Indians; older daughter
apparently kidnapped.
Paper & date: EPT May 18, 1883
Date & place of death: 15 yrs. ago, 75 mi. from Ft. Concho, Texas

CHAUNCEY, ____ Shot by mob.
Paper & date: EPT Apr. 16, 1883
Date & place of death: Last week, Gatesville, Texas

CHAVES, _____ - child, 14 mos.; pneumonia; fa.-TELESFERO CHAVES.
   Paper & date: RGR June 9, 1883
   Date & place of death: June 6, 1883, Las Cruces, N. M.

CHAVEZ, Mrs. _____ - age 89; son: JUAN CHAVEZ
   Paper & date: EPDH Oct. 12, 1881
   Date & place of death: Last week, San Antonio, Texas

CHAVES, ANDRES - Brutally beaten at Bernalillo, N. M. by MANUEL GARCIA;
   Bro.
   Paper & date: LS May 13, 1885
   Date & place of death: May 10, 1885, Pajarito, N. M.

CHAVEZ, ARIAS - Fell through ice on river and washed under.
   Paper & date: LS Jan. 28, 1885
   Date & place of death: Jan. 22, 1885, Alameda, N. M.

CHAVES, BENITO of Albuquerque, N. M. ; stabbed while in the home of two
   Mexican women of ill repute.
   Paper & date: LS Dec. 31, 1881
   Date & place of death: Dec. 28, 1881

CHAVEZ, CAMILIO - Killed by CLEOFUS ROMERO in self defense.
   Paper & date: LS Nov. 14, 1885
   Date & place of death: N. M.

CHAVES, CARLOS - Shot by mob after jail break; convicted murderer of
   Chinaman near Ft. Bayard, N. M. in Feb. 1883
   Paper & date: LS Mar. 12, 1884; LS Aug. 22, 1884
   Date & place of death: Mar. 10, 1884, near Silver City, N. M.

CHAVES y PINO, JUAN --murder by _____LOGWOOD and _____ HOUSE.
   Paper & date: LS July 29, 1882
   Date & place of death: Lincoln co., N. M.

CHAVEZ, JULIAN - Killed by a train.
   Paper & date: LS Oct. 3, 1885
   Date & place of death: Sept. 29, 1885, near Las Vegas, N. M.

CHAVEZ, Padre MANUEL of Los Lunas, N. M. ; son: DEMETRIO CHAVEZ.
   Paper & date: LS Nov. 30, 1881
   Date & place of death: Nov. 26, 1881

CHAVEZ, Sra. MICACIA GARCIA DE - age 120 at death; she had 6 ch.; 36
   grch.; 112 ggrch.; 37 gggrch.; 1 ggggrch.; youngest dtr. Srta. ASCEN-
   CION CHAVEZ, 88.
   Paper & date: LS Sept. 12, 1885
   Date & place of death: Last week, San Mateo, N. M.

CHEROKEE JIM - Mangled.
   Paper & date: LS Oct. 21, 1885
   Date & place of death: Near ABBOTT ranch, N. M.

CHICO, PEPE - Lawyer; stabbed by bro. over woman.
   Paper & date: EPT June 10, 1885
   Date & place of death: June 8, 1885, Guanajuato, Mex.

CHILDRESS, _____ - Murdered by 6 men.
   Paper & date: EPMS Dec. 14, 1884
   Date & place of death: San Saba, Texas

CHILDS, JOHN W. - shot by city marshal.
   Paper & date: LS Nov. 22, 1884 (Saturday)
   Date & place of death: Friday night (probably a week ago), Palestine,
   Texas

CHIN HUNG - Killed by HUNG AH HUNG
   Paper & date: LS May 2, 1885
   Date & place of death: July 1884, San Angelo, Texas

33

CHIPMAN, H. - Ex-ranger, not 20 yrs. old; shot by Mexicans; formerly
    lived on the Salado near San Antonio, Texas
    Paper & date: EPDH Sept. 7, 1881
    Date & place of death: Sept. 3, 1881, Pittsburg, near El Paso, Tex.

CHISUM, JOHN - Had been at Hot Springs, Ark. for some months for his
    health; for so long a leading cattleman of our territory (N. Mex.)
    Paper & date: RGR Jan. 3, 1885
    Date & place of death: Recently

CHRISTIE, _____ - Suicide; bro. in San Jose, California
    Paper & date: LS Nov. 7, 1883
    Date & place of death: Alameda, Calif.

CHRISTMUS, P. T. - Shot by PREY HUMPHREYS
    Paper & date: LS Nov. 7, 1885
    Date & place of death: Near Uvalde, Texas

CISCK, GEORGE - Fell three stories - died of internal injuries.
    Paper & date: LS May 26, 1883
    Date & place of death: Dallas, Texas

CISCO, _____ - Murdered by MILES BOSS
    Paper & date: LS Oct. 4, 1884
    Date & place of death: Few months ago, Marlin, Texas

CISNEROS, CONCEPCION- Pneumonia
    Paper & date: RGR Mar. 22, 1884
    Date & place of death: Last week, Las Cruces, N. M.

CLAIBORNE, Col. J. F. H. (Historian) - 77 yrs.
    Paper & date: LS May 24, 1884
    Date & place of death: May 17, 1884, Natchez, Miss.

CLAIBORNE, JAMES (miner) - Killed by WILLIAM COVINGTON, miner.
    Paper & date: LS May 13, 1885
    Date & place of death: May 1, 1885, Crittenden, Ariz.

CLARA, Capt. JESSE - age 83; 35 yrs. in Texas; Vet. of Tex. Rev.
    Paper & date: EPT Apr. 27, 1883
    Date & place of death: Recently, Texas

CLARK, _____ - Suicide; middle-aged teamster; no other name could be
    found; bur. on the spot.
    Paper & date: RGR July 7, 1883
    Date & place of death: June 23, 1883, at Whitewater between Ft. Sel-
    den and Ft. Stanton, N. M.

CLARK, _____ - Negro; killed by _____ JACKSON, Negro.
    Paper & date: LS June 27, 1883
    Date & place of death: Asia, San Jacinto co., Texas

CLARK, _____ - Killed by Indians.
    Paper & date: LS Dec. 26, 1885
    Date & place of death: Cactus Flat, N. M. or Ariz.

CLARK, Mrs. _____ - daus.: EMMA and AMANDA
    Paper & date: EPT Sept. 9, 1883
    Date & place of death: Jan. 1883, Gainesville, Texas

CLARK, BUSH - Hung by mob.
    Paper & date: EPDH Oct. 12, 1881
    Date & place of death: Oct. 6, 1881, Socorro, N. M.

CLARKE, C. C. - Friends believed to be in Ill.
    Paper & date: LS Mar. 31, 1883
    Date & place of death: Near Whitewater, N. M.

CLARK, CAGE of Bonham, Tex.; killed by lightning
    Paper & date: LS Nov. 12, 1881/ Date & place: Oct. 24, 1881

CLARK, Col. E. D. - Pneumonia; Ass't Sec'y of Interior; formerly of
   Vicksburg, Miss; bur. Holly Springs, Miss; bro.: LEIGH CLARK of El
   Paso, Texas; wife.
   Paper & date: EPT Mar. 24, 1885
   Date & place of death: Mar. 23, 1885, Washington, D. C.

CLARKE, F. P. - House bought by Capt. THATCHER for his family in Nash-
   ville.
   Paper & date: LS Jan. 11, 1882
   Date & place of death: before Jan. 1882

CLARK, FRED W. - age 31 yrs. 11 mos.; congestion of brain and apoplectic
   fits; bur.: Aug. 26, 1883; wife.
   Paper & date: EPT Aug. 28, 1883
   Date & place of death: Aug. 25, 1883, Deming, N. M.

CLARKE, GAYLORD JUDD - Tragic; b. Feb. 28, 1830; Founder of St. Clement's
   Episc. Ch., El Paso, Texas; dau.: CLEMENT who died in El Paso; wife
   Paper & date: EPDH Apr. 13, 1896
   Date & place of death: Dec. 7, 1870, El Paso, Texas

CLARK, JENNIE - Murdered by FRED GLOVER; convicted June Court.
   Paper & date: LS Mar. 18, 1885
   Date & place of death: N. M.

CLARK, Capt. W. P. - Indian fighter; 2nd Cavalry; att'd to Lt. Gen. SHER-
   MAN's staff.
   Paper & date: EPT Sept. 24, 1884
   Date & place of death: Sept. 21, 1884, Washington, D. C.

CLAY, JOHN - Skull broken in negro gambling house.
   Paper & date: LS Oct. 22, 1884
   Date & place of death: Recently, Waco, Texas

CLEMENTS, L. M. - Killed by Mexicans, NICHOLAS OLGUIN and ten others.
   Paper & date: LS Dec. 29, 1883; LS Dec. 22, 1883
   Date & place of death: Dec. 10, 1883, Clifton, Ariz.

CLEMMONS, H. E., JR.
   Paper & date: EPT Oct. 30, 1884
   Date & place of death: Marshall, Texas

CLEVELAND, G. W. - Negro shot by mob after jail break.
   Paper & date: LS Mar. 12, 1884
   Date & place of death: Mar. 10, 1884, near Silver City, N. M.

CLEVELAND, W. R. - Fell off cars on Sunset line
   Paper & date: LS Oct. 1, 1884
   Date & place of death: Sept. 24, 1884, Texas

CLIFTON, _____ Murdered by KID LEWIS
   Paper & date: EPT Sept. 15, 1883
   Date & place of death: Some time ago, Silver City, N. M.

CLIFTON, A. - Shot himself accidently
   Paper & date: LS June 23, 1883
   Date & place of death: Dublin, Texas

CLOTH, Sgt. CHRISTIAN, 8th Cav.; suicide-shot himself.
   Paper & date: LS Aug. 22, 1883
   Date & place of death: Meyers Spring, Texas

CLOUGH, _____ - Wife of Socorro, N. M.
   Paper & date: BU Nov. 7, 1885
   Date & place of death: Baltimore, Md.

COALBACK, Maj. GEORGE at San Antonio, Texas; fight at Lee's Creek.
   Paper & date: LS Jan. 27, 1883
   Date & place of death: Jan. 21, 1883

COATS, SAM - R. R. engineer;   train accident on Louisville, New Orleans
   & Texas R. R.
   Paper & date: LS Jan. 23, 1884
   Date & place of death: Jan. 18, 1884, near Ft. Gibson.

COCHISE - Rumored to have died as a result of a fight in Sonoro, Mex.
   Paper & date: TB Aug. 23, 1871
   Date & place of death:.........

COCHRAN, ANDREW of Longview, Texas;   killed by HIRAM GIVENS - justified.
   Paper & date: EPT Apr. 24, 1883
   Date & place of death: Apr. 21, 1883, Lordsburg, N. M.

COCIGAN (?), SALVATOR -Italian;   drowned swimming in the Bosque River.
   (Bad film)
   Paper & date: LS June 6, 1883
   Date & place of death: near Waco, Texas

COCKRANE, W. R. - Crushed by another tender in roundhouse as he was
   cleaning one.
   Paper & date: LS Oct. 22, 1884
   Date & place of death: Last week in Palestine, Texas

CODINGTON, JOSIAH - Suicide by cutting artery in left arm.
   Paper & date: LS Feb. 21, 1885
   Date & place of death: Few days ago, Albuquerque, N. M.

CODY, THEODORE -
   Paper & date: LS Aug. 20, 1884
   Date & place of death: Last week, San Saba, Texas

COLDWELL, EDWARD from New York;   shot by miners for murdering ROBERT
   MORRISON.
   Paper & date: LS May 23, 1883
   Date & place of death: May 20, 1883, San Augustin, N. M.

COLE, A. B. - Lawyer in Dallas, Texas;   run over by cars.
   Paper & date: LS Nov. 15, 1882
   Date & place of death: Last week

COLE, Mrs. C. F. - is dying;   hus.: C. F. COLE.
   Paper & date: LS Nov. 10, 1883
   Date & place of death: San Angelo, Texas

COLE, JAMES E. - Murdered by JOEL FOWLER
   Paper & date: EPDH Jan. 27, 1884
   Date & place of death: Nov. 1883, Socorro, N. M.

COLE, NATHAN (negro) - Brains beat out while acting as peace-maker.
   Paper & date: LS Nov. 22, 1884
   Date & place of death: Nov. 16, 1884, Kildare, Texas

COLEMAN, CHARLES, JR.
   Paper & date: LS Mar. 31, 1883
   Date & place of death: Mar. 29, 1883, Las Cruces, N. M.

COLLINS, _____ - Messenger;   killed by robbers including JACOB ELMER
   and CHARLES HINSLEY near Tucson, Ariz.
   Paper & date: EPT Oct. 6, 1883
   Date & place of death: Aug. 10, 1883

COLLINS, _____ - Shot by GEO. NEILL, a bar tender.
   Paper & date: LS Mar. 7, 1883
   Date & place of death: Seguin, Texas

COLLINS, Judge - in Las Vegas, N. M.; effects of whiskey; talented law-
   yer, late of California.
   Paper & date: LS Dec. 9, 1882
   Date & place of death: Dec. 4, 1882

COLLINS, CLARA - Accidentally shot by a young lady friend.
    Paper & date: LS July 25, 1883
    Date & place of death: Ft. Worth, Texas

COLLINS, GEORGE - Shot by JOHN RYAN, foreman of Bobtail Mine.
    Paper & date: RGR Jan. 5, 1884
    Date & place of death: Dec. 24, 1883, Hillsboro, N. M.

COLLINS, PAT - Conductor; stabbed by a lunatic.
    Paper & date: RGR Dec. 6, 1884
    Date & place of death: Deming, N. M.

COLLINS, T. - Killed by Lt. THURSTON in self-defense.
    Paper & date: LS Oct. 31, 1885
    Date & place of death: Ft. McIntosh

COMON, WM. - Run over by train.
    Paper & date: LS Aug. 1, 1885
    Date & place of death: Beaumont, Texas

COMSTOCK, _____ - Shot by son TOM COMSTOCK in dispute over crop division
    Paper & date: LS Nov. 11, 1885
    Date & place of death: Wise co., Texas

COMSTOCK, F. J. - IOFF member; Surv.: widowed mo. and sis.
    Paper & date: EPDH Jan. 27, 1884
    Date & place of death: ....

CONANT, FRED H. - Young journalist; bur. Aug. 31, 1884, Colorado Springs,
    Colo. from home of W. L. CONANT; fa.: W. A. CONANT, Winslow, Ariz.;
    wife.
    Paper & date: EPT Sept. 11, 1884
    Date & place of death: Aug. 1884, Colorado Springs, Colo.

CONE, JOHN - Negro; hanged for rape.
    Paper & date: LS Jul. 11, 1883
    Date & place of death: Jul. 6, 1883, Houston, Texas

CONE, WALTER - Former telegraph editor of New Mexican, Albuquerque.
    Paper & date: LS Sept. 13, 1882
    Date & place of death: Sept. 7, 1882, Denver, Colo.

CONGER, DEL - Premature discharge of cannon.
    Paper & date: LS July 12, 1884
    Date & place of death: July 4, 1884, Centralia, Mo.

CONKLIN, A. M. - Editor of Socorro, N. M.; murdered - shot by EUNOFRIO
    BACA; wife
    Paper & date: LS Nov. 12, 1881; EPDH Dec. 14, 1884
    Date & place of death: Dec. 25, 1880

CONKLIN, JAMES - Said to have been first American settler in Santa Fe,
    arriving in June, 1822.
    Paper & date: LS June 9, 1883
    Date & place of death: Santa Fe, N. M.

CONNELL, W. W. - Shot and killed by JAKE DAVIS or FRITZ DAVIS, driver
    for the transfer company; CONNELL was S. P. brakeman.
    Paper & date: LS Oct. 11, 1882; EPDH Oct. 11, 1882
    Date & place of death: Oct. 8, 1882, El Paso, Texas

CONNELLY, J. B. - Fell from wagon.
    Paper & date: LS Dec. 23, 1885
    Date & place of death: Near Bowie, Texas

CONNOLLY, C. P. of Sulphur Springs, Texas; bur. Nov. 18, 1881 with Mason-
    ic honors.
    Paper & date: LS Nov. 26, 1881
    Date & place of death: ....

CONNORS, JOE - Shot by _____ WAZBURG while entering his home intoxicated
Paper & date: LS Nov. 12, 1884
Date & place of death: Nov. 7, 1884, Prescott, Ariz.

CONNER, M. - Suicide; ill and despondent? Not a soldier, but he went
to Ft. Bliss Hospital for help; refused. A guard did give him a
blanket and a place to sleep. Probably from Benson, Ariz or Los Angeles.
Paper & date: LS Jan. 18, 1882
Date & place of death: last week

CONNOR, R. J. - Sher. of Burnet co., Texas; remains sent to Georgia.
Paper & date: LS Nov. 23, 1881
Date & place of death: ....

CONSADINE, SIMON - Explosion on R. R. south of Benson, Ariz. Territory
Paper & date: LS Jan. 21, 1882
Date & place of death: Jan. 12. or 19, 1882

CONSINDINE, _____ at Deming, N. M.; shot by Dty. Sher. while trying
to escape.
Paper & date: LS Nov. 25, 1882; LS Sept. 27, 1882
Date & place of death: last week, near Rincon, N. M.

CONTRERAS, JUAN - No immediate survivors.
Paper & date: RGR Aug. 29, 1885
Date & place of death: Aug. 21, 1885, Chamberino, N. M.

CONVEL, MATHIAS - Killed by JIM GRAY
Paper & date: LS Dec. 12, 1885
Date & place of death: Floresville, Texas

COOK, _____ Killed by lightning.
Paper & date: LS Aug. 29, 1885
Date & place of death: Purmela, Texas

COOK, Col. ABNER HUGH -
Paper & date: LS Feb. 27, 1884
Date & place of death: Feb. 22, 1884, Austin, Texas

COOK, B. F. - age 24; consumption; Par. of Westport, Kans.
Paper & date: SH July 26, 1885; EPT July 28, 1885
Date & place of death: July 25, 1885 El Paso, Texas

COOK, Judge HENRY C. of El Paso, Texas; bro.: M. L. COOK of San Joa-
quin, California.
Paper & date: LS June 9, 1883
Date & place of death: May 25, 1883, San Joaquin, Calif.

COOPER, Judge HENRY, ex-Senator of Tenn.; murdered and robbed.
Paper & date: LS Feb. 16, 1884
Date & place of death: Short time ago near Caliocan, Chih. Mex.

COOPER, PETER - Built Copper Union (Cooper Union?)
Paper & date: EPT Apr. 15, 1883
Date & place of death: ....

COOPER, Mrs. ROBERT (Negro); cut in abdomen by hus.; hus.: ROBERT COOPER
Paper & date: LS Oct. 22, 1884
Date & place of death: Oct. 16, 1884, Galveston, Texas

COOPS, JOHN - Shot while asleep on porch. Wife's bro. BEN MILLER is
accused.; wife.
Paper & date: LS Aug. 6, 1884
Date & place of death: Last week, Gatesville, Texas

COPINGER, PATRICK - Miner; aged 32, unmarried; accidently shot by PAT-
TRICK CANNON.
Paper & date: RGR Dec. 8, 1883; LS Dec. 15, 1883
Date & place of death: Dec. 5, 1883, Lake Valley, N. M.

CORKEY, J. J. of St. Louis, Mo. injured when stage overturned; will die; stage from Abilene, accident near Rocky Bluff.
Paper & date: EPT June 18, 1885
Date & place of death: San Angelo, Texas

CORN, JASPER N. - Dty. Sher. Lincoln co.; shot by NICOLAS ARAGON while resisting arrest at Gallinas Springs, San Miguel co., N. M.
Paper & date: LS Nov. 5, 1884
Date & place of death: Few days ago, Lincoln co., N. M.

COSGROVE, _____ - Infant girl; Par.: M./M. C. COSGROVE
Paper & date: TB Nov. 1, 1871
Date & place of death: Thurs. Oct. 2, 1871, Las Cruces, N. M.

COSSAD, FRANK P. - Murdered in camp.
Paper & date: LS Aug. 29, 1885
Date & place of death: Aug. 27, 1885, Vinita, Indian Terr.

COSTILLO family - Killed by Indians; nine members of family - 3 generations - grfather and grmother near 80; their son and wife and 5 chi.
Paper & date: EPDH Sept. 13, 1882
Date & place of death: near Calabasas, Mex.

COSTILLO, JUAN of Raton, N. M.; lynched - enticed a little girl away from home.
Paper & date: RGR May 30, 1885
Date & place of death: Aug. 30, 1884

COTTON, ANNIE of Dallas, Texas; suicide, arsenic.
Paper & date: LS Jan. 11, 1882
Date & place of death: Jan. 3, 1882

COULTER, ED. - "The Kid" - lynched.
Paper & date: LS Nov. 19, 1881
Date & place of death: About two weeks ago, Tierra Amarilla, N. M.

COURIER, JEAN (COUPIER?) - Jugular vein cut by Italian tramp, whom a posse hanged.
Paper & date: LS Aug. 30, 1882
Date & place of death: Aug. 27, 1882, Deming, N. M.

COWAN, W. B. of Nappanee, Indiana; oldest of children;   bro.: Dr. COWAN of Las Cruces; sis.: Mrs. P. C. MESSICK; bro.: JOHN COWAN of Goshen; late fa.: Hon. JOSEPH COWAN of New Paris.
Paper & date: RGR Dec. 20, 1884
Date & place of death: Dec. 8, 1884

COWART, HARRY - Convict working on CLAY's Plantation tried to escape.
Paper & date: LS Oct. 14, 1885
Date & place of death: Oct. 10, 1885, near Millican, N. M.

COWDREY, N. A. - Heart disease; well-known in Texas, Mexico and El Paso.
Paper & date: EPT Oct. 28, 1885
Date & place of death: Oct. 19, 1885, New York.

COX, _____ - Sher. and posse broke up a gang of horse thieves; COX was leader of the gang.
Paper & date: LS Aug. 12, 1882
Date & place of death: A few days ago near Sherman, Texas

COX, _____ - Daughter killed by Indians; fa.: HENRY COX and family.
Paper & date: EPT June 5, 1885
Date & place of death: Few years ago, New Mexico.

COX, BARNY - aged 50 yrs; pneumonia - ill 48 hours.
Paper & date: RGR Jan. 24, 1885
Date & place of death: Before Jan. 20, 1885, Lake Valley, N. M.

COX, Judge THOMAS B. - suddenly
Paper & date: LS Sep. 27, 1884/ Date & place: Sep. 19,1884,Bonham, TX

CRABTREE, RUSSEL - aged 18, of Sulphur Springs; attempted suicide by
    shooting himself in the shoulder.
    Paper & date: EPMS Nov. 27, 1884
    Date & place of death: ....

CRAIG, DAVID - Waylaid and killed by JAMES LYLE - old feud.
    Paper & date: LS Dec. 16, 1885
    Date & place of death: Panola, Texas

CRAIG, E. F. - Killed in fight at NED BOUND's home during a dance.
    Paper & date: EPT Feb. 13, 1885; LS Feb. 14, 1885
    Date & place of death: Feb. 11, 1885, Chickasaw Nation, Ind. Terr.

CRAMER, HENRY - Found dead in bed; formerly with Denver & Rio Grande RR
    Paper & date: EPT Dec. 5, 1885
    Date & place of death: Dec. 3, 1885, Salida, Colo.

CRANE, WALTER - Killed by Sher. ROBB
    Paper & date: LS Feb. 25, 1882
    Date & place of death: Feb. 18, 1882 near Uvalde, Texas

CRANSTON, ROBERT - Run over by Mexican Central R. R. cars on Dec. 7, 1881;
    fa. from Atlanta, Georgia.
    Paper & date: LS Dec. 21, 1881
    Date & place of death: Dec. 16, 1881

CRARY, CHARLES P. - age 34; drowned in acequia while drunk; wife- no ch.
    both frm Cincinnati, Ohio.
    Paper & date: LS Sept. 26, 1885; EPT Sept.25, 1885
    Date & place of death: Sept. 23, 1885, El Paso, Texas

CRAWFORD, BEN - Sher. of Graham co., Ariz.; killed by Indians.
    Paper & date: EPT Dec. 4, 1885
    Date & place of death: Near Wilcox, Ariz.

CRAWFORD, Mrs. JACK - body taken to Philadelphia for bur.; hus.
    Paper & date: RGR Mar. 8, 1884
    Date & place of death: Mar. 1, 1884, El Paso, Texas

CRAWFORD, WM. S. - of Albuquerque, N. M. ; shot by JAY ELLIOT; Crawford
    was one of PAT GARRETT's deputies.
    Paper & date: LS Dec. 24, 1881
    Date & place of death: Dec. 18, 1881

CRESPIN, _____ - Murdered by young _____ LUCAS.
    Paper & date: LS Oct. 21, 1882
    Date & place of death: A month ago, Golden, N. M. (Colo.?)

CREWS, SAM - 14 yrs. old ; drowned.
    Paper & date: LS Aug. 25, 1883
    Date & place of death: Near Hancock Springs on Lampasas River, Texas

CRITTENDEN, WILLIAM - Shot self.
    Paper & date: LS Aug. 13, 1884
    Date & place of death: Denver, Colo.

CRIZLE, CHRIS -
    Paper & date: EPDH Oct. 18, 1882
    Date & place of death: Oct. 16, 1882, El Paso, Texas

CROCKETT, _____ - Young man; murdered by JOHN M. OLIVER
    Paper & date: LS Mar. 11, 1885
    Date & place of death: Few days ago, Chickasaw Nation, Ind. Terr.

CROSBY, FRANK of Galveston, Texas; drowned; wrecked boat found.
    Paper & date: LS Feb. 8, 1882
    Date & place of death: Recently

CROSS, CHARLES - Typhoid; a native of Derbyshire, England, and Supt. of
    Mr. SCHAUBLIN's mill. Family in England; 2 daus.; bur. Masonic Cem.

CROSS, CHARLES (cont'd):
   Paper & date: RGR Oct. 13, 1883; RGR Dec. 1, 1883
   Date & place of death: Oct. 7, 1883, Las Cruces, N. M.

CROSS, SARAH - Relict of FRANCIS CROSS; son: CHARLES CROSS of Las Cruces, N. M.
   Paper & date: RGR July 28, 1883
   Date & place of death: May 23, 1883, Penley, England.

CROSS, THOMAS - aged 45; an old miner - "leaded"; lead poisoning - held to be death from natural causes; had worked in Penn. and latest at Socorro, N. M.
   Paper & date: RGR Jul. 26, 1884
   Date & place of death: Jul. 21, 1884

CROUCH, Capt. J. S. (or S. C.) - Old settler
   Paper & date: EPMS Jan. 3, 1885; EPT Jan. 9, 1885
   Date & place of death: Dec. 31, 1884, Deming, N. M.

CROW, GEORGE - Injured March 2, 1885; tenderly cared for; "May the crows on the fence, In your hearing play; Five corns on your dying day."
   Paper & date: RGR Mar. 7, 1885
   Date & place of death: Mar. 5, 1885

CROWLEY, PETER J. - aged 39 yrs.; shot by _____ GRIFFITH; b. Mass.; bro.: J. J. CROWLEY, San Antonio, New Mexico; wife in Milwaukee.
   Paper & date: BU Aug. 22, 1885
   Date & place of death: Aug. 19, 1885, at his ranch, 40 mi. east of Carthage, N. M.

CRUMMING (CRUMMEY?), _____ - son, age 5 yrs.; thrown from burro and dragged; fa.: GEORGE CRUMMING.
   Paper & date: LS Sept. 30, 1885
   Date & place of death: Las Vegas, N. M.

CRUMP, WILLIAM (Negro) - Shot
   Paper & date: LS Aug. 1885
   Date & place of death: Found Aug. 22, 1885, near Las Vegas, N. M.

CUARON, CONCEPCION - Shot by OCTAVIANO GARCIA
   Paper & date: LS Feb. 2, 1884
   Date & place of death: Jan. 31, 1884, Paso del Norte, Mex.

CUMMINGS, Dr. S. M. - Shootout by JAMES MANNING, owner of Coliseum and another person; bro.-in-law of DALLAS STOUDENMIRE.
   Paper & date: LS Feb. 15, 1882; EPDH Feb. 15, 1882
   Date & place of death: Feb. 14, 1882

CUNNINGHAM, Dr. _____ - Shot by STERLING KING.
   Paper & date: LS Apr. 18, 1885
   Date & place of death: Duffau, Erath co., Texas

CUNNINGHAM, S. S. - Shot by RICHARD BREEDLOVE.
   Paper & date: LS July 25, 1883
   Date & place of death: Socorro, N. M.

CURLEY, BILL - Hung
   Paper & date: LS Nov. 28, 1883
   Date & place of death: Grant co., N. M.

CURRAN, EDWARD - Congestion of bowels; bro.: JOHN CURRAN of Mex. Cen. RR
   Paper & date: EPT June 7, 1883
   Date & place of death: June 3, 1883, Chihuahua, Mexico

CURRIE, JAMES R. of Marshall, Texas; shot and killed; Sher. JESSE LEE, _____ KIMBERLY and McCALL (or _____ McPHAUL) were tried; HICKENBAUGH also listed as killer; bro.: JOHN CURRIE
   Paper & date: EPT Mar. 18, 19, 20, 1885; LS Apr. 1, 1885; LS May 9, 1885
   Date & place of death: Mar. 16, 1885, Springer, N. M.

CURRIE, JOHN - Shot; Sher. JESSE LEE, ____ KIMBERLY, ____ McCALL (McPHAUL)

41

CURRIE, JOHN (cont'd):
    and HICKENBAUGH - tried; bro.: was JAMES R. CURRIE of Marshall, Texas
    Paper & date: LS May 9, 1885; EPT Mar. 19,20, 1885
    Date & place of death: Mar. 18, 1885, Springer, N. M.

CURTIS, Mrs. ALICE - Took poison; Mrs. Curtis was of York (state not
    given.)
    Paper & date: LS Dec. 30, 1882
    Date & place of death: Lordsburg, N. M.

CURTIS, J. W., JR. - aged 17; strangulated hernia; fa.: J. W. CURITS, SR.
    of South Fork, N. M.
    Paper & date: RGR Nov. 14, 1885
    Date & place of death: Oct. 17, 1885

CURTIS, JACK - Run over by train
    Paper & date: EPT Apr. 12, 1883
    Date & place of death: Apr. 10, 1883, near Santa Rosalia, Mex.

CURTIS, NELSON - a cowboy; killed by two Mexicans.
    Paper & date: LS Mar. 28, 1883
    Date & place of death: Valencia co., N. M.

CUSHING, Col. LEE - Killed by COCHISE' band in Whetstone Mountains.
    Paper & date: TB May 18, 1871
    Date & place of death: May 5, 1871, Whetstone Mountains

CUSICK, S. - Consumption
    Paper & date: EPDH Feb. 15, 1882
    Date & place of death: Feb. 14, 1882, El Paso, Texas

CUTLER, CON.(?) of California; yellow fever
    Paper & date: EPT Sept. 27, 1885
    Date & place of death: Sept. 25, 1885, Hermosillo, Mexico

DAGGETT, Mrs. _____
    Paper & date: LS Oct. 1, 1884
    Date & place of death: Ft. Worth, Texas

DAILEY, BRADFORD - Killed by Indians; widow, married _____ REA, lives in
    Tucson, Ariz.
    Paper & date: EPDH Dec. 3, 1895
    Date & place of death: 22 years ago, near Las Cruces, N. M.

DAILY, GEORGE - In Dona Ana co., N. M.*
    Paper & date: LS Jan. 7, 1882; EPDH Dec. 28, 1881; RGR Dec. 15,1883
    Date & place of death: Aug. 1881, Lake Valley, N. M.
    (* Killed by Indians led by Chief NANE; Post office named for him..
    DALY at Silver Camp, Dona Ana co., N. M.)

DALAY, JOHN - Apache; killed by Maj. RANDALL's scouts.
    Paper & date: TB July 11, 1874
    Date & place of death: June 14, 1874, Arizona

DAILY, THOMAS - Shot and killed
    Paper & date: LS Mar. 1, 1882
    Date & place of death: Last week, Gallup Station, N. M.

DALLAS, _____ (Negro) - Slipped while hopping on train
    Paper & date: LS Jan. 11, 1882
    Date & place of death: Last week, near Waco, Texas

DAMERON, DAN - Lingering on verge of grave for months; one of the first
    American settlers of the valley; b. Cape Girardeau co., Mo. about 46
    years ago. Went to Calif. at an early day. 1862 to N. M. with First
    Regiment of Calif. Column. First Sgt. in RYNERSON's Co.
    Paper & date: RGR Feb. 28, 1885
    Date & place of death: Feb. 24, 1885

DANBURY, GUS - Cutting affray.
    Paper & date: LS Dec. 30, 1885
    Date & place of death: Seay, Texas

DANIELS, HENRY (Negro) - Murdered
    Paper & date: LS June 2, 1883
    Date & place of death: Recently near Austin, Texas

DANIELS, WILLIAM A. - Killed by Indians - Apaches.
    Paper & date: LS June 13, 1885
    Date & place of death: June 9, 1885, near Bisbee, Arizona

DAP,_____ - Dty. Sher. of Henderson co., Texas; killed by Rev. HENRY
    SMITH, Baptist preacher.
    Paper & date: LS May 23, 1883
    Date & place of death: 3 years ago.

D'ARCAMBAL, CHARLES - aged 64; Veteran of Texas Navy, Badge of Honor from
    SAM HOUSTON. Descendant of noble family of France. Grandfather was
    consul at Baltimore, Md. under NAPOLEON. An uncle still lives in
    France, a member of nobility.
    Paper & date: SH Apr. 26, 1885
    Date & place of death: Few days ago, Kalamazoo, Michigan

DAVENPORT, WILLIAM - Son of Judge T. OEPPERWEIN charged with murder.
    Paper & date: LS July 16, 1884
    Date & place of death: July 6, 1884 Leon Springs (Bexar co.-Pecos?)

DAVEY, WILLIAM - Bewildered by fire; literally roasted alive.
    Paper & date: RGR July 12, 1884
    Date & place of death: June 24, 1884, Lake Valley, N. M.

DAVIS, _____ - Boy age 14; chilled to death; mo.: Mrs. Davis
    Paper & date: EPMS Dec. 17, 1884
    Date & place of death: Dec. 13, 1884, near Merkel, Texas

DAVIS, _____ - Shot and stabbed by Dr. _____ DAVIS. WHITTINGTON also
    arrested.
    Paper & date: EPT Oct. 5, 1883
    Date & place of death: Oct. 2, 1883, near Franklin, Texas

DAVIS, Judge _____- Elderly gentleman of Bryan, Texas
    Paper & date: EPDH Sept. 28, 1881; EPDH Oct. 5, 1881
    Date & place of death: Sept. 27, 1881, El Paso, Texas

DAVIS, Mrs. _____ - House burned
    Paper & date: LS June 23, 1883
    Date & place of death: Paris, Texas

DAVIS, Mrs. ALICE - Puerperal fever; hus.: CHARLES DAVIS; 3 small child-
    ren.
    Paper & date: EPDH Jan. 11, 1882
    Date & place of death: Jan. 8, 1882, El Paso, Texas

DAVIS, Mrs. ANNA E. of Las Cruces, N. M.; shot herself over grief for her
    son HARRY who died about 2 mos ago and violent death of hus.
    Paper & date: EPT Aug. 31, 1883; RGR Sept. 1, 1883; LS Sept. 1, 1883
    Date & place of death: Aug. 29, 1883, Organ, N. M.

DAVIS, C. C. -Committed suicide
    Paper & date: LS Mar. 4, 1882
    Date & place of death: Ysleta, N. M., Feb. 26, 1882

DAVIS, Mrs. CHARLES - Bur.: Concordia Cemetery; hus.
    Paper & date: LS Jan. 5, 1884
    Date & place of death: El Paso, Texas

DAVIS, CHRIS - Poisoned by_____ SAYRE with carbolic acid.
    Paper & date: LS Dec. 22, 1883
    Date & place of death: About 10 days ago, Socorro, N. M.

DAVIS, GEORGE W. - aged 32 of Rincon, N. M.; native of Worcester, Mass.
    Paper & date: EPT Nov. 11, 1884
    Date & place of death: Nov. 5, 1884, Santa Fe, N. M.

DAVIS, HARRY - Little boy; Mo.: Mrs. ANNA E. DAVIS
    Paper & date: EPT Aug. 31, 1883
    Date & place of death: Two mos. ago, Las Cruces, N. M.

DAVIS, HARRY - Blacksmith; struck by lightning
    Paper & date: LS Aug. 1, 1883
    Date & place of death: Near Whitesboro, Texas

DAVIS, I. H. of San Fe; shot accidently and killed
    Paper & date: LS Oct. 26, 1881
    Date & place of death: Last week

DAVIS, JACK - Run over by his wagon while in town trading.
    Paper & date: LS Jan. 10, 1885
    Date & place of death: Jan. 8, 1885, Waco, Texas

DAVIS, JAMES - Bullet in his heart; not known whether accidental or sui-
    cide.
    Paper & date: RGR Apr. 4, 1885
    Date & place of death: Last Monday at La Luz, N. M.

DAVIS, MARTIN - age 22; Private C Troop 10th Cavalry; killed in action
    with Indians.
    Paper & date: EPT Jun. 27, 1883
    Date & place of death: Jul. 30, 1880, Eagle Springs, Texas

DAVIS, SARAH (Negro) - Second try at suicide by morphine.
    Paper & date: LS Aug. 22, 1885
    Date & place of death: Denison, Texas

DAVIS, TEMPY - Negro woman; visited Brenham, Texas; returned home; be-
    lieve poisoned.
    Paper & date: LS Feb. 2, 1884
    Date & place of death: Texas

DAVIS, TOM - Confidence man formerly of Las Vegas, N. M. shot by JAMES
    T. HOLLAND, a Texan from Abilene. JOHN T. HILL, Abilene marshal,
    accessory.
    Paper & date: LS Sept. 2, 1885; LS Sept. 5, 1885
    Date & place of death: Sept. 1, 1885, New York.

DAWSON, CHARLES - Old feud; shot by JNO. H. GOOD; Mo.: Mrs. DAWSON who
    killed ROBERT BLACK in Socorro a little over a year ago; step-son:
    WILLIAM RAPER.
    Paper & date: RGR Dec. 12, 1885; LS Dec. 16, 1885; RGR Dec. 19,1885
    Date & place of death: Dec. 8, 1885, La Luz, N. M.

DEAL, BARRON FERGUSON of El Paso; native of Iowa, age 26; consumption;
    wife and relatives; issued first newspaper in El Paso, Apr. 2, 1881,
    the "Herald".
    Paper & date: EPT May 19, 1885; LS May 20, 1885; SH May 24, 1885
    Date & place of death: May 16, 1885, Warrensburg, Mo.

DE BERRY, JOHN - Stabbed by CLYDE MADDOX
    Paper & date: LS Oct. 4, 1884
    Date & place of death: Sept. 27, 1884, Gainesville, Texas

DE FORREST, JOHN - Shot by father-in-law, _____ BOLTON; surv.: wife
    Paper & date: LS Feb. 25, 1882
    Date & place of death: Feb. 21, 1881, White Oaks, N. M.

DE GAMBS, ROBERT - Shot by _____ THOMPSON, self defense.
    Paper & date: LS Feb. 27, 1884
    Date & place of death: Feb. 21, 1884, Lake Valley, N. M.

DEGREFENERD, JOE - Stabbed 21 times in fight in a saloon with J. W. JONES,

DEGREFENERD (cont'd):   a school teacher.
    Paper & date: LS Sept. 23, 1882
    Date & place of death: Sept. 16, 1882, Whitney, Texas

DE GRESS, Col. FRANCIS; bro. Col. J. C. DE GRESS, Mayor of Austin, Tex.;
    sis.: Mrs. A. F. STEINBUCH of El Paso, Texas
    Paper & date: EPDH Jan. 21, 1883; EPDH Apr. 9, 1894
    Date & place of death: Mexico City, death announced.

DE HAGUE, J. A. (J. C.)- heart disease; wife
    Paper & date: LS June 20, 1885; EPT June 20, 1885
    Date & place of death: June 18, 1885, El Paso, Texas

DELAMU, WILLIAM - Insane man accidently shot and killed himself
    Paper & date: LS Mar. 4, 1882
    Date & place of death: Feb. 26, 1882, Socorro, N. M.

DELANY, FLORENCE B. - hus.: W. E. DE LANY (son of post trader at the
    Fort.)
    Paper & date: RGR July 14, 1883
    Date & place of death: Recently, Ft. Stanton, N. M.

DELANEY, WILLIAM - To be hanged for murder (Bisbee, Ariz.)
    Paper & date: LS Mar. 26, 1884
    Date & place of death: Mar. 28, 1884, Tombstone, Ariz.

DELARD, CHARLES - Murdered by Indians between Casas Grandes and Gavilan
    on way to Silver City, N. M.
    Paper & date: TB Mar. 16, 1871
    Date & place of death: ....

DELEON, BENITO - To be shot for wrecking and robbing train in Nov. 1883
    Paper & date: EPT Aug. 13, 1885
    Date & place of death: Nuevo Laredo, Mex.

DENHAM, CHAS. - Murdered by WM. JONES and C. C. TOWNER.
    Paper & date: LS Nov. 25, 1885
    Date & place of death: Near Lincoln, N. M.

DENNINGHOFF, THOMAS and wife and 3 children; drowned in floods.
    Paper & date: EPT May 30, 1885
    Date & place of death: May 27-28, 1885, Waco, Texas

DENNY, FRANK - Exposure on hunting trip.
    Paper & date: LS Jan. 10, 1885
    Date & place of death: Grafton, N. M.

DENVER, J. C. - Shot by _____ ALLISON.
    Paper & date: LS Dec. 2, 1885; EPT Dec. 2, 1885
    Date & place of death: Ft. Worth, Texas

DEPPE, CHAS. - Suicide by morphine; barber; oldest resident German sett-
    ler.
    Paper & date: LS Jan. 24, 1883
    Date & place of death: Jan.19, 1883, Dallas, Texas

DEUS, J. P. - G. W. WAHL, Adm. of estate, Ysleta, Texas
    Paper & date: EPDH Aug. 5, 1883
    Date & place of death: ....

DEVEREAUX, E. C. - bro.: J. J. DEVEREAUX of El Paso, Texas
    Paper & date: LS Sept. 17, 1884
    Date & place of death: Sept. 14, 1884, Laurence, Kansas

DEVINA, JOHN - While on a spree went to sleep on R. R. track - run over
    by train.
    Paper & date: LS Mar. 18, 1885
    Date & place of death: Houston, Texas

DEVINE, JOHN - Double pneumonia; an old resident of Lake Valley, N. M.
Paper & date: RGR Jan. 17, 1885
Date & place of death: Jan. 10, 1885

DEWALL, A. of Houston, Texas; Left note planning suicide - unheard of
since; wife and children.
Paper & date: EPT Aug. 16, 1885
Date & place of death: ....

DIBBLE, _____ - Young; murdered by BONITO's band of Indians; bro.:
Judge _____ DIBBLE, New Orleans, La.
Paper & date: EPT Sept. 15, 1883; EPDH Jan. 11, 1890
Date & place of death: Last spring,near Winchester, Ariz.

DIBBLE, FRANK - Shot and died; bur.: in Las Vegas, N. M.
Paper & date: LS Dec. 28, 1881
Date & place of death: Dec. 20, 1881, Santa Fe, N. M.

DICKSON, _____ - Brakeman AT & SF; train accident.
Paper & date: LS Apr. 11, 1883
Date & place of death: Apr. 7, 1883, near La Junta, Col.

DICKSON, WILLIAM - Run over by train
Paper & date: LS Aug. 15, 1883
Date & place of death: Clear Creek, Texas

DIETER, GEORGE - Well-known in El Paso; suicide - shooting; bros.: J.P.
DIETER and A. C. DIETER of El Paso, Texas
Paper & date: LS Dec. 30, 1885; EPT Dec. 30, 1885
Date & place of death: Dec. 27, 1885, Wichita, Kansas

DIETZ, _____ - Shot by Indians - must die (according to the surgeon at
Ft. Bayard.)
Paper & date: TB Mar. 30, 1871
Date & place of death: at Lone Mountain.

DILVERY, _____ - R. R. Engineer; train accident
Paper & date: LS Nov. 3, 1883
Date & place of death: Oct. 28, 1883, near Aguas Calientes, Mex.

DINAN, _____ - Child; aged 5 months; fa.: MICHAEL DINAN, clerk at
RANDALL Quarry.
Paper & date: RGR Aug. 1, 1885
Date & place of death: July 30, 1885

DITY, SAM (Negro) - Burned in court house fire; all records destroyed.
Paper & date: LS Nov. 18, 1882
Date & place of death: Nov. 13, 1882, Crocket, Houston co., Texas

DIVIVE, HENRY - Newspaperman of Illinois; consumption
Paper & date: LS May 27, 1885
Date & place of death: Armijo House, Albuquerque, N. M.

DIXON, E. S. - Killed by bro.-in-law, F. B. DAWSON
Paper & date: LS July 18, 1885
Date & place of death: McMullen co., Texas

DOAN, R. C. - a member of Congress
Paper & date: LS Dec. 17, 1881
Date & place of death: Dec. 10, 1881, Austin, Texas

DODGE, _____ - Ex-policeman; dropped dead
Paper & date: LS Dec. 5, 1883
Date & place of death: Deming, N. M.

DODGE, Sen. _____ of Iowa; son: A. V. DODGE well known in El Paso.
Paper & date: EPT Dec. 20, 1885
Date & place of death: ....

DODGE, Gen. & Mrs. G. M. - Pres. of Construction Co.; train collision
    Paper & date: EPDH Feb. 8, 1882
    Date & place of death: Feb. 7, 1882, near Waco, Texas

DOEMICH, OSCAR - Found dead in bed, suffocated; native of Hesse Cassel,
    Germany; would be 21 yrs. old Jan. 1886; uncle: GUSTAV BILLING of
    Socorro, N. M.; cousin: JUSTUS JUNGK of Socorro, N. M.
    Paper & date: LS Nov. 18, 1885; BU Nov. 21, 1885
    Date & place of death: last week, Socorro, N. M.

DOMINGUEZ, JUAN " DEAF JUAN" - Found dead
    Paper & date: EPMS Nov. 27, 1884
    Date & place of death: Nov. 21, 1884, San Antonio, Texas

DOMINGUEZ, MARIANO - Killed by Indians
    Paper & date: EPT Oct. 20, 1885
    Date & place of death: near Ramos, Mex.

DONAHUE, _____ - bro.: JNO. JACKSON DONAHUE of El Paso, Texas (known as
    EL NINO EDDIE); uncle: DAVE BIDDLE of New Orleans.
    Paper & date: EPT July 14, 1884
    Date & place of death: ....

DONAHUE, JOHN - Section hand; run over by train.
    Paper & date: LS June 27, 1883
    Date & place of death: Houston, Texas

DONAHUE, MICHAEL - Fell off train - broke neck.
    Paper & date: LS Sept. 3, 1884
    Date & place of death: Sept. 2, 1884, near Eagle Ford, Texas

DONAVAN, _____ - a young man; killed by stone falling on him.
    Paper & date: LS June 2, 1883
    Date & place of death: Coyote, Canyon, N. M.

DONLEY, R. M. of Dallas, Texas; young lawyer; shot and killed by C. M.
    BURGESS; he had spoken ill of candidate Burgess who lost election.
    Paper & date: LS Nov. 15, 1882
    Date & place of death: Nov. 9, 1882

DORIAN, PATRICK - Skull crushed plus cuts and bruises; believed waylaid
    during a major fire.
    Paper & date: EPT Aug. 23, 1885
    Date & place of death: Aug. 21, 1885, Texarkana, Texas

DORIS, ALEX.- Shot by H. M. ST. CYR of Texas; in self-defense.
    Paper & date: EPT Oct. 20, 1884
    Date & place of death: Oct. 11, 1884, Chiquito Jaquino Mining Camp,
    Mexico.

DORSEY, CORA IRENE - Infant dau. of the late P. DORSEY.
    Paper & date: BU Aug. 1, 1884
    Date & place of death: July 5, 1884, Socorro, N. M.

DORSEY, PATRICK - b. possibly Ontario, Canada; moved to Penn. with bro.
    TOM; later to Calif. and in 1881 to Socorro; wife and family.
    Paper & date: BU Nov. 1, 1883
    Date & place of death: Oct. 22, 1883, Socorro, N. M.

DOUGLASS, _____ (negro) - Lynched for rape of Mrs. ROGERS.
    Paper & date: EPT June 28, 1883
    Date & place of death: June 27, 1883, Jefferson, Texas

DOUGLASS, CHARLES - Sher. BLACKER (BLACKLEY)(BLAKELY) acquitted. Sheriff
    BLAKELY accidentally dropped a pistol.
    Paper & date: LS May 26, 1883; EPT May 25, 1883; LS May 30, 1883
    Date & place of death: Last winter, Fort Bend co., Texas

DOUGLASS, FRED - Murder
    Paper & date: LS Feb. 18, 1882/Date & place: Feb. 2,1882-between Vil-

la and Los Compos, Texas.

DOWD, DAN - To be hanged for murder (Bisbee, Ariz.)
   Paper & date: LS Mar. 26, 1884
   Date & place of death: Mar. 28, 1884, Tombstone, Ariz.

DOWELL, Mrs. LAURA B. - Formerly of Galveston, Texas; died at home of
   her son-in-law, Houston, Texas; wife of the late Dr. GREENVILLE DOWELL
   Paper & date: EPMS Dec. 4, 1884
   Date & place of death: Nov. 28, 1884, Houston, Texas

DOWLIN, WILL - Formerly of Dowlin's Mills, Lincoln co., N. M.; bro.:Capt
   PAUL DOWLIN; wife and 3 sons.
   Paper & date: RGR Dec. 20, 1884
   Date & place of death: Dec. 11, 1884, at Pueblo Asylum for the In-
   sane.

DOWNEY, DAN - Dynamite blast
   Paper & date: LS Mar. 28, 1885
   Date & place of death: 9 mi. Wichita Falls, Texas

DOWNEY (DOWNING), JOHN - Pvt. in 13th Infantry; murder by WM. S. PEARL
   and ALBERT FRANK; wife and family in Kansas.
   Paper & date: RGR May 10, 1884; LS Jan. 31, 1883
   Date & place of death: Jan. 19, 1883, Fort Stanton, N. M.

DOWNING, SARAH C. - age 23 yrs.; paralysis of the heart; hus.: W. J.
   DOWNING.
   Paper & date: LS Aug. 26, 1882
   Date & place of death: Aug. 23, 1882

DOWNS, Maj. W. T. - Body sent to Atchison, Kans.; well known R. R. man.
   Paper & date: LS Mar. 17, 1883
   Date & place of death: Las Vegas Hot Springs, N. M.

DOWNS, WILLIAM - Clubbed by _____ TATUM.
   Paper & date: LS Oct. 8, 1884
   Date & place of death: Few days ago, Longview, Texas

DOYLE, JOHN - Shot himself.
   Paper & date: LS July 18, 1883
   Date & place of death: Santa Fe, N. M.

DRAKE, THOMAS - Quarrel after election with STEPHEN LEWIS
   Paper & date: LS Dec. 20, 1882
   Date & place of death: last week, Santiago, Texas

DRAPER, JAMES - Caught in shaft at rolling mill.
   Paper & date: LS Nov. 15, 1884
   Date & place of death: Houston, Texas

DRAWN, Mrs. E. A. - Shot while assisting JAMES PITTS to escape; dau.:
   Mrs. JAMES PITTS.
   Paper & date: EPT Feb. 24 and 25, 1885
   Date & place of death: Feb. 21, 1885, New Braunfels, Texas

DRESSER, GEORGE E. - Pneumonia; relatives in Stockbridge, Mass.
   Paper & date: EPT Jan. 23, 1885
   Date & place of death: June 7, 1879, El Paso, Texas

DRESSER, JOHN T. - over 45; suicide by hanging; wife and daughter.
   Paper & date: LS July 8, 1885
   Date & place of death: July 4, 1885, Silver City, N. M.

DRIDEN, A. B. - Had taken refuge in old church building which then blew
   down.
   Paper & date: LS Jan. 3, 1883
   Date & place of death: last week, near Riverside, Texas

DRINKARD, Dty. Sher. _____- Killed while making an arrest

DRINKARD (cont'd):
    Paper & date: LS Oct. 31, 1885
    Date & place of death: Headville, Texas

DRISCOLL, TOM - Palo Blanco cattleman; shot by Dty. Sher. PETER BURLESON
    Paper & date: LS Jan. 12, 1884; LS Jan. 19, 1884
    Date & place of death: Jan. 16, 1884, Springer, N. M.

DU___S, J. PETER - Suit in Paso del Norte, Mex. on the estate for 5 yrs
    and 10 mos.
    Paper & date: LS July 28, 1883
    Date & place of death: before 1878, Mexico

DU BOIS, DAN - Well known in N. M.; found dead
    Paper & date: EPT Sept. 4, 1884
    Date & place of death: few days ago.

DUBOIS, JOHN - Killed by JAMES ELMORE; employee of J. W. FLEMING, Gila
    River area, N. M.
    Paper & date: LS Mar. 22, 1884
    Date & place of death: N. M.

DUFFY, JAS. - Relatives in the East
    Paper & date: BU May 1, 1883
    Date & place of death: last summer, San Marcial or Hachito, N. M.

DUNCAN, BEN - (Negro) - shot by TOBE ESTER (negro) while pecan hunting.
    Paper & date: LS Nov. 8, 1884
    Date & place of death: Nov. 1, 1884, Belton, Texas

DUNCAN, LALLIE - Consumption; ta.: ALEXANDER D. DUNCAN of Duncan's Mills,
    Calif.; sis.: Mrs. PYATH.
    Paper & date: LS Sept. 27, 1882
    Date & place of death: Sept. 25, 1882 at Central Hotel, El Paso, Tex.
    while enroute from Florida.

DUNLAP, _____ - Fell from scaffolding.
    Paper & date: LS Feb. 11, 1885
    Date & place of death: Paris, Texas

DUNLAP, _____ - Killed by mob in defense of his bro.-in-law's, ___ HAYS,
    home.
    Paper & date: EPT Oct. 10, 1884
    Date & place of death: Sipe Springs, Texas (near Waco.)

DUNN, Dr. J. S.
    Paper & date: EPDH Dec. 28, 1881
    Date & place of death: May 25 - June 1, 1881, San Elizario, Texas

DUNN, JAMES "PRETTY JIM" - Small pox; formerly of San Antonio, Texas
    Date & place of death: Recently, El Paso, Texas
    Paper & date: EPDH Jan. 28, 1883

DUNN, Mrs. LULU - Consumption; hus.; bro.: C. B. KING
    Paper & date: RGR July 19, 1884
    Date & place of death: Organ, N. M., July 14, 1884

DUNN, W. L. - Suicide
    Paper & date: LS Oct. 31, 1885
    Date & place of death: Weatherford, Texas

DUPER, CHRISTIAN - age 55; paralysis of the heart; ad for estate settle-
    ment Nov. 24, 1883; wife: Mrs. DOLORES DUPER; b. Philadelphia June 25,
    1828; in Army, Capt. & Brevet Maj. L. P. GRAHAM's Co. D, Regiment of
    Dragoons in New Mexico; War of Rebellion - Union side; youngest dau.
    m. to Sher. WHITE of El Paso, Tex.; dau.: Mrs. W. L. JERRELL; dau.-
    unmarried; 2 sons.
    Paper & date: RGR Nov. 10, 1883; RGR Nov. 24, 1883
    Date & place of death: Nov. 3, 1883

DURAN, ABEL - To be hanged for murder of Chinaman near Ft. Bayard, N.M. last Feb.
Paper & date: LS Aug. 22, 1883
Date & place of death: N. M.

DURAN, JUAN - Will be hanged for murder of a chinaman, Ft. Davis, Texas; actual hanging, Dec. 14, 1883 at Withera Wells, Texas
Paper & date: LS Oct. 3, 1883; LS Oct. 17, 1883; LS Dec. 19, 1883
Date & place of death: Dec. 14, 1883, Presidio co., Texas

DURAN, MANUEL - Shot Oct. 5 by MARCELINO GUARDIA; probably fatal
Paper & date: LS Oct. 7, 1885; EPT Oct. 6, 1885
Date & place of death: Concordia, Texas

DURAN, RAFAEL - Killed by VICTORIANO MEDINA
Paper & date: LS Feb. 9, 1884
Date & place of death: Feb. 7, 1884, Ysleta, Texas

DURAN, TIBURCIO (Constable) - Shot and killed while attempting to arrest ANASTACIO DELFIN, a desperado.
Paper & date: LS Nov. 21, 1885; LS Dec. 2, 1885
Date & place of death: Nov. 18, 1885, Tularosa, N. M.

DURAND, DOLLY (notorious thief) - Killed
Paper & date: LS Oct. 7, 1882
Date & place of death: Oct. 1, 1882, San Antonio, Texas

DURE, _____ - Shot and killed by two men; DURE was Postmaster at Mahomet and on way home.
Paper & date: LS Dec. 30, 1882
Date & place of death: last week, Mahomet, Texas

DURFE, E. R. - of Jacksonville, Ill.; consumption; bur. in Jacksonville, Ill.; mo.: Mrs. Durfe
Paper & date: LS Feb. 28, 1883
Date & place of death: Feb. 26, 1883, Las Cruces, N. M.

DUSCHE, JOHN - Fell from wagon which then ran over him.
Paper & date: LS Sept. 3, 1884
Date & place of death: Pit's Bridge, Texas

DUTCH CHARLEY - aged less than 20; shot by WM. MARTIN of Mesilla, N. M.; CLEMENTE CASTILLO, J. P., and LEWIS KAHLER, Clerk, empaneled a jury and acted as coroner; Verdict: "Deceased came to his death by means of a bullet." Jury later named WM. MARTIN as the assassin.
Paper & date: RGR Dec. 8, 1883
Date & place of death: Nov. 30, 1883, Palomas, N. M.

DUTCH JOE - Whiskey to blame.
Paper & date: LS Feb. 14, 1885
Date & place of death: Gallup, N. M.

DWELLE, RICHARD G. - Welchman about 45 yrs; suicide - shot himself; un-married.
Paper & date: RGR Jan. 3, 1885; EPMS Jan.4, 1885; EPDS Jan. 7, 1885; RGR Jan. 10, 1885
Date & place of death: Las Cruces, N. M., Jan. 4, 1885

DWYER, JOHN - Wounded by Indians a month ago.
Paper & date: LS Dec. 23, 1885
Date & place of death: Kingston, Ariz.

DWYER, Maj. JOSEPH E. - Bro.-in-law: Mayor JOSEPH MAGOFFIN of El Paso, Texas.
Paper & date: LS Sept. 17, 1884
Date & place of death: Sept. 14, 1884, San Antonio, Texas

DYER, CHARLES - Saloon man of San Antonio, Tex.; missing-wife fears foul play.
Paper & date: LS Jan. 5, 1884/ Date & place: ......

DYER, SAM & ELI - Murderers of RAGSDALE and BUCHANAN
    Paper & date: LS June 13, 1885
    Date & place of death: Bonham, Texas; Lynched

EANES, CLAUDE - age 8; murdered possibly by mo. and _____ COURTNEY.
    Paper & date: EPT Dec. 27, 1885
    Date & place of death: Clarksville, Texas

EANES, HUGH - Poisoned; wife & _____ COURTNEY suspected; surv.: wife
    and son, CLAUDE
    Paper & date: EPT Dec. 27, 1885
    Date & place of death: last August, Clarksville, Texas

EASELL, SAMUEL and young daughter - killed his dau. and himself.
    Paper & date: EPT Dec. 16, 1884
    Date & place of death: Greenville, Texas

EASTON, CLARENCE - age 9; shot by playmate LUCAS DOURTE trying to fright-
    en him. Not expected to live.
    Paper & date: LS July 18, 1883
    Date & place of death: Raton, N. M.

EATON, K. T. - Murder; J. D. GILLENWATERS arrested in San Antonio, Tex.
    $2,000 had been offered for his capture.
    Paper & date: LS Mar. 29, 1882
    Date & place ot death: last year, Arkansas

EBLEN, JAMES G., Capt. - Paralysis; bur. Sept. 8, 1883, Dallas, Texas;
    about 35 years old, of El Paso, Texas; Co. Atty; native of Tenn.;
    lived Dallas and Ind. Terr. about 12 years.; surv.: wife and 3 sons;
    bro.-in-law: CHARLES A. WORK, 320 Pearl St., Dallas, Texas.
    Paper & date: EPT Sept. 9, 1883; EPT Sept. 11, 1883; LS Sept.12, 1883
    Date & place of death: Sept. 7, 1883, Dallas, Texas

EDGERTON, GEO. O. - Short illness; came here in 1850 - m. into an esti-
    mable Mex. family; wife and 4 ch.
    Paper & date: EPT Jan. 1, 1885
    Date & place of death: Dec. 31, 1884, Paso del Norte, Mex.

EDWARDS, _____ Killed by _____ KENNEDY.
    Paper & date: BU Nov. 14, 1885
    Date & place of death: ca 1886, Colfax co., N. M.

EDWARDS, Capt. A. D.
    Paper & date: LS Apr. 1, 1882
    Date & place of death: Mar. 25, 1882, Terrell, Texas

EDWARDS, JOHN F. - Formerly of El Paso, Texas
    Paper & date: LS Oct. 28, 1885
    Date & place of death: few days ago, Columbia, Mo.

EDWARDS, Mrs. JOSEPH - surv.: hus.
    Paper & date: LS Aug. 1, 1885
    Date & place of death: Houston, Texas

EDWARDS, WILLIAM (or E.) - Shot by townspeople while causing trouble;
    alias ED COLLINS; originally from Ky.; was in Silver City last winter.
    Paper & date: EPDH Nov. 9, 1881; LS Nov. 9, 1881
    Date & place of death: Nov. 2, 1881, Camp Rice, Texas

EGGERSON, _____ - Young; kicked to death by horse; a farmer
    Paper & date: EPT July 9, 1884
    Date & place of death: near Uvalde, Texas

EGGLESTON, EVERARD T. - Cashier State Nat'l Bank
    Paper & date: LS Oct. 14, 1885
    Date & place of death: Austin, Texas

EICHLER, _____ - Reported killed by Indians; former resident of Socorro

EICHLER (cont'd) - N. M.
    Paper & date: BU Dec. 19, 1885
    Date & place of death: Southwest

ELDRIDGE, _____ - of Jefferson, Texas; train accident.
    Paper & date: LS Feb. 25, 1885
    Date & place of death: near Mt. Vernon, Ind.

ELLER, WASHINGTON - age 11; accidentally shot by brother HENRY, age 14.
    Paper & date: EPT Aug. 26, 1884
    Date & place of death: Aug. 23, 1883, near McKinney, Texas

ELLIOTT, RILEY (Negro) - Called to door and shot; he was a witness again-
    st cow theives.
    Paper & date: LS June 6, 1885
    Date & place of death: May 31, 1885 at 3 a.m., 8 mi. from Greenville,
    Texas.

ELLIS, Mrs. _____ (Negro) - Beaten to death by estranged hus. GREEN ELLIS
    negro.
    Paper & date: LS Aug. 4, 1883
    Date & place of death: Longview, Texas

ELLIS, CHARLES E. - Sher.; murdered during San Elzeario riot.
    Paper & date: LS Aug.20, 1884
    Date & place of death: ....

ELLISON, SAMUEL - Old resident; paralyzed and dying.
    Paper & date: LS Mar. 5, 1884
    Date & place of death: Santa Fe, N. M.

ELMER, JACOB - Robber; killed by posse for murder.
    Paper & date: EPT Oct. 6, 1883
    Date & place of death: Oct. 3, 1883, near Tucson, Ariz.

ELMORAN, FRENCHY - Hung by mob.
    Paper & date: EPDH Oct. 12, 1881
    Date & place of death: Oct. 6, 1881, Socorro, N. M.

ELSINGER, ROBERT - Killed by ROBERT COURTWRIGHT, and JAMES McINTIRE and
    W. C. MOORE and _____ SCOTT and _____ CASEY.
    Paper & date: LS June 2, 1883; EPT Oct. 21, 1884; EPT Oct. 17,1885
    Date & place of death: May 5, 1883, Socorro co., N. M.

ELY, G. S. or S. G. - Accident; fell down mine shaft.
    Paper & date: LS Aug. 22, 1883; LS Aug. 25, 1883
    Date & place of death: near Hillsboro, N. M., near Animas Peak

ELY, T. J. - Engraver for "Texas Siftings"
    Paper & date: SH Oct. 19, 1884
    Date & place of death: few days ago, Austin, Texas

EMMETT, TOM - Englishman; suicide
    Paper & date: LS Mar. 22, 1884
    Date & place of death: Mar. 16, 1884, Hillsboro, N. M. (Tex.?)

ENCARNACION, _____ - Shot by men from Paso del Norte, Mex.; surv.:family
    Paper & date: LS Nov. 10, 1883; EPT Nov. 18, 1883
    Date & place of death: Nov. 8, 1883, Canutillo, Texas

ESPARZO, JAMES - Two escaped Mexican convicts shot him and robbed him.
    Paper & date: LS Nov. 22, 1882
    Date & place of death: recently, DeWitt co., Texas

ESPERANZA, JUAN - Shot
    Paper & date: LS Jan. 31, 1885
    Date & place of death: Jan. 24, 1885, Eagle Pass Rd., Dimmitt co.,
    Texas

ESPERENZA, PASCUAL - Italian; shot by ___ DAVIS & ____ SANDOVAL

ESPERENZA (cont'd):
Paper & date: LS July 25, 1883
Date & place of death: recently, Las Vegas, N. M.

ESQUIBEL, REFUGIO - Died of thirst; surv.: son-in-law, MATIAS CONTRERAS
of La Joya, N. M.
Paper & date: BU Oct. 3, 1885
Date & place of death: Sept. 16-25, 1885, near La Joya, N. M.

ESTES, WILLIAM A. - Contractor on Mex. Cen. R. R.; bur. on Apr. 14, 1883;
formerly of Lawrence co., Mo.
Paper & date: EPT Apr. 16, 1883
Date & place of death: Apr. 12, 1883, Santa Rosalia, Mex.

ESTEYS, W. H. of San Saba, Texas; runaway stage; broke his leg; later
amputated; he is "very low"; near Senterfeit.
Paper & date: LS Oct. 28, 1882

ESTRADO, SOSTENOS - Killed by Indians
Paper & date: EPDH Oct. 5, 1881
Date & place of death: between Willcox and San Carlos, Ariz.

EVANS, _____ - 12 yr. old son; disappeared - thought to be dead; fa.:
Dr. EVANS
Paper & date: LS May 16, 1883
Date & place of death: Ft. Worth, Texas

EVANS, _____ (train engineer) - scalded in train accident at Providence,
Louisiana.
Paper & date: LS Dec. 2, 1885
Date & place of death: Nov. 27, 1885, Marshall, Texas

EVANS, JOHN - Went to sleep on tracks and was mangled by train.
Paper & date: LS May 12, 1883
Date & place of death: Mount Pleasant, Texas

EVARTS, Judge G. A. - 86 years
Paper & date: LS Feb. 9, 1884
Date & place of death: Feb. 1, 1884, Ft. Worth, Texas

EVEANS, Mrs. DOLORES - age 40; hus.: JOHN EVEANS
Paper & date: EPT Sept. 17, 1885
Date & place of death: Sept. 16, 1885, El Paso, Texas

EVERETTS, _____ - R. R. Conductor; train accident; Missouri-Pacific
Paper & date: EPT Apr. 11, 1883
Date & place of death: Apr. 10, 1883, near Baker, Texas

EWING, E. W. - Suicide - illness
Paper & date: LS Feb.18, 1885
Date & place of death: Feb. 11, 1885, Brenham, Texas

FADDIS, J. C. - age 90; son R. P. FADDIS of Socorro, N. M.
Paper & date: BU Oct. 31, 1885
Date & place of death: last week, Lawrence co., Penn.

FALES, NED - Hung by mob for killing W. C. O'BOYLY
Paper & date: EPT Sept. 5, 1884
Date & place of death: Ariz.

FALVEY, PATRICK - Miner; accidentally shot
Paper & date: BU May 1, 1883
Date & place of death: Socorro, Merritt Mine, N. M.

FANNICK, GEORGE - early 20's; murder and suicide pact with ANNIE MANLER
Paper & date: EPT Sept. 30, 1884
Date & place of death: Sept. 28, 1884, Dallas, Texas

FARLEY, LUCIEN - Result of wounds several months ago inflicted by shot by

FARLEY (cont'd):
   GEORGE RAINS of Belton, Texas
   Paper & date: LS Dec. 14, 1881
   Date & place of death: Dec. 3, 1881, Corsicana, Texas

FARR, TOM is dead; "an old resident"
   Paper & date: LS Oct. 28, 1882
   Date & place of death: San Saba, Texas

FAULKNER, SAMUEL - fight
   Paper & date: LS Aug. 9, 1884
   Date & place of death: Fredonia, Texas

FAY, JAMES - Shot in neck by ELLIOTT, the cook; Jury - "Justifiable homi-
   cide."
   Paper & date: RGR Feb. 16, 1884
   Date & place of death: Feb. 15, 1884

FEATHERSTON, Mrs. MARY A. - b. Washington co., Ark.; hus. and 8 ch. of
   Socorro, N. M.
   Paper & date: BU July 1, 1883
   Date & place of death: May 20, 1883, San Marcial, N. M.

FELIPE, JUAN - Credited with being 106-120 years old. Half Pueblo Indian
   ....."it is said that he nursed the father of Padre BACA when he was
   a child, and the Padre is near to 80 years old."
   Paper & date: RGR Dec. 26, 1885
   Date & place of death: last week

FELLOWS, O. - Duel with Mr. LANE
   Paper & date: LS July 26, 1882
   Date & place of death: July 22, 1882, Collinsville, Texas

FERNANDEZ, ALEXANDER - Killed in a fight with JAMES G. WHITNEY; body
   sent to San Francisco, Calif.
   Paper & date: EPT Aug. 20, 1883; EPT Aug. 21, 1883; LS Aug. 22,1883;
   LS Sept. 15, 1883
   Date & place of death: Punta de Agua, Valencia co., N. M.

FERNANDES, Mrs. SAMUEL C. - age 27; suddenly; hus. and 2 little girls of
   El Paso. Her rel. live in Eastern Texas
   Paper & date: EPDH May 3, 1882
   Date & place of death: May 2, 1882, El Paso, Texas

FERNDON, W. H. - about 30 yrs. old; poss. suicide; orig. Sullivan co.,
   N. Y.
   Paper & date: EPT May 7, 1884
   Date & place of death: May 6, 1884, Paso del Norte, Mex.

FERRIN, MIKE - Murdered by JOHN YOUNG
   Paper & date: EPT Nov. 11, 1884
   Date & place of death: Austin, Texas

FETNER, _____ - Murdered by ALLY ARNOLD
   Paper & date: LS Dec. 3, 1881
   Date & place of death: Cooke co., Texas

FEWELL, _____ - Infant; bur. Apr. 19, 1883; fa.: Mr. FEWELL
   Paper & date: EPDH Apr. 22, 1883
   Date & place of death: El Paso, Texas

FIELD, ARABELLA - Cerebral apoplexy; surv.: bro.; body to be exhumed and
   sent to Brooklyn, N. Y.
   Paper & date: LS Nov. 21, 1885; EPT Nov. 21, 1885; LS Nov. 28,1885;
   LS Dec. 12, 1885
   Date & place of death: Nov. 19, 1885, El Paso, Texas

FIELD, D. C. - Suicide
   Paper & date: LS Oct. 6, 1883
   Date & place of death: Sept. 29, 1883, Charleston, Ariz.

FIELDS, _____ - Justifiable killing by J. R. JOHNSON
    Paper & date: LS Jan. 20, 1883
    Date & place of death: a few days ago, Hillsboro, N. M.

FIERRO, ANDREAS - Crushed by falling wall.
    Paper & date: EPDH Nov. 18, 1883
    Date & place of death: El Paso, Texas

FIFE, Mrs. WM. N. - Murdered by _____ FRANCISCO; hus.: and 7 yr. old dau
    Paper & date: EPT Sept. 19, 1884
    Date & place of death: Sept. 11, 1884, in Chiricahua Mtns near Tomb-
    stone, Ariz.

FINCH, HENEAGE from England; age 36; EARL OF AYLESFORD; inflammation of
    the bowels; bur. in England; no male desc.-bro. CHARLES, 2 daus. in
    England; turned cowboy.
    Paper & date: LS Jan. 17, 1885; LS Jan. 21, 1885
    Date & place of death: Jan. 13, 1885, Big Springs, Texas

FINDLAY, JOHN - Shot and killed by JORDAN; Jury verdict: Justifiable
    homicide.
    Paper & date: LS Nov. 15, 1882
    Date & place of death: recently, White Oaks, N. M.

FINKS, JOE - Premature cannon discharge
    Paper & date: LS July 12, 1884
    Date & place of death: July 4, 1884, Centrailia, Mo.

FINLEY, _____ - Drowned; wrecked boat found
    Paper & date: LS Feb. 8, 1882
    Date & place of death: recently, Galveston, Texas

FINN, PATRICK - of Deming, N. M.; Captured - probably killed by Indians;
    partner C. D. FITCH of Deming, N. M.
    Paper & date: EPT June 7, 1883; EPT June 12, 1883; EPT June 30,1883
    Date & place of death: 40 mi. from Casas Grande, Mex.

FINNEGAN, JAMES - Killed; Mex. Cen. R. R.
    Paper & date: EPDH Jan. 20, 1884
    Date & place of death: July 26, 1883, Mex.

FISHER, _____ Reported killed by Indians; former resident of Socorro,
    N. M.
    Paper & date: BU Dec. 19, 1885
    Date & place of death: Southwest

FISHER, J. K. "KING" about 27 yrs.; Dty. Sher. of Uvalde co.; shot down
    in self defense by JOE C. FOSTER and JACOB S. COY; wife and children
    in Uvalde, Texas
    Paper & date: EPDH Mar. 16, 1884; LS Mar. 22, 1884
    Date & place of death: Mar. 11, 1884, Austin, Texas

FISHER, W. K. - Collision of 2 trains.
    Paper & date: LS Sept. 24, 1884
    Date & place of death: Sept. 20, 1884, near A & P Junction, El Paso

FISKE, Mrs. E. A. - Suddenly died; bur. in Springfield, Ohio
    Paper & date: LS Apr. 5, 1882
    Date & place of death: last week, Santa Fe, N. M.

FITZGERALD, JOHN - Shot by FRANK PRUITT of Texas; supposed to be mor-
    tally wounded.
    Paper & date: LS Sept. 12, 1885
    Date & place of death: Sept. 7, 1885, Las Vegas, N. M.

FITZMAURICE, JOHN - An old resident of Santa Fe
    Paper & date: LS Feb. 25, 1882
    Date & place of death: Feb. 19, 1882, Santa Fe, N. M.

FITZPATRICK, JAMES - Formerly of Gainsville, Tex.; run over

FITZPATRICK (cont'd):
    Paper & date: LS Feb. 14, 1885
    Date & place of death: Atoka, Ind. Terr.

FITZPATRICK, JAMES R. - Struck over head with chair by J. M. BROWN
    Paper & date: LS Oct. 3, 1883; EPT Sept. 22, 1883
    Date & place of death: Sept. 21, 1883, Deming, N. M.

FLEMING, _____ - Horse thief; fight with posse from Texas
    Paper & date: EPT May 5, 1883
    Date & place of death: May 2, 1883, near Darlington, Ind. Terr.

FLEMING, H. WARD - age 19; consumption; (Law Clerk in office of Judge
    S. B. NEWCOMB); youngest son of ANDREW J. and E. FLEMING; d. at home
    of his uncle G. W. McCUMBER of Elmira
    Paper & date: RGR July 11, 1885
    Date & place of death: Jun. 23, 1885

FLEMING, J. W. - Shot by E. L. CUNNINGHAM
    Paper & date: LS Nov. 10, 1883
    Date & place of death: Nov. 7, 1883, Galveston, Texas

FLEMING, WILLIAM CHAMBERLAINE - age 42; consumption; native of Baltimore,
    Md.
    Paper & date: LS Jan. 9, 1884
    Date & place of death: Jan. 7, 1884, El Paso, Texas

FLETCHER, JAMES - Pneumonia; old resident
    Paper & date: LS Feb. 14, 1885
    Date & place of death: Georgetown, N. M.

FLETCHER, WM. - Shot and killed while assisting in arrest of BURL BURLE-
    SON; also listed at Milican, Texas
    Paper & date: LS Jan. 27, 1883; LS Jan. 20, 1883
    Date & place of death: Jan. 15, 1883, Wellborn, Texas

FLIESCHEIG, RICHARD EMIL - Murdered in 1884 by HENRY MEYER, CHARLES JUNE-
    MAN, W. F. ALLEN: all under arrest. CLIFFORD PORTER also implicated.
    Paper & date: EPDH June 1, 1889; EPDH June 6, 1889
    Date & place of death: 1884

FLORES, FRANCISCO - Run over by emigrant train; he had lived at Carri-
    zal, Mexico.
    Paper & date: LS Oct. 21, 1882
    Date & place of death: Oct. 17, 1882, San Marcial, N. M.

FLORES, GERONIMO - Shot by drunk Mexican
    Paper & date: LS May 23, 1885
    Date & place of death: Eagle Pass, Texas

FLORES, MANUEL - Hanged by mob.
    Paper & date: EPT Mar. 4, 1885
    Date & place of death: Feb. 28, 1885, Dimmett co., Texas

FLORES, MATIAS - Was Mayor Domo of Acequias, Las Cruces, N. M.; wife and
    family.
    Paper & date: TB Feb. 28, 1872
    Date & place of death: recent death

FLORES, MEQUIADES - Shot by rustlers on a drunken spree; Rustlers in-
    cluded: BILLY WILSON, TOM PICKETT, YANK BEALE, PONEY WILLIAMS
    Paper & date: RGR Jan. 19, 1884
    Date & place of death: Jan. 15, 1884, Seven Rivers (near Tularosa),
    New Mexico

FLORES, Mrs. RAFAELA PEREZ DE - age 60; bur. Aug. 12 or 13, 1883; dau.:
    Mrs. MANUEL E. FLORES, wife of El Paso Co. Clerk who is also her step-
    son.
    Paper & date: EPDH Aug. 19, 1883; EPT Aug. 14, 1883
    Date & place of death: Aug. 11, 1883, Las Cruces, N. M.

FLORMAN, ERNEST EUGENE - aged 3 yrs., 7 mos. and 10 days; Par.: ERNES-
TINE & ROLE FLORMAN.
Paper & date: TB July 19, 1871
Date & place of death: July 14, 1871, Silver City, N. M.

FLUMMERFELT, PHILLIP G. - Apoplexy; old soldier
Paper & date: LS Feb. 21, 1885
Date & place of death: Mora, N. M.

FLY, ROBERT C. - Shot by M. WARD; son of mine owner in Mexico
Paper & date: LS Sept. 15, 1883
Date & place of death: Sept. 11, 1883, Hondo City, Texas

FLYNN, Dr. WILLIAM H. - Formerly of Boston; shot by MARTIN NELSON
Paper & date: LS May 9, 1885
Date & place of death: May 5, 1885, Bonito, N. M.

FOGG, _____ - Young man; lockjaw in Ft. Selden Hospital after accidental
shot in thigh.
Paper & date: LS Aug. 30, 1882
Date & place of death: recently, Rincon, N. M.

FOGG, J. F. - of California; beaten to death by his partner.
Paper & date: LS Jan. 30, 1884
Date & place of death: Jan. 27, 1884, Ft. Worth, Texas

FOLEY, JOHN - Froze to death
Paper & date: LS Jan. 10, 1885
Date & place of death: near Albuquerque, N. M.

FONTAINE, Mrs. ELIZABETH - hus.: A. G. FONTAINE
Paper & date: LS Feb. 27, 1884
Date & place of death: Feb. 23, 1884, Albuquerque, N. M.

FOO FONG - A Chinaman; killed by AH CHEE; surv.: bro.
Paper & date: EPT July 13, 1883; EPT_ July 14, 1883
Date & place of death: July 10, 1883, Deming, N. M.

FOOTE, Mrs. _____ - Died in a saloon; woman of easy virtue from Silver-
ton, Colorado.
Paper & date: LS Jan. 10, 1883
Date & place of death: Jan. 5, 1883, Deming, N. M.

FOOTE, Mrs. A. H. - Blood poisoning; hus.: Judge A. H. FOOTE
Paper & date: LS Apr. 12, 1884
Date & place of death: Lawrence, (Kansas?)

FORBA, _____ (woman) - Shot by LEVI VARGAS
Paper & date: LS Mar. 3, 1883
Date & place of death: Feb. 23, 1883, San Antonio, N. M.

FORD, _____ - Aged 9 months, boy; lingering illness; only child of M/M
EDWARD FORD
Paper & date: RGR Dec. 15, 1883
Date & place of death: Dec. 9, 1883

FORD, ED - Murdered by Apaches; of Blue Creek, Grant co., N. M
Paper & date: RGR June 27, 1885
Date & place of death: recently

FORICH, _____ - Pallbearers: Masonic Order
Paper & date: LS Oct. 4, 1884
Date & place of death: few days ago, Hidalgo co., Texas

FORNARA, JOE - Native of Italy; here 3 years
Paper & date: EPDH June 22, 1884
Date & place of death: June 18, 1884, El Paso, Texas

FORREST, _____ - old negro; pneumonia - not expected to recover
Paper & date: LS Dec. 5, 1883/ Place: Silver City, N. M.

57

FORSTER, Mrs. SUSAN - Hydrophobia
    Paper & date: LS June 16, 1883
    Date & place of death: Cooper, Delta co., Texas

FOSTER, IRVIN (Negro) - Shooting scrape - shot by GENERAL SEYMORE (negro)
    both bad cases
    Paper & date: LS Apr. 29, 1885
    Date & place of death: last week, Hearne, Texas

FOSTER, JOE - Wound he received at the time he killed BEN THOMPSON
    Paper & date: LS Mar. 26, 1884; EPDH Mar. 23, 1884
    Date & place of death: Mar. 22, 1884, Austin, Texas (or San Antonio,
    Texas)

FOSTER, LEWIS (Negro) - Lynched
    Paper & date: LS Oct. 31, 1883
    Date & place of death: Shulenberg, Texas

FOUNDATION, JOHN - Shot by THOMAS M. BOYD, JR.
    Paper & date: EPT Aug. 20, 1884; LS Aug. 23, 1884
    Date & place of death: Aug. 16, 1884, Lake Valley, N. M.

FOUNTAIN, BABY - hrs. old; Par.: M/M A. J. FOUNTAIN and twin
    Paper & date: NTF June 18, 1881
    Date & place of death: June 17, 1881, Las Cruces, N. M.

FOWLER, JOEL A.- Lynched - body cut down by Sher. SIMPSON; jury decided
    death from strangulation at hands of parties unknown. Body placed in
    $225 metal coffin and shipped to Ft. Worth, Texas for bur. - former
    home; surv.: wife - JOSIE, Bastrop, Texas; bro.: J. P. FOWLER.
    Paper & date: LS Dec. 12, 1883; LS Jan. 26, 1884; RGR Jan. 26, 1884;
    LS Jan, 30, 1884; EPDH Jan. 27, 1884
    Date & place of death: Jan. 23, 1884, Socorro, N. M.

FOWLER, WILLIAM - Blind; fractured skull by SAM DAGGETT, negro.
    Paper & date: LS Aug. 8, 1883
    Date & place of death: Ft. Worth, Texas

FOX, Mrs. _____ - Stabbed by hus.
    Paper & date: LS Nov. 19, 1884
    Date & place of death: Houston, Texas

FRAMBOW, JOHN - Murdered by STEDMAN WARD, alias CHARLES JOHNSON - arrest-
    ed in Las Vegas, N. M.
    Paper & date: EPT Apr. 14, 1885
    Date & place of death: Dec. 3, 1884, Decatur, Texas

FRANCISCO, CHARLES - Brakeman, age 25; run over by switch engine; here
    about 1 ½ mo.; native of Cleveland, Ohio; fa.: yardmaster at Tulare,
    Calif.; wife at Geneva, Ohio
    Paper & date: LS Sept. 16, 1885; EPT Sept. 15, 1885
    Date & place of death: Sept. 14, 1885, El Paso, Texas

FRANCOIS, _____ - Killed by blast while digging well
    Paper & date: LS Sept. 27, 1884
    Date & place of death: San Antonio, Texas

FRANK, ARNOLD of St. Louis, Mo.; crushed by R. R. cars
    Paper & date: LS Mar. 29, 1882
    Date & place of death: last week, Price's Station near Palestine, Tx.

FRANK, JACOB H. - Young German; suicide by morphine
    Paper & date: LS Feb. 27, 1884
    Date & place of death: Feb. 23, 1884, Albuquerque, N. M.

FRANKLIN, _____ - bro.-in-law: _____ McCUISTION, alderman of Socorro, N.M.
    Paper & date: BU Oct. 24, 1885
    Date & place of death: this week,Hillsboro, N. M.

FRANKLIN, WILKES (Negro) - of Bastrop, Tex.; murdered; accused was TOM

FRANKLIN (cont'd): PEARSON of Sherman, Texas
Paper & date: LS Oct. 25, 1882
Date & place of death: 1873

FRASCHEL, JOHN - of Blue Creek, Grant co., N. M.; murdered by Apaches.
Paper & date: RGR June 27, 1885
Date & place of death: recently

FRAZIER, JOHN (R.A.?) - Shot by tramps on train (JOHN PRICE & JOHN WRIGHT)
sruv.: wife; he was conductor on International R. R.
Paper & date: LS Jan. 24, 1885; LS Jan. 31, 1885; EPT Jan. 21,1885
Date & place of death: Jan. 20, 1885, near Houston, Texas

FRAZIER, JOHN of Laramie City; old prospector
Paper & date: LS May 16, 1885
Date & place of death: Deming, N. M.

FREDERICKS, GEORGE - Murdered by ORTH STEIN
Paper & date: EPMS Dec. 16, 1884
Date & place of death: Leadville, Colo.

FREDERICKS, P. J. (a baker) - "has mixed his last batch"
Paper & date: LS Apr. 18, 1885
Date & place of death: Silver City, N. M.

FRENCH, Capt. _____ - wife - now Mrs. LEHY of Concordia, Texas
Paper & date: EPT May 22, 1884

FREUDENTHAL, RACHEL - aged 6 mos. and 10 days; Par.: MORRIS and MINNA
FREUDENTHAL
Paper & date: RGR July 25, 1885
Date & place of death: July 23, 1885

FREUND, Dr. M. - Died in bed
Paper & date: LS Sept. 17, 1884
Date & place of death: Sept. 11, 1884, Houston, Texas

FREY, JOHN - Shot by HORACE SMITH
Paper & date: LS Aug. 11, 1883
Date & place of death: near Clifton, Ariz.

FRIER, _____ - Old man; burned in LILLIE's cabin by Indians in Mogollons
Paper & date: EPT Dec. 15, 1885
Date & place of death: Dec. 8, 1885, near Silver City, N. M.

FRIETZE, FREDERICK of Mesilla, N. M.; shot by Mexican customs when he
did not hear their order to stop; he did not hear any of the warning
shots since he was a deaf mute. Custom Officer EVARISTO TELLES had
lived at Las Cruces and had known young FRIETZE well. Surv.: par.
Paper & date: LS Oct. 11, 1882
Date & place of death: Oct. 7, 1882

FRIETZE, GUILLERMO - aged nearly two years; par.: ALBINA Y MA. GUADA-
LUPE FRIETZE
Paper & date: RGR Mar. 28, 1885
Date & place of death: Mar. 20, 1885, Mesilla, N. M.

FRIEZE, FRANK - Stabbed by H. M. MARTIN
Paper & date: LS Feb. 14, 1885; LS Feb. 18, 1885
Date & place of death: Weatherford, Texas

FRIOR, _____ - Killed by Indians in Mogollons
Paper & date: RGR Dec. 19, 1885
Date & place of death: last week

FRITZ, CHARLES - age 55; b. Jan. 19, 1831, Stuttgart, Germany; to Mon-
trose, Penn. 1855; to this area 1869 when he visited his brother Col.
EMIL FRITZ; widow and 7 children (had 4 boys and 4 girls)
Paper & date: RGR Dec. 19, 1885
Date & place of death: Dec. 3, 1885, Lincoln co., N. M.

FRITZ, Mrs. CHARLES - hus.; 4 dau. and 4 sons (one dau. Mrs. JAMES M. DOLAN)
Paper & date: RGR Jan. 19, 1884
Date & place of death: last week, Spring Ranch, 8 mi. below Lincoln, N. M.

FRITZ, WINFIELD S. - Murdered by outlaws
Paper & date: LS Oct. 18, 1884
Date & place of death: found Oct. 4, 1884, RAFFERTY Ranch, SW corner Cochise co., Ariz.

FRITZ, Mrs. WINFIELD S. - Murdered
Paper & date: LS Oct. 18, 1884
Date & place of death: found Oct. 4, 1884, RAFFERTY Ranch, SW corner Cochise co., Ariz.

FROST, Mrs. _____ - Died at her old home; hus.: Col. MAX FROST
Paper & date: LS Sept. 5, 1883
Date & place of death: Aug. 27, 1883, Troy, Mo.

FULTON, Mrs. BELLE - Took morphine; hus.: a TP engineer
Paper & date: EPMS Dec. 13, 1884
Date & place of death: Toyah, Texas

FUNKE, LOUIS - Caught in fly wheel of mill
Paper & date: LS Jan. 19, 1884
Date & place of death: Jan. 17, 1884, Albuquerque, N. M.

FUTH, CHARLES - Young German; shooting by negro COMPTON; drinking and wanting to kill a Mr. WOODS
Paper & date: LS Feb. 15, 1882
Date & place of death: a few days ago, Randall Station, N. M. 3 mi. above Ft. Selden, N. M.

GABNER, _____ Young; accidently shot himself
Paper & date: LS Sept. 24, 1884
Date & place of death: Sept. 18, 1884, near San Antonio, Texas

GABRIELA (Senora) - "nearly as old as Methusela"
Paper & date: LS Feb. 17, 1882
Date & place of death: Las Cruces, N. M. the other day

GADWOOD, MOSES - a brakeman; run over by train
Paper & date: LS Oct. 18, 1882
Date & place of death: Oct. 13, 1882, Las Vegas, N. M.

GAIGALBY, _____ - Killed by _____ GONZALES at Tularosa, N. M.
Paper & date: RGR Feb. 16, 1884
Date & place of death: about 10 days ago

GAINES, Mrs. - widow of Col. GAINES
Paper & date: LS Apr. 16, 1884

GALBREATH, WILLIAM - Shot 5 times by CHARLES DARNELL (dispatch from Galveston, Texas, May 15, 1883); surv.: divorced wife of Darnell is a cousin of Galbreath; also leaves wife and several small children.
Paper & date: EPT May 16, 1883; LS May 19, 1883
Date & place of death: near Armesboro or Winesboro, Texas

GALE, CHARLES OLIVER - Last heard of Ft. Wingate, July, 1882. Lived in Albuquerque, N. M. Formerly of Boston, Mass.
Paper & date: BU Dec. 29, 1891
Date & place of death: missing

GALER, W. C. of Ft. Worth, Texas; shot dead by SIMON GOBERT, both cotton buyers.
Paper & date: LS Dec. 20, 1882
Date & place of death: last week

GALINDA, BERNARDA (Widow) - THOMAS LICON stabbed her. Little hope for
her recovery. surv.: 2 small children
Paper & date: RGR Mar. 8, 1884
Date & place of death: Mar. 1, 1884

GALINDO, JOSEFA- Killed by her seducer, a half-breed, WILLIAM ADAMS
Paper & date: LS Mar. 18, 1885
Date & place of death: Mar. 12, 1885, Eagle Pass, Texas

GALLAGHER, JOHN J. of Atlanta, Ga.; heart disease, pericardia in conjunc-
tion with typhus-malaria fever. Age 23 or 24; bur.: July 24, in
Ysleta, Texas (Roman Catholic); surv.: par. and bro.
Paper & date: LS July 18, 1883; LS July 25, 1883; EPDH July 29,1883;
EPT July 25, 1883
Date & place of death: July 23, 1883, El Paso, Texas

GALLEGOS, JOSE TRUJILLO and family - Riddled by posse; he murdered his
wife and 10 yr. old dau.; he murdered MIGUEL MONTANO and wife; 3 yr.
old son sent to El Pino, N. M.; considered to be insane.
Paper & date: LS Mar. 4, 1885; EPT Feb. 27, 1885
Date & place of death: recently, San Miguel co;, M. M.

GALLEGOS, JUAN JOSE - Stabbed in stomach by JULIAN ABEYTIA.
Paper & date: LS Apr. 1, 1885
Date & place of death: Socorro, N. M.

GALLEGOS, VICTOR - Hanged
Paper & date: LS Aug. 23, 1884
Date & place of death: near Brownsville, Texas on Mexican side of
river.

GALLOWAY, JOHN - Killed by policeman - JAMES RUSHING.
Paper & date: LS Aug. 6, 1884; EPMS Nov. 29, 1884
Date & place of death: July 31, 1884, Ft. Worth, Texas

GALVAN, JESUS - To be shot for wrecking and robbing train in Nov. 1883
Paper & date: EPT Aug. 13, 1885
Date & place of death: Nuevo Laredo, Mexico

GALVAN, THOS. (JOHN?) - Killed by JOHN WALSH (WELCH?)
Paper & date: LS May 2, 1883; EPT May 3, 1883
Date & place of death: Apr. 28, 1883, Lordsburg, N. M.

GANDREW, THOMAS - Killed by Apaches.
Paper & date: LS Sept. 30, 1885
Date & place of death: Tombstone, Ariz.

GARCIA, _____ - Killed by two dty. shers. He was a Mexican desperado.
Paper & date: LS Feb. 25, 1882
Date & place of death: one day last week, near San Antonio, Texas

GARCIA, ABEJO - Poisoned by wife, Mrs. MARIA RUPERTA ARRIOLA de GARCIA.
Hus. and dog both died after supper of atole and and strychnine.
Paper & date: LS Jan. 10, 1883; RGR Sept. 8, 1883
Date & place of death: La Union, N. M.

GARCIA, Dona ANA MARIA MONTOYA de - bur.: Aug. 26, 1885
Paper & date: BU Aug. 29, 1885
Date & place of death: San Antonio, N. M.

GARCIA, ANTONIO - Shot
Paper & date: LS Jan. 31, 1885
Date & place of death: Jan. 24, 1885, Eagle Pass Rd., Dimmitt co.Tx.

GARCIA, ATILANO - Killed by Texas cow driver
Paper & date: LS June 24, 1885
Date & place of death: Zuni Mtns., N. M.

GARCIA, JOSE- Stabbed by JUAN MORUYO
Paper & date: LS Feb. 18, 1885/ D & P: Feb. 15,1885,Pinos Altos, N.M.

GARCIA, JOSE S. de - aged 11 mos. and 10 days; par.: JESUS S. & AMELIA
A. de GARCIA
Paper & date: RGR Jan. 10, 1885
Date & place of death: Jan. 2, 1885

GARCIA, JUAN MARIA - age 53 or 54; widow and dau., Mrs. FELIPE BACA
Paper & date: EPT May 6, 1885; BU May 5, 1885
Date & place of death: May 4, 1885, Socorro, N. M.

GARCIA, OCTAVIANO - Sentenced to death for murder and other crimes.
Paper & date: LS Feb. 2, 1884; EPDH Feb. 3, 1884
Date & place of death: Feb. 3, 1884, Paso del Norte, Mex.

GARCIA, PABLINA - 105 yrs. old; married 4 times; mother of 22 children
Paper & date: LS Apr. 14, 1883
Date & place of death: last week, Manzano, N. M.

GARCIA, PANCHO - Assassinated
Paper & date: LS Oct. 24, 1885
Date & place of death: Uvalde, Texas

GARCIA, RAMON (Mex. cattleman) - shot by Sgt. BROWN of Eng. parentage
but Mex. native in self defense.
Paper & date: LS Jan. 24, 1885
Date & place of death: Jan. 14, 1885, Los Vacos, Mex. opposite Del
Rio, Texas

GARCIA, TORIBIO - Cold-blooded murder - shot in back while defending life
of neighbor and friend by HITTSON's gang of cattle thieves. Quiet
inoffensive fellow.
Paper & date: TB Sept. 28, 1872
Date & place of death: ....

GARDNER, RALPH - Shot by Dty. Sher. ALEXANDER and VAN RIPER; alias GEORGE
HENDERSON.
Paper & date: EPT May 6, 1883
Date & place of death: May 2, 1883, San Antonio, Texas

GARIESSEN (GARREINSEN?), OSCAR -
Paper & date: LS Aug. 9, 1884
Date & place of death: Aug. 7, 1884, Galveston, Texas

GARLOCK, WILLIAM - Paralysis
Paper & date: LS Feb. 11, 1885
Date & place of death: Galveston, Texas

GARRETT, ED (Negro) - Hanged for his wife's murder.
Paper & date: LS Jan. 31, 1883
Date & place of death: Jan. 26, 1883, of Texarkana, Texas

GARRETT, MARY - Murdered by hus. with an axe and threw body in river; he
was found guilty; surv. hus. ED GARRETT
Paper & date: LS Dec. 20, 1882
Date & place of death: Jan. 1, 1882, Texarkana, Texas

GARRETT, O. C. - Suicide - shot himself; bro. PAT GARRETT, ex-Sher. of
Lincoln co., N. M.
Paper & date: LS Aug. 29, 1883
Date & place of death: Palestine, Texas

GARRITY, THOMAS - Found on the beach
Paper & date: LS Dec. 30, 1885
Date & place of death: Galveston, Texas

GARTRELL, THOMAS & NELLIE - Found dead; may have been from California
Paper & date: EPDH Oct. 19, 1881
Date & place of death: about a month ago, Rio Chico, Mex.

GASCOIGNE, Mrs. W. O. -aged 64; formerly a resident of Las Cruces; dau:
Mrs. T. F. PRICE (wife of the Public School Spt., Las Cruces, N. M.

GASCOIGNE (cont'd):
    Paper & date: RGR June 21, 1884
    Date & place of death: Wichita, Kansas

GASS, S. - Consumption; a waiter at Central Hotel
    Paper & date: LS Dec. 17, 1881
    Date & place of death: Dec. 16, 1881, El Paso, Texas

GATEWOOD, BEVERLY - 12 yrs. old; drowned
    Paper & date: LS July 28, 1883
    Date & place of death: Houston, Texas

GENTRY, M/M. LAFKIN and children- Cyclone destroyed home.
    Paper & date: EPT Apr. 24, 1885
    Date & place of death: Apr. 22 or 23, 1885, near Mexia, Texas

GENTZ, OTTO F. - Congestion of the brain.
    Paper & date: RGR July 11,1885; BU July 11, 1885; LS July 15, 1885
    Date & place of death: June 30, 1885, Hillsboro, N. M.

GEORGE, _____ - Killed by Indians near Black Diamond Springs, Dragoon
    Mtns., Arizona
    Paper & date: EPDH Jan. 21, 1883
    Date & place of death: recently

GEORGE, A. C. - To be hanged for murder of E. KNEESECK (KNESECK)
    Paper & date: LS June 3, 1885
    Date & place of death: June 26, 1885

GEORGE, Col. W. F. - Heart disease
    Paper & date: EPT Apr. 18, 1883
    Date & place of death: Apr. 14, 1883, Cleburne, Texas

GERONIMO's son - age 13; killed by Lt. DAY's troops; sur.: GERONIMO and
    his 3 wives and children (5). The wives and children were captured.
    Paper & date: EPT Aug. 19, 1885
    Date & place of death: Aug. 7, 1885, near Makavi, Mexico.

GERHOUSE, CHARLES - Suicide by morphine
    Paper & date: LS Jan. 17, 1883; EPDH Jan. 17, 1883
    Date & place of death: Jan. 15, 1883, El Paso, Texas

GERUIRE, _____ (a German) - Killed by a cowboy
    Paper & date: LS May 24, 1884
    Date & place of death: last week, in the Mogollons, N. M.

GEYER, ALBERT ("King of Sweden") - Frozen to death
    Paper & date: LS Jan. 21, 1885
    Date & place of death: Albuquerque, N. M.

GIBBS, _____ - Killed by E. F. BROOKS of Wharton, Texas; wife: Mrs. FAN-
    NIE E. GIBBS.
    Paper & date: LS Nov. 7, 1885
    Date & place of death: Texas

GIBBS, R. T. - He got a license to marry MATTIE JOHNSON but when he ar-
    rived with the preacher she refused. He got a bottle of laudanum, a
    bottle of Fowler's solution of arsenic, a lot of morphine and a lot
    of sulphate of zinc and took the whole thing. The inquest was held
    the next day.
    Paper & date: LS Apr. 7, 1883
    Date & place of death: Ft. Worth, Texas

GIBSON, _____ - Murdered on Mescalero Reservation by MUCHACHO NEGRO.
    Paper & date: RGR May 26, 1883
    Date & place of death: New Mexico

GIBSON, ARCHIE (Negro) - To be hung for murdering his wife.
    Paper & date: LS May 13, 1885
    Date & place of death: May 29, 1885, Richmond, Texas

GIBSON, Mrs. ARCHIE (negro) - murdered by hus. ARCHIE GIBSON
Paper & date: LS May 13, 1885
Date & place of death: Texas

GIBSON, EMMA - (Negro) - Suicide by morphine
Paper & date: LS Aug. 8, 1883
Date & place of death: San Antonio, Texas

GIBSON, WILLIAM of Raymond, Neb.- Typhoid fever
Paper & date: EPDH June 28, 1882
Date & place of death: June 27, 1882, El Paso, Texas

GILBERT, _____ Young man; accidentally shot by JOE WALKS before May 30.
Paper & date: LS June 3, 1885
Date & place of death: other day, Houston, Texas

GILBERT, Mrs. _____ - Wandered away and found dead.
Paper & date: LS Jan. 30, 1884
Date & place of death: Houston, Texas

GILBERT, S. C. - age 26
Paper & date: LS Apr. 11, 1885
Date & place of death: Metropolitan Hotel, Deming, N. M.

GILES, Mrs. _____ - Surv. son ALFRED GILES of Comfort, Boerne, San Antonio, Texas, El Paso and other Tex. cities - lost three fingers from
gunshot.
Paper & date: EPT Nov. 3, 1885
Date & place of death: recently

GILL, JENNIE (?) - Burned while lighting fire with coal oil.
Paper & date: LS July 11, 1883
Date & place of death: Dallas, Texas

GILLEM, JOHN - Apaches at Pino Alto attacked a hay camp. Gillem had
lived 3 years in area on Gila River near Pino Alto; a native of Paris, Texas
Paper & date: MT June 30, 1861
Date & place of death: June 18, 1861

GILLESPIE, Dr. C. - Suicide by morphine or accidental overdose. Connec-
tions in Mexico and San Antonio, Texas
Paper & date: LS Aug. 29, 1883; EPT Aug. 28, 1883
Date & place of death: Aug. 27, 1883, Cleburne, Texas

GILLESPIE, JESSIE - Par.: S. S. GILLESPIE. This is second child he's
lost in a short time.
Paper & date: LS Jan. 10, 1885
Date & place of death: Jan. 7, 1885, El Paso, Texas

GILLETT, - baby; Par.: M/M JAMES B. GILLETT, ass't Marshall.
Paper & date: LS Sept. 12, 1883
Date & place of death: Sept. 10, 1883, Ysleta, Texas

GILMAN, CHARLES - surv.-wife
Paper & date: LS Mar. 10, 1883
Date & place of death: Denison, Texas

GILMORE, Mrs. CHARLOTTE - Shot by gun trap set by W. A. ALLEN
Paper & date: LS Apr. 26, 1884
Date & place of death: Apr. 22, 1884, El Paso, Texas

GILPIN, DOC - former sher.' shot Apr. 10 by C. H. ROBERTS
Paper & date: LS Apr. 15, 1885
Date & place of death: Apr. 11, 1885, Deming, N. M.

GIVENS, Mrs. SARAH - Bad health since April; fa: WM. WAITS
Paper & date: RGR July 26, 1884
Date & place of death: July 19, 1884, Organ, N. M.

GODEMAIRE, FRANK of Las Cruces
    Paper & date: RGR Nov. 29, 1884
    Date & place of death: few days ago, Tularosa, N. M.

GODFROY, Maj. F. C. (GODFREY) - Formerly agent for Mescalero Reservation
    Paper & date: RGR June 6, 1885
    Date & place of death: May 15, 1885, Plattsburg, N. Y.

GOLDTHWAITE, HAMPTON V. - Left Nevada for Arizona 1881 and into Mexico;
    info. needed; sis.: Mrs. A. W. G. DACIE, New York City
    Paper & date: BU Mar. 8, 1892

GOMEZ, Mrs. _____ - Murder by hus.
    Paper & date: LS Oct. 21, 1882
    Date & place of death: Mesilla, N. M.

GOMEZ, Mrs. _____ - Killed by hus.
    Paper & date: LS Oct. 31, 1885
    Date & place of death: near Laredo, Texas

GOMEZ, BRANLIO - Killed by Indians
    Paper & date: EPDH Oct. 5, 1881
    Date & place of death: between Wilcox and San Carlos, Arizona

GOMEZ, MANUEL - Murdered by CHESTER COUSINS. This is same as NAVOR or
    NABOR GOMEZ.
    Paper & date: LS June 2, 1883; LS Feb. 21, 1883; LS June 9, 1883
    Date & place of death: 4 mos. ago, San Marcial, N. M.

GOMEZ, MAXIMO (Milkman) - Murdered on way to deliver milk.
    Paper & date: LS Aug. 19, 1885
    Date & place of death: near Rio Grande City, Texas

GONZALES, Mrs. ANTONIO - Suicide
    Paper & date: LS Apr. 8, 1885
    Date & place of death: Eagle Pass, Texas

GONZALES, CARMEN - fa.: JOSE M. GONZALES
    Paper & date: LS May 9, 1883
    Date & place of death: May 6, 1883, Ysleta, Texas

GONZALES, COYETTEZNO - Fight with soldiers; a bandit (contraband)
    Paper & date: EPDH July 12, 1882
    Date & place of death: July 9, 1882, near Piedras Negras, Mexico

GONZALEZ, JUAN (Indian Scout) - Shot by rancher while out of uniform.
    Paper & date: LS Sept. 9, 1885
    Date & place of death: some mos. ago, Grant co., N. Mexico

GONZALES, JUAN of Tecolote, N. M.; killed by CHATO's Indians; wife & dau.
    Paper & date: EPDH Sept. 9, 1883
    Date & place of death: Spring 1855, near San Miguel, New Mexico

GONZALEZ, LUZ - 12 year old boy; accidentally shot himself
    Paper & date: LS Aug. 8, 1883
    Date & place of death: Aug. 7, 1883, El Paso, Texas

GONZALES, Mrs. NESTOR - Accidentally shot by husband; hus: NESTOR GON-
    ZALES
    Paper & date: LS Feb. 18, 1885
    Date & place of death: about Feb. 6, 1885, Limitar, New Mexico

GONZALES, SEFERINO - Run over by train; died of injuries
    Paper & date: LS July 7, 1883
    Date & place of death: El Paso, Texas

GOODIN, A. L. - Salesman; Pasons(or Parsons?), Kans.; possible suicide
    Paper & date: LS Apr. 7, 1883
    Date & place of death: last week, Austin, Texas

GOODMAN, _____ Killed by Indians
    Paper & date: EPDH May 10, 1882
    Date & place of death: near Galeyville, Arizona

GOODPASTER, WILLIAM F. - Consumption
    Paper & date: LS May 24, 1884
    Date & place of death: May 22, 1884, at home, Owingsville, Ky.

GOODWIN, THOMAS - Shot by partner JOHN WALSH
    Paper & date: EPT Apr. 28, 1883
    Date & place of death: Apr. 28, 1883, Lordsburg, New Mexico

GOODYKOONTZE, A. P. - Murdered in camp; white citizen of Cherokee Nation;
    m. an Indian
    Paper & date: LS Aug. 29, 1885; EPT Aug. 25, 1885
    Date & place of death: Aug. 20, 1885, Vinita, Indian Territory

GORDON, _____ - Shot by CRAIG - self defense following argument.
    Paper & date: LS Jan. 28, 1885
    Date & place of death: Jan. 23, 1885, Indian Territory

GORDON, BILL - Killed by 3 Mexicans on Mex. Central R. R.; well-known in
    El Paso, Texas
    Paper & date: LS Sept. 29, 1883
    Date & place of death: Sept. 26, 1883, near Lerdo, Mexico

GORDON, JOHN - MUCHACHO NEGRO tried for his murder. Judge instructed
    jury to bring in not guilty verdict. Muchacho Negro is known as a
    bad Indian.
    Paper & date: RGR Mar. 21, 1885
    Date & place of death: about 2 years ago

GORMAN, JAMES - Struck by locomotive at Kingman Sta.
    Paper & date: NTF June 18, 1881
    Date & place of death: few days ago, Santa Fe, New Mexico

GORZA, ANTONIO - Killed with sword by GUADALUPE FEJO - old quarrel
    Paper & date: LS Feb. 18, 1885
    Date & place of death: Brownsville, Texas

GOSLING, HAL L. - U. S. Marshal; - murdered by CHARLES YEAGER (YEGGER?
    YERGER?) & JAMES PITTS (Pitts did the shooting); wife and mo. of
    Castroville, Texas; ch. and sis.; bro.-in-law Dr. DEVEREAUX formerly
    of Medina co., Texas, currently Montclova, Mexico
    Paper & date: LS Feb. 25, 1885; SH July 19, 1885
    Date & place of death: Feb. 21, 1885, near New Braunsfel, Texas

GOULD, A. G. of Liverpool
    Paper & date: LS May 9, 1885
    Date & place of death: Santa Fe, N. M.

GOULD, C. H. - Telegraph operator on Sonora R. R.; yellow fever
    Paper & date: EPT Oct. 14, 1883
    Date & place of death: Guaymas, Mexico

GRAFFEN, S. M. - Pneumonia
    Paper & date: LS Nov. 14, 1883
    Date & place of death: Nov. 8, 1883, Silver City, N. M.

GRAFTON, Gen. B. F. - Associated with BOB INGERSOLL in Ivanhoe mine in
    Black Range, N. M.
    Paper & date: BU Nov. 1, 1883
    Date & place of death: ......

GRAHAM, _____ - Firm: GRAHAM, COLLINS & CO.; killed by fa. of his victim
    _____HEWLETT; surv.: fa. of the firm
    Paper & date: EPT Sept. 3, 1884
    Date & place of death: Sept. 2, 1884, near Gatesville, Texas

GRAHAM, _____ - from the east; yellow fever

66

GRAHAM (cont'd):
    Paper & date: EPT Sept. 18, 1885
    Date & place of death: Sept. 10, 1885, Guaymas, Mexico

GRAHAM, W. L. of McKinney, Texas; formerly of Rusk, Texas; dropped dead-
    heart disease.
    Paper & date: LS Nov. 11, 1882
    Date & place of death: a few days ago.

GRANGER, Gen. GORDON - Union general; b. 1826
    Paper & date: EPDH Jan. 10, 1895
    Date & place of death: Jan. 10, 1876, Santa Fe, New Mexico

GRANGINE, Pvt. _____ - Co. G, 23rd Inf.; typhoid-pneumonial bur. at Ft.
    Bliss.
    Paper & date: LS Jan. 12, 1884
    Date & place of death: Ft. Bliss, Texas

GRANT, BEN (Negro) - HENRY CUMBY, negro, arrested on suspicion of murder
    Paper & date: LS Aug. 15, 1883
    Date & place of death: 10 mi. from Marshall, Texas

GRANT, LUCIEN - Murdered by DOCK WALKER, who was hanged in Texarkana,
    June 27, 1884
    Paper & date: LS July 2, 1884
    Date & place of death: ......

GRAVES, Rev. H. T. of Brenham, Texas; Pastor of Baptist Church; age 69 yrs
    Paper & date: LS Nov. 19, 1881
    Date & place of death: Nov. 4, 1881

GRAVES, Mrs. J. R.
    Paper & date: LS Jan. 21, 1885
    Date & place of death: Jan. 17, 1885, Las Vegas, N. M.

GRAY, _____ Killed resisting arrest.
    Paper & date: LS Oct. 6, 1883
    Date & place of death: Sept. 29, 1883, near Weatherford, Texas

GRAY, FOSTER - Shot by SWEENY when Gray boarded the train and started
    shooting. Both are negroes.
    Paper & date: LS Dec. 10, 1881
    Date & place of death: Dec. 5, 1881, Lamy, N. M.

GRAY, R. L. - Shot by JOHN CALISHAN in self defense.
    Paper & date: LS Feb. 7, 1885
    Date & place of death: TERRY's Ranch, 7 mi. above Kerrville, Texas

GRAY, WILLIAM - Wife: CAROLYN GRAY sues Texas and Mex. R. R. for damages
    Paper & date: LS Sept. 15, 1883
    Date & place of death: Texas

GRAY, WM. A. of Little Rock, Ark.; caused by Dr. RICHARD H. L. BIBB-
    arrested in Saltillo, Mex.
    Paper & date: LS Feb. 7, 1883

GRAY, ZACK - Duel with BILL DOUGHERTY
    Paper & date: EPT Aug. 15, 1884
    Date & place of death: Aug. 10, 1884, Sand Prairie near Terrell,Tex.

GREEN, _____ - Murdered by Indians led by CHIEF NANE
    Paper & date: RGR Dec. 15, 1883
    Date & place of death: ca 1880, Lake Valley, N. M.

GREEN, _____ - Murder by step-son, STEELE; wife-Mrs. GREEN; bro.-_____
    GREEN.
    Paper & date: LS Aug. 16, 1882
    Date & place of death: last week, Denton, Texas

GREEN, _____ - Shot by Indians June 2; not expected to live

GREEN (cont'd):
    Paper & date: LS June 6, 1885
    Date & place of death: ANCHETA's Ranch, Pinos Altos, N. M.

GREENE, BOSS - JIM & D. BAILEY arrested for murder.
    Paper & date: LS Aug. 4, 1883; LS Nov. 21, 1883
    Date & place of death: 5 (7?) yrs. ago, Comanche, Texas

GREEN, GEORGE - Texas Veteran - age 72
    Paper & date: LS May 23, 1885
    Date & place of death: Milam co., Texas

GREEN, JESSE - Hanged by mob; nephew of BILL BAB, once famous
    Paper & date: EPT Oct. 2, 1884
    Date & place of death: Sept. 26, 1884, near Gatesville, Texas

GREENWALD, ETHEL BEATRICE - Infant, 5 mos. 16 days; par: M/M JOHN GREEN-
    WALD
    Paper & date: BU Dec. 1, 1883
    Date & place of death: last month, Socorro, N. M.

GREER, Hon. JNO. F. - fa.: Dr. GREER of San Augustine, Texas
    Paper & date: LS Dec. 7, 1881
    Date & place of death: Nov. 25, 1881, Kaufman, Texas

GREGG, J. A. - Suicide
    Paper & date: LS May 2, 1885
    Date & place of death: Apr. 15, 1885, near Bryan, Texas

GREGORY, MAGGIE of Palestine, Texas; threw herself under a train; unre-
    quited love.
    Paper & date: LS Jan. 31, 1883
    Date & place of death: Jan. 26, 1883

GREGORY, Judge R. C. - Son: Capt. ____ GREGORY of El Paso
    Paper & date: EPT Jan. 27, 1885
    Date & place of death: Jan. 25, 1885, Lafayette, Indiana

GRENET, H. of San Antonio, Texas; died suddenly; a prominent merchant
    Paper & date: LS Mar. 1, 1882
    Date & place of death: Feb. 22, 1882

GRESHAN, GEORGE - Apoplexy
    Paper & date: LS Aug. 20, 1883
    Date & place of death: Paris, Texas

GRIBBLE, ASHBY LEE - Quick consumption
    Paper & date: LS Jan. 25, 1882
    Date & place of death: Jan. 20, 1882, Waco, Texas

GRIFFIN, _____ - Murdered; claimed to be from El Paso
    Paper & date: EPDH Oct. 25, 1882
    Date & place of death: 1882, Portland, Ark.

GRIFFIN, TOM - Cherokee outlaw; shot while robbing a store
    Paper & date: LS Aug. 23, 1884
    Date & place of death: Indian Territory

GRIFFIN, WILLIS - Killed in a fight
    Paper & date: LS Jan. 2, 1884
    Date & place of death: Dec. 26, 1883, McDade, Texas

GRIGGS, GEORGE L. - foul play
    Paper & date: LS Sept. 15, 1883
    Date & place of death: Mexia, Texas

GRINER, HENRY - Shot by Mexicans
    Paper & date: LS May 31, 1884
    Date & place of death: Kinney co., Texas

GRISWOLD, MACE R. - Druggist; hunting accident
Paper & date: LS Sept. 29, 1883; LS Oct. 10, 1883
Date & place of death: Las Vegas, N. M.

GROMICHA, GEORGE (Aged German) - beaten by negro robber.
Paper & date: LS Jan. 24, 1885
Date & place of death: Galveston, Texas

GROSTETTE, ALEXIS L. (C.?) - Killed by ROBERT COURTWRIGHT, JAMES MC IN-
TIRE, W. C. MOORE, _____ SCOTT & _____ CASEY.; m. just 9 days to Miss
CLEMENCE POURADE; mo. and bros.
Paper & date: LS June 2, 1883; EPT May 18, 1883; EPT Oct. 17, 1885
Date & place of death: May 5, 1883, near BISHOP Ranch, Socorro co.,
New Mexico

GROUND HOG - Cherokee - sentenced to be executed
Paper & date: EPT July 11, 1884
Date & place of death: Sept. 20, 1884, Koowees, Cowee Dist., Chero-
kee Nation, Indian Territory

GRUBERT, CHARLES - (German) drowned in Guadalupe River
Paper & date: LS Oct. 18, 1884
Date & place of death: Oct. 11, 1884, near Cuero, Texas

GRUENLER, A. - of Saxony; suddenly; formerly employed in El Paso
Paper & date: LS Oct. 21, 1885; EPT Oct. 18, 1885
Date & place of death: Oct. 17, 1885, Chihuahua, Mexico

GUICERO, _____ - Hanged - probably by DAN DOWD's friends for assisting
in his capture.
Paper & date: LS Jan. 30, 1884
Date & place of death: Tombstone, Arizona

GURLACH, RUDOLPH - Fell from bridge over the San Joaquin while drunk
Paper & date: LS Sept. 27, 1884
Date & place of death: Sept. 21, 1884, Fresno, Ariz. Terr.

GUSSETT, NERWICK (NOSGELLE?) - Black spider bite; fa.: Col. N. GUSSETT,
banker.
Paper & date: LS Sept. 2, 1885; EPT Sept. 2, 1885
Date & place of death: Aug. 29, 1885, Corpus Christi, Texas

GUTHRIE, _____ - Well caved in on him; suffocation
Paper & date: LS July 15, 1885
Date & place of death: July 7, 1885, Luling, Texas

GUTHRIE, GEORGE - Shot by bros. _____ & FRANK NEELEY (NEAGLIE)
Paper & date: LS Feb. 23, 1884; LS Sept. 6, 1884
Date & place of death: Feb. 18, 1884, Richmond, Arizona

GUTIERREZ, _____ - Shot by IGNACIO VARGAS
Paper & date: EPDH July 1, 1883
Date & place of death: Paso del Norte, Mexico

GUTIERRES, SIATO - Shot by rustlers on a drunken spree. Rustlers includ-
ed BILLY WILSON, TOM PICKETT, YANK BEALE & PONEY WILLIAMS
Paper & date: RGR Jan. 19, 1884
Date & place of death: Jan. 15, 1884, Seven Rivers near Tularosa,NM

GUTIERRES, Mrs. TOMAS C.
Paper & date: LS Mar. 5, 1884
Date & place of death: Mar. 1, 1884, near Albuquerque, N. M.

GUY, Sgt. _____ of Indian Police; killed while with a posse attempt-
ing to arrest stock thieves.
Paper & date: LS May 9, 1885
Date & place of death: LEE's Ranch, Indian Territory

HACKENBERRY, _____ - Murdered by 3 men
    Paper & date: LS Sept. 6, 1884
    Date & place of death: San Jose, N. M.

HADDON (?), JAS. - Struck by lightening, near Anderson, Texas
    Paper & date: LS Aug. 25, 1883
    Date & place of death: Pine Grove, Texas

HADLEY, JAMES A. - Body found by a group of "Drovers" - dead for 3-4 wks
    murdered by Indians in Bent co., N. M.- recently of Emporia, Kansas.
    Sis.: SARAH; Fa.: of Dublin, Indiana; sweetheart
    Paper & date: TB Oct. 18, 1871
    Date & place of death: Oct. 12, 1871

HADLEY, LUKE (Negro) - Lynched for rape and attempted rape of several
    white women.
    Paper & date: EPT June 28, 1884
    Date & place of death: June 24, 1884, Whitney, Texas

HAGAR, JOHN W. - Adm. of Estate, R. P. KELLEY, Dona Ana co., N. M.
    Paper & date: MT June 30, 1861
    Date & place of death: before June 1, 1861

HAGUE, _____ - Infant son; pneumonia; Par.: M/M J. P. HAGUE (EPT New
    Years Special Edition 1882 - biog. sketch of father.)
    Paper & date: LS Feb. 21, 1885; EPT Feb. 21, 1885
    Date & place of death: Feb. 19, 1885 El Paso, Texas

HAILING(HALLING), JACOB - Killed by Apaches - lately from New Orleans
    Paper & date: LS Nov. 11, 1885; EPT Nov. 12, 1885; RGR Nov. 14,1885
    Date & place of death: Nov. 8, 1885 near Lake Valley, N. M.

HAINEY, THOMAS - Knife fight 27 Feb. with JAMES PUTNAM - not expected
    to live.
    Paper & date: LS Feb. 28, 1885
    Date & place of death: Gallup, N. M.

HALCOMB, MASON - To die for murder in Indian Territory
    Paper & date: EPT Feb. 1, 1885
    Date & place of death: Apr. 7, 1885, Ft. Smith, Arkansas

HALE, JOHN - Shootout, DALLAS STOUDENMIRE - "two of the roughs."
    Paper & date: EPDH Dec. 28, 1881; NTF Apr. 20, 1881
    Date & place of death: Sunday, Apr. 17, 1881, Las Cruces, N. M.

HALEY, BOB - Killed by _____ MARTIN
    Paper & date: LS Dec. 12, 1883
    Date & place of death: few days ago, Cleburne, Texas

HALEY, Capt. C. Q. - a San Jacinto veteran
    Paper & date: LS Nov. 4, 1882
    Date & place of death: Oct. 30, 1882 in Kosse, Texas

HALEY, DANIEL "PEGLEG" - died
    Paper & date: EPDH Oct. 18, 1882
    Date & place of death: El Paso, Texas

HALL, _____ - Stabbed by _____ DEASON. A sewing machine agent. (does
    not state that he died.)
    Paper & date: LS Dec. 13, 1882
    Date & place of death: (?) Dec. 5, 1882, Ft. Worth, Texas

HALL, Capt. _____ - Rumored killed by maurauding Mexican Nationals
    Paper & date: EPT Feb. 12, 1885
    Date & place of death: Dimmett co., Texas

HALL, FRANK - age 22; rabies - bitten by rabid rat about 10 days ago.
    Fa.: Rev. Mr. HALL.
    Paper & date: LS Apr. 5, 1882
    Date & place of death: of Hutchins, Texas

HALL, W. D. - Shot by WILLIAM CATHEY, JR.
    Paper & date: LS Sept. 20, 1884
    Date & place of death: near Belton, Texas

HALLETT, NEWT - yellow fever; wife: BELLE SIDDONS HALLETT of St. Louis,
    Mo. Later known as MONTE VERDE and Mme. VESTAL.
    Paper & date: EPDH Nov. 2, 1881
    Date & place of death: between 1871 and 1877, Houston, Texas

HALLWAGGER, GEORGE of Ft. Worth, Texas; suicide; from Lexington, S. C.
    Paper & date: LS Nov. 26, 1881
    Date & place of death: last week

HAMIER, LAURA - drowned
    Paper & date: EPT Oct. 24, 1884
    Date & place of death: Oct. 22, near Virginia Point, near Galveston,
    Texas

HAMILTON, CHARLES - Shot by firing squad for murder of soldier. Well
    known on West Coast and other terr.
    Paper & date: SH July 27, 1884
    Date & place of death: July 27, 1884, Mexico City, Mexico

HAMILTON, J. H. of Albuquerque, N. M.; "departed by the morphine route"
    Paper & date: LS Dec. 17, 1882
    Date & place of death: last week

HAMILTON, PETE (Negro) - shot
    Paper & date: LS Aug. 18, 1883
    Date & place of death: near Waco, Texas

HAMMER, R. F. abt. 28 yrs.; found dead in bed; believed suicide by poi-
    son; well known in El Paso, Texas; family in United States; mo. in
    Germany.
    Paper & date: EPT Aug. 29, 1885; LS Sept. 2, 1885; EPT Sept. 2,1885
    Date & place of death: Aug. 28, 1885, Mexico City, Mex.

HAMPE, _____ - Assault by drunken negro, PITTS. City Marshall HAMPE
    was beaten savagely and shot 4 times. PITTS gave himself up.
    Paper & date: LS Feb. 3, 1883
    Date & place of death: Jan. 27, 1883, New Braunfells, Texas

HANCOCK, DOCK - Shot by FRANK JOHNSON, ex-sher. of Parker co.
    Paper & date: LS Nov. 12, 1884
    Date & place of death: Nov. 4, 1884, Springtown, Texas

HANCOCK, J. P. - Drowned
    Paper & date: LS July 29, 1885
    Date & place of death: Waco, Texas

HANCOCK, Mrs. W. H. - age 40; outraged and murdered; hus. and ch.
    Paper & date: EPT Dec. 27, 1885; LS Dec. 30, 1885
    Date & place of death: Dec. 1885, Austin, Texas

HANDY, LOUIS of Rio Grande City, Texas; murdered 6 miles below Rio Grande
    City, Texas; apparently he was Dty. Sher.
    Paper & date: LS Dec. 10, 1881
    Date & place of death: Dec. 1, 1881, Rio Grande City, Texas

HANEHAN, JOHN of Laredo, Texas - wounds in shoot-out with Sher.'s posse
    on Oct. 18.
    Paper & date: LS Oct. 29, 1881
    Date & place of death: Oct. 19, 1881

HANNON, Mrs. L. A. - Hus.-car repairer; baby-3 weeks old
    Paper & date: RGR Jan. 5, 1884
    Date & place of death: Dec. 31, 1883, Rincon, N. M.

HARDCASTLE, B. L. -(of the "News")
    Paper & date: LS Sept. 26, 1885/ Place - Texas

HARDEMAN, _____ - Dty. Marshal - killed at Variety Theater.
Paper & date: LS June 10, 1885
Date & place of death: Colorado City, Texas

HARDIE (HARDY?), ROBERT M. - Shot by HENRY OMANA (OTANA?), a congress-
man of Mex., over a woman.
Paper & date: EPT June 2, 1885; EPT Dec. 9, 1885
Date & place of death: June 1, 1885, Mexico City

HARDIN, _____ - Infant dau.; par.: M/M DAVID HARDIN
Paper & date: BU Aug. 1, 1884
Date & place of death: June 23, 1884, Merrimac, St. Louis co., N. M.

HARENS, ED - Brakeman on S. P.; fell under train; bur.: El Paso, Texas
Paper & date: EPDH June 28, 1882
Date & place of death: June 25, 1882, near Sierra Blanca, Texas

HARGROVE, _____ - an Englishman; kicked to death by ____ MARSHALL.
Paper & date: LS May 30, 1883
Date & place of death: Galveston, Texas

HARMON, C. H. - Killed by ____ HITCHCOCK
Paper & date: LS Nov. 7, 1885
Date & place of death: near Hackberry, Ariz.

HARRIMAN, JACK - of Wallace, N. M.; shot by WM. MOSIER in Wallace some
weeks ago; died Sister's Hospital.
Paper & date: LS Feb. 13, 1884; LS Jan. 26, 1884
Date & place of death: Jan. 22, 1884, Santa Fe, N. M.

HARRINGTON, PAT - Killed; R. R. man; wife - Mrs. CATHERINE HARRINGTON -
recovered $5000 from R. R.
Paper & date: LS Dec. 2, 1882; LS June 27, 1885

HARRIS, _____ - Beat over head by WILLIAM BUTCHER. May die.
Paper & date: EPT Oct. 3, 1883
Date & place of death: Comanche, Texas

HARRIS, _____ - Child; fa.: JOHN HARRIS.
Paper & date: EPT June 5, 1885
Date & place of death: June 3, 1885, El Paso, Texas

HARRIS, ANNIE - Poisoned herself.
Paper & date: EPMS Dec. 11, 1884
Date & place of death: Dec. 5, 1884, Kingston, Ariz.

HARRIS, D. A. - R. R. Conductor, Mex. Cen.; fell from cars; body sent to
Cedar Rapids, Iowa; friends in El Paso, Texas
Paper & date: LS Nov. 17, 1883
Date & place of death: Nov. 14, 1883, Sacramento, near Chihuahua,Mex.

HARRIS, ETHEL - Killed by Indians.
Paper & date: LS Dec. 16, 1885
Date & place of death: on Snow Creek, in Mogollon mtns., N. M.

HARRIS, JACK - Killed by BEN THOMPSON, ex-city marshal of Austin, Texas;
in a theater at San Antonio.
Paper & date: LS Jan. 6, 1883; EPDH July 26, 1882
Date & place of death: San Antonio, Texas; recently.

HARRIS, ORLANDO - Killed by ALLEN HILL, alias JOHN KEEN.
Paper & date: EPDH Mar. 5, 1896
Date & place of death: 15 yrs. ago, Mineral Wells, Texas

HARRIS, R. H. - Overdose of morphine.
Paper & date: LS Jan. 11, 1881
Date & place of death: Jan. 4, 1881 - of Brenham, Texas

HARRIS, W. W. - Thrown from horse - concussion.
Paper & date: LS Oct. 18, 1884
Date & place of death: Oct. 13, 1884, Tom Green co., Texas

HARRISON, _____ - Young man; murdered.
    Paper & date: EPDH June 10, 1883
    Date & place of death: After Civil War, 20 miles above El Paso, Tex.

HARRISON, WILLIAM - Killed by Indians.
    Paper & date: LS Dec. 2, 1885
    Date & place of death: On Turkey Creek near Ft. Apache, Ariz.

HARRISON, WILLIAM - Excessive use of liquor.
    Paper & date: LS Oct. 18, 1884
    Date & place of death: Last week near Trickham, Texas

HARROUM, H. D. - heart disease - sudden
    Paper & date: LS Dec. 2, 1885
    Date & place of death: Silver City, N. M.

HART, C. D. - Cancer - son of W. D. HART of Minden, Nebraska
    Paper & date : RGR Mar. 29, 1884; RGR May 3, 1884
    Date & place of death: ...of Jarilla Tanks, N. M.

HART, DUNCAN C. - Suicide by shooting; from New Haven, Conn.; bro.: of
    Grant co., New Mexico
    Paper & date: LS Feb. 24, 1883
    Date & place of death: Feb. 16, 1883, Grant co., N. M.

HART, JAMES - Killed by BOB PERRY.
    Paper & date: LS Sept. 15, 1883
    Date & place of death: July or August 1882, Indian Territory

HARVEY, GEORGE - Shot by REDDY MC CANN.
    Paper & date: LS Aug. 11, 1883
    Date & place of death: Santa Fe, N. M.

HARVEY, J. F. - age 45; hung self with his drawers.
    Paper & date: LS Sept. 24, 1884
    Date & place of death: last week - Honey Grove, Texas

HARWOOD, Mrs. _____ of Missouri; L. B. HARWOOD, son of Las Cruces; Gov.
    MARMADUKE, bro. of Mo.?
    Paper & date: RGR July 18, 1885
    Date & place of death: July 14, 1885

HASH, JOHN - Killed by his brother
    Paper & date: LS Feb. 6, 1884
    Date & place of death: Feb. 2, 1884, Dallas, Texas

HASKELL, GEORGE S.
    Paper & date: LS May 2, 1885
    Date & place of death: Chloride, N. M.

HASTINS, HARRY - Fell from tree gathering pecans.
    Paper & date: EPMS Dec. 17, 1884
    Date & place of death: Paluxy, Texas

HATCH, Mrs. _____ ; hus. Gen. Hatch.
    Paper & date: EPDH Oct. 5, 1881; EPDH Oct. 26, 1881
    Date & place of death: Washington, D. C.

HATCH, S. W. - Suicide
    Paper & date: LS May 23, 1885
    Date & place of death: Gainesville, Texas

HATHERTON, JAS. or HATHORN, JASON - (Negro) - Lynched
    Paper & date: LS July 15, 1885; EPT July 8, 1885
    Date & place of death: July 5, 1885, Trinity, Texas

HAUDENSCHILD, J. W. -(called WEST) -hack driver; accidentally shot him-
    self about midnight.
    Paper & date: LS Oct. 11, 1884
    Date & place of death: Oct. 8, 1884, El Paso, Texas

HAUGHN, ..(Judge) - Shot
    Paper & date: LS July 7, 1883
    Date & place of death: Jefferson, Texas

HAWES, GEORGE (Negro) - Shot in fight with vigilantes.
    Paper & date: EPT Sept. 5, 1884
    Date & place of death: Aug. 27, 1884, Refugio, Texas

HAWKINS, BEN (Negro) - Hung by mob for murder.
    Paper & date: EPT Feb. 6, 1885
    Date & place of death: Feb. 4, 1885, Franklin, Texas

HAWORTH, Maj. J. L. - Sudden; he was supt. of all Indian schools in the
    nation. Wife and 2 m. daus.
    Paper & date: EPT Mar. 13, 1885
    Date & place of death: Mar. 12, 1885, Albuquerque, N. M.

HAY, GEORGE C. - Killed on NOEL's Ranch; age 50' Apaches led by GERONIMO
    at Mule Spring Canyon.
    Paper & date: LS Nov. 11, 1885; RGR Nov. 14, 1885
    Date & place of death: Nov. 8, 1885 near Ft. Cummings, N. M.

HAYNE, ARTHUR - (Mining expert); well known in N. M. and Ariz.
    Paper & date: LS Nov. 3, 1883
    Date & place of death: Oct. 25, 1883 San Francisco, California

HAYNIE (HAINES?), ELLA - (Negro); accidentally shot by voodoo Dr. JONES
    (Negro)
    Paper & date: LS Nov. 18, 1885
    Date & place of death: Palestine, Texas

HAYNES, J. R. - Shot in his yard. Mr. DUNLAP wounded.
    Paper & date: EPT Oct. 14, 1884
    Date & place of death: Oct. 11, 1884 near Comanche, Texas

HAYS, _____ - Young boy; killed by mob in defense of his home; par.
    Paper & date: EPT Oct. 10, 1884
    Date & place of death: Oct. 8, 1884, Sipe Springs, Tex. (near Waco)

HAYS, Mrs. _____ - Run over and killed by street car.; age 72
    Paper & date: LS Feb. 4, 1882
    Date & place of death: last week. Of Houston, Texas

HAYS, Col. JOHN COFFEE of Texas Rangers; bur.: 24 Apr. Oakland, Calif.;
    service: St. John's Episcopal Church; burial: Mtn. View Cem.
    66 yrs. old; native of Tenn.; wife, son and dau.
    Paper & date: EPT Apr. 28, 1883; EPT May 2, 1883
    Date & place of death: Apr. 21, 1883 near Piedmont, California

HAYES, JOSEPH - Mine cave in
    Paper & date: EPT May 19, 1884
    Date & place of death: May 18, 1884, Grass Valley, (N. M. or Calif.?)

HAYES, THOMAS - Shot by J. PENDLETON.
    Paper & date: EPT Sept. 20, 1883
    Date & place of death: Sept. 19, 1883, Coleman, Texas

HAYES, WASH (Negro) - Accidentally shot by Mr. _____DEMAY.
    Paper & date: EPT Aug. 26, 1884
    Date & place of death: Aug. 24, 1884, Richmond, Texas

HAYWARD, _____ - Knights of Honor Benefit filed Jan. 20, 1885 - pd. Mar.
    9, 1885
    Paper & date: EPT Mar. 10, 1885
    Date & place of death: El Paso, Texas

HAZELL, Mrs. _____ - Outraged and murdered;one was JOHN MARTIN; hus.& ch.
    Paper & date: LS June 27, 1885
    Date & place of death: Elkhart, Texas

HAZELWOOD, JOHN of Baird, Texas - Suicide
    Paper & date: LS Dec. 19, 1883
    Date & place of death: Sweetwater, Texas

HEACOCK, C. - Murdered by wife; wife: EFFIE HEACOCK - got life imprison-
    ment.
    Paper & date: LS Dec. 7, 1881
    Date & place of death: July 1880 of Wills Point, Texas

HEALY, _____ - Murder; W. C. COOK was acquitted in this trial at George-
    town, Texas
    Paper & date: LS Aug. 9, 1882
    Date & place of death: at Taylor, Texas

HEARNE, _____ - ELPIJO BACA charged with killing.
    Paper & date: LS May 13, 1885
    Date & place of death: last fall San Francisco, Socorro co., N. M.

HEATH, JOHN - Lynched for murder. Formerly of Dallas, Texas
    Paper & date: LS Feb. 27, 1884
    Date & place of death: Tombstone, Ariz.

HEDGES, GEORGE M. - Died; formerly worked in El Paso, Texas
    Paper & date: EPDH Dec. 9, 1883
    Date & place of death: last week, Oakland, California

HEDGES, R. S. - Shot by "REDDY", a saloonkeeper.
    Paper & date: LS Oct. 10, 1883
    Date & place of death: Oct. 5, 1883, White Oaks, N. M.

HEFFERIN, MICHAEL - age abt. 30
    Paper & date : EPDH Oct. 5, 1881
    Date & place of death: Oct. 3, 1881, El Paso, Texas

HEGAN, FRANK - Killed by MERVILL PARKS, convicted at Weatherford, Texas
    Apr. 21, 1883
    Paper & date: EPT Apr. 25, 1883
    Date & place of death: Texas

HEISE, Mrs. MARGARET - Grave broken into, apparently to steal jewelry re-
    ported to have been buried on her.
    Paper & date: LS Dec. 16, 1882
    Date & place of death: Las Vegas, N. M.

HELLIN, J. R. - Suicide; shot himself
    Paper & date: LS July 28, 1883
    Date & place of death: Pine Hill, Texas

HELPER, JOHN A. - Suicide; he had been on a spree; nephew of late JOHN
    ADAMS.
    Paper & date: LS Aug. 19, 1882
    Date & place of death: a few days ago; of Paris, Texas

HEMPHILL, Cpl. _____ - Co. C; killed during thunder storm while asleep
    Paper & date: EPT Sept. 1, 1883
    Date & place of death: Aug. 26, 1883, Ft. McDowell

HENDERSON, DON - Shot by BURT GARLAND
    Paper & date: LS Aug. 29, 1885; LS Sept. 2, 1885
    Date & place of death: Forney, Texas

HENDERSON, PRESS - (Negro)- shot, mutilated and skull crushed by CHARLES
    WINTERS (Negro)
    Date & paper: LS Oct. 18, 1884
    Date & place of death: Oct. 13, 1884, Hearne, Texas

HENDERSON, ROBERT -(Engineer) shot by WILLIAM M. GIBBS for insulting his
    wife.
    Paper & date: LS June 16, 1883; LS June 20, 1883
    Date & place of death: Raton, N. M.

HENDERSON, TOM - Formerly of Springer, N. M.; shot himself accidentally
Paper & date: LS Apr. 25, 1885
Date & place of death: Stoneville, Montana

HENRI, WM. HENRY of Chilili
Paper & date: LS Mar. 26, 1884; RGR Mar. 29, 1884
Date & place of death: Mar. 22, 1884, Albuquerque, N. M.

HENRIS, GABE (Negro) - fight with another negro
Paper & date: LS June 9, 1883
Date & place of death: Austin, Texas

HENRY, _____ - To be hung for murder in Crockett co., Texas, Nov. 13,
1885
Paper & date: LS Oct. 17, 1885

HENRY, ABE - Run over by load of coal
Paper & date: LS Jan. 31, 1885
Date & place of death: Dallas, Texas

HENRY, BOB of N. Y.; probably by Apaches
Paper & date: EPT Sept. 29, 1884
Date & place of death: recently; mtns. 300 mi. beyond Chihuahua, Mex.

HENRY, JULIA of Indian Territory; age 25; shot herself - suicide.
Paper & date: LS Oct. 29, 1884
Date & place of death: Oct. 24, 1884, near Dallay

HENRY, WM. - Convict; struck over head with shovel.
Paper & date: LS Apr. 7, 1883
Date & place of death: Apr. 1, 1883, Hawkins, Texas

HENTIG, _____ - Killed by Indians in fight; probably an army man.
Paper & date: EPDH Sept. 7, 1881
Date & place of death: Arizona

HEPBURN, G. B. of Scotland; assassinated during a riot; younger bro.:
ARCHIBALD BUCHAW HEPBURN of Scotland.
Paper & date: EPT June 27, 1883; EPT June 12, 1884
Date & place of death: some time ago, Pinas Altos, Mexico

HEPNER, GUS - Murdered by Indians between Casas Grandes and Gavilan on
way to Silver City, N. M.
Paper & date: TB Mar. 16, 1871

HERBERT, Mrs. _____ - hus. and dau: EVA
Paper & date: BU Dec. 5, 1885
Date & place of death: 3 yrs. ago, Sabinal, N. M.

HERBERT, EVA - almost 7 yrs.; bur. in Sabinal, N. M. beside mo.; niece
of M/M A. L. STRAUSS; fa.; uncle: S. LEVY, all of Socorro, N. M.
Paper & date: BU Dec. 5, 1885
Date & place of death: Dec. 2, 1885, Socorro, N. M.

HERBERT, HENRY - Shot by PETER CARL, a gambler.
Paper & date: LS Sept. 3, 1884
Date & place of death: Aug. 30, 1884, Rincon, N. M.

HERBIG, JULIUS - Hanging - suspected suicide
Paper & date: LS Oct. 11, 1884
Date & place of death: Oct. 4, 1884 near San Antonio, Texas

HERDON, Mrs. DEINA
Paper & date: LS Aug. 5, 1885
Date & place of death: Albuquerque, N. M.

HERFF, Dr. JOHN - Pertitonitis by eating imported sausages
Paper & date: LS Jan. 11, 1882
Date & place of death: Jan. 5, 1882; of San Antonio, Texas

HERRERA, JOSE MARIA - Heart disease
    Paper & date: EPDH Feb. 18, 1883
    Date & place of death: last week, Paso del Norte, Mexico

HERRING, J. W. - (Hackman) - Suicide by poison because wife left him and
    entered house of ill-fame.
    Paper & date: LS Nov. 22, 1884
    Date & place of death: San Antonio, Texas

HESLAND, Mr. and 10 yr. old son - Struck by lightening
    Paper & date: LS May 26, 1883
    Date & place of death: near Busby Knob, Texas

HESTER, SAM - Shot by VAN R. ELLIOT and bro. R. H. ELLIOT for making in-
    discreet proposals to VAN ELLIOT's wife.
    Paper & date: LS May 5, 1883; LS May 9, 1883
    Date & place of death: May 6, 1883, Organ, N. M.

HEWITT, Mr. _____ - Murdered by ADDIE LOWE, a negro
    Paper & date: LS Dec. 9, 1885
    Date & place of death: Falls co. , Texas

HEWLETT, _____ - Shot by _____ GRAHAM, over deaths of their sons.
    Paper & date: EPT Sept. 3, 1884
    Date & place of death: Sept. 2, 1884, near Gatesville, Texas

HIBBARD, MATTHEW - Consumption
    Paper & date: LS June 13, 1885
    Date & place of death: Silver City, N. M.

HICKEY, Mrs. JANE C. - aged 46; hus.: MARTIN L. HICKEY (or MAURICE) of
    Las Cruces. She was born at Wheatland, N. Y and had lived for some
    years at Mesilla and near Dona Ana.
    Paper & date: RGR Dec. 8, 1883; LS Dec. 12, 1883
    Date & place of death: Dec. 1, 1883, Mesilla Valley, N. M.

HICKSON, JOE - Murdered by partners FRANK BRECK and TOM WELSH(or FRANK
    BECK & TOM WELLET)
    Paper & date: LS Nov. 5, 1884; EPT Nov. 4, 1884
    Date & place of death: Oct. 28, 1884, Good Hope Mining Camp, N. M.

HIGHLANDER, W. H. - Old citizen; killed by 2 highwaymen
    Paper & date: LS Dec. 23, 1885
    Date & place of death: Dallas co, Texas

HILDRETH, _____ - Shot by HOG DAVIS (a professional gambler) at a Baile
    at Silver City, N. M.
    Paper & date: TB Sept. 7, 1872; TB Sept. 28, 1872

HILL, _____ - Senator; 30,000 attended
    Paper & date: LS Aug. 26, 1882
    Date & place of death: buried Aug. 19, 1882, at Atlanta, Texas (or
    Allonto, Texas)

HILL, CHARLIE - Drunken shoot out with Col. EATON and Ch. of Police MON-
    ROE; bro.: BUTCH HILL
    Paper & date: LS Dec. 31, 1881
    Date & place of death: Dec. 25, 1881, Socorro, N. M.

HILL, GEORGE - Overdose of Fowler's solution
    Paper & date: LS Nov. 28, 1883
    Date & place of death: Nov. 18, 1883, Shakespeare, N. M.

HILL, JOHN A. - Old miner in Grant co., N. M.; suddenly
    Paper & date: LS Dec. 15, 1883
    Date & place of death: Dec. 7, 1883, Ivanhoe, N. M.

HILT, G. - Rheumatism of the heart
    Paper & date: LS Jan. 11, 1882
    Date & place of death: Jan. 6, 1882, Las Vegas, N. M.

HILTON, JOHN - Train engineer; three men robber train.
Paper & date: LS Sept. 30, 1885
Date & place of death: 2 yrs. ago. Coolidge, Texas

HILZINGER, GROVER CLEVELAND - died aged 1 mo. 10 days. JOSEPH T. & ALLIE
HILZINGER, par.
Paper & date: LS Dec. 23, 1884
Date & place of death: Dec. 22, 1884, El Paso, Texas

HINCH, BROWN - Murdered by JAMES WINGFIELD, aka JAKE MAXEY. Murderer
captured Jan. 29, 1885 by Sher. MURPHY of Lake Valley and is being
held in Hillsboro, N. M. jail for Missouri officials.
Paper & date: RGR Feb. 21, 1885
Date & place of death: Dec. 25, 1883 at Sligo Iron Furnace, Dent co.,
Missouri

HINDOO, JAMES - Mangled
Paper & date: LS Oct. 21, 1885
Date & place of death: "near ABBOTT ranch",N. M.

HINKLE, THOMAS E. of Matton, Ill.; nephew Dr. J. M. MILLER, Socorro, N.M.
Paper & date: BU July 25, 1885
Date & place of death: July 21, 1885, Socorro, N. M.

HINSLEY, CHAS. - Robber; killed by posse for murder
Paper & date: EPT Oct. 6, 1883
Date & place of death: Oct. 4, 1883 near Tucson, Ariz.

HITCH, JOHN - Stabbed by HENRY BETTS
Paper & date: LS July 25, 1885
Date & place of death: July 18, 1885, Gainesville, Texas

HITE, _____ - 6 yr. girl; loaded pistol accidently knocked off a shelf
by negro servant. Mo.: Mrs. Hite
Paper & date: LS Jan. 7, 1882
Date & place of death: Dec. 28, 1881, Jacksonville, Texas

HOAG, _____ - Bitten by tarantula; will probably die
Paper & date: LS Aug. 15, 1883
Date & place of death: Santa Rita, N. M.

HOBECK. J. G. (R. R. fireman) - train accident on T & P
Paper & date: EPT Mar. 17, 1885
Date & place of death: Mar. 15, 1885, near Arlington, Texas

HOBRECHT, WILLIAM - Suicide
Paper & date: LS Nov. 14, 1885
Date & place of death: San Antonio, Texas

HODGE, _____ - Sta. Mtr. of Enical Sta., Texas; murdered by MENDIOLA, a
Mexican.
Paper & date: LS May 27, 1885
Date & place of death: Texas

HODGES, G. M. - Murdered by JOSE MARIA MENDELA
Paper & date: LS Nov. 28, 1885
Date & place of death: Cotulla, Texas

HOECK, Mrs. J. F. - Received word last week; hus. and 4 ch.; son: FRED P.
HOECK of El Paso, Texas
Paper & date: EPDH Apr. 3, 1882
Date & place of death: Appenade, Germany

HOECK, JESSIE - bur. Leavenworth, Kans.; hus.: F. P. HOECK; fa.: Major
VAUGHN; par.
Paper & date: LS Aug. 30, 1882; EPDH Aug. 30, 1882
Date & place of death: Aug. 28, 1882, El Paso, Texas

HOFF, WM. - Bequeathed $8,000 property to cities of Galveston and Pales-
tine, Texas for charitable purposes. Had lived in Palestine, Texas

HOFF (cont'd):
    Paper & date: LS Nov. 29, 1882
    Date & place of death: recently in "Old Country" of Germany

HOFFMAN, H. O. - Suicide in jail by hanging
    Paper & date: LS Nov. 25, 1885
    Date & place of death: Brenham, Texas

HOGAN, _____ - 2 trains collided
    Paper & date: LS Sept. 24, 1884
    Date & place of death: Sept. 20, 1884 near A & P Junction, El Paso,
    Texas

HOGAN, Miss ELIZABETH - Had lived in Texas since 1839 and in Houston...
    since 1845.
    Paper & date: LS Dec. 28, 1881
    Date & place of death: Dec. 20, 1881, Houston, Texas

HOGAN, Mrs. J. C. - Suicide
    Paper & date: LS Aug. 20, 1884
    Date & place of death: last week, Gainesville, Texas

HOGAN, JOHN - Killed by Miss JESSIE WELLS
    Paper & date: EPT May 2, 1883
    Date & place of death: last Jan., Chihuahua, Mexico

HOGAN, MICHAEL -
    Paper & date: EPDH Dec. 28, 1881
    Date & place of death: Aug. 10-17, Paso del Norte, Mex.

HOGAN, MICHAEL
    Paper & date: LS Mar. 1, 1884
    Date & place of death: Feb. 27, 1884, Albuquerque, N. M.

HOHSTADT, _____ - Young; killed by CHATO's band
    Paper & date: EPT Aug. 26, 1885
    Date & place of death: Ojo de Agua (Ariz.?)

HOLBROOK, M. A. - Jailer; killed by JOSEPH CASEY in escape attempt
    Paper & date: LS June 23, 1883; EPT May 1, 1883
    Date & place of death: Apr. 29, 1883, Tucson, Arizona

HOLCOMB, J. B. - Shot - he was alias "CHARLEY GREEN"
    Paper & date: LS Jan. 4, 1882
    Date & place of death: Dec. 27, 1881, Lake Valley, N. M.

HOLLAND, _____ (Negro) - Heart Disease
    Paper & date: LS Mar. 18, 1885
    Date & place of death: Las Vegas, N. M.

HOLLAND, JOE, a difficulty with TOM DELOACH (formerly of White Oaks) at
    a Hay Ranch - 16 miles from El Paso
    Paper & date: RGR Sept. 12, 1885

HOLLAND, WILLIAM - Shot by JOHN BUSTER over card game
    Paper & date: EPMS Dec. 16, 1884
    Date & place of death: other day - Seven Rivers, N. M.

HOLLERAN, MICHAEL - died in hospital; had a small trading stand, left es-
    tate of $10,000
    Paper & date: LS Nov. 15, 1882
    Date & place of death: recently, Houston, Texas

HOLLINGSWORTH, LESLIE MARMADUKE - little boy; named for old friend of
    S. C. SLADE, El Paso, in Mo.; fa.: CHARLEY HOLLINGSWORTH
    Paper & date: EPT Oct. 8, 1884

HOLMES, JERRY - Killed in saloon brawl
    Paper & date: LS May 2, 1883
    Date & place of death: Del Rio, Texas

HOLMES, JOHN F. of Rochester, N. Y.; hemorrhage of the lungs.
Paper & date: LS Jan. 16, 1884
Date & place of death: Jan. 7, 1884, Las Vegas, N. M.

HOLMES, JOSEPH (Negro) - Murdered
Paper & date: LS Aug. 4, 1883
Date & place of death: near Corsicana, Texas

HOLMES, S. N. -(Editor) - burned; former Lt. court martialed at Ft. Bliss
surv.: wife
Paper & date: BU Mar. 1, 1884; LS Feb. 20, 1884; RGR Feb. 23, 1884
Date & place of death: Feb. 15, 1884, Prescott, Ariz.

HOOPER, FRED - Murdered by CELSO LOPEZ on a horse ranch (partly illegible)
Paper & date: LS Sept. 9, 1882
Date & place of death: recently, New Mexico

HOPKINS, _____ - R. R. engineer; train accident
Paper & date: LS Nov. 3, 1883
Date & place of death: Oct. 28, 1883, near Agua Calientes, Mex.

HOPKINS, MATHEW
Paper & date: LS Nov. 28, 1883
Date & place of death: Nov. 23, 1883, Austin, Texas

HORN, GEORGE - Killed by Indians
Paper & date: EPT Sept. 16, 1885
Date & place of death: Sept. 13, 1885, near Lake Valley, N. M.

HORN, JNO. - Indian raid
Paper & date: LS Sept. 19, 1885
Date & place of death: near Georgetown, N. M.

HORNER, JAMES - fireman on Santa Fe R. R. - train accident
Paper & date: LS Apr. 11, 1883
Date & place of death: Apr. 6, 1883, near La Junta, Col.

HOSKINS, CHARLIE - Shot by DAVE WOODS (Negro)
Paper & date: LS Sept. 23, 1885
Date & place of death: near McDade

HOUSTON, BILL - (Negro) - shot and killed during a melee by W. P. WRIGHT
(white). Houston was a musician at a house.
Paper & date: LS Jan. 27, 1883
Date & place of death: Jan. 22, 1883, at Waco, Texas

HOWARD, _____ - boy; suffocated accidentally; fa.: J. T. HOWARD
Paper & date: EPT Apr. 16, 1883
Date & place of death: Apr. 15, 1883, Ft. Worth, Texas

HOWARD, _____ - Run over by Ft. Worth Street railroad car; fa.: ALLEN
HOWARD sued the R. R. for $10,000 for killing his son.
Paper & date: LS Oct. 11, 1882
Date & place of death: Ft. Worth, Texas

HOWARD, _____ - Murdered
Paper & date: LS July 7, 1883
Date & place of death: El Paso co., Texas?

HOWARD, ("TEX"?) - To be hanged for murder (Bisbee, Ariz.)
Paper & date: LS Mar. 26, 1884
Date & place of death: Mar. 28, 1884, Tombstone, Ariz.

HOWARD, FRANK - Murdered
Paper & date: LS Dec. 10, 1881
Date & place of death: Nov. 25, 1881; of Albuquerque, N. M.

HOWARD, JOE - Killed by TOM DELOACH during argument in self-defense;bur.:
at Concordia; no known relatives; believed to have come from Ind.Terr.
Paper & date: LS Sept. 9, 1885; EPT Sept. 9, 1885

HOWARD, JOE (cont'd):
    Date & place of death: Sept. 8, 1885, near El Paso, Texas

HOWARD, JOHN - Fireman; train wreck
    Paper & date: LS May 23, 1883
    Date & place of death: Badger Station on Denver and Rio Grande R. R.

HOWARD, MINNIE - age 7 yrs.; burned to death
    Paper & date: LS Apr. 21, 1883
    Date & place of death: Ft. Worth, Texas

HOWARD, SAMUEL - drowned
    Paper & date: LS June 9, 1883
    Date & place of death: near Palestine, Texas

HOWARD, TOM - Killed by CLEM CHILDERS; trial in Ysleta, Texas
    Paper & date: EPT Apr. 25, 1883
    Date & place of death: abt 5 yrs. ago, Presidio co., Texas

HOWE, FRED - Found dead, riddled with bullets. Suspician toward JESUS
    MARIO RODRIGUEZ
    Paper & date: LS Oct. 11, 1882
    Date & place of death: last week near Georgetown, N. M.

HOWE, ISAAC - age 70; b. in Ky.; surv.: wife and several grown sons.
    Paper & date: LS Apr. 1, 1885
    Date & place of death: Raton, N. M.

HOWELL, JAMES - Shot by drunken cowboy; bullet entered back of his head
    and came out the front; he lived 34 hours; WM. EISENSMIDT, THOS.
    GRADY and JESUS BOSTUS charged with murder; all 3 acquitted because
    could not show which one fired fatal shot.
    Paper & date: RGR Oct. 4, 1884; RGR Oct. 11, 1884
    Date & place of death: Lake Valley, N. M.

HOWLETT, RICHARD - Murdered by TOM BOWE (BOWIE) in 1877
    Paper & date: LS May 14, 1884; LS Jan. 30, 1884
    Date & place of death: Silver City, N. M.

HOY, ABBIE - aged 4; fell from a dry goods box - internal injuries; bur.:
    May 20, 1884; fa.: J. M. HOY of Rincon, N. M.
    Paper & date: RGR May 31, 1884
    Date & place of death: last week

HOYT, SQUIRREL - Shot and killed by Sher. LUCAS of Choctaw Nation.
    Paper & date: EPT Dec. 25, 1884
    Date & place of death: (Okla.) Indian Territory

HUBBARD, HARRY - Killed by PETER CARROLL
    Paper & date: EPT Sept. 3, 1884
    Date & place of death: Sept. 1, 1884?, Rincon, N. M.

HUBBELL, JOHNNIE - Shot
    Paper & date: LS Nov. 26, 1881
    Date & place of death: last week; of Bernalillo, N. M.

HUBBELL, Capt. SANTIAGO J. - Apoplexy; b. in New England 1822, to N. M.
    as a youth; m. sister of Judge TOMAS GUTIERREZ and cousin of Col.
    FRANCISCO CHAVEZ; surv.: widow, 2 sons and 5 daus.; 1st Coll. of Cus-
    toms in El Paso.
    Paper & date: LS Feb. 11, 1885; EPT Feb. 7, 1885
    Date & place of death: Feb. 7, 1885, Albuquerque, N. M. or Pajarito,
    N. M.

HUBER, HARRY - Shot by PETE CARL
    Paper & date: RGR Sept. 6, 1884
    Date & place of death: Sept. 1, 1884, Rincon, N. M.

HUCKLEBY, THOMAS - Caught between two R. R. cars
    Paper & date: LS Nov. 30,1881/ D & P: Nov. 21,1881, Ft. Worth, Texas

HUGHES, _____ 7 yr. old girl - burned; fa.: WILLIAM HUGHES
    Paper & date: LS Aug. 8, 1883
    Date & place of death: near Cedar Hill, Texas

HUGHES, Mrs. JIM - Murdered by hus. JIMMY HUGHES, known as "Pet of the
    San Simon". M. in Clifton, N. M.
    Paper & date: EPT Aug. 23, 1884
    Date & place of death: 18 mos. ago. Texas

HUGHES, TOM - Murdered by Indians led by Chief NANE
    Paper & date: RGR Dec. 15, 1883
    Date & place of death: c. 1880, Lake Valley, N. M.

HUGHES, WILLIAM - Apoplexy. Old Soldier.
    Paper & date: LS Feb. 21, 1885
    Date & place of death: Mora, New Mexico

HUGHSTON, BUD - Killed by W. R. ORMAN.
    Paper & date: LS Oct. 28, 1885
    Date & place of death: Waco, Texas

HULL, Mrs. ELLEN - Died in Dentist's chair. Hus.: Santa Fe R. R. brake-
    man.
    Paper & date: LS Nov. 10, 1883
    Date & place of death: Oct. 31, 1883, Galveston, Texas

HULT, HALO HALE (infant son) - Fa.: E. G. HULT
    Paper & date: BU July 1, 1884
    Date & place of death: June 1884, Socorro, New Mexico

HUMBLE, G. B. - Axed
    Paper & date: LS Jan. 31, 1885
    Date & place of death: near Boerne, Texas

HUMMEL, OSCAR - Run over by train. Probably murdered and body placed on
    tracks long before the train came, one mile West of train depot. Age
    25; Ft. Bliss Quartermaster clerk from Texas interior.
    Paper & date: LS Aug. 9, 1882; EPDH Aug. 9, 1882
    Date & place of death: Aug. 6, 1882, El Paso, Texas

HUNNINGTON, FRANK - (Hackman) - shot.
    Paper & date: LS Nov. 4, 1885
    Date & place of death: Brownwood, Texas

HUNT, Mrs. MARY - age 35/36 - strychnine in room at HILL's old theatre
    bldg. Effects left to Miss EDWARDS, % GARDNER, #36 Main St., Los
    Angeles, California
    Paper & date: LS Aug. 5, 1882
    Date & place of death: Aug. 4, 1882, El Paso, Texas

HUNTER, ALLEN - (Negro) - Shot by PRES WILSON (Negro) argument over cards
    Paper & date: LS Dec. 26, 1885
    Date & place of death: Bosqueville, Texas

HUNTINGTON, F. - Murdered by Apaches
    Paper & date: RGR June 27, 1885
    Date & place of death: recently, of Sonora

HUNTON, ROBERT M. - age 21 - bur. in Va. Native of Warrenton, Va. Uncle
    Gen. EPPA HUNTON of Va.; bro.: JAMES H. HUNTON of the South.
    Paper & date: BU Dec. 5, 1885
    Date & place of death: Dec. 4, 1885

HURLEY, JOHN - Dty. Sher. shot while aiding in the arrest of NICHOLAS
    ARAGON. b. near Chaperito, N. M.
    Paper & date: LS Jan. 28, 1885
    Date & place of death: Jan. 26, 1885 near Las Vegas, N. M.

HURLOCK, HENRY - Shot.; fa.
    Paper & date: LS Sept. 15, 1883/ Place: Trinity Sta., Texas

HUSSEY, _____ - Suicide - shot himself; son: THOMAS HUSSEY
      Paper & date: LS July 22, 1885
      Date & place of death: two yrs. ago. Galveston, Texas

HYDE, _____ (Old man) - Killed by youth _____ COCKERELL -family feud.
      Paper & date: LS Apr. 12, 1884
      Date & place of death: Canton, Van Zandt co., Texas

IBECK, JULIUS of Corsicana, Texas; suicide by laudanum.
      Paper & date: LS Jan. 25, 1882
      Date & place of death: Jan. 19, 1882

ILFELD, HERMAN of Santa Fe, New Mexico
      Paper & date: LS Mar. 22, 1884
      Date & place of death: Mar. 15, 1884, New York, N. Y.

INABRIENT, (?), Dr. - Killed by DUTCH RA--ES?; bro.
      Paper & date: LS June 16, 1883
      Date & place of death: 4 yrs. ago, Terrell, Texas

INGRAM, JAMES - age 80
      Paper & date: LS Aug. 27, 1884
      Date & place of death: Aug. 11, 1884, Victoria, Texas

IRIGOYEN, JUAN - Fight with smugglers across Rio Grande.
      Paper & date: EPDH Jan. 6, 1884
      Date & place of death: Dec. 31, 1883, Paso del Norte, Mexico

IRVINE, A. G. - Pneumonia
      Paper & date: LS Feb. 17, 1882
      Date & place of death: Feb. 13, 1882

IRVING, JIM - Murdered by GOLD BLIFFLE
      Paper & date: LS Oct. 8, 1884
      Date & place of death: 1879, Johnson county, Texas

IRWIN, Mrs. ANNA - as a young girl, buckled on Gen. SAM HOUSTON's sword
      just before the Battle of San Jacinto.
      Paper & date: LS Jan. 26, 1884
      Date & place of death: Few days ago near Bryan, Texas

IRWIN, JAMES (Negro) - murdered; mail hack driver between San Antonio &
      Stockdale. The mail sacks had been rifled.
      Paper & date: LS Aug. 9, 1882
      Date & place of death: a few days ago, Texas

IRWIN, JO - Shot by unknown thru window after his arrest for murdering
      _____ SCOTT.
      Paper & date: LS Dec. 31, 1881
      Date & place of death: abt. 27 Dec. 1881, near Richmond, N. M.

JACKSON, _____ - adopted child; given morphine for quinine.
      Paper & date: LS May 23, 1883
      Date & place of death: Corsicana, Texas

JACKSON, _____ (Negro) - Killed resisting arrest.
      Paper & date: LS Nov. 7, 1885
      Date & place of death: Gordonville, Texas

JACKSON, Mrs. A. - Murdered by hus.; suspicion he killed wife and baby;
      hus.: A. JACKSON.
      Paper & date: LS Oct. 7, 1882
      Date & place of death: Ft. Worth, Tex.

JACKSON, ANDREW (Negro) - Badly decomposed body believed to be Jackson,
      who was taken from jail by a mob and not heard from since.
      Paper & date: LS Dec. 2, 1885
      Date & place of death: BELL's Sta., Texas

JACKSON, C. T. - Consumption
Paper & date: LS Nov. 28, 1883
Date & place of death: Nov. 27, 1883, El Paso, Texas

JACKSON, JOHN or JAMES - Killed by WILLIAM STAGG and CHARLES LONGWORTHY.
Relatives in New Orleans. Bro.: of Lake Valley
Paper & date: LS June 20, 1885; BU June 27, 1885
Date & place of death: June 15, 1885 near Lake Valley, New Mexico

JACKSON, SAMUEL - Pneumonia; had lived in Dallas, Texas
Paper & date: LS Dec. 30, 1882
Date & place of death: Dec. 27, 1882, El Paso, Texas

JACOBSON, Mrs. P. J. C. - hus.: PETER J. C. JACOBSON
Paper & date: BU Oct. 10, 1885
Date & place of death: Sept. 17, 1885, Luna Valley, New Mexico

JAGER, EDDIE of Nutt; pneumonia; fa.: F. G. JAGER
Paper & date: RGR Feb. 23, 1884
Date & place of death: recently

JAGER, GEORGIE - age 2
Paper & date: LS May 30, 1885
Date & place of death: Watrous, N. M.

JAMES, JESSE - Biog. of JAMES family and connections.
Paper & date: EPDH May 3, 1882

JAMES, JESSE - Murdered by BOB FORD
Paper & date: LS Apr. 8, 1885

JANTIQUE, JESUS - Killed; a well known character in New Mexico
Paper & date: LS Nov. 29, 1882
Date & place of death: Nov. 18-25, 1882 , Chihuahua, Mexico

JAQUEZ, Judge _____
Paper & date: EPT Aug. 11, 1885
Date & place of death: Aug. 9, 1885, Chihuahua, Mexico

JAQUES, THOMAS - Shot fatally - on point of death
Paper & date: LS May 16, 1883
Date & place of death: May 13, 1883, San Marcial, New Mexico

JARAMILLO, RAFAEL & CASIMIRO - Premature blast at mine.
Paper & date: LS Apr. 25, 1885
Date & place of death: last week, Georgetown, New Mexico

JEANERETT, JULIUS - Suicide - despondent. A Mexican wife. No children.
Paper & date: RGR Nov. 8, 1884
Date & place of death: Nov. 2, 1884

JEFFRIES, FRANK - Murder - two bullet holes in head; body found in Prair-
ie Creek in Waxahachie, Ellis co., Texas
Paper & date: LS Oct. 12, 1881
Date & place of death: Prairie Creek, Ellis co., Texas

JENNINGS, Mrs. _____ - Suffering from bone felon
Paper & date: LS Oct. 8, 1884
Date & place of death: last week, Sulphur Springs, (Tex. or N. M.)

JERRELL, WM. L. of Las Cruces, N. M. - Shot during robbery of stage coach
in which he was riding between Concho, Texas and Abilene, Texas. Bur.
in San Angelo, Texas; wife and 3 ch.; Sher. WHITE, bro-in-law.
Paper & date: LS Feb. 6, 9 & 13, 1884; EPT June 27, 1884; LS Oct. 7,
1885
Date & place of death: Feb. 5, 1884, Texas

JEWETT, Mrs. Col. _____
Paper & date: LS Feb. 21, 1883
Date & place of death: White Oakes, N. M.

JOHNSON, _____ Ex-Marshall of El Paso, Texas;killed by his successor
    DALLAS STOUDENMIRE. BELLE COFFIN, house of ill fame, is claiming to
    be his wife and trying to get his property in Kansas. She had at
    least been his mistress. Johnson fired a shot gun at Studemeir with-
    out killing him.
    Paper & date: NTF Apr. 20, 1881; EPDH Dec. 28, 1881; LS Aug. 2, 1882
    Date & place of death: Apr. 17, 1881, El Paso, Texas

JOHNSON, _____ - 18 mo. old girl; fa.: Justice JOHNSON, of Concordia,Tx.
    3 miles below El Paso; smallpox.
    Paper & date: LS Feb. 8, 1882
    Date & place of death: Feb. 4, 1882

JOHNSON, _____ negro, desperate character; killed by JOE ATKINSON
    Paper & date: LS Mar. 28, 1883
    Date & place of death: Mar. 24, 1883, Deming, New Mexico

JOHNSON, _____ - Brakeman, train accident.
    Paper & date: PET May 1, 1883
    Date & place of death: on T & P R. R., near Ft. Worth, Texas

JOHNSON, _____ negro boy- run over by train
    Paper & date: LS June 16, 1883
    Date & place of death: San Antonio, Texas

JOHNSON, _____ - Lynched for murder of THOMAS BRANT.
    Paper & date: LS Dec. 5, 1883
    Date & place of death: Dec. 1, 1883, Coolidge, Texas

JOHNSON, _____ little girl; accidentally shot; fa.: LOTT JOHNSON
    Paper & date: LS July 16, 1884
    Date & place of death: Moore Sta. near San Antonio, Texas

JOHNSON, ALEX - Suicide; a Swede
    Paper & date: LS Feb. 25, 1882
    Date & place of death: Feb. 18, 1882, Dallas, Texas

JOHNSON, ANDREW - carpenter, age 63
    Paper & date: LS Oct. 1, 1884
    Date & place of death: Sept. 27, 1884, Raton, New Mexico

JOHNSON, ANDREW - Killed by W. J. PERKINS
    Paper & date: LS Feb. 13, 1884
    Date & place of death: last week, Cedar Bayo, Texas

JOHNSON, DICK - Negro; shot by unknown; body found 5 mi. west of Paris,
    Texas
    Paper & date: LS Dec. 7, 1881
    Date & place of death: before Nov. 22, 1881

JOHNSON, Rev. FELIX
    Paper & date: LS Dec. 19, 1883
    Date & place of death: Paris, Texas

JOHNSON, HENRY - "YELLOW HENRY" - Killed by irate citizens.
    Paper & date: LS Sept. 20, 1884
    Date & place of death: Clay, Texas

JOHNSON, HENRY - To be hanged
    Paper & date: LS Nov. 11, 1885; LS Nov. 18, 1885
    Date & place of death: Nov. 13, 1885, Crockett, Texas

JOHNSON, J. E. or J. R. "ADOBE" - Shot by WM. MEAD; a m. niece in St.
    Louis and minor children.
    Paper & date: RGR Mar. 1, 1884; LS Feb. 27, 1884
    Date & place of death: Feb. 23, 1884, Hillsboro, N. M.

JOHNSON, JOE - (Negro) - shot by TOM SMITH over Smith's wife.
    Paper & date: LS Mar. 4, 1885
    Date & place of death: Mar. 1, 1885, El Paso , Tex.

JOHNSON, JOHN - Street car driver
    Paper & date: LS Apr. 11, 1885
    Date & place of death: Albuquerque, New Mexico

JOHNSON, JOHNNY? - Murdered; bur. by Sr. TRENES PACHECO and a companion;
    Left Deming, N. M. about 10 days ago with Mr. C. CHAPMAN of Lake Val-
    ley, N. M.
    Paper & date: EPT June 26, 1883
    Date & place of death: at Espia near Janos, Mexico

JOHNSON, PETER - Shot in head, hands tied behind back
    Paper & date: LS Nov. 12, 1884
    Date & place of death: Nov. 7, 1884, near Brackett, Texas

JOHNSON, R. A. - Heart disease
    Paper & date: LS Aug. 22, 1885
    Date & place of death: Texarkana, Texas

JOHNSON, ROBERT - Murder; bail refused for _____ CADE by appeal court at
    Galveston; reversed district court decision at Nacogdoches co., Texas
    Paper & date: LS Jan. 28, 1882
    Date & place of death: Texas

JOHNSON, ROBERT - age 23 or 24; possibly mountain fever; fa.: Policeman
    J. W. JOHNSON of El Paso.
    Paper & date: LS July 11, 1883; EPDH July 15, 1883
    Date & place of death: July 10, 1883, El Paso, Texas

JOHNSON, THOMAS - Cowboy row
    Paper & date: LS June 30, 1883
    Date & place of death: Colfax co., N. M.

JOHNSON, TOM - Killed by Indians
    Paper & date: EPDH Sept. 13, 1882
    Date & place of death: Sonora State, Mexico

JOHNSON, WILLIAM - Shooting fray with JOHN BROPHY - neither expected to
    live.
    Paper & date: LS Dec. 23, 1885
    Date & place of death: Liberty, N. M.

JOHNSON, WILLIAM and 12 yr. old boy - killed by Indians; wife missing-
    presumed killed also.
    Paper & date: EPT Dec. 2, 1885
    Date & place of death: Dec. 1, 1885 near Wilcox, Arizona

JOHNSTON, HARRIS J. - abt. 37 yrs.; native of Missouri
    Paper & date: EPDH Oct. 5, 1881
    Date & place of death: Sept. 22, 1881, El Paso, Texas

JONES, _____ - Suicide - morphine; eloped with Miss KNIGHT from Marshall,
    Texas a few days ago.
    Paper & date: LS Sept. 24, 1884
    Date & place of death: Sept. 18, 1884

JONES, ALEX. of Marfa, Texas - murdered
    Paper & date: EPT Oct. 18, 1885
    Date & place of death: near Ruidoso, New Mexico

JONES, Dr. B. C. - Assassinated by unknown parties
    Paper & date: LS Jan. 7, 1882
    Date & place of death: Dec. 23, 1881, Eagle Pass, Texas

JONES, Mrs. E. A. - Cut her throat; hus.: Col. E. A. JONES; her family
    old and aristocratic of Maryland
    Paper & date: LS Oct. 18, 1884
    Date & place of death: Oct. 12, 1884, Waco, Texas

JONES, E. E. - Killed by JOHN R. THOMAS
    Paper & date: LS Oct. 1, 1884 (no place or date)

JONES, ED - Killed by Indians near Lucero, Chihuahua, Mexico
    Paper & date: LS Nov. 9, 1881
    Date & place of death: aft. Oct. 24 and before Nov. 9, 1881

JONES, FRANK - Hack driver; shot by BOB LANE
    Paper & date: LS Jan. 14, 1885
    Date & place of death: Jan. 10, 1885, Dallas, Texas

JONES, HILLIS - Assassinated; B. W. EDGALL (Editor) and others charged.
    son: BILL, age 16
    Paper & date: LS Jan. 24, 1885; LS Mar. 11 and 18, 1885
    Date & place of death: Jan. 11, 1885, Vernon, Texas

JONES, Col. SAMUEL J. - Paralysis; b. Fluvanna co., Va., 16 Apr. 1827;
    m. MARY C. FRAYSER, Cumberland co., Va., 6 May 1847; 1855 moved to
    Douglas co., Kansas; 1858 collector of Customs at Las Cruces, N. M.;
    Nov. 1878 stricken with paralysis and lost use of right hand and voc-
    al cords.
    Paper & date: LS Dec. 15, 1883; RGR Dec. 15, 1883
    Date & place of death: Dec. 10, 1883

JONES, T. - (Negro) - dropped dead after being on a spree.
    Paper & date: LS June 2, 1883
    Date & place of death: Sherman, Texas

JONES, " AUNT TEMPLE" (Negro) - Burned
    Paper & date: LS Nov. 7, 1885
    Date & place of death: Austin, Texas

JONES, THOMAS - Accidentally shot by C. L. "LINK" FOREST (C. S. MUIRHEAD
    alias C. L. FOREST); bro.: WILL JONES
    Paper & date: LS Feb. 25, 1885; EPT Nov. 6 & 18, 1885
    Date & place of death: Feb. 23, 1885, El Paso, Texas

JONES, TOM - Killed by cousin WM. JONES
    Paper & date: LS Nov. 1, 1882
    Date & place of death: Oct. 26, 1882 of Galveston, Texas

JONES, WALTER of Dallas, Texas; by Indians
    Paper & date: LS Apr. 7, 1883
    Date & place of death: recently on the Gila River

JONES, WM. - Stabbed by a Mexican; soldier of Troop I, 8th Cavalry
    Paper & date: LS Jan. 24, 1883
    Date & place of death: Jan. 11, 1883; date of stabbing in Brownsville,
    Texas

JONES, WILLIAM CLAUDE - (Old) - 1st Lt. in Seminole War; served in Mex.
    War; well known in Las Cruces, N. M.
    Paper & date: EPT May 5, 1884
    Date & place of death: Apr. 3, 1884, Wailukee? Sandwich Islands

JOSEPHINE, SISTER - Nun
    Paper & date: LS Aug. 26, 1885
    Date & place of death: Albuquerque, N. M.

JUAREZ, Gen. DOMINGO - Shot by soldiers; article datelined Monterrey,
    Mexico, July 31.
    Paper & date: EPT Aug. 1, 1884
    Date & place of death: last week, Capula, Mexico

JUH_, Indian Chief; reported killed at wedding of his dau. in Sierra Mad-
    res; actually drowned swimming Casas Grande River; b. Warm Springs, N.
    M. - son of Apache girl and Jesuit Priest - 1832; son & dau. survive.
    Paper & date: LS Sept. 26, 1883; EPT Sept. 30 & Oct. 11, 1883; EPDH
    Apr. 29 & Nov. 11, 1883
    Date & place of death: Jan. 15, 1883, Mexico

JUH's wife - Killed by Mexicans.
    Paper & date: EPDH June 21, 1882/ D & P: May 11,1882,Casas Grandes,Mx.

JUMENEZ, Gen. - Shot by soldiers; article datelined Monterrey, Mexico, July 31.
  Paper & date: EPT Aug. 1, 1884
  Date & place of death: near Satuta, Mexico

JUNEMANN, Mrs. CHARLES - Beaten over head with hammer by RICHARD RIC-
  BARCK (?)
  Paper & date: LS Aug. 27, 1884
  Date & place of death: Galveston, Texas

KALLENBERG, Dr. _____ of Lake Valley, N. M.- shot by CHRIS MOESNER
  Paper & date: LS Dec. 14, 1881
  Date & place of death: May 4, 1881

KANE, JOHN H. - abt. 27; came from Janesville, Wisconsin about 4 yrs ago.
  Paper & date: LS May 16, 1885
  Date & place of death: Silver City, N. M.

KAPLAN, JACOB - formerly El Paso, Texas; bro.: H. KAPLAN, El Paso, Texas
  Paper & date: EPT Oct. 2, 1883
  Date & place of death: Sept. 25, 1883, San Francisco, California;
  bur.: 26 Sept.

KATZ, ARVY - Murdered
  Paper & date: EPT July 2, 1885
  Date & place of death: Mar. 1885, 60 mi. SW of Tucson, Arizona

KAUFFMAN, _____ from Geauge co., Ohio; hanged himself.
  Paper & date: LS July 8, 1885
  Date & place of death: July 2, 1885, Silver City, N. M.

KEARL, CHARLES M/M - Murdered by Indians between Casas Grandes and Gavilan on way to Silver City, N. M.; Mrs. Kearl's scalp found after an
  attack on Indians by Capt. RUSSELL near Ralston; also found glove belonging to Mr. Kearl.
  Paper & date: TB Mar. 16, 1871; TB Apr. 13, 1871
  Date & place of death: .....

KEATING, _____ - Killed by Apaches
  Paper & date: EPT Oct. 4, 1885
  Date & place of death: Oct. 2, 1885, White Trail Canyon, San Simon
  Valley, Arizona

KEATING, PAULINE (Infant dau.) 18 mo's; croup; par.: M/M PAUL KEATING;
  only child
  Paper & date: LS Apr. 26, 1884; EPDH Apr. 27, 1884
  Date & place of death: Apr. 24, 1884, El Paso, Texas

KEATING, "OLD TOMMY"
  Paper & date: LS Mar. 18, 1882
  Date & place of death: Mar. 16, 1882, El Paso, Texas

KEATS, _____ - Killed by Indians
  Paper & date: LS Oct. 3, 1883
  Date & place of death: Oct. 1, 1883, N. M.

KEGHEY, W. S. - San Jacinto Veteran; survived by son.
  Paper & date: LS Sept. 17, 1884
  Date & place of death: last week; Jasper, Texas

KELIHER, MICHAEL of N. M.; murder by JOHN J. WEBB.
  Paper & date: LS Dec. 7, 1881
  Date & place of death: March 1880

KELLY, _____ Cowboy; shot in fight citizens and rangers.
  Paper & date: EPDH July 22, 1883
  Date & place of death: Toyah, Texas

KELLY, Mrs. _____ - Burns in yard east of Willis; son ALFRED, insane.

Mrs. KELLY (cont'd):
Paper & date: LS Apr. 12, 1884
Date & place of death: Apr. 8, 1884, Willis, Texas

KELLEY, ("TEX?") - To be hanged for murder (Bisbee, Arizona)
Paper & date: LS Mar. 26, 1884
Date & place of death: Mar. 28, 1884, Tombstone, Arizona

KELLEY, E. M. - To be hanged. 30 day reprieve by Pres. of U.S.A. Paper
of Mar. 18, 1882 reprieve until Apr. 17. Paper of Mar. 11, 1882, ...
will be next Saturday.
Paper & date: LS Feb. 18, 1882
Date & place of death: in Santa Fe, New Mexico

KELLEY, EUGENE - Drowned; son of JOHN KELLEY, N. Y. banker.
Paper & date: LS May 27, 1885
Date & place of death: May 18, 1885, Lampazas, Mexico

KELLY, FANNY - during surgery.
Paper & date: LS Sept. 13, 1884

KELLY, FRED (Negro) - Fractured skull - clubbed by SAM JOHNSON, negro.
Paper & date: LS June 23, 1883
Date & place of death: Tyler, Texas

KELLY, HORACE A. - Asthma; had started El Paso's Daily Independent a
year ago; family in California; originally from Cincinnati, Ohio;
came recently from Albuquerque, New Mexico.
Paper & date: LS Jan. 20, 1883; EPDH Jan. 17, 1883
Date & place of death: Jan. 16, 1883, Ysleta, Texas

KELLEY, JAMES L. - age 69
Paper & date: LS Nov. 5, 1884
Date & place of death: Sept. 29, 1884, Ennis, Texas

KELLY, JOHN - of Benton, California; found dead in mine shaft.
Paper & date: LS Feb. 27, 1884
Date & place of death: Florida Mtns., N. M.

KELLY, JOHN (Negro) - known as JIM; heart disease; long time Army man.
Paper & date: LS Aug. 25, 1883; EPT Aug. 25, 1883
Date & place of death: Aug. 23, 1883, El Paso, Texas

KELLEY, MARTIN - 10th Cav.; in action with Indians.
Paper & date: EPDH Sept. 1883
Date & place of death: July 26, 1880, Eagle Springs, Texas (in Eagle
Mountains)

KELLEY, WILLIAM, Major - d. at Denver - enroute from El Paso to Laramie.
Suffered a painful illness - unable to sit up.
Paper & date: TB Jan. 10, 1872
Date & place of death: Dec. 28, 1871

KELSEY, Pvt. ----- of Ft. Craig, N. M.; killed by Pvt. RICHARDSON, deserter.
Paper & date: LS Nov. 26, 1881

KELSEY, O. D. - recently stabbed in Lincoln co., N. M.; died near Fort
Stanton, bur. in fort cemetery; DAN MC CARTY found guilty.
Paper & date: RGR May 30, 1885; LS Apr. 4, 1885
Date & place of death: recently near Ft. Stanton

KENDALL, _____ - from Illinois; consumption
Paper & date: EPT Nov. 20, 1884
Date & place of death: Nov. 19, 1884, El Paso, Texas

KENNEDY, _____ - (baby); killed by fa.; mo. survives.
Paper & date: BU Nov. 14, 1885
Date & place of death: 1868-69, Colfax co., New Mexico

KENNEDY, _____ - Lynched for 21 murders; wife survives.
Paper & date: BU Nov. 14, 1885
Date & place of death: 1869, Colfax co., New Mexico

KENNEDY, JAMES - of Beaumont, Texas; fell dead while working at his car-
penter bench.
Paper & date: LS Oct. 26, 1881
Date & place of death: week before

KENNEDY, JAMES - (a miser) - fever and lacking necessities of life.
Paper & date: LS Oct. 22, 1884
Date & place of death: Oct. 15, 1884, Galveston, Texas

KENNEDY, THOS. G.
Paper & date: LS Oct. 22, 1884
Date & place of death: Oct. 16, 1884, Plano, Texas

KENNEDY, WILLIAM - Kicked to death by vicious horse.
Paper & date: LS Nov. 12, 1881
Date & place of death: a few days ago,near Ft. Worth, Texas

KENNEY, MARY A. - Attack by ferocious cow.
Paper & date: LS Nov. 2, 1881
Date & place of death: last week, near Dallas, Texas

KERN, _____ - Dty. Sher. of Lincoln co.; murdered by ARAGON.
Paper & date: RGR Nov. 15, 1884

KERR, J. V. - Murdered - J. S. IRVINE charged.
Paper & date: LS Oct. 21, 1885
Date & place of death: Bowie, Texas

KERR, MOSES -(little) - accidentally shot by bro. W_____; fa. M. P.
KERR.
Paper & date: LS Mar. 1, 1884
Date & place of death: Feb. 22?, 1884, Cameron, Texas

KERR, WILLIE - age 3 or 4; drowned in acequia; par.: M/M THOMAS S. KERR.
Paper & date: EPT May 1, 1884; LS May 3, 1884
Date & place of death: Apr. 30, 1884, El Paso, Texas

KERSECK, E. - Shot by 3 men.
Paper & date: EPT Oct. 4, 1884
Date & place of death: Oct. 2, 1884, New Prague Sta., near Flatonia,
Texas

KESNER, HARRY - Shot and killed by JIM HARLAN.
Paper & date: LS Dec. 31, 1881
Date & place of death: the other day, Lamy, Texas

KESSE, _____ - (child) - "gun wasn't loaded but went off".
Paper & date: LS Apr. 16, 1884
Date & place of death: last week, Ovilla, Texas

KESTER, JOHN - 40 yrs.; long illness- inflammation of stomach; bur. Nor-
ristown, Penn.; was a native of Norristown.
Paper & date: EPT Jan. 4, 1885; EPMS Jan. 4, 1885
Date & place of death: Jan. 3, 1885, El Paso, Texas

KEUFFEL, _____ - Murdered by robbers.
Paper & date: EPT Nov. 25, 1883
Date & place of death: Nov. 23, 1883, Feodor, Texas near Giddings.

KIDD, JAMES - age 92; veteran of War of 1812.
Paper & date: LS Mar. 28, 1885
Date & place of death: a few days ago, Grayson co., Texas

KIEF, Mr. _____ - Suicide.
Paper & date: TB May 8, 1872
Date & place of death: May 1, 1872, Central City, New Mexico

KIEFER, MABEL CLAIRE - Inf. dtr.; age 8 mo. 13 days; par.: CHARLES C. &
    AMY E. KIEFER.
    Paper & date: EPT Oct. 13, 1885; LS Oct. 14, 1885
    Date & place of death: Oct. 12, 1885, El Paso, Texas

KIERSKI, MORITZ - age 71 yrs. 7 mo.; obit in San Francisco "Chronicle"
    Sept. 2, 1882; sons: WILLIAM & JOHN S. KIERSKI of El Paso, Texas
    Paper & date: EPDH Sept. 6, 1882
    Date & place of death: San Francisco, California

KILGORE, _____ - Postmaster; wife: FIDELIA KILGORE
    Paper & date: LS Oct. 10, 1885
    Date & place of death: Longview, Texas

KIMBALL, D. P. - Typhoid pneumonia
    Paper & date: LS Nov. 28, 1883
    Date & place of death: Nov. 25, 1883, St. David's on the San Pedro,
    Cochise co., Arizona

KING, _____ - Family killed by Indians
    Paper & date: BU May 26, 1885
    Date & place of death: Mogollons, Near Arizona border, New Mexico

KING, _____ - (Negro) - Shot by Dty. Sher. BELLOW while making an arrest
    Paper & date: LS Oct. 28, 1885
    Date & place of death: McKinney, Texas

KING, _____ - Ex.- Sheriff; killed by _____ PARROTT
    Paper & date: LS Aug. 1, 1885
    Date & place of death: Jacksboro, Texas

KING, CHAS. - Murdered by his farm hands for his money.
    Paper & date: LS Nov. 5, 1881
    Date & place of death: last week near Rio Grande City, Texas

KING, DANIEL - Murder; Gov. SHELDON offered $250 reward for arrest of
    FRANCISCO TRUJILLO in this connection.
    Paper & date: LS Aug. 9, 1882
    Date & place of death: 1878 in Colfax co., New Mexico

KING, DENNIE (Negro) - Shot by sher. while trying to escape jail.
    Paper & date: LS May 20, 1885
    Date & place of death: May 15, 1885, Marshall, Texas

KING, ED - Shoot out with police
    Paper & date: LS Mar. 18, 1885
    Date & place of death: Springer, New Mexico

KING, Capt. RICHARD - Cancer of stomach
    Paper & date: EPT Apr. 15, 1885
    Date & place of death: Apr. 14, 1885, San Antonio, Texas

KING, " SANDY" - Hanged; rustler
    Paper & date: LS Nov. 16, 1881; LS Nov. 28, 1883
    Date & place of death: last week, Grant co., N. M.

KING, W. M. - Drowned; was son of Confederate officer killed at Shiloh.
    Paper & date: BU Nov. 1, 1883
    Date & place of death: recently near Las Vegas, New Mexico

KINNEY, _____ - Killed by Indians
    Paper & date: LS Dec. 26, 1885
    Date & place of death: Cactus Flat, Ariz. or New Mexico

KINNEY'S INDIAN - Shoot out with constable
    Paper & date: EPMS Dec. 11, 1884
    Date & place of death: Dona Ana, New Mexico

KINSMAN, WILLIAM - Shot by paramour, Mrs. _____ WOODMAN
    Paper & date: LS Feb. 28, 1883/D & P: Feb. 23, 1883,Tombstone, Ariz.

KIRBY, WILLIAM - of San Antonio, Texas
Paper & date: LS Dec. 14, 1881
Date & place of death: Dec. 4, 1881

KISER, FRANK - (a miner); shot by PETER MACKEL; will die and Mackel may
die also; Kiser had been seeing Mackel's daughter.
Paper & date: LS Mar. 21, 1883
Date & place of death: few days ago, White Oaks, N. M.

KISTLER, WILLIAM F. - age 24; drowned while fording Rio Grande.
Paper & date: EPT Aug. 11, 1884
Date & place of death: Aug. 7, 1884, near Ft. Quitman, Texas

KITCHEN, JOHN - bro.: CHARLES-Omaha, Neb.
Paper & date: LS May 31, 1884
Date & place of death: Las Vegas, N. M.

KITTENBRUCK, WALTER - (Mine manager); shot from ambush
Paper & date: EPT May 9, 1885
Date & place of death: May 7, 1885, Pachuca, Mexico

KJALSTROM, ALBERT - Tragic death; killed by _____ WALKER; relatives
Paper & date: BU Jan. 1, 1885; LS Jan. 17, 1885
Date & place of death: last Friday, Socorro, N. M.

KLEIN, JAMES - of Phoenix, Ariz.; run over by train
Paper & date: LS Sept. 20, 1884
Date & place of death: Sept. 19, 1884, Dallas, Texas

KNEES, _____ - Murder by "roughs" along R. R.
Paper & date: LS Feb. 17, 1882
Date & place of death: a few days ago- Crane's Sta., N. M.

KNEESECK, E. - Murdered by 3 men; A. C. GEORGE & H. M. SHARPE convicted.
Paper & date: LS Oct. 8, 1884; LS June 3, 1885
Date & place of death: last week - New Prague, Texas

KNOBB, GUSTAVE - Run over by train
Paper & date: LS Jan. 16, 1884
Date & place of death: San Antonio, Texas

KNOX, LEE - Murder; (Richmond?, Texas)
Paper & date: LS Dec. 21, 1881
Date & place of death: between Dec. 7 and 11, 1881, near Richard, Tx

KOEHL, GEORGE - Drowned
Paper & date: EPT Oct. 24, 1884
Date & place of death: Oct. 22, 1884, near Virginia Point, near Gal-
veston, Texas

KOEHLER, HATTIE - 9 nos. old; bur. Aug. 15, 1883; par.: M/M J. U. KOEHLER
Paper & date: EPT Aug. 15, 1883
Date & place of death: El Paso, Texas

KOENIG, JOHN - DE MARS & SILVA under bond; DODD discharged
Paper & date: EPT July 3, 1884; LS July 19, 1884
Date & place of death: July 1, 1884, Albuquerque, N. M.

KORN, JASPER - Dty. Sher.; killed in attempted arrest of NICOLAS ARAGON
Paper & date: LS Jan. 31, 1885
Date & place of death: last Oct.

KRAMER, _____ - of Milton, Penn.; consunption; bro. took body home.
Paper & date: EPT Jan. 17, 1884
Date & place of death: Jan. 14, 1884, El Paso, Texas

KRAMER, JOHN - of Denver, Colo.; murdered; traveling salesman
Paper & date: EPT Dec. 20, 1885
Date & place of death: over a year ago near Leadville, Colo.

KREIGTER, JOHN - age 19; fell dead from heart disease
    Paper & date: LS Sept. 20, 1882
    Date & place of death: last week in Galveston, Texas

KREMPKAU, GUS - young; shoot-out by JOHN HALE
    Paper & date: EPDH Dec. 28, 1881; NTF Apr. 20, 1881
    Date & place of death: Apr. 17, 1881

KROHN, MAX - of Cincinnati, Ohio; disappeared in Socorro - Silver City
    area after withdrawing large amount of money to buy cattle in Aug. or
    Sept. 1884; relatives in Cincinnati.
    Paper & date: BU Feb. 1, 1885
    Date & place of death: New Mexico

KRUG, RUDOLPH G. - Young man; neglect - far from home and friends
    Paper & date: LS Oct. 6, 1883
    Date & place of death: Albuquerque, N. M.

KRUZ, CHAS. - Killed by a Mex. who confessed before dying last week at
    Punta del Agua, Mexico; KRUZ was editor of "Gringo and Greaser".
    Paper & date: BU Oct. 24, 1885

KUEMMERLE, Mrs. JULIUS - lived here for more than a year; hus.'s where-
    abouts unknown; bro.: JAMES REPINE of Leavenworth, Kansas; removed
    remains to that place.
    Paper & date: RGR Jan. 3, 1885
    Date & place of death: Dec. 27, 1884, Las Cruces, N. M.

KUHLMAN, HENRY - (German) - Murdered with an axe.
    Paper & date: LS Jan. 10, 1885
    Date & place of death: dead sev. days - near Uvalde, Texas

KUNTZ, Mrs. JOSEPH - Shot by hus.: JOSEPH KUNTZ
    Paper & date: LS July 16, 1884
    Date & place of death: July 9, 1884, Sherman, Texas

KUSZ, CHARLES L. - Shot by unknown
    Paper & date: LS Apr. 2, 1884
    Date & place of death: Mar. 28, 1884, Manzano, N. M.

KYLE, _____ - chg'd - released on $8000 bail each were HUSE & WALL MER-
    CHANTS.
    Paper & date: LS Nov. 14, 1885
    Date & place of death: Clay co., Texas

LABONNE, E. - (old citizen) - heart disease; Knights of Honor.
    Paper & date: EPMS Dec. 5, 1884; EPT Dec. 5, 1884
    Date & place of death: Dec. 4, 1884, at residence, Ysleta, Texas

LACEY, _____ (Negro); lynched for rape of Mrs. ROGERS
    Paper & date: EPT June 28, 1883; LS June 30, 1883
    Date & place of death: June 26, 1883, Marion co., Texas

LACKEY, HENRY - Shot from ambush by GEORGE DICKEY, JAMES M. & EDWARD
    THOMAS BENNETT near Las Tabias
    Paper & date: EPT Aug. 20, 1884; LS Aug. 27, 1884
    Date & place of death: Aug. 16, 1884, White Oaks, N. M.

LAFFERR, JOSEPH W. - Killed by escaped convicts - KIT JOY and his gang;
    six children.
    Paper & date: LS Mar. 12, 1884; LS Mar. 22, 1884; RGR Mar. 15, 1884;
    LS Feb. 11, 1885
    Date & place of death: Mar. 10, 1884, near Silver City, New Mexico

LAMB, _____ - Affray with Mex. police
    Paper & date: EPMS Dec. 11, 1884
    Date & place of death: Nov. 23, 1884, Sonora State, Mex.

LAMB, ALEXANDER - Desperate character; shot by Dty. Sher. _____ NORRIS of

LAMB, (cont'd) - Kinney co.; resisting arrest.
    Paper & date: LS Aug. 1, 1883; EPDH Aug. 5, 1883
    Date & place of death: July 25, 1883 near Langtry, Tex._(at Osman)

LAMPSON, J. A. - Struck in breast by stone.
    Paper & date: LS Mar. 14, 1883
    Date & place of death: last week in stone quarry near Chihuahua, Mex.

LAMPTON, _____ - (young man) abt. 20 yrs. old; crushed while coupling
    R. R. cars.
    Paper & date: LS Oct. 22, 1884
    Date & place of death: few days ago, Colorado City, Texas

LANDERS, _____ - Young; shot by GEORGE CHRISTY
    Paper & date: EPT Dec. 13, 1884
    Date & place of death: Indian Nation

LANDIS, J. H. - Shot by _____ VARNELL; dau.
    Paper & date: LS Mar. 14, 1883
    Date & place of death: few days ago - Hubbard City, Texas

LANE, BOB - (desperate character of Red River co., Texas); shot by Sher.
    _____ BLAIR and city Marshall _____ THORNTON; cannot possibly recover
    Paper & date: EPT Sept. 2, 1884
    Date & place: Bonham, Texas

LANSING, PETER - at San Antonio, Sonora, Mexico; murder - a miner in Mex.
    Paper & date: LS July 26, 1882
    Date & place of death: recently

LAPPENBOCK, A. P. - (Postmaster); killed himself
    Paper & date: EPT Apr. 13, 1883
    Date & place of death: Apr. 12, 1883, Castroville, Texas

LARA, AURELIO - New trial for murder ordered (prev. sentenced to death)
    Paper & date: LS Feb. 27, 1884
    Date & place: Grant co., N. M.

LARA, RUPERTO - Hanged for murdering NESMITH family.
    Paper & date: LS May 2, 1885
    Date & place of death: Apr. 30, 1885, Las Cruces, N. M.

LARIS, E. F. - Train wreck caused by EMANUEL CORTEZ, JERRY MARTIN & JESSE
    HENDERSON.
    Paper & date: LS Apr. 8, 1885
    Date & place of death: Nov. 14, 1885, Waller co., Texas

LASIO, KARLO - Murdered by STEFANO VIBUTICHO (?)
    Paper & date: LS June 23, 1883
    Date & place of death: on Island near Corpus Christi, Texas

LATCH, _____ - child; carbolic acid by mistake; mo.: LAURA LATCH.
    Paper & date: LS Aug. 4, 1883
    Date & place of death: Dallas, Texas

LAUN, GEORGE - Killed over poker debt.
    Paper & date: EPDH Oct. 12, 1881
    Date & place of death: Oct. 5, 1881, El Paso, Texas

LAWLER, MIKE - Old man from Mass.; Lung congestion
    Paper & date: EPDH Dec. 7, 1881
    Date & place of death: Dec. 4, 1881, El Paso, Texas

LAWRENCE, Dr. CALHOUN - Shot by L. V. SIMPSON in argument.
    Paper & date: EPMS Dec. 4, 1884
    Date & place of death: Dec. 2, 1884, Nechesville, Texas

LAWRENCE, JAS. - Mine cave-in.
    Paper & date: EPT May 19, 1884
    Date & place of death: May 18, 1884, Grass Valley, (N.M.?/Calif.?)

LAWS, Mrs. ____-hus.; son ROBERT H. LAWS; suit to recover property.
    Paper & date: EPT July 29, 1885
    Date & place of death: 1861, Dallas?, Texas

LEACH, J. A.-Shot & killed by BEN HUNT; a seduction case caused trouble.
    Paper & date: LS Jan. 28, 1882
    Date & place of death: Jan. 22, 1882, Caldwell, Texas

LEAKY, N. M. "MIKE"-of Uvalde, Texas; shot by stockman.
    Paper & date: EPT Dec. 3, 1885
    Date & place of death: Nov. 28, 1885, Marfa, Texas

LEAKEY, SAM or TOM-Shot by ROBERT DOWE or BOB LOW; Leakey had killed 2
    men; bro.: N. M. LEAKY of Uvalde, Texas.
    Paper & date: LS Aug. 13, 1884; EPT Aug. 9, 1884 & Dec. 3, 1885
    Date & place of death: Aug. 6, 1884, Eagle Pass, Texas

LECHUGA, MARQUETA-Murdered by Apaches; -of Silver City, N. M.
    Paper & date: RGR June 27, 1885
    Date & place of death: recently

LEDUC, EUGENE-Lung hemorrhage; rel. in France died recently leaving him
    a fortune.
    Paper & date: EPT Nov. 19, 1884
    Date & place of death: Nov. 19, 1884, El Paso, Texas

LEE, ____ - (American teamster) - shot in affray with Mex. police.
    Paper & date: EPMS Nov. 29, 1884
    Date & place of death: Nov. 23, 1884, Canon, Socorro St., Mex.

LEE, JAMES -Killed by J. H. MILLIKEN; self-defense.
    Paper & date: EPT Sept. 30, 1888; LS July 11, 1885
    Date & place of death: May 1885, Granbury, Tex. or Weatherford, Tex.

LEE, JIM & PINK ot Cook co., Texas; killed resisting arrest; notorious
    outlaws.
    Paper & date: LS Sept. 12, 1885; EPT Sept. 13, 1885
    Date & place of death: Sept. 9, 1885 near Dexter, Texas

LEE, MITCH -Hung by mob after jail break.
    Paper & date: LS Mar. 12, 1884
    Date & place of death: Mar. 10, 1884, near Silver City, N. M.

LEE SHUM - Chinaman; sentenced to death for murder.
    Paper & date: LS Jan. 30, 1884
    Date & place of death: Las Vegas, N. M.

LEEPER, JOHN -Shoot-out with PASCHAL LEONARD.
    Paper & date: LS Apr. 16, 1884
    Date & place of death: Apr. 12, 1884, Henrietta, Texas

LEFIAND, ____-child; rat poison; fa.: THOMAS and family.
    Paper & date: LS Oct. 1, 1884
    Date & place of death: Texas

LEGG, JOSEPH -Lay down on tracks and was run over.
    Paper & date: LS July 18, 1883
    Date & place of death: Cleburne, Texas

LEIBA, ROBERTO - Fight with Indians.
    Paper & date: EPT Oct. 20, 1885
    Date & place of death: Oct. 11, 1885, near Ramos, Mexico

LEISWITZ, R. -(a German) - suicide by poison.
    Paper & date: LS Nov. 26, 1884
    Date & place of death: Nov. 23, 1884, Brenham, Texas

LEMON, Judge ____-Killed by mob; son: JOHN LEMON.
    Paper & date: EPT July 24, 1890
    Date & place of death: 1871, Las Cruces, N. M.

LENNOIR, EUGENE (Mexican)
Paper & date: LS Oct. 18, 1884
Date & place of death: Found Oct. 11, 1884 near Las Vegas, N. M.

LENOX, F. B. of Globe, Ariz.; killed by Indians; wife and family.
Paper & date: EPDH May 3, 1882
Date & place of death: Before Apr. 24, 1882, between Silver City, N. M. and Clifton, Ariz.

LENTGGER (LEINGGER?), HENRY - Stabbed by MANUEL & DALZIO
Paper & date: LS Jan. 31, 1885
Date & place of death: Jan. 24, 1885 - 15 mi. N. of San Angelo, Tex.

LENTON, Mrs. JOSEPH & baby; carried off June 4, 1885 by Indians; believed dead; hus. and 1 dau.; formerly of Dallas, Texas
Paper & date: EPT June 25, 1885
Date & place of death: near Silver City, N. M.

LEO, Hon. A. J. - Poison fly bite on his face.
Paper & date: LS Dec. 8, 1883
Date & place of death: recently, Edinburg, Texas

LEONARD, J. L. -
Paper & date: EPT June 17, 1883
Date & place of death: June 12, 1883, Dallas, Texas

LEONARD, Mrs. J. L. of Dallas, Texas; sickness caused by constant watch-ing at bedside of her sick son; husband J. L.; son (not named)
Paper & date: LS Jan. 11, 1882; EPT June 17, 1883
Date & place of death: Jan. 3, 1882

LEONARD, JAMES - Brakeman; fell under train; par.: in Rockford, Ill.
Paper & date: EPT July 15, 1885
Date & place of death: July 13, 1885, Ashfork, Ariz.

LERMO, JUAN - Shot by rustlers on a drunken spree at Seven Rivers (near Tularosa), N. M.; rustlers included BILLY WILSON, TOM PICKETT, YANK BEALE, PONEY WILLIAMS.
Paper & date: RGR Jan. 19, 1884
Date & place of death: Jan. 15, 1884

LESLIE, W. P.
Paper & date: EPDH Feb. 8, 1882
Date & place of death: Feb. 6, 1882, El Paso, Texas

LESTER, RUSSELL
Paper & date: EPDH Apr. 22, 1883
Date & place of death: Vinita, Indian Territory

LETOT, _____ - Accidental-shot glanced off tree; bro.
Paper & date: LS Jan. 24, 1885
Date & place of death: near Dallas, Texas

LEVALLE, CHARLES - (little boy) - fell in river and drowned.
Paper & date: LS May 9, 1883
Date & place of death: San Antonio, Texas

LEWIS, _____ - Murder; body riddled by bullets when he attempted to ar-rest some escaping prisoners from S. A. jail.
Paper & date: LS Dec. 20, 1882
Date & place of death: last week in San Antonio, Texas

LEWIS, A. W. - Murder by bullet - sheep man
Paper & date: LS Dec. 20, 1882
Date & place of death: recently, near Pleasanton, Texas

LEWIS, ANDREW - Fell in front of a mowing machine
Paper & date: LS June 16, 1883
Date & place of death: near Round Rock, Texas

LEWIS, HOWARD & sister & 3 ch.- drowned in floods
    Paper & date: EPT May 30, 1885
    Date & place of death: May 27-28, 1885, Waco, Texas

LEWIS, JOSEPH - (miner) - Mine cave-in; wife and 2 ch. in Pennsylvania
    Paper & date: LS Aug. 15, 1885; BU Aug. 6, 1885
    Date & place of death: Aug. 6, 1885, Socorro, N. M.

LEWIS, MARK - Shot by DAN LEWIS
    Paper & date: LS Oct. 10, 1883
    Date & place of death: last week, Dos Cabezas, Ariz.

LEWIS, PETER - Murder by JOHN MC GILVARY at Solitaire Mine, N. M. near
    Lake Valley, N. M.
    Paper & date: LS Oct. 18, 1882
    Date & place of death: last week, N. M.

LEWIS, T. - Killed by Indians near Lucero, Chihuahua, Mexico
    Paper & date: LS Nov. 9, 1881; EPDH Nov. 2, 1881
    Date & place of death: after Oct. 24, 1881

LEWIS, WM. - (ex-Judge) = Died in exterme proverty; known as an author,
    lexturer and politician.
    Paper & date: LS Feb. 17, 1883
    Date & place of death: Feb. 11, 1882, Dallas, Texas

LIDY, Mrs. _____ - age 63; son: S. B. LIDY of Socorro, N. M.
    Paper & date: BU Aug. 8, 1885
    Date & place of death: Aug. 2, 1885, West Alexander, Pennsylvania

LIGHTFOOT, _____ - Hanged; horse thief - by mob in Coryell co., Texas
    Paper & date: LS Oct. 22,1881
    Date & place of death: week before Oct. 22

LIGON, MUNFORD - Fell from cow-catcher of Houston & Texas Central engine,
    head struck a tie and burst his skull.
    Paper & date: LS June 4, 1884
    Date & place of death: May 27, 1884 near Walker's Creek, Courtney,Tx

LILLY, Capt. ED - age 52 yrs.
    Paper & date: LS Jan. 28, 1882
    Date & place of death: Jan. 18, 1882, San Antonio, Texas

LILLIE (LILLEY), JOHN H. - Killed by Indians; administrator notice.
    Paper & date: EPT Dec. 15, 1885; LS Dec. 16, 1885; BU May 8, 1886
    Date & place of death: Dec. 8, 1885, in Mogollons near Silver City,
    New Mexico

LIND, C. H. - Shot and killed by CLAY DRYE; Lind was a noted gambler.
    Paper & date: LS Dec. 9, 1882
    Date & place of death: recently at Eagle Pass, Texas

LINDSAY, _____ - Murdered by step-son RUFE LINDSAY; step-father and sis-
    ter both murdered.
    Paper & date: LS Sept. 27, 1884
    Date & place of death: few weeks ago, Arlington, Texas

LINSAY, GEORGE - Accidentally shot by his uncle M. M. SILVY
    Paper & date: LS Jan. 2, 1884
    Date & place of death: near Milano, Texas

LINENBERG, Mrs. MARY - Suicide - shot herself.
    Paper & date: LS Aug. 12, 1885
    Date & place of death: Brenham, Texas

LINN, "BUCK" CHARLES M. - Killed at the Gem Theatre by ROBERT CAHILL; in
    self-defense.
    Paper & date: LS Apr. 15, 1885; EPT Apr. 16, 1885
    Date & place of death: Apr. 15, 1885, El Paso, Texas

LINO, _____ of Las Vegas, N. M.; murder by DAVE RADABAUGH, jailer.
      Paper & date: LS Dec. 7, 1881
      Date & place of death: April 1880

LIP--EN, WILLIAM, JR. - Thrown from horse
      Paper & date: LS June 27, 1883
      Date & place of death: San Saba, Texas

LITONA(?), G. B. - by falling log.
      Paper & date: LS Oct. 1, 1884
      Date & place of death: last week 130 mi. W. of Socorro, N. M.

LITTLE, Mrs. _____ - Malarial fever contracted at Rincon, N. M.; husband
      Paper & date: EPDH Nov. 9, 1881
      Date & place of death: Nov. 3, 1881, El Paso, Texas

LITTLE, BEN (Negro) - Hanged by mob.
      Paper & date: LS Oct. 14, 1885
      Date & place of death: Oct. 10, 1885, Mount Pleasant, Texas

LITTLEFIELD of Cooke county, Texas; murder by ALLY ARNOLD
      Paper & date: LS Dec. 3, 1881

LIVING, GABE (Negro) - Murdered
      Paper & date: LS June 6, 1883
      Date & place of death: near Waco, Texas

LIVINGSTON, JOHN of Terrell, Texas; dead in bed in a hotel.
      Paper & date: LS Sept. 26, 1885
      Date & place of death: Sept. 22, 1885, Fort Worth, Texas

LLOYD, ANDY (Negro) - Shot by ELI SMITH, negro - love of same woman
      Paper & date: LS June 27, 1883
      Date & place of death: Jacksonville, Texas

LO, Mrs. - (Indian Squaw) - Struck by lightning while cooking dinner;
      near Elk Springs (N. M.?)
      Paper & date: RGR July 26, 1884
      Date & place of death: July 19, 1884

LOBATO, NICHOLAS - Accidentally shot himself while hunting.
      Paper & date: LS Dec. 9, 1885
      Date & place of death: Lincoln co., N. M.

LOCKHART, DEL - Lynched
      Paper & date: LS Nov. 19, 1881
      Date & place of death: about two weeks ago

LOCKIE, Miss _____ - Killed by step-father AL LOCKIE
      Paper & date: LS Aug. 29, 1885
      Date & place of death: Aug. 24, 1885, Blanco county, Texas

LOCKIE, M/M _____ - Killed by his bro. AL LOCKIE
      Paper & date: LS Aug. 29, 1885
      Date & place of death: Aug. 24, 1885, Blanco county, Texas

LOCKIE,(LOCKEY), AL - Hanged by mob.
      Paper & date: LS Aug. 29, 1885
      Date & place of death: Aug. 24, 1885, Blanco county, Texas

LOCKIE, Mrs. HENRY - Killed by husband's step-father AL LOCKIE; hus.:
      HENRY
      Paper & date: LS Aug. 29, 1885
      Date & place of death: Aug. 24, 1885, Blanco county, Texas

LOCKWOOD, JAMES - Accidental discharge of his gun at Alamosa, Bernalillo
      county, N. M.
      Paper & date: LS Jan. 13, 1883
      Date & place of death: Jan. 7, 1883, Bernalillo co., N. M.

LOCO's son - (Indian) - Killed by troops in fight; fa.: LOCO
    Paper & date: EPDH May 3, 1882
    Date & place of death: Apr. 28, 1882, Animas Mtns., Arizona

LOCO, AURELIO - To be hanged for murder of Chinamen near Ft. Bayard, N.
    M. last Feb.
    Paper & date: LS Aug. 22, 1883
    Date & place of death: New Mexico

LOGAN, Col. J. C. - Stage coach overturned; died of injuries later; bur.
    in California
    Paper & date: EPMS Dec. 16, 1884; LS Dec. 5, 1883
    Date & place of death: Nov. 20, 1883 between Kingston and Lake Valley
    New Mexico.

LOGAN, WILLIAM - Shot by (F?) WOOD
    Paper & date: LS July 7, 1883
    Date & place of death: Georgetown, N. M.

LON CHON - (Chinese age 24) - Typhoid fever
    Paper & date: EPDH Sept. 27, 1882
    Date & place of death: San Antonio, Texas

LONG, Mr. _____ - Massacred by Indians, San Pedro Valley
    Paper & date: TB May 4, 1871
    Date & place of death: Apr. 13, 1871

LONG, HENRY - His body identified as one found recently in desert on the
    JAMES ACKENBACK ranch; M. L. HICKEY (his neighbor) indicted for his
    murder; Son CHARLES HICKEY also indicted but he has gone to Texas.
    Paper & date: RGR Mar. 1, 1884; RGR Apr. 26, 1884
    Date & place of death: 2 years ago near Las Cruces, New Mexico

LONG, M. from near Colorado City, Texas; suicide; member of Lodge of Hon-
    or of Brownsville, Miss.; wife: Mrs. ANNA LONG living near Painted
    Cave, Texas.
    Paper & date: LS Mar. 31, 1883; EPT Apr. 12, 1883
    Date & place of death: found Mar. 30, 1883, El Paso, Texas

LONG, M. - burned
    Paper & date: LS Mar. 10, 1883
    Date & place of death: Mar. 5, 1883, Houston, Texas

LONGERVILLE, FERNAND - age 35-40; run over by R. R. pushcar - accident;
    Belgian by birth - letter in pocket from Brussels.
    Paper & date: BU May 19, 1885
    Date & place of death: May 13, 1885, Socorro, N. M.

LONGWORTH, TOM "PINTO TOM" - Consumption
    Paper & date: LS June 4, 1884
    Date & place of death: May 26, 1884, Lincoln, N. M.

LONN, Mrs. MARY - Shot herself
    Paper & date: LS Sept. 2, 1885
    Date & place of death: near Brenham, Texas

LONOIRE, JOHN - Caught in cotton gin machinery
    Paper & date: EPMS Dec. 10, 1884
    Date & place of death: Grand Bluff, Texas

LOPEZ, _____ - Girl murdered by mother because 17 yr old girl insisted
    on marrying against mo.'s wishes; mo.: JUANA LOPEZ of Mesilla, N. M.;
    fa.: JESUS LOPEZ
    Paper & date: NTF Apr. 30, 1881
    Date & place of death: Apr. 28, 1881

LOPES, ANISETO - His gun discharged while trying to control a runaway
    team of oxen; bro.
    Paper & date: LS Feb. 10, 1883
    Date & place of death: last Monday near Anthony, Texas

LOPEZ, JOSE - Murdered
    Paper & date: LS June 27, 1883
    Date & place of death: Mangus Spring ranch, Grant co., New Mexico

LOPEZ, Don JUAN - old resident
    Paper & date: LS Jan. 24, 1885
    Date & place of death: Santa Fe, New Mexico

LOPEZ, Dona ROSA (over 100 yrs.) - formerly of Las Cruces, New Mexico
    Paper & date: LS Jan. 31, 1885; RGR Jan. 31, 1885
    Date & place of death: Silver City, New Mexico

LORD, JAMES A. - (actor) - erysipelas; bur. - Chicago
    Paper & date: LS Jan. 21, 1885
    Date & place of death: Jan. 18, 1885, Socorro, New Mexico

LORD, SAMUEL - suicide
    Paper & date: LS Sept. 23, 1882
    Date & place of death: a day or two ago, Albuquerque, New Mexico

LORD, SCOTT - JOHN E. LORD, son, well known in El Paso
    Paper & date: EPT Oct. 13, 1885
    Date & place of death: lately, New York City

LORENZETTE, COSTANTINO - Italian roustabout - suicide
    Paper & date: EPT Dec. 23, 1884
    Date & place of death: Dec. 22, 1884, El Paso, Texas

LOSSON, HARRY S.M.-5 yrs. 8 mos.; fa.: C. C. LOSSON and family; came from
    the East.
    Paper & date: EPT May 13, 1883
    Date & place of death: May 5, 1883, Chihuahua, Mexico

LOVELACE, _____ - Encounter with Dty. Sher. ANDERSON
    Paper & date: LS Aug. 5, 1885
    Date & place of death: Milam county, Texas

LOWE, EUSTACE B. - 16 yrs.; on trip to the Arctic Ocean from San Francis-
    co; fa.: R. G. LOWE of Galveston, Texas. - oldest son.
    Paper & date: LS Jan. 23, 1884
    Date & place of death: Apr. 8, 1883 aboard ship "Dawn"

LOWRY, _____ - Shot - negro arrested on suspicion; wound may be fatal.
    Paper & date: LS Aug. 18, 1883
    Date & place: North of Kosse, Texas

LOYA, JUAN - Shot by a Mexican; is in dying condition.
    Paper & date: EPT Dec. 25, 1884; EPDH Dec. 28, 1884
    Date & place: near Concordia, Texas

LUBBE, Rev. Father - Consumption
    Paper & date: LS Jan. 12, 1884
    Date & place of death: Jan. 10, 1884, Ysleta, Texas

LUBURG, FRED - Murdered; fa.: of San Antonio, Texas
    Paper & date: LS Nov. 22, 1884
    Date & place of death: Nov. 17, 1884 near New Orleans

LUCAS, _____ - Suicide; (he had murdered _____ CRESPIN); he was spoken
    of as "Young Lucas"; bro. and fa.
    Paper & date: LS Oct. 21, 1882
    Date & place of death: a few days ago at Golden, Colorado

LUCE, NAT - Murdered by Apaches. (see LUSE, NAT)
    Paper & date: RGR June 27, 1885
    Date & place of death: recently - of Alma, N. M.

LUCERO, JUAN M. - age 87
    Paper & date: LS Apr. 22, 1885
    Date & place of death: El Prado, Taos county, New Mexico

LUCERO, VICENTE - Accidentally dropped his pistol and shot himself at
Providencia - 12 or 14 mi. from Deming, New Mexico; freighter from
Mesilla, N. M. returning from Deming.
Paper & date: RGR Aug. 22, 1885
Date & place of death: Aug. 16, 1885

LUCIO, _____ - Killed by a son of LUCIANO ABALOS (AVALOS?)
Paper & date: LS Feb. 13, 1884
Date & place of death: week ago, Tularosa, N. M.

LUCRECIO, J. I. - Drinking
Paper & date: LS July 4, 1883
Date & place of death: Los Alamos, N. M.

LUDWIG, _____ - Found dead last Sat. (30 Oct.); suspect foul play.
Paper & date: LS Nov. 5, 1881
Date & place of death: near Cerrillos, N. M.

LUNA, ANTONIO JOSE of Los Lunas, N. M.; son, Hon. TRANQUILLINO LUNA, N.M.
delegate in Congress
Paper & date: LS Dec. 24, 1881
Date & place of death: Dec. 20, 1881

LUNA, FREDERICO - Shot by JOHN A. SICHLER
Paper & date: EPT Sept. 19, 1883
Date & place of death: Los Lunas, N. M.

LUSE, NAT - Killed with companion - probably by GERONIMO's band.
Paper & date: LS & EPT May 23, 1885
Date & place of death: May 22, 1885 near Silver City, N. M.

LUSSON, HARRY of Fort Worth, Texas; bitten by rabid cat on last Monday
Paper & date: LS Jan. 20, 1883 (Sat.)

LUTTER, CHRISTIAN - Murdered by Apaches; of Blue Creek, Ariz.
Paper & date: RGR June 27, 1885
Date & place of death: recently

LYONS, _____ - Dropped dead
Paper & date: LS Oct. 15, 1884
Date & place of death: Oct. 9, 1884, Houston, Texas

LYONS, W. E. (E. F.? or E. W.?) - GERONIMO and his Apaches
Paper & date: LS May 27, 1885; BU June 2, 1885; RGR June 27, 1885
Date & place of death: Alma, N. M. vicinity

LYONS, J. J. of Gilmore, Texas; murder, possibly by printer, ASHLEY.
Editor of "New Issue".
Paper & date: LS Apr. 8, 1882
Date & place of death: Apr. 5, 1882

McAASBAN, PAUL Brenham, Texas; formerly of LaGrange, Texas; suddenly age
55.
Paper & date: LS May 27, 1885
Date & place of death: May 12, 1885, Columbus, Texas

McADAMS, IKE - Murder - TOM BRUMLEY & GRADE SMITH charged; claim self-
defense.
Paper & date: LS Sept. 17, 1884
Date & place of death: near Caddo Mills, Texas

McATEER, _____ - Killed in a fight in the court room.
Paper & date: LS Dec. 5, 1883
Date & place of death: Dec. 1, 1883, Prescott, Ariz.

McCABE, Mrs. _____ - Heart disease in open court
Paper & date: LS Sept. 26, 1885
Date & place of death: Sept. 25, 1885, Galveston

McCABE, DON (DAN?) - Killed in saloon; gambler; pugnacious; mo. & sister
at Wilkesbarre, Penn.
Paper & date: RGR Jan. 5 & 12, 1884
Date & place of death: Dec. 31, 1883, Lake Valley, N. M.

McCAIN, _____ - a young man; stabbed by drunken policeman, Serg't McHENRY
Paper & date: LS Nov. 29, 1882
Date & place of death: a few nights ago, Galveston, Texas

McCALL, FRANK - Accidentally shot himself
Paper & date: RGR May 29, 1866
Date & place of death: May 22, 1866, Santa Fe, N. M.

McCALL, MATT - (young man) - drowned during late flood
Paper & date: LS May 6, 1885
Date & place of death: White Rock Creek, Dallas co., Texas

McCANN, PAT - Old railroad employee - No clergyman available, so conductor ALLEN presided at the ceremony. When body was lowered into the
ground, Allen sang out: "Well boys, one by one the roses fall." "Yes",
said CHARLEY WING, by way of response, "Step by step to h--l we go."
These solemn words concluded the funeral service.
Paper & date: RGR Feb. 16, 1884
Date & place of death: not long ago

McCARTHY, PAT - Stabbed by MIKE O'DONNEL - found guilty.
Paper & date: LS Feb. 1 & 17, 1882
Date & place of death: 3 weeks ago, Paso del Norte, Mexico

McCARTY, _____ - wife: KATE
Paper & date: LS Sept. 17, 1884
Date & place of death: 4 yrs. ago on L & GN R. R., Tyler, Texas

McCAVERY, OLIVER - Burned in court house fire at Crocket, Houston county,
Texas. All records destroyed.
Paper & date: LS Nov. 18, 1882
Date & place of death: Nov. 13, 1882, Crocket, Texas

McCAY, TOM - Dynamite blast
Paper & date: LS Mar. 28, 1885
Date & place of death: 9 mi- Wichita Falls, Texas

McCLELLAND, WM. - Internal injuries from a fall from his horse.
Paper & date: LS May 23, 1883
Date & place of death: Silver City, New Mexico

McCLENAND, WILLIAM - Dty. Sher.; shot by unknown.
Paper & date: LS July 12, 1884
Date & place of death: Giddings, Texas

McCLUSKY (or McCLOSKY), Cardinal - relative A. J. McCLUSKY of Socorro,
New Mexico
Paper & date: BU Oct. 17, 1885
Date & place of death: New York

McCOLLOCK, _____ of Tascosa, Texas; killed by a gambler; Sheriff
Paper & date: LS Aug. 16, 1882
Date & place of death: recently

McCOMAS, CHARLEY - 6 yr. old son of Judge and Mrs. H. C. McCOMAS; beaten
to death by Indians after being kidnapped; bro's: DAVID & WILLIAM
McCOMAS.
Paper & date: LS June 30, 1883; LS Sept. 19 & 22, 1883; EPT July 18,
1883; EPDH Aug. 10, 1883
Date & place of death: June 1883, Mexico

McCOMAS, Judge HAMILTON C. & Mrs. JUNIATTA W. - Killed by Indians, CHATO
& PENALTISCH in the group; son CHARLIE kidnapped; son DAVID of Lords-
burg, N. M.; son: WILLIAM of Shakespeare, N. M.; 2 dau's.
Paper & date: LS Mar. 31, May 9 & 23, Apr. 18 & Sept. 22, 1883; EPT

McCOMAS (cont'd): Apr. 22, July 18, Aug. 25 & Sept. 25, 1883
    Date & place of death: Mar. 28, 1883, between Paschal and Lordsburg,
    New Mexico.

McCONNELL, _____ - child murdered by fa.; fa.: ELI McCONNELL arrested &
    in Weatherford jail.
    Paper & date: LS Dec. 16, 1882
    Date & place of death: 3 weeks ago, Parker co., Texas

McCORMICK, Miss ELLA - Sis. of Ex-Attorney General McCORMICK.
    Paper & date: LS Nov. 14, 1885
    Date & place of death: Nov. 9, 1885, Austin, Texas

McCUEN, J. G. of Atl. & Pac. R. R. - heart disease; formerly of Mex. Cen-
    tral R. R.
    Paper & date: EPT Nov. 21, 1885
    Date & place of death: Nov. 19, 1885, Albuquerque, N. M.

McCULLOCH (or McCULLOUGH) GREEN - Lynched for murdering CHARLES (A.?) H.
    BRAGG; wife.
    Paper & date: LS Aug. 16, 1884; EPT Aug. 15, 1884
    Date & place of death: Aug. 13, 1884, Cotulla, Texas

McCULLOUGH (or McCULLOCH), W. H. - Body identified near Savoya - killed
    by white men; 3 Indians accused; bro.: W. B. of Marshaltown, Iowa; a
    native of New York state.
    Paper & date: BU May 1 & July 1, 1884; BU Oct. 3, 1885; BU May 29,
    1886
    Date & place of death: Mogollon Mtns, Ariz. missing several months;
    presumed dead.

McCURRY, OLIVER - Burned in jail fire.
    Paper & date: LS Dec. 12, 1883
    Date & place of death: Nov. 1883, Houston, Texas

McDANIELS, JAMES - Shot by officers.
    Paper & date: EPT July 8, 1885
    Date & place of death: near San Geronimo, Texas

McDERMOTT, JAMES - Killed by Apaches
    Paper & date: LS Sept. 30, 1885
    Date & place of death: Tombstone, New Mexico (Ariz.?)

McDONALD, _____ - Killed by Indians
    Paper & date: EPT Dec. 30, 1885
    Date & place of death: near Duncan, Arizona

McDONALD, - 4 youngest children - aged 2 - 7 yrs.; burned to death; fa.:
    MICHAEL McDONALD.
    Paper & date: LS Feb. 24, 1883
    Date & place of death: last week, McKinney co., Texas

MacDONALD, ANDREW - Run over by train.
    Paper & date: EPT May 15, 1883
    Date & place of death: May 4, 1883, Ortis Sta., out of Chihuahua, Mex.

McDONALD, DAN - Texas Ranger; relatives in Illinois.
    Paper & date: LS Jan. 6, 1883
    Date & place of death: a few days ago.

McDONALD, JOHN - Fell dead
    Paper & date: LS Aug. 18, 1883
    Date & place of death: Silver City, N. M.

McDONALD, Hon. JOHN M.
    Paper & date: EPT Apr. 18, 1883
    Date & place of death: Apr. 14, 1883, San Antonio, Texas

McDONALD, W. D. - Killed by Indians in Chocolate Pass, Mexico; a Grant co.
    N. M. miner.

McDONALD (cont'd):
    Paper & date: LS Dec. 9, 1882
    Date & place of death: recently

MacDONNELL (or McDONALD) - Infant son; inflammation of the bowels; fa.:
    Rev. R. W. MacDONNELL.
    Paper & date: LS Aug. 20, 1884; EPT Aug. 18, 1884
    Date & place of death: Aug. 18, 1884, El Paso, Texas

McDONOUGH, T. J. - Murdered by son-in-law JAMES SCOTT; dau.: Mrs. JAMES
    SCOTT.
    Paper & date: LS Nov. 28, 1885; EPT Nov. 28, 1885
    Date & place of death: Nov. 17, 1883, Dallas, Texas

McDOWELL, ROBT. J. - Fight with Dr. _____ RENFRO.
    Paper & date: LS June 6, 1883; EPT Oct. 30, 1884
    Date & place of death: Killeen, Texas

McFARLANE, Mrs. ____
    Paper & date: LS Nov. 15, 1884
    Date & place of death: Funeral Nov. 12, 1884, Las Vegas, N. M.

McFARLIN, Rev. DANIEL - age 75; paralysis; Methodist.
    Paper & date: LS Jan. 14, 1885
    Date & place of death: Jan. 10, 1885, Marshall, Texas

McGARRITY, J. A. - Fight; shot in face by HAINSA McQUESTEIR.
    Paper & date: LS Oct. 15, 1884
    Date & place of death: Oct. 10, 1884, near Corsicana, Texas

McGONIGLE, ____ - Young man; murdered.
    Paper & date: EPDH June 10, 1883
    Date & place of death: after Civil War, 20 mi. above El Paso, Texas

McGORMAN, ____ - Pile driver.
    Paper & date: LS Jan. 14, 1882
    Date & place of death: Jan. 9, 1882, Laguna, New Mexico

McGRAW, Dty. Sher. of Trinidad, New Mexico; killed by GEORGE GOODELL.
    Paper & date: LS Aug. 23, 1882
    Date & place of death: Aug. 19, 1882

McGUIRE, GEORGE - Young; suicide - believed unintentional.
    Paper & date: EPDH Apr. 8, 1883
    Date & place of death: recently near Three Rivers, N. M.

McINTIRE, Mrs. R. J. - Smallpox; hus. bookkeeper for Wells Fargo - R. J.
    McIntire.
    Paper & date: EPDH June 3, 1883; EPDH Jan. 6, 1884
    Date & place of death: May 30, 1883, El Paso, Texas

McKELLER, ____ - Run over by train while drunk.
    Paper & date: LS Aug. 19, 1882
    Date & place of death: a few days ago near Atlanta, Texas

McKENZIE, ____ - Murdered by Indians.
    Paper & date: TB May 4, 1871
    Date & place of death: Apr. 13, 1871, San Pedro Valley

McKENZIE, Mrs. CATHERINE - son: Brig. Gen. R. S. McKENZIE
    Paper & date: LS May 2, 1883
    Date & place of death: recently, Santa Fe, New Mexico

McKERNAN, THOS. - Explosion on R. R. south of Benson, Arizona Territory.
    Paper & date: LS Jan. 21, 1882
    Date & place of death: Jan. 12-19, 1882

McKINERY, DANIEL - in coal mine.
    Paper & date: LS July 7, 1883
    Date & place of death: Gallup, New Mexico

McKINLEY, DAN - formerly of Lincoln co., N. M.; accidentally shot him-
self at a hay camp.
Paper & date: LS Nov. 7, 1885
Date & place of death: New Mexico

McKINN, _____ 2 sons; Indian raid; fa.: JOHN McKINN
Paper & date: LS Sept. 19, 1885
Date & place of death: near Georgetown, N. M.

McKINNEY, EVA - age 2
Paper & date: LS June 3, 1885
Date & place of death: Las Vegas, N. M.

McKINNEY, JOHN - Apple vendor; drunken brawl
Paper & date: LS June 2, 1883
Date & place of death: May 30, 1883, Paso del Norte, Mexico

McKNIGHT, MAUD - age 5 mos.; par.: R. A. & R. McKNIGHT.
Paper & date: EPT Oct. 27, 1885
Date & place of death: Oct. 26, 1885, El Paso, Texas

McKURTAN, P. - of Sonora; murdered by Apaches
Paper & date: RGR June 27, 1885
Date & place of death: recently

McLACHLEN, Mrs. A. M. - hus.: A. M. McLACHLEN, Washington, D. C.; bro.-
in-law: W. B. McLACHLEN, El Paso, Texas
Paper & date: SH Aug. 17, 1884
Date & place of death: Aug. 14, 1884, Washington, D. C.

McLANE, T. J. - Duel with O. FELLOWS
Paper & date: LS July 26, 1882
Date & place of death: Collinsville, Texas, July 22, 1882

McLAUGHLIN, Pvt. CHAS. - formerly of Boston, Mass.; shot 3 Sept. by HEN-
RY J. BERRY - dying at Ft. Bliss. LOU BAXTER, a woman, implicated.
Paper & date: LS Sept. 5, 9, 12, 1885; EPT Sept. 11, 1885; SH Sept.
6, 1885
Date & place of death: Sept. 7, 1885, El Paso, Texas

McLAUGHLIN, PETER - Murder by J. WHITNEY. McLaughlin was quarry contrac-
tor on Palo Pinto co., Texas court house.
Paper & date: LS Sept. 16, 1882
Date & place of death: Sept. 8, 1882

McLEAN, HARRY - Stabbed by JOHN HOGAN, native of St. Louis and nephew of
JOHN HOGAN, Congressman; son of former editor of "Free Press", San
Buena, Ventura, Calif. Bur.: 27 May, Concordia Cem. Native of Calif.
Paper & date: LS May 28, 1884; EPT May 28, 1884
Date & place of death: May 25, 1884

McLEMOORE, THOMAS - Lynched
Paper & date: LS Jan. 2, 1884
Date & place of death: Dec. 25, 1883, McDade, Texas

McLEMOORE, WIGHT - Lynched
Paper & date: LS Jan. 2, 1884
Date & place of death: Dec. 25, 1883, McDade, Texas

McLENNON, _____ of Lampasas co., Texas; shot attempting escape.
Paper & date: EPT Mar. 22, 1885
Date & place of death: Grimes co., Texas

McLEOD, GEORGE
Paper & date: LS Mar. 5, 1884
Date & place of death: Feb. 27, 1884, Silver City, New Mexico

McMAHON, JOHN - Probable suicide
Paper & date: LS Sept. 17, 1884
Date & place of death: Sept. 12, 1884, Grand Prairie, Texas

McMARTIN, SAMUEL - bro.. of Raton, New Mexico
    Paper & date: BU Aug. 1, 1884
    Date & place of death: July 1884, Socorro, New Mexico

McMARTRIE, JAMES - Murdered by Mexican who escaped into Mexico
    Paper & date: LS May 6, 1885
    Date & place of death: 65 mi. from Laredo, Texas on Rio Grande

McMILAN, _____ - Murdered by WILLIAM and ROBERT EANES
    Paper & date: LS Jan. 30, 1884
    Date & place of death: Williamson co., Texas

McMILLAN, _____ - Murdered by Papago Indian (this may be D. A. McMILLAN)
    Paper & date: LS July 9, 1884
    Date & place of death: between Gunsight and Sonoyta

McMILLAN, D. A. - Murdered in Mexico. Not the same D. A. McMillan of Organ, New Mexico.
    Paper & date: RGR Dec. 20, 1884
    Date & place of death: lately

McMURRAY, Mrs. JOHN - Accident - shot by husband JOHN McMURRAY.
    Paper & date: LS Aug. 22, 1883
    Date & place of death: Henrietta, Texas

McNEIL, Dr. _____ - Shot by BILL PREYER
    Paper & date: LS Sept. 27, 1884
    Date & place of death: Sept. 21, 1884, 6 mi. N. of Paige, Texas

McNEAL, WILLIAM - Thrown from horse against a tree.
    Paper & date: LS Aug. 27, 1884
    Date & place of death: Cameron, Texas

McPHAIL, _____ - Shot by police officer McLEOD in house of ill repute.
McPhail, young man, ex-convict.
    Paper & date: LS Jan. 11, 1882
    Date & place of death: Jan. 2, 1882, Austin, Texas

McPHERSON, _____ - Killed by 3 unknown men in Red River, 20 mi. N. W.
of Paris, Texas
    Paper & date: LS Jan. 7, 1882
    Date & place of death: Dec. 27, 1881, near Paris, Texas

McRAE, W. E. - Run over by train
    Paper & date: LS Mar. 18, 1885
    Date & place of death: Galveston, Texas

McROY, _____ - Kicked by horse which fell on him.
    Paper & date: LS May 5, 1883
    Date & place of death: Bryan, Texas

McWILLIAMS, Miss _____ - Suicide supposed - drowned.
    Paper & date: LS Oct. 1, 1884
    Date & place of death: Sept. 24, 1884, Gatesville, Texas

McWIRTER, JACK - Assassinated
    Paper & date: LS Dec. 24, 1881
    Date & place of death: Dec. 15, 1881, Rogers, Texas

MABRY, Gen. W. H. of Ft. Worth, accidentally shot himself.
    Paper & date: LS Mar. 26, 1884
    Date & place of death: Sherman, Texas

MACÉ, _____ famous French barber; formerly lived Las Vegas, N. M.;
hair dresser for CARLOTTA, wife of MAXIMILLIAN.
    Paper & date: LS Feb. 13, 1884
    Date & place of death: Feb. 8, 1884, Paso del Norte, Mexico

MACKLEY, Miss IDA - a girl (age is illegible) heart disease; fa.

MACKLEY (cont'd):
    Paper & date: LS Jan. 17, 1883
    Date & place of death: El Paso, Texas

MADDEN, M. L.
    Paper & date: LS Jan. 20, 1883
    Date & place of death: ca. Jan. 18/19, 1883, El Paso, Texas

MADDOX, _____ - Surgeon (Army), killed by Indians.
    Paper & date: LS Dec. 23, 1885; EPT Dec. 25, 1885
    Date & place of death: Dec. 19, 1885, White House, N. M.

MADDOX, WALTER - Caught in saw at mill
    Paper & date: LS Sept. 24, 1884
    Date & place of death: near Alvarado, Texas

MADRID, MANUEL - 14 yrs.; shot himself
    Paper & date: LS Nov. 18, 1885
    Date & place of death: Turkey Mountains, New Mexico

MADRID, SANTA CRUZ - Shot by GABRIEL MORA
    Paper & date: LS June 20, 1883
    Date & place of death: Socorro, New Mexico

MAES, EPIFANIO - Struck by lightening July 18 ..will probably die.
    Paper & date: LS July 25, 1885
    Date & place: Santa Fe, New Mexico

MAESTAS, _____ - Infant daughter; fa.: PEDRO MAESTAS
    Paper & date: LS Apr. 4, 1885
    Date & place of death: Watrous, New Mexico

MAGRE, _____ Senor of Matamoras, Mexico; explosion in fire works fact-
    ory; Sr. Magre and 4 others burned to death.
    Paper & date: LS (Sat.) Feb. 3, 1883
    Date & place of death: Jan. 31. 1883

MANLER, ANNIE - ca. 18 yrs.; murder and suicide pact with GEORGE FANNICK
    Paper & date: EPT Sept. 30, 1884
    Date & place of death: Sept. 28, 1884, Dallas, Texas

MANNING, CHARLES of Jack co., Texas; shot
    Paper & date: EPT Oct. 7, 1883
    Date & place of death: Day or two ago, Fort Worth, Texas

MANTOYA, MIGUEL of San Mateo, New Mexico; "unloaded pistol"
    Paper & date: LS Nov. 2, 1881
    Date & place of death: Oct. 26, 1881

MANZANARES, _____ - Infant son; suddenly; par.: Hon. & Mrs. F. A. MAN-
    ZANARES
    Paper & date: BU Oct. 31, 1885
    Date & place of death: Oct. 26, 1885, Arriba del Las Vegas, N. M.

MANZANARES, _____ - Killed by Indians
    Paper & date: EPT May 20, 1883
    Date & place of death: May 10, 1883, Hacienda del Carmen, Mexico

MARBLE, B. - Old man age 60; run over by train
    Paper & date: LS July 25, 1885
    Date & place of death: near Mesquite, Texas

MARKHAM, THOMAS - Arm torn off in cotton gin and it is thought he will
    die.
    Paper & date: LS Sept. 20, 1882
    Date & place of death: near Fort Worth, Texas

MARKLEY, Judge J. of Ft. Worth, Texas; congestion of lungs; bur.: Ft.
    Worth, Texas
    Paper & date: LS Nov. 15, 1882

MARKLEY (cont'd):
    Date & place of death: last Fri., San Augustin, New Mexico

MARMOLEJO, Father
    Paper & date: EPT Sept. 3, 1885
    Date & place of death: Sept. 1, 1885, Leon, Mexico

MARQUEZ, FELIX of Silver City, N. M.; murdered by Apaches
    Paper & date: RGR June 27, 1885
    Date & place of death: recently

MARQUEZ, MARIA of Silver City, N. M.; murdered by Apaches
    Paper & date: RGR June 27, 1885
    Date & place of death: recently

MARR, JOE - Little boy; measles; bur. May 18, 1883; fa.: Col. JAMES MARR
    Paper & date: EPT May 18, 1883; EPDH May 20, 1883
    Date & place of death: May 17, 1883, El Paso, Texas

MARR, W. - Killed by JOHN YATES
    Paper & date: LS Oct. 28, 1885
    Date & place of death: Pleasanton, Texas

MARSDEN, S. - Can of coal-oil on fire instead of coffee pot.
    Paper & date: LS Feb. 25, 1882
    Date & place of death: a few days ago, near Dallas, Texas

MARSH, Mrs. ELLEN E.
    Paper & date: EPT Sept. 25, 1883
    Date & place of death: Sept. 24, 1883, El Paso, Texas

MARTIN, _____ - Old man; murdered by TOM BROWN who was later lynched
    Paper & date: LS Jan. 26, 1884
    Date & place of death: last summer, Texas

MARTIN, Mrs. ENCAMBRIAN - Brained with an axe by her hus. ENCAMBRIAN MAR-
    TIN
    Paper & date: LS Mar. 7, 1883
    Date & place of death: Watrous, New Mexico

MARTIN, FRANK - R. R. laborer; murder by 17 yr. old lad
    Paper & date: LS Nov. 16, 1881
    Date & place of death: Nov. 9, 1881, near Liberty Hill, Texas

MARTIN, J. E. - of Rio Grande City, Texas; sher.; murdered 6 miles be-
    low Rio Grande City, Texas
    Paper & date: LS Dec. 10, 1881
    Date & place of death: Dec. 1, 1881

MARTIN, Hon. J. M. - State senator from 11th Dist. of Texas; formerly
    editor of Gainesville Register, Texas.
    Paper & date: LS Mar. 15, 1882
    Date & place of death: Mar. 9, 1882, Saundersville, Tenn.

MARTIN, JOHN - Lynched; murderer of Mrs. HAZELL, Elkhart, Texas
    Paper & date: LS July 11, 1885

MARTIN, JOHN "TENNESSEE" - Killed by Indians
    Paper & date: EPT Nov. 11, 1885
    Date & place of death: near Rincon, N. M.

MARTIN, JOHN - Lynched for shooting his wife.
    Paper & date: LS Nov. 14, 1883
    Date & place of death: Luling, Texas

MARTIN, Mrs. JOHN - Shot by husband
    Paper & date: LS Nov. 14, 1883
    Date & place of death: Nov. 7, 1883, Luling, Texas

MARTIN, JOSE - NARCISSUS SALAZAR of Rio Arriba co., N. M. on trial for

MARTIN (cont'd): his murder.
    Paper & date: LS Jan. 14, 1885
    Date & place of death: New Mexico

MARTIN, K. A. - Murdered; Dr. LEACHES held without bail.
    Paper & date: LS July 15, 1885
    Date & place of death: Comanche, Texas

MARTIN, M. DENT of St. Louis, Missouri; drinking excessively.
    Paper & date: LS Sept. 13, 1884
    Date & place of death: Sept. 7, 1884, Albuquerque, New Mexico

MARTIN, W. R. - Suicide
    Paper & date: EPT Aug. 25, 1885
    Date & place of death: Colorado City, Texas

MARTINAS, MELQUIADES - Shot by Indians
    Paper & date: TB Dec. 20, 1871
    Date & place of death: Dec. 18, 1871, Chambarino, New Mexico

MARTINEZ, PEDRO - to be shot for wrecking and robbing train in Nov. 1883
    Paper & date: EPT Aug. 13, 1885
    Date & place of death: Nuevo Laredo, Mexico

MARTINEZ, POOLER - Shot by HILL and LONGSTON
    Paper & date: LS Apr. 16, 1884
    Date & place of death: Vermejo, New Mexico

MARTINEZ, Dona VICTORIA of Las Cruces, New Mexico; age 100 years
    Paper & date: LS Nov. 2, 1881
    Date & place of death: Oct. 21, 1881

MARX, MUNROE of New York, New York; inflammation of the brain
    Paper & date: LS Aug. 13, 1884
    Date & place of death: Aug. 12, 1884, El Paso, Texas

MASCARENOS, AMADOR - 11 yrs.; shot by FRANK PHILLIPS, 9 yrs. son of Rev.
    MAXWELL PHILLIPS.
    Paper & date: LS Mar. 3, 1883
    Date & place of death: Feb. 23, 1883, Mora, New Mexico

MASON, _____ - Little boy drowned in river; surv.: mother
    Paper & date: EPDH Dec. 28, 1881
    Date & place of death: June 29-July 6, 1881, near Ft. Bliss, Texas

MASON, _____ (Head brakeman) Mo.-Pac. train went through burning bridge
    (news release from Denison, Texas); family in Buffalo, New York
    Paper& date: EPT July 11, 1884
    Date & place of death: 8/9 July 1884, near Checotali, (Indian Terr.?
    or Texas?)

MASON, _____ - Killed by NAT TANTON
    Paper & date: LS Mar. 10, 1883
    Date & place of death: last Jan., Sulphur Springs, Texas

MASON, _____ - Shoot-out with rangers at Green Lake (fence cutter)
    Paper & date: LS Aug. 20, 1884
    Date & place of death: July 26, 1884, Edwards co., Texas

MASON, JOSEPH - Old citizen
    Paper & date: LS Nov. 12, 1884
    Date & place of death: Nov. 6, 1884, Marshall, Texas

MATCHET, Dr. _____ of Brenham, Texas
    Paper & date: EPDH Dec. 28, 1881
    Date & place of death: Apr. 3, 1881, El Paso, Texas

MATTHEWS, Mrs. _____ of Smith co., Texas; suicide; surv.: hus.
    Paper & date: LS Jan. 12, 1884
    Date & place: ....

109

MATHEWS, "ROCKY" H. O. - Agent for Mr. SAYLOR; well-known in Socorro, N.
M. in earlier days; bur.: in Jimulco, Mexico; sis.: in Rockford, Colo.
Paper & date: LS Jan. 24, 1885; EPT Jan. 22, 1885; BU Aug. 29, 1885
Date & place of death: Jan. 18, 1885, road from Jimulco, Mexico to
state of Durango, Mexico

MATTHEWS, WILLIAM - Matthews eloped with the wife of JAMES SECRIST and
later tried to get her personal effects from the husband who shot him
Paper & date: LS July 18, 1885
Date & place of death: Comanche co., Texas

MAUPIN, THOMAS C. - b. 2 Sept. 1796 in Madison co., Ky.; d. home of Col.
G. B. STEVENSON, Isleta, Texas; wife died 6 years ago; 11 children,
only 1 living; Baptist; bur. July 31, 1885; dau.: Mrs. G. B. STEVEN-
SON.
Paper & date: LS Aug. 15, 1885
Date & place of death: July 30, 1885, Isleta, Texas

MAXWELL, GEORGE - Fight with HAWKE's PETE in which Maj. COALBACK was mor-
tally wounded also.
Paper & date: LS Jan. 27, 1883
Date & place of death: Jan. 21, 1883, Lee's Creek, Texas

MAY, _____ - Child; measles; youngest child of JOHN L. & ELIZABETH MAY
Paper & date: TB May 22, 1872
Date & place of death: May 17, 1872

MAY, _____ - Killed in fight with _____ PLASBY.
Paper & date: LS Aug. 1, 1883
Date & place of death: near Denison, Texas

MAY, Mrs. C. M. of Tom Green co., Texas; suddenly; widow of the late
County Judge C. M. MAY in Baird, Texas
Paper & date: LS Aug. 30, 1882
Date & place of death: Aug. 24, 1882

MAY, CHARLES - Engineer on Mex. Cent.
Paper & date: EPT Aug. 23, 1885
Date & place of death: Aug. 18, 1885, Silao, Mex.

MAYBERRY, _____ - boy; murdered by MARTIN NELSON; bur. with his father;
sis.: PET (NELLIE)
Paper & date: RGR May 16, 1885
Date & place of death: May 4, 1885, Bonito, New Mexico

MAYBERRY, EDDIE - age 6; murdered by MARTIN NELSON; sis.: PET (NELLIE)
Paper & date: RGR May 16, 1885
Date & place of death: May 4, 1885, Bonito, New Mexico

MAYBERRY, M. S. - murdered by MARTIN NELSON; dau.: PET (NELLIE), sent to
childless uncle in Iowa.
Paper & date: RGR May 16, 1885; LS May 9, 1885
Date & place of death: May 4, 1885, Bonito, New Mexico

MAYBERRY, Mrs. M. S. and 1 dau. - murdered by MARTIN NELSON; was soon to
become a mother; dau.: PET (NELLIE)
Paper & date: RGR May 16, 1885; LS May 9, 1885
Date & place of death: May 4, 1885, Bonito, New Mexico

MAYNARD, A. M. - Raided by Apaches; 17 people killed
Paper & date: LS (Wed.) Jan. 11, 1882
Date & place of death: recently, near Onova, Mexico

MAYS, DICK - Killed by Indians
Paper & date: EPT Dec. 4, 1885
Date & place of death: Dec. 3, 1885, Coronado Ranch on Gila River,
Arizona

MEAD, JOSEPH H. - Dropsy; bur.: Sept. 13, 1883
Paper & date: EPT Sept. 14, 1883/D & P: Sep. 12,1883,Deming, N. M.

MEADOWS, WM. - To die for murder in Indian Territory.
    Paper & date: EPT Feb. 1, 1885
    Date & place of death: Apr. 7, 1885, Ft. Smith, Arkansas

MECKLEY, J. A. - Consumption; well-known and former resident of El Paso,
    Texas; family
    Paper & date: EPT Nov. 25, 1884
    Date & place of death: Nov. 22, 1884, Keokuk, Iowa

MEDRAN, CAYETANO - Shot by PONCIANO FRANCO
    Paper & date: LS July 25, 1883
    Date & place of death: Toyah Creek, Pecos co., Texas

MEEKER, Miss JESSIE - Consumption
    Paper & date: LS Apr. 11, 1885
    Date & place of death: Albuquerque, N. M.

MEEKER, N. C. - Tortured to death by Ute Indians in massacre; dau*- 1882
    in Washington, D. C. of pneumonia.(*JOSEPHINE C. MEEKER, d. Dec.)
    Paper & date: LS Jan. 3, 1883
    Date & place of death: 1879

MEIR, Mrs. _____ - of Las Cruces, N. M.;sis.: Dona MANUELA ALBILLAR.
    Paper & date: LS Nov. 2, 1881
    Date & place of death: 'three weeks before"

MELEADY, CHARLES - Shot by IKE GREATHOUSE; bur. same day
    Paper & date: LS Apr. 18, 1883
    Date & place of death: Apr. 15, 1883, Las Vegas, New Mexico

MELEY, JOHN F. (MILEY,MEELY) - Took morphine
    Paper & date: LS July 29, 1885
    Date & place of death: Dallas, Texas

MENCHACA, ANTONIO of San Antonio, Texas; powder exploded; mo. and 2 sis.;
    uncle JESUS CUELLAR; aunt TERRESA CUELLAR (sis. of JESUS)
    Paper & date: EPDH Aug. 2, 1882
    Date & place of death: July 18, 1882, near Del Rio, Texas

MENDELA, JOSE MARIA - Sentenced to hang for murder of G. M. HODGES
    Paper & date: LS Nov. 28, 1885
    Date & place of death: Cotulla, Texas

MENDOSA, SIDRO
    Paper & date: RGR June 9, 1883
    Date & place of death: June 5, 1883, Las Cruces, New Mexico

MENTZGER, HENRY - Stabbed by Mexican named MANUEL _____ & DALZIO
    Paper & date: EPT Jan. 27, 1885
    Date & place of death: Jan. 25, 1884, near San Angelo, Texas

MERCHANT, HARRY - Shot by CHARLEY HINSON; fa.: wealthy cattleman of Tex.
    Paper & date: EPT July 24, 1883
    Date & place of death: July 21/22, 1883, Baird, Texas

MERRIAN, JOSEPH C. of Boston, Mass.
    Paper & date: LS Mar. 11, 1882
    Date & place of death: Mar. 4, 1882, Dallas, Texas

MERRICK, _____ - Murdered by J. ADAMS
    Paper & date: LS Oct. 21, 1885
    Date & place of death: Kaufman co., Texas

MERRILL, _____ - U. S. Dty. Marshall; killed while attempting to arrest
    whiskey peddlers.
    Paper & date: LS Oct. 3, 1883
    Date & place of death: Sept. 28, 1883, near Webber's Falls, Ind.Terr.

MERRILL, M/M THOMAS - Recently married; murdered by axes; last seen on
    Christmas day; Mrs. MERRILL ca. 20 yrs; mo. of Mrs MERRILL lives in

MERRILL (cont'd): - Dallas, Texas; Mrs. MERRILL niece of Capt. J. D.
Reed, Fort Worth, Texas; m. ca. Apr. or May 1884
Paper & date: LS Dec. 30, 1884; EPT Dec. 30, 1884; EPT May 29, 1885
Date & place of death: Discovered Dec. 28, 1884, near Sierra Blanca,
Texas

MERRILL, TIP - Accidentally shot by HENRY ABLES
Paper & date: LS Sept. 21, 1885
Date & place of death: near Tyler, Texas

MESSENGER, WINNIE - burns
Paper & date: EPMS Dec. 4, 1884
Date & place of death: Dec. 3, 1884, El Paso, Texas

METCALF, JOHN W. - age 36; "a malady"; an early pioneer and founder of
Silver City; surv.: by a bro. - native of Wayne co., Ky.
Paper & date: TB Mar. 27, 1872
Date & place of death: ca. Mar. 14, 1872

MEYER, _____ - a Jew; murdered by PATRICIO CHARLES - convicted at Lar-
edo, Texas, Feb. 19, 1883
Paper & date: LS Feb. 24, 1883
Date & place of death: Texas

MEYER, CHARLES - Stabbed by 2 tenants on fa.'s farm; surv.: fa.
Paper & date: LS June 24, 1885
Date & place of death: near Hubbard City, Hill co., Texas

MEYER, FRANK - Murdered; HENRY BROWN convicted at Las Vegas, New Mexico
Paper & date: LS Mar. 21, 1883
Date & place of death: N. M.

MICHAEL, _____ of San Antonio, Texas; drank lye; _____ - age 4 yrs; fa.:M.
MICHAEL.
Paper & date: LS Dec. 13, 1882
Date & place of death: recently

MICHEL, ALEXANDER - bro.-in-law: BARNEY OPPENHEIMER of San Antonio, Tex.
Paper & date: SH Apr. 5, 1885
Date & place of death: past week, San Antonio, Texas

MICHELBOROUGH, _____ - Suicide; dau.: MARY
Paper & date: EPT June 30, 1884
Date & place of death: June 19/20, 1884 Millican, Texas

MICHELBOROUGH, Mrs. _____ - Killed by husband; dau.: MARY
Paper & date: EPT June 30, 1884
Date & place of death: June 19/20, 1884 Millican, Texas

MIDDLETON, W. G. of Albuquerque, N. M.; consumptive - died of heart di-
sease; bur. in Concordia, Texas; surv.: sis; formerly of N. Y.
Paper & date: LS Jan. 31, 1885; EPT Jan. 30, 1885; EPDH Feb. 1,1885
Date & place of death: Jan. 29, 1885, on incoming Santa Fe train

MIER, JAS. of Waco, Texas; "destitute old man".
Paper & date: LS Jan. 25, 1882
Date & place of death: Jan. 20, 1882

MILES, JAMES - Stepped off speeding train while intoxicated.
Paper & date: LS Aug. 8, 1885
Date & place of death: near Dallas, Texas

MILK, Mrs. LEMUEL of Kankakee, Ill.; pneumonia; doctor was Dr. JUSTICE;
surv.: son, in delicate health; hus.: - back in Ill.
Paper & date: LS Dec. 7, 1881
Date & place of death: Dec. 7, 1881, El Paso, Texas

MILLER, _____ - child; dose of medicine from wrong bottle; mo: Mrs.Mil-
ler.
Paper & date: LS Aug. 20,1884/ D&P: Rhea's Mills, Collin co., Texas

MILLER, Mr. _____ - Stabbed
    Paper & date: LS Oct. 21, 1885
    Date & place of death: Hawkins, Texas

MILLER, _____ - (a German) - murdered by _____ FAUGHT
    Paper & date: LS Apr. 16, 1884
    Date & place of death: Apr. 5-12, 1884, Troupe, Texas

MILLER, ALBERT - Negro gambler; shot himself.
    Paper & date: LS June 9, 1883
    Date & place of death: San Antonio, Texas

MILLER, CHARLES - Shot by Dty. Sher. MART MERRILL while resisting arrest;
    fa.: Sher. MARION MILLER
    Paper & date: EPT Oct. 18, 1885
    Date & place of death: Sherwood, Texas (near San Angelo).

MILLER, CHAS. - DICK ROGERS accused.
    Paper & date: EPMS Dec. 10, 1884
    Date & place of death: Oct. 1883, Raton, N. M.

MILLER, CHAS. - (Train engineer) - Scalded when engine overturned pin-
    ning him underneath.
    Paper & date: LS May 27, 1885
    Date & place of death: May 17, 1885, Eagle Pass, Texas

MILLER, DAVID - Negro; run over by train
    Paper & date: LS June 9, 1883
    Date & place of death: Texarkana, Texas

MILLER, EDWARD - Run over by train
    Paper & date: LS Nov. 14, 1883
    Date & place of death: few nights ago near Dallas, Texas

MILLER, Mrs. EMILY
    Paper & date: EPMS Nov. 27, 1884
    Date & place of death: Nov. 19, 1884, Eagle Pass, Texas

MILLER, FRANK of Laredo, Texas; shot and stabbed - will probably die -
    killed a policeman; former Texas Ranger.
    Paper & date: EPT Aug. 15, 1883
    Date & place of death: Monterrey, Mexico

MILLER, J. J. - Shot in his home
    Paper & date: LS Nov. 7, 1885
    Date & place of death: Nacogdoches, Texas

MILLER, JOHN - Shot by BUTLER CARPENTER and possibly _____ CARPENTER.
    Paper & date: EPDS Apr. 22, 1883
    Date & place of death: Apr. 8, 1883, Sherman, Texas

MILLER, JOHN - Merchant; killed by a Mexican.
    Paper & date: LS Aug. 5, 1885
    Date & place of death: Casa Salazar, N. M.

MILLER, JOHN S. - Shot by IKE JORDAN
    Paper & date: LS Nov. 24, 1883; LS Nov. 28, 1883
    Date & place of death: Nov. 19, 1883, San Antonio, Texas

MILLER, JOSEPH - Accidentally shot by playmate OVID CLARK, age 8, with
    old rusty pistol he had found.
    Paper & date: LS Apr. 28, 1883
    Date & place of death: Dallas, Texas

MILLER, RUFUS - Accidentally shot himself
    Paper & date: LS Dec. 16, 1885
    Date & place of death: Comanche co., Texas

MILLETT, EDWARD - Killed by LARRY ROBERTS
    Paper & date: LS Nov. 14, 1885; D & P: near Weimar, Texas

MILLEY (MILEY), _____ of White Oaks, N. M.; result of injuries caused
    the five yr. old boy's death; fa.: HENRY MILLEY
    Paper & date: LS Dec. 27, 1882; LS Jan. 10, 1883
    Date & place of death: other day

MILLIKEN, Mrs. W. C. of Weatherford, Texas; hus.: Dr. W. C. MILLIKEN
    Paper & date: LS Aug. 19, 1882
    Date & place of death: a few days ago

MILLIO, CLEMENTIO - age 14; suicide
    Paper & date: LS Nov. 25, 1885
    Date & place of death: Lincoln, N. M.

MILLS, _____ - Bro. of Major MILLS; Indian massacre at COOK's Canon in
    Grant co., N. M.. Mail route was run by GEORGE GIDDINGS. Coach found
    overturned by ALEJANDRO DEGARE of El Paso, freighting copper. Col.
    BAYLOR sent detail and found bodies of MILLS, ROESCHLER, PURTELL and
    AVELINE on top of COOK's Peak (inside a 2 ft. stone fortification).
    WILSON's body 150 ft. away - only 2 or 3 scalped. Afterwards story
    came from Mexicans of Janos that MANGUS COLORADO and COCHISE were both
    in the fight which lasted 3 days. MANGUS lost 40 men and withdrew af-
    ter 2 days. COCHISE remained and killed all others left.
    Paper & date: EPT Jan. 20, 1887
    Date & place of death: June 1860

MILLS, Hon. JOHN S. of Navasota, Texas; congestion caused by bathing too
    soon after dinner; age ca 46 and unmarried.
    Paper & date: LS Dec. 3, 1881
    Date & place of death: Nov. 22, 1881

MILLSPAUGH, PHILLIP, JR. - Drowned - body not recovered; native of New
    York; bro.: also a member of same surveying party.
    Paper & date: TB July 17, 1872
    Date & place of death: between Franklin and Las Cruces

MINTON, JACOB - Old citizen
    Paper & date: EPMS Nov. 30, 1884
    Date & place of death: few days ago, Denton, Texas

MITCHELL, _____ (8 yr. old dau.); burned to death; fa.: ANDREW MITCH-
    ELL.
    Paper & date: LS Sept. 24, 1884
    Date & place of death: last week, Kildare, Texas

MITCHELL, ALLEN - Surv.: Mrs. W. H. DODGE, St. Louis, Missouri
    Paper & date: BU Apr. 5, 1892
    Date & place of death: last heard of 1880 in Shakespeare, Grant co.,
    New Mexico

MITCHELL, CHARLES - Found June 5 - dead about 6 days
    Paper & date: EPT June 9, 1883
    Date & place of death: Playito opp. Guaymas, Mex.

MITCHELL, CHAS. - Negro; hung by mob - ravisher of Mrs. WADDELL; her hus.
    was believed to have hired him.
    Paper & date: LS Nov. 8, 1884
    Date & place of death: Nov. 3, 1884, Little Rock, Arkansas

MITCHELL, HUGH - Stabbed by J. M. WHEELIS
    Paper & date: LS Nov. 22, 1884
    Date & place of death: Overton, Texas

MITCHELL, JAMES - 40 yrs. in Texas; heart disease
    Paper & date: LS Mar. 18, 1885
    Date & place of death: recently, Bryan, Texas

MITCHELL, Mrs. MARTHA of Bastrop, Tex.; 83 yrs. old
    Paper & date: EPT Apr. 27, 1883
    Date & place of death: Apr. 23, 1883, Belton, Texas

MITCHELL, Capt. P. J. and oldest son; killed by Navajos while prospecting
with another man, also killed; he was supt. of Santa Rita mine and
Golden Rule mine.
Paper & date: EPT July 14, 1884
Date & place of death: about 3 weeks ago in Arizona

MITCHELL, W. P. - Running a switch engine; J. N. SELBY of Greenville, Tx
wrote Albuquerque Journal for information re the cause of death.
Paper & date: LS Jan. 20, 1883
Date & place of death: last Apr. 1882, Coolidge, New Mexico

MIX, Mr. _____ Shot - will probably die.
Paper & date: LS Apr. 5, 1884
Date & place of death: Apr. 3, 1884, Alvarado, (Tex.? or N. M.?)

MIX, Maj. JOHN of Ft. Cummings, N. M. - Suicide
Paper & date: LS Nov. 2, 1881
Date & place of death: Oct. 25, 1881

MOBLEY, J. W. - Killed by JOHN REEVES
Paper & date: LS June 2, 1883
Date & place of death: Baird, Texas

MODE, THOMAS P. - (Policeman) age 34, dark hair and eyes, over 6' tall,
nearly 200 lbs., native of Missouri, fa. d. while he was small; mo.
remarried; had lived in Colorado, Kansas, Nebraska and Waco, San Antonio and El Paso, Texas and had been a Texas Ranger; killed by HOW-
ARD H. DOUGHTY, formerly of Norwalk, Conn. and Detroit, Michigan, age
ca 25, 5'7", 145 lbs; bur. July 11, 1883, Ft. Bliss Cemetery; surv.:
wife, no children.
Paper & date: LS July 14, 1883; LS July 11, 1883; LS Apr. 16, 1884;
EPT July 12, 1883; EPT July 18, 1883
Date & place of death: July 11, 1883, in what was later the county
jail of El Paso, Texas

MODIE, Mrs. R. L. (nee ELIZABETH McINTOSH, b. Mora, N. M., 26 yrs. ago);
hus. - m. 2½ yrs. ago.
Paper & date: BU Aug. 1, 1884
Date & place of death: July 22, 1884, Socorro, N. M.

MOLINO, JOSE LIND - Cook; killed by Indians
Paper & date: EPDH Oct. 5, 1881
Date & place of death: between Wilcox and San Carlos, Arizona

MOLLY, J. A. "TEX" - Lumber business; shot by robbers
Paper & date: LS Dec. 12, 1883
Date & place of death: Dec. 10, 1883, Bisbee, Arizona

MONJEAU, LOUIS - Killed by JOHN N. HUDGENS, claimed self-defense, caused
by whiskey; bro.: Rev. MONJEAU, Baptist preacher at Topeka, Kansas.
Paper & date: LS Jan. 21, 1885; EPT Jan. 18, 1885
Date & place of death: Jan. 5, 1885, White Oaks, N. M.

MONROE, WILLIAM - Murdered and robbed; railroad agent at Webb Sta., Texas
Paper & date: LS Feb. 21, 1883
Date & place of death: Feb. 14, 1883

MONTALBO, JOSE LOPEZ of Laredo, Texas; shot by PEDRO ARGUINDIGUI
Paper & date: LS July 15, 1885
Date & place of death: July 5, 1885, Nuevo Laredo, Mexico

MONTANO, Don MIGUEL & WIFE - Murdered by JOSE TRUJILLO GALLEGOS
Paper & date: LS Feb. 21, 1885; EPT Feb. 27, 1885
Date & place of death: Feb. 17, 1885, near Ft. Sumner, N. M. (Las
Norias)

MONTERA, SANTIAGO - Found with bullet hole in his head.
Paper & date: LS May 23, 1883
Date & place of death: Socorro, New Mexico

MONTE(S), CARPIO - Mescalero Apache Indian in jail at Santa Fe - to be
hanged for murder - d. in cell of consumption
Paper & date: RGR May 24, 1884; LS Apr. 18, 1883; LS Feb. 27, 1884
Date & place of death: recently

MONTES, JOSE DE LA LUZ - age 59; apoplexy; uncle of mayor-elect ESPIRI-
DION PROVENCIO of Paso del Norte, Mex.; two bro. inherit.
Paper & date: LS Dec. 23, 1885; EPT Dec. 23, 1885
Date & place of death: Dec. 21, 1885, Paso del Norte, Mexico

MONTES, Sra. JOSEFA - Widow of JOSE DE LA LUZ JAQUES (MONTES?); mo.-law
of Mr. E. PROVENCIO.
Paper & date: EPT Mar. 14, 1885
Date & place of death: Mar. 13, 1885, Paso del Norte, Mex. or El Paso,
Texas (?)

MONTGOMERY, JIM (JAMES) - GERONIMO and his Apaches
Paper & date: LS May 27, 1885; EPT May 28, 1885
Date & place of death: Alma, New Mexico vicinity

MONTGOMERY, JOHN - Fell from scaffold into machinery; bur. in El Paso,
Texas; originally from Lambton, Canada where relatives still live;
aka - JACK STACEY
Paper & date: LS May 13, 1885; EPT May 14, 1885; SH May 17, 1885
Date & place of death: May 11, 1885, Sierra Blanca, Texas

MONTGOMERY, WM. - Fight with BUD ARNOLD; not expected to live
Paper & date: LS Aug. 8, 1885
Date & place: near Texarkana, Texas

MONTOYA, A. - Struck by lightening
Paper & date: LS Aug. 19, 1885
Date & place of death: no. of Wallace, N. M.

MONTOYA, ANDRES - Former sher.
Paper & date: LS June 13, 1883
Date & place of death: Socorro co., N. M.

MONTOYA, Mrs. DOLORES - Formerly of Santa Fe, N. M.
Paper & date: LS Sept. 22, 1883
Date & place of death: Sept. 18, 1883, Las Vegas, N. M.

MONTOYA, DOMINGO - Suicide after murdering his wife, (JOSEFA MELENDRES);
3 young ch. who cannot be found.
Paper & date: RGR Apr. 5, 1884
Date & place of death: Mar. 31, 1884

MONTOYA, ESTANISLAO - age 68; family; oldest miner in Socorro; worked
Merrit mine 1840.
Paper & date: LS Aug. 16, 1884; BU Sept. 1, 1884
Date & place of death: Aug. 8, 1884, San Antonio, N. M.

MONTOYA, JOSE - (Young) - accidentally shot himself through the head.
Paper & date: LS June 20, 1885
Date & place of death: near Cimarron, N. M.

MONTOYA, JOSEFA MELENDRES - Shot by hus., DOMINGO MONTOYA of Dona Ana;
jealous; 3 young ch. who cannot be found.
Paper & date: RGR Apr. 5, 1884
Date & place of death: Mar. 31, 1884

MONTOYA, LUPITA LUNA de - Surv.: hus. and family
Paper & date: BU Sept. 1, 1884
Date & place of death: Aug. 23, 1884, San Antonio, N. M.

MONTOYA, NESTOR - Prominent citizen of Bernalillo co., New Mexico
Paper & date: RGR Aug. 4, 1883
Date & place of death: recently

MONTOYA, R. - Heart disease; came to El Paso from Tucson, Arizona.

MONTOYA (cont'd):
    Paper & date: EPDH Sept. 16, 1883
    Date & place of death: this week, El Paso, Texas

MOOD, Rev. F. A. - Regent of Southwestern University, Georgetown, Texas
    Paper & date: EPT Nov. 14, 1884
    Date & place of death: Nov. 12, 1884, Waco, Texas

MOON, PETE - Lynched
    Paper & date: EPT June 18, 1885
    Date & place of death: June 16, 1885, Indian Territory

MOON, WM. - Killed by CALVIN SMITH, colored
    Paper & date: LS Apr. 28, 1883
    Date & place of death: few months ago, Texas

MOONEY, TOM - Shot accidentally by AUGUST CLINE
    Paper & date: LS Aug. 15, 1885
    Date & place of death: near Lincoln, New Mexico

MOORE, _____ - Killed in fight in the court room
    Paper & date: LS Dec. 5, 1883
    Date & place of death: Dec. 1, 1883, Prescott, Arizona

MOORE, _____ - Infant dau.; par.: M/M B. C. MOORE; erected 1st tombstone
    in city.
    Paper & date: LS Mar. 21, 1883
    Date & place of death: 3 mos. ago, El Paso, Texas

MOORE, _____ - 12 yr. old son thrown from horse
    Paper & date: LS Mar. 3, 1883
    Date & place of death: last week, Dallas co., Texas

MOORE, _____ - a boy; lynched
    Paper & date: EPT June 30, 1885
    Date & place of death: a week ago, near Headtown, New Mexico

MOORE, CHAS. - Fight with Indians in Steins Peak range.
    Paper & date: LS Oct. 19, 1881
    Date & place of death: Oct. 13, 1881 near Lordsburg, New Mexico

MOORE, CHAS. - Killed by Indians
    Paper & date: BU Nov. 7, 1885; RGR Nov. 14, 1885
    Date & place of death: Nov. 2, 1885, Lake Valley, New Mexico

MOORE, ELI - Shot and killed by A. P. CRISWELL
    Paper & date: LS Mar. 8, 1882
    Date & place of death: Feb. 21, 1882, Texarkana, Texas

MOORE. JOHN - Shot by herders while trying to rob them.
    Paper & date: EPDH Nov. 29, 1882
    Date & place of death: few days ago, Gallinas, Mexico

MOORE, TOM - Consumption
    Paper & date: LS Apr. 22, 1885
    Date & place of death: Albuquerque, N. M.

MOORHEAD, Col. WM. A. - son: JAMES A MOORHEAD, foreman of Sierra Bella
    Mine; from Washington, D. C.; head of Treasury Pension Bureau; Col.
    Moorhead was uncle by marriage to Dr. MERRIL, dentist.
    Paper & date: RGR Oct. 4, 1884
    Date & place of death: Sept. 27, 1884

MORALES, Mrs. MARTINA - age 101
    Paper & date: LS Aug. 29, 1883
    Date & place of death: San Antonio, Texas

MORALES, PANCHA - Shot by MANUEL DEALLAS
    Paper & date: LS Aug. 4, 1883
    Date & place of death: Ft. Ewell, La Salle co., Texas

MORALES, PANCHO - Shot
    Paper & date: LS Jan. 31, 1885
    Date & place of death: Jan. 24, 1885, Eagle Pass Rd., Dimmitt co.,Tx

MORALES, TRINIDAD - Shot
    Paper & date: EPT Dec. 16, 1883
    Date & place of death: Dec. 15, 1883, near Ft. Davis, Texas

MORELAND, HARVEY - Killed by Indians; fa.: JAMES MORELAND
    Paper & date: EPT May 27, 1885
    Date & place of death: May 23, 1885, near Grafton, New Mexico

MORGAN, ANNIE - Fell from trapeze - broke her neck
    Paper & date: LS Aug. 4, 1883
    Date & place of death: Aug. 3, 1883, Silver City, New Mexico

MORGAN, FRANK - Lynched
    Paper & date: EPT June 30, 1885
    Date & place of death: a week ago, near Headtown, Texas

MORGAN, GEORGE - Lynched
    Paper & date: EPT June 18, 1885
    Date & place of death: June 16, 1885, Indian Territory, Ok.

MORGAN, JOHN G. - City Marshall; shot by S. E. STILES
    Paper & date: LS July 19, 1884
    Date & place of death: July 15, 1884, Taylor, Texas

MORGAN, KATE - 14/15 yrs. old; drowned in San Gabriel river.
    Paper & date: LS May 9, 1885
    Date & place of death: near Taylor, Texas

MORGAN, W. S. - Stranger
    Paper & date: LS Feb. 2, 1884
    Date & place of death: this week, Tucson, Ariz.

MORLEY, W. R. of Las Vegas, N. M.; accidentally shot himself in Chihuahua on Mexican Central R. R. near Santa Rosalio, Mex.; chief engineer;
prominent N. M. man; surv.: wife in Washington City, 3 chil.
    Paper & date: LS Jan. 6, 1883

MORRILL, _____ - age 22, U. S. Marshal; shot by whiskey peddlers JOHN
BANK (BURKE?) & JOHN M. JACKS, Cherokee Ind.
    Paper & date: EPT Sept. 29, 1883
    Date & place of death: Sept. 27, 1883, between Childress Sta. and
Webb Falls, Ind. Terr., Ok.

MORRILL, Judge AMOS
    Paper & date: LS Mar. 8, 1884
    Date & place of death: Mar. 5, 1884, Austin, Texas

MORRIS, AARON - Young; while hunting, gun discharged prematurely; fa.:
HENRY MORRIS recently of Ysleta, Texas
    Paper & date: LS Sept. 29, 1883
    Date & place of death: Sept. 21, 1883, near Silver City, N. M.

MORRIS, CULLEN - Kicked by WM. GANSON
    Paper & date: EPT Aug. 31, 1883
    Date & place of death: Texarkana, Tx.-Ark.

MORRIS, J. W. of Corsicana, Texas; murder by FRANK CLANTON
    Paper & date: LS Aug. 12, 1882
    Date & place of death: last spring

MORRIS, JOHN C. - a gambler; shot by WM. R. RAYNER, Dty. U. S. Revenue
    Collector
    Paper & date: LS Dec. 31, 1881; LS Feb. 22, 1882
    Date & place of death: Dec. 20, 1881, Fort Worth, Texas

MORRIS, JNO. P. - Sher.; shoot-out with Rangers; wife in Pecos, Texas

MORRIS (cont'd):
  Paper & date: LS Aug. 22, 1885; EPT Aug. 20, 1885; EPT Aug. 21,1885
  Date & place of death: Aug. 18, 1885, Toyah, Texas

MORRISON, RAY - Assassinated; B. W. EDGALL (Editor) chg'd with others.
  Paper & date: LS Jan. 24, 1885; LS Mar. 18, 1885
  Date & place of death: last week, Vernon, Texas

MORRISON, ROBERT H. - Shot by EDWARD COLDWELL; came to N. M. 6 mos. ago
    from Gainesville, Texas
  Paper & date: LS May 23, 1883; RGR May 26, 1883
  Date & place of death: May 20, 1883, San Augustin, N. M.

MOTH, THOMAS - Run over by train
  Paper & date: LS Aug. 26, 1882
  Date & place of death: Aug. 24, 1882, El Paso, Texas

MOUSER, W. of Dallas, Texas; became insane and died; young son of F. M
    MOUSER.
  Paper & date: LS Sept. 20, 1882
  Date & place of death: Sept. 15, 1882

MUCKLEROY, W. H. - Killed by J. M. and WM. GREER
  Paper & date: LS Dec. 2, 1885
  Date & place of death: Livingston, Texas

MUDD, _____ - Lynched for murder of _____ WYCKLAND
  Paper & date: EPT May 16, 1883; EPT May 17, 1883
  Date & place of death: May 15, 1883, Monterrey, Mexico

MULGROVE, MARTIN - Murdered
  Paper & date: LS May 16, 1883
  Date & place of death: near Corsicana, Texas

MULICK, ALFRED of Big Spring, Texas; inflammation of the brain.
  Paper & date: LS Feb. 24, 1883
  Date & place of death: Feb. 23, 1883, El Paso, Texas

MULLEN, LOUIS A. - Editor; sudden
  Paper & date: LS Aug. 13, 1884
  Date & place of death: Aug. 6, 1884, Yuma, Ariz.

MULLER, Dr. of Washington, Texas (or MOELLER); shot and killed by Con-
    stable ALF GEE; old feud; a dentist
  Paper & date: LS Jan. 28, 1882
  Date & place of death: recently

MULLER, Miss ELVINA - age 65; suicide by strychnine
  Paper & date: LS May 2, 1885
  Date & place of death: Apr. 25, 1885, San Antonio, Texas

MULLIGAN, JIM - Stabbed; a song and dance man who had appeared at Coli-
    seum some time ago
  Paper & date: LS Apr. 8, 1882
  Date & place of death: recently, Denver, Colo.

MUNCEY, ALEXANDER M. (A.?)
  Paper & date: LS Nov. 26, 1884
  Date & place of death: Nov. 23, 1884, San Antonio, Texas

MUNGER, Miss NELLIE of Las Cruces, N. M.
  Paper & date: LS Jan. 17, 1883
  Date & place of death: a few days ago, South Fork, Lincoln co., N. M.

MUNOZ, MANUEL L. - Lawyer
  Paper & date: EPT Oct. 21, 1885
  Date & place of death: last week, Velazquez, Chihuahua, Mexico

MURCHISON, MATTIE - Negro; HENRY, negro, to be hung Nov. 13, 1885 for her
    murder.

MURCHISON (cont'd)
    Paper & date: LS Oct. 17, 1885
    Date & place of death: Crockett co., Texas

MURPHY, _____ Struck by lightening; surv.: wife
    Paper & date: LS Feb. 7, 1883; LS Feb. 10, 1883
    Date & place of death: last week, near Huntsville, Texas

MURPHY, E. F. - Injured Oct. 26; later died
    Paper & date: EPDH Jan. 20, 1884
    Date & place of death: Nov. 25, 1883, Mex. Cen. R. R., Mexico

MURPHY, E. H. - Heart disease; gentile of Salt Lake City, Utah & Calif.
    Paper & date: LS May 24, 1884

MURPHY, JAMES _ Murder; a miner in Mexico
    Paper & date: LS July 26, 1882
    Date & place of death: recently, San Antonio, Sonoro, Mexico

MURPHY, JNO. - Suicide
    Paper & date: LS Feb. 14, 1885
    Date & place of death: Ft. Worth, Texas

MURPHY, LEE - Shot by BILL BLACKMAN, a negro
    Paper & date: LS Dec. 19, 1885
    Date & place of death: near Belden, Texas

MURPHY, NED - Probably by Apaches
    Paper & date: EPT Sept. 29, 1884
    Date & place of death: recently, mtns. 300 mi. beyond Chihuahua, Mex.

MURRAY, PETER "LAUGHING PETE" - Brakeman; rail accident; bur. El Paso,
    Texas; mo. in Boston, Mass.
    Paper & date: EPT June 17, 1885; EPT June 18, 1885
    Date & place of death: June 16, 1885, near Sanderson, Texas

MYER, _____ - Child; fa.: Mr. MYER
    Paper & date: EPT July 24, 1883
    Date & place of death: July 22, 1883, El Paso, Texas

MYERS, GEORGE of Missouri
    Paper & date: LS Feb. 14, 1885
    Date & place of death: Las Vegas, N. M.

NACK, CHARLES - Thrown from horse probably fatal
    Paper & date: LS July 11,1885
    Date & place of death: Silver City, N. M.

NANA, Chief - Killed by Maj. DAVIS' command; dispatch says Lt. DAY killed
    Nana and 2 others, Aug. 18, 1885
    Paper & date: EPT Aug. 20, 1885; BU Aug. 22, 1885
    Date & place of death: Aug. 7, 1885, 200 mi. into Mex. (Makavi, Mex.)

NAPIER, C. G.
    Paper & date: EPDH Nov. 22, 1882
    Date & place of death: few days ago, Laredo, Texas

NASH, TETE - 14 yr. old boy; thrown from horse
    Paper & date: LS Aug. 15, 1883
    Date & place of death: Kaufman, Texas

NAVARRO, FRANCISCO - Stabbed
    Paper & date: LS Apr. 8, 1885
    Date & place of death: Brownsville, Texas

NAVARRO, Mrs. JESUS - Stabbed by husband
    Paper & date: LS Oct. 21, 1885
    Date & place of death: Huntsville, Texas

NEAL, JOHN A. - of Boston, Mass.; murdered and robbed; bros. in Mass.
   Paper & date: EPT May 4, 1883
   Date & place of death: (Okla.) Ind. Terr. on ranch of Kans. City
   Cattle Co.

NEELY, W. L. - Shot by a boy
   Paper & date: LS Nov. 12, 1884
   Date & place of death: Nov. 7, 1884, Ft. Worth, Texas

NEGGLI (NIGGLI?), FERDINAND - Shot by Sheriff THUMM
   Paper & date: LS Sept. 5, 1885
   Date & place of death: Castroville, Texas

NEGRO BILL (Negro) - Shot by masked men - will probably die
   Paper & date: EPMS Dec. 14, 1884
   Date & place: Baird, Texas

NEILL, _____ - Little boy; accidentally shot by nurse; fa.: Co. Atty.
   G. F. NEILL.
   Paper & date: EPDH Dec. 28, 1881
   Date & place of death: Dec. 9, 1881, El Paso, Texas

NEIS, KATIE
   Paper & date: LS Mar. 7, 1883
   Date & place of death: last week in Albuquerque, N. M.

NELBEY(?), WILLIAM - Shot - mysterious circumstances
   Paper & date: LS Jan. 16, 1884
   Date & place of death: Las Vegas, N. M.

NELSON, JOHN D. - Dty. Sher. of Kerr co., Texas; shot by TOM BAKER
   Paper & date: LS Nov. 22, 1882
   Date & place of death: last week

NELSON, MARTIN -(from Nebraska 4 yrs. ago); shot down after murdering 8
   people.
   Paper & date: LS May 9, 1885
   Date & place of death: May 5, 1885, Bonito, New Mexico

NELSON, N. - Suicide by morphine
   Paper & date: LS July 18, 1883
   Date & place of death: Burnet, Texas

NELSON, PETER - Shot by MARTIN NELSON (no relation)
   Paper & date: LS May 9, 1885
   Date & place of death: May 5, 1885, Bonito, New Mexico

NERISICKS, Sister M. (of Sisters of Loretto at Mora, N. M.); pneumonia
   Paper & date: LS Mar. 14, 1885
   Date & place of death: Mar. 9, 1885, Las Vegas, N. M.

NERO, JOE (Negro) - Shot in head by TOM MARSHALL. Native of Indianapolis,
   Ind.; ordained Las Vegas, N. M. last year.
   Paper & date: LS Jan. 12, 1884
   Date & place of death: Marshall, Texas

NESMITH, GEORGE W.,his wife and adopted daughter - Murdered - bodies were
   found on an unfrequented prairie between Las Cruces and Tularosa, N.M.
   RUPERTO LARA, whose friend was MAXIMO APODACA. LARA & APODACA have
   confessed. GEORGE W. NESMITH (of Tularosa) and wife LUCY NEWCOMB NEW-
   SMITH of Franklin, N. C., m. ca 30 June 1868. Quoted from Santa Fe,
   New Mexican June 30, 1868. PAT COGHLAN arrested for complicity.
   Paper & date: RGR Mar. 21, 1885; RGR Apr. 4, 1885; RGR Nov. 27, 1886;
   BU May 5, 1885
   Date & place of death: Sept. 1882

NEWSMITH, LUCY NEWCOMB - Murdered; (see record of GEORGE W. NESMITH, her
   husband)
   Paper & date: RGR Mar. 21, 1885; RGR Nov. 27, 1886
   Date & place of death: Sept. 1882, near Tularosa, N. M.

121

NETTLETON, Mrs. M. C. - hus. and ch.
    Paper & date: LS Dec. 30, 1885
    Date & place of death: Dec. 26, 1885, Albuquerque, N. M.

NEUENDORF, Judge MAX - Sudden - suicide by poison suspected.
    Paper & date: LS Nov. 11, 1885
    Date & place of death: San Antonio, Texas

NEVAREZ, G. - aged 13; congestive fever; uncle: MANUEL NEVAREZ
    Paper & date: RGR June 1884
    Date & place of death: June 8, 1884

NEVARES, Mrs. JULIANA - age 65; hus.: FELIPE NEVARES; br.-in-law: MANUEL
    NEVARES.
    Paper & date: RGR Nov. 3, 1883
    Date & place of death: Oct. 31, 1883

NEVAREZ, Mrs. MANUEL - Lingering illness; hus.; blind dau. aged 18
    Paper & date: RGR June 2, 1883
    Date & place of death: Thurs.

NEVAREZ, Dona PETRA - hus.: Don RAMON NEVAREZ
    Paper & date: RGR June 21, 1884
    Date & place of death: June 14, 1884, Las Cruces, New Mexico

NEW, J. N. - Shot by JOHN S. NEEL (NEAL), aged 17, who is being held by
    Sher. POE of Lincoln co.
    Paper & date: LS July 11, 1883; RGR July 14, 1883
    Date & place of death: June 19, 1883, Lincoln co., N. M.

NEWALL, HALL - Shot by BUCK ROBINSON
    Paper & date: LS Feb. 18, 1885
    Date & place of death: Howard's Canyon on North Concho, 60 mi. from
    San Angelo, Texas

NEWBERRY, Dr. _____ - Son of Prof. NEWBERRY of Columbia College (Univ.)
    Paper & date: EPDH Feb. 15, 1882
    Date & place of death: Feb. 10, 1882, Corralitos, Mexico

NEWMAN, FANNIE M. - (young girl age 17) - lingering illness at home of
    EZEKIEL S. NEWMAN, uncle; bur. St. Louis, Mo.; par.: Hon. H. L. and
    SALLIE M. NEWMAN and sis., all of St. Louis, Mo.
    Paper & date: LS Mar. 5, 1884; EPDH Mar. 9, 1884
    Date & place of death: Mar. 4, 1884, El Paso, Texas

NEWMAN, LILLIAN - (6 mo, 17 days) - Inflammation of the bowels; par.: S.
    H. & JESSE NEWMAN
    Paper & date: LS Aug. 4, 1883
    Date & place of death: Aug. 1, 1883, El Paso, Texas

NEWMAN, Miss MYRA in New York City; pneumonia; par.: HENRY L. & SALLIE E.
    NEWMAN of St. Louis; uncles and aunts in El Paso: E. S. NEWMAN, G. T.
    NEWMAN, LUCY AUSTIN, Mrs. C. R. MOREHEAD.
    Paper & date: LS Oct. 4, 1882
    Date & place of death: Oct. 1, 1882

NEWMAN, Dr. S. T. - age 67; native of Miss.; bur.: Bellefontaine Cemetery
    at St. Louis; Surv.: wife, 6 children, 6 gr-children; oldest son died
    4 yrs. ago; son S. H. NEWMAN of El Paso, Texas.m. 1839.
    Paper & date: LS July 18 & 28, 1883
    Date & place of death: July 11, 1883, St. Louis, Missouri

NEWMAN, TOMMY - 3½ yrs. old; fall from wagon; par.: M/M G. T. NEWMAN;
    second child; bur.: May 29 in Concordia Cemetery
    Paper & date: LS May 28, 1884
    Date & place of death: May 27, 1884, Antelope Springs Ranch

NEWTON, Mrs. SAM - Murdered by hus. SAM NEWTON, Choctaw Indian
    Paper & date: LS Nov. 7, 1885
    Date & place of death: Ind. Terr.

NEWTON, Col. - (formerly of Marshall, Texas); Col., wife and two ch. all
    murdered at their ranch in Western Texas by Indians. He was formerly
    a merchant and druggist.
    Paper & date: LS Dec. 6, 1882
    Date & place of death: a few days ago

NICHOLS, AL. - Shot by ZACK FOSTER
    Paper & date: LS Apr. 15, 1885
    Date & place of death: near Palestine, Texas

NICHOLS, JAMES M.
    Paper & date: LS Oct. 31, 1885
    Date & place of death: Santa Fe, N. M.

NICHOLS, JOHN - V. P. City National Bank; dropped dead while opening safe
    Paper & date: LS Aug. 22, 1885
    Date & place of death: Ft. Worth, Texas

NICHOLS, WILLIAM of Dallas, Texas; killed on train by CHARLES K. ADAMS
    of Carrolton, Ill.
    Paper & date: EPT May 6, 1883
    Date & place of death: May 4, 1883, near Montrose, Mo.

NICHOLSON, Mrs. INDIA L. - bro.: Sher. _____ WHITE of El Paso, Texas
    Paper & date: EPT May 10, 1885
    Date & place of death: May 5, 1885, Petersburg, Va.

NINOS, REFUGIO - Exposure and old age; bur. as a pauper
    Paper & date: LS Mar. 4, 1882
    Date & place of death: 3 days before

NIXON, MILTON V. - Friend of JOHN SUTTON who eloped with wife of JOHN
    JAMES - Nixon and Sutton killed by settlers.
    Paper & date: LS July 30, 1884; RGR July 26, 1884
    Date & place of death: July 16, 1884, Lincoln co., New Mexico

NIXON, WM. -(Negro) - to die for murder in Indian Territory
    Paper & date: EPT Feb. 1, 1885
    Date & place of death: Apr. 7, 1885, Ft. Smith, Arkansas

NODINE, GEORGE - Accident - shot by JOHN W. SCOTT - bear hunting; wife &
    family of Pueblo Springs, N. M.
    Paper & date: BU July 25, 1885; BU Aug. 1, 1885
    Date & place of death: few days ago, Mogollon Mtns., N. M.

NOLAN, JOHN - Drowned in 10 inches of water while drunk
    Paper & date: LS June 27, 1883
    Date & place of death: Houston, Texas

NOLAN, Maj. NICHOLAS - 3rd Cav.; wife through El Paso going east; he was
    commanding officer of Ft. Apache, Ariz.
    Paper & date: LS Oct. 31, 1883; LS Nov. 3, 1883
    Date & place of death: .....

NOONAN, MIKE - Killed by Indians
    Paper & date: EPT Oct. 10, 1885
    Date & place of death: Dragoon Mtns., Cochise co., Ariz.

NORMAN, ORLOF - Wounded on Sunday, Oct. 10, in Albuquerque, N. M.; d. of
    the wounds; accidently shot by DANA COBB, Wells Fargo agent; bullet
    went thru a thin partition and wounded innocent bystander. Son: WILLIE
    NORMAN, clerk in store of J. SCHUTZ, El Paso, Texas; dau.: Mrs. DAVIS
    of Las Cruces, N. M.
    Paper & date: LS Oct. 15, 1881
    Date & place of death: after Oct. 10 and before Oct. 15, 1881

NORMAN, WILLIAM
    Paper & date: LS Sept. 27, 1884
    Date & place of death: Seeley Mine at Blossburg, N. M.

NORRIS, J. W. of Rice, Texas; murder by 2 strangers. Postmaster of Rice.
    Paper & date: LS Mar. 1, 1882
    Date & place of death: Feb. 21, 1882

NORRIS, W. C. - Shot by GEORGE COLLINS, (known as "Shotgun" COLLINS).
    Paper & date: LS Feb. 4, 1885
    Date & place of death: Montrose

NORVELL, W. R. - Murder by SHOCK COLDWELL - executed at McKinney, Texas,
    Aug. 18, 1882
    Paper & date: LS Aug. 23, 1882
    Date & place of death: 1880

NOWLAN, Maj. ____ - fever last week.
    Paper & date: EPT Nov. 4, 1883
    Date & place of death: Holbrook, Ariz.

NOYES, FRANK S. - bro.: ED administrator, Raton, N. M.
    Paper & date: LS July 11, 1885
    Date & place of death: ....

NUNEZ, CLATO - powder exploded.
    Paper & date: EPDH Aug. 2, 1882
    Date & place of death: July 19, 1882 near Del Rio, Texas

NYE, TOM or NIGH, T. P.- (Ranger); shootout with Sher. JNO. P. MORRIS.
    Paper & date: LS Aug. 22, 1885; EPT Aug. 20 & 26, 1885
    Date & place of death: Aug. 18, 1885 Toyah, Texas

OBERSCHELP, G. -(German) - Run over by cars.
    Paper & date: LS Mar. 11, 1882
    Date & place of death: Mar. 6, 1882 Brenham, Texas

O'BOYLY, W. C. of Silver King, Ariz.; killed by NED FALES.
    Paper & date: EPT Sept. 5, 1884
    Date & place of death: Pinal, Ariz.

O'BRIEN, _____ -(girl) - Suicide, over disappointed love; fa.: Dr. J. F.
    O'BRIEN
    Paper & date: LS Mar. 8, 1882
    Date & place of death: Mar. 1, 1882-of Salado, Bell co., Texas

O'BRIEN, _____ of Alleyton, Texas
    Paper & date: LS Sept. 20, 1884
    Date & place of death: Sept. 14, 1884 aboard passenger train.

O'BRIEN, MACK - Killed by bro.-in-law FRANK HYLES.
    Paper & date: LS Nov. 25, 1882
    Date & place of death: Nov. 20, 1882 Hico, Texas

OBSIECHT, GEORGE - age 99; soldier under NAPOLEON I (BONAPARTE); Mason
    since 1814.
    Paper & date: LS Jan. 14, 1882
    Date & place of death: Jan. 5, 1882 Fredricburg, Texas.

OCHOA, _____ - Killed by Indians.
    Paper & date: EPT June 12, 1885
    Date & place of death: June 10, 1885 near Bisbee, Ariz.

OCHOA, _____ - Killed by _____ SILVA.
    Paper & date: LS Nov. 5, 1884; EPT Nov. 3, 1884
    Date & place of death: Nov. 2, 1884 Paso del Norte, Mexico.

OCHOA, ANTONIO - Former Gov. of Chihuahua.
    Paper & date: EPT July 17, 1883
    Date & place of death: July 13, 1883 Chihuahua, Mexico

O'CONNELL, _____ - Murder. Rancher.
    Paper & date: LS Mar. 29, 1882 D/P: on Gila River, N. M. or Ariz.

O'CONNELL, EUGENE, (Irish exile) - Shot Saturday night.
    Paper & date: EPT Apr. 2, 1881
    Date & place of death: Mar. 31, 1881 El Paso, Texas

O'CONNOR, Mrs. _____ - gave birth to triplets recently.
    Paper & date: LS Nov. 7, 1885
    Date & place: Austin, Texas

O'CONNOR, JOHN -Shot by JOB O'BRIEN;probably fatal.
    Paper & date: EPT Apr. 16, 1883
    Date & place: near Leon, Texas

ODELL, Mrs. WALTER
    Paper & date: LS Apr. 26, 1884
    Date & place of death: Mar. 25, 1884 Stapleton, Staten Island

ODGERS, HENRY - Former resident of Silver City - accidentally shot by
    shotgun in his wagon.
    Paper & date: LS Nov. 19, 1884
    Date & place of death: between Silver Cliff, Col. & Silver City, N.M.

O'DONNELL, _____ - Murdered by YOUNG bros.
    Paper & date: EPT Oct. 6, 1883
    Date & place of death: Nov. 1878 Tilden?, Texas

OGLESBY, _____ - Murdered - possibly by ARTHUR LORD.
    Paper & date: LS Apr. 16, 1884
    Date & place of death: Jones Co., Texas?

OGLESBY, Sher. _____ - Rumored killed by maurauding Mexican Nat'ls.
    Paper & date: EPT Feb. 12, 1885
    Date & place of death: Dimmitt Co., Texas

OHLSEN, OLE - Found dead by JESUS SERNA beside trail 4 miles above town-
    motive robbery.
    Paper & date: RGR July 5, 1884
    Date & place of death: Rincon, N. M.

OHLSON, CHARLES - Killed by F. MATCHET (?) in self-defense.
    Paper & date: EPT Oct. 4, 1884
    Date & place of death: Sept. 29, 1884 Houston, Texas

O'KEEFE, PAT -Found dead.
    Paper & date: LS July 28, 1883
    Date & place of death: 25 mi. No. of Santa Fe, N. M.

OLGUIN, BERNARDO (nearly 75 yrs. old) - Pneumonia after falling from
    train. Pueblo Indian Chief. Indian Scout - bro.SIMON was, too. Bro.
    killed by VICTORIO's band about 2 yrs. ago.
    Paper & date: LS Apr. 11, 1883; EPT Apr. 12, 1883; EPDH Apr. 22, 1883
    Date & place of death: Apr. 10, 1883 Ysleta, Texas

OLGUIN, NEMECIO of Socorro, Texas - run over by train; age 18.
    Paper & date: LS Aug. 15, 1883; EPDH Aug. 19, 1883
    Date & place of death: Aug. 14, 1883 Ysleta, Texas

OLIVER, JOHN M. - Shot by posse while resisting arrest for murder.
    Paper & date: LS Mar. 11, 1885
    Date & place of death: few days ago, Chickasaw Nation, Ind. T. Okla.

OLNEY, SAMUEL - Feared dead.
    Paper & date: LS Aug. 8, 1883
    Date & place: of Silver City, N. M.

O'MEARA, THOMAS - Congestion of brain. Found June 4, 1883.
    Paper & date: EPT June 9, 1883
    Date & place of death: At a deadfall of the Mole, Mex.

O'NEAL, HENRY - Oldest Amer. inhabitant.
    P/D: LS Sept. 8, 1883   D/P: Sept. 4, 1883 Santa Fe, N. M.

O'NEAL, WM. - Beaten on Nov. 4, 1884 by _____ GRADY - later died.
    Paper & date: LS Nov. 22, 1884
    Date & place of death: Houston, Texas

ORD, Gen. E. G. O. - Yellow fever; dau.: REBECCA.
    Paper & date: EPT July 24, 1883; EPT Dec. 4, 1885
    Date & place of death: July 22, 1883 Havana, Cuba

O'REAR, TOMMY (infant) Par.: M/M GEO. O'REAR.
    Paper & date: BU Apr. 1, 1884
    Date & place of death: Mar. 16, 1884 Socorro, N. M.

ORELA, QUINTO - Killed by Indians.
    Paper & date: EPT Sept. 16, 1885
    Date & place of death: Sept. 13, 1885 near Lake Valley, N. M.

ORMSBY, WILLIAM B. - Suicide by morphine. Wife & 5 ch.
    Paper & date: LS Sept. 29, 1883; EPT Sept. 26, 1883
    Date & place of death: Sept. 25, 1883 Socorro, N. M.

ORRANTIA, IGNACIO - DOLORES P. ORRANTIA, adm. of estate.
    Paper & date: LS Aug. 20, 1884; RGR Sept. 6, 1884
    Date & place of death: Aug. 18, 1884 Chamberino, N. M.

ORTEGA, PEDRO - Murdered by CELSO GRIJALVA.
    Paper & date: EPT June 21, 1884
    Date & place of death: June 20, 1884 Phoenix, Ariz.

ORTIZ, Mrs. ANNA MARIA of Santa Fe, N. M.
    Paper & date: LS Nov. 19, 1881
    Date & place of death: Nov. 13, 1881

ORWIG, CALVIN (ED.) - killed by Indians;GERONIMO's band;surv.by wife.
    Paper & date: EPT May 24, 1885; BU Dec. 17, 1887
    Date & place of death: May 22, 1885 near Silver City, N. M.

OTERO, _____ dau.; fa.: FELIX OTERO.
    Paper & date: BU Oct. 17, 1885
    Date & place of death: Oct. 1885 Cuba, N. M.

OTERO, MANUEL   - a wealthy Mexican.
    Paper & date: LS Mar. 4, 1882
    Date & place of death: Feb. 25, 1882 Valencia co., N. M.

OTERO, MANUAL B.- murder. JAMES G. WHITNEY acquitted Apr. 30, 1884 -
    self-defense.
    Paper & date: LS May 3, 1884; LS Aug. 22, 1883; EPT Aug. 21, 1883
    Date & place: Punta de Agua, Valencia, N. M.

OTERO, SANTIAGO - age 83.
    Paper & date: LS Sept. 6, 1884
    Date & place of death: Aug. 29, 1884 San Miguel co., N. M.

O'TOOL, _____ - Fell over 150 ft. bluff.
    Paper & date: LS Jan. 14, 1882
    Date & place of death: Jan. 7, 1882 near San Antonio, Texas

O'TOOLE, _____- Killed - supposed accident in trying to resist officers.
    fa.: of Carlisle, N. M.
    Paper & date: EPMS Dec. 14, 1884
    Date & place of death: Carlisle, N. M.

OTT, PETER - Bursting of an over-loaded gun.
    Paper & date: LS July 18, 1883; RGR July 14, 1883
    Date & place of death: Recently, Silver City, N. M.

OVERSTREET, Rev. Mr. _____-Murdered by _____ WILLIAMS.
    Paper & date: LS Dec. 19, 1885
    Date & place of death: Texas

OVERTON, _____ Infant boy; horses ran away throwing the family from the buggy. Par.: M/M WILLIAM OVERTON; gr.-mo.: Mrs. WILLICK, mo. of Mrs. OVERTON.
Paper & date: EPMS Dec. 17, 1884
Date & place of death: Dec. 8, 1884 near Dallas, Texas

OWEN, AGNES HELEN (Inf. dau.)-age 6 mo. 20 days. Mo.: the late AGNES HELEN OWEN; Fa.: O. DARWIN OWEN.
Paper & date: LS Oct. 17, 1885
Date & place of death: Oct. 17, 1885 El Paso, Texas

OWEN, Mrs. AGNES HELEN - age 27 - puerperal peritonitis; Hus.: O'DARWIN OWEN; sis.: Miss BESSIE CAIRNS; dau.: AGNES HELEN
Paper & date: LS Apr. 8, 1885; EPT Apr. 9, 1885
Date & place of death: Apr. 8, 1885 El Paso, Texas

OWEN, ARNET R.
Paper & date: LS Apr. 11, 1883
Date & place of death: Apr. 7, 1883 Albuquerque, N. M.

OWEN, EXILIA (EMILIA?) - only child; Par.: W. G. & NELLIE OWEN. Notice to Richmond, Va. & Danville, Ill.
Paper & date: EPT Aug. 8, 1884
Date & place of death: Aug. 8, 1884 El Paso, Texas

OWEN, Judge J. L. of Nacogdoches, Texas; falling of a tree.
Paper & date: LS Mar. 4, 1882
Date & place of death: Feb. 14, 1882

OWEN, Capt. R. - B. F. PASCHALL chg'd with murder.
Paper & date: LS Feb. 21, 1885
Date & place of death: Denton?, Texas

OWENS, _____ - Young man; consumption
Paper & date: LS June 20, 1885
Date & place of death: CLINE's Ranch, Lincoln co., N. M.

OWENS, Mrs. CALLIA - burned.
Paper & date: LS Nov. 15, 1884
Date & place of death: Nov. 10, 1884 near Waco, Texas

OWENS, CASEY (female) - Beaten by MAUD RAYNOR, female desperado of Texas & Indian Territory.
Paper & date: LS Jan. 21, 1885
Date & place: Abilene, Texas

OWENS, P. B. - Murdered by R. P. MUSICK.
Paper & date: LS Dec. 19, 1885
Date & place of death: of Rusk, Texas

OWENS, TOMMY (mail carrier) - Killed by Indians.
Paper & date: EPDH Oct. 5, 1881
Date & place of death: Sept. 1881 near Camp Apache, Ariz.

PACHECO, CRECENCIO - Adm. SABINA de PACHECO & JUAN D. PACHECO.
Paper & date: BU May 12, 1885
Date & place of death: Sabinal, N. M.

PACHECO, SAVAS - Shot.
Paper & date: LS Nov. 3, 1883
Date & place of death: Oct. 31, 1883 Tucson, Ariz.

PADILLA, EDDIE - Funeral today, Aug. 11, 1883, from residence of Capt. VAN PATTEN.
Paper & date: RGR Aug. 11, 1883
Date & place of death:.......

PADILLO, JACINTO - to be shot for wrecking & robbing train in Nov. 1883
Paper & date: EPT Aug. 13, 1885
Date & place of death: Nuevo Laredo, Mex.

127

PADILLA, LEANDRO - Killed by train.
    Paper & date: LS Oct. 3, 1885
    Date & place of death: Sept. 29, 1885 near Las Vegas, N. M.

PAGE, W. M. of El Paso, Tex. shot by _____ CARR in self defense. Bro.:
    R. M. PAGE of East Texas.
    Paper & date: LS May 30, 1883; EPT June 26, 1883
    Date & place of death: May 27, 1883 San Augustin, N. M.

PALMER, P. - Murdered by Apaches. Of Sonora.
    Paper & date: RGR June 27, 1885
    Date & place of death: recently

PALMER, Dr. RALPH - Suicide
    Paper & date: LS Nov. 12, 1884
    Date & place of death: Nov. 6, 1884 Gila Bend, Ariz.

PARKER, JACK - Pneumonia. Young man from Llano co., Texas. Texas Rang-
    er.
    Paper & date: LS Mar. 15, 1882
    Date & place of death: Mar. 14, 1882 El Paso co., Texas

PARKER, PAT (negro) age 125.
    Paper & date: LS Dec. 16, 1885
    Date & place of death: Dallas Co. Poor Farm, Texas

PARHAM or PARKHAM, _____ - ELPIJO BACA chgd. with killing.
    Paper & date: LS May 13, 1885
    Date & place of death: last fall, San Francisco, Socorro co., N. M.

PARKS, GEORGE - Engineer on Rio Grande R. R.; family in Hornellsville,
    New York.
    Paper & date: EPT Sept. 15, 1883
    Date & place of death: Sept. 14, 1883 Douglass, Colo.

PARKS, M/M HENRY - Murdered.
    Paper & date: EPT Aug. 20, 1884
    Date & place of death: on Big Creek, Ind. Terr. (Okla.)

PARSONS, _____ - Suicide.
    Paper & date: LS Jan. 24, 1883
    Date & place of death: Jan. 16, 1883 Lordsburg, N. M.

PARTEIL (PURTELL), JOHNNY - Indian massacre by COCHISE. See MILLS, ____
    bro. of Maj. MILLS.
    Paper & date: EPT Jan. 20, 1887
    Date & place of death: June 1860 Cook's Peak, Grant co., N. M.

PATRICK, JAMES M. of Sturgeon, Mo. - age 27; sick and deranged; disap-
    peared - believed dead. Mo.: Mrs. SARAH PATRICK, Sturgeon, Mo.
    Paper & date: LS Feb. 6, 1884
    Date & place of death: Mar. 1882 between Las Cruces, N. M. and Kan-
    sas City, Mo.

PATRICK, REUBEN - Killed by bro. SID over ownership of dog.
    Paper & date: NTF June 18, 1881
    Date & place of death: Georgetown, Colo.

PATRON, JUAN B. - Shot by MITCHELL MANEY son of Judge MANEY, Pearsall,
    Tex.; CRESENCIANO, bro.-in-law.
    Paper & date: LS Apr. 16, 1884; EPMS Dec. 10, 1884
    Date & place of death: Apr. 9, 1884 Puerta De Luna, N. M.

PATTON, JAMES - Run over by train.
    Paper & date: EPMS Dec. 13, 1884
    Date & place of death: Texarkana, Texas

PATTON, JOHN S. - Permission granted to his sons (JOHN F. & FELIPE S.
    PATTON) to move body from graveyard at Mesilla, N. M. to Masonic ceme-
    tery near town. Funeral notice at time of his death - "He was the

PATTON (cont'd): oldest American resident in New Mexico, having come from Boone co., Mo. in 1824.
Paper & date: RGR June 27, 1885
Date & place of death: Mar. 13, 1866

PAUCLEY, _____ - Lynched for murder of WYCKLAND. Name given as PAUST also.
Paper & date: EPT May 16 & 17, 1883
Date & place of death: May 15, 1883 Monterrey, Mexico.

PAUR, ALEXANDER - Heart disease - suddenly; died far from relatives in a foreign land.
Paper & date: EPMS Jan. 4, 1885; EPT Jan. 4 & 6, 1885
Date & place of death: Jan. 3, 1885 Paso del Norte, Mexico

PAYETTE, MORGAN - Murdered by JAMES GADDIS.
Paper & date: LS Oct. 24, 1885; BU Oct. 24, 1885
Date & place of death: Oct. 13, 1885 Alma, N. M.

PAYNE, DAVID L. (Okla. "boomer") - died eating breakfast.
Paper & date: EPT Nov. 29, 1884
Date & place of death: Nov. 28, 1884 Wellington, Kansas

PEARL, WILLIAM S. - Lynched by mob for murder of JOHN DOWNEY.
Paper & date: LS Jan. 31, 1883; RGR May 10, 1884
Date & place of death: Jan. 22-24, 1883 Lincoln, N. M.

PEARSALL, _____ (little boy) - shot accidentally; fa.: J. PEARSALL.
Paper & date: LS Jan. 7, 1882
Date & place of death: Jan. 1, 1882 Carbonateville, N. M.

PEARSON, ANDY - Shot by R. B. HICKMAN.
Paper & date: LS Oct. 1, 1884
Date & place of death: Sept. 25, 1884 East Dallas, Texas

PEARSON, JAMES (stonemason) - Shot during attempted bank robbery.
Paper & date: EPT Sept. 25, 1884
Date & place of death: Sept. 24, 1884 - of Las Vegas, N. M.

PEARSON, JAMES of Kansas City - consumption; former R. R. news agent; no home or relatives.
Paper & date: BU Aug. 22, 1885
Date & place of death: Aug. 21, 1885 Socorro, N. M.

PEARSON, WILLIAM - Shot in cold blood by MARCELIUS M. COSTLY; fa. surv.
Paper & date: LS June 27, 1883
Date & place of death: Bellville, Texas

PEAS - an aged Comanche Indian; naturalized and a good democrat.
Paper & date: LS Mar. 7, 1883
Date & place of death: Feb. 28, 1883 Waco, Texas

PEASE, Mrs. GEORGE of Santa Fe, N. M. - Murder by hus.; she was his wife or mistress; hus.: GEORGE PEASE.
Paper & date: LS July 29, 1882
Date & place of death: about a year ago

PEASE, Capt. W. B. of Cabra Springs, N. M. - died in Las Vegas, N. M.; Postmaster at Cabra Springs, N. M.
Paper & date: LS Nov. 11, 1882
Date & place of death: Nov. 7, 1882

PECKHAM, _____ - Murdered - ELFEGO BACA indicted in Socorro, N. M.
Paper & date: BU Dec. 5, 1885
Date & place of death: N. M.

PEDRAZA, EUGENIO of La Mesa, N. M. - Killed for rustling by Capt. SALA-ZAR's Militiamen. El Paso locality. Age 28, 6' tall.
Paper & date: LS Feb. 28, 1883; EPDH Mar. 18, 1883
Date & place of death: Feb. 20, 1883 N. M.

PEEL, R. - Murdered; fa.: Judge B. L. PEEL.
Paper & date: EPDH May 10, 1882
Date & place of death: recently, Charleston, Ariz.

PELTETIER, Capt. ____ - bur. in New Mexico.
Paper & date: LS July 1, 1885
Date & place of death: Astor House, New York.

PENA, Srta. FAUSTINA - consumption; age 18.
Paper & date: LS Mar. 25, 1882
Date & place of death: Mar. 23, 1882 Paso del Norte, Mexico

PENDERGRAFT, PAT - Cut own throat - will probably die.
Paper & date: LS June 3, 1885
Date & place: MOLLY BROWN's house, Tyler, Texas

PENDLETON, JOHN (Constable) - Shot accidently during a quarrel. MIKE
HOUSTON, gambler, & CHAS. KEENA, bartender, quarrel at Conelio?, Tex.
(Canutillo?)
Paper & date: LS Jan. 7, 1882
Date & place of death: Dec. 26, 1881

PENROSE, JOHN - small pox.
Paper & date: RGR Jan. 12, 1884
Date & place of death: Jan. 5, 1884 Silver City, N. M.

PERDOMO, Mrs. JUANA C. (b. Havana) - aged 90 years; rel.: QUINTIN
VILLEGAS.
Paper & date: LS Feb. 7, 1885
Date & place of death: Feb. 6, 1885 Laredo, Texas

PERDUE, JAMES - age 48 (native of Indiana) - Shot by young employee LAW-
SON or Indians?; died in El Paso, Texas; fa., bro., bro.-in-law; re-
mains exhumed and sent to Paola, Kansas.
Paper & date: LS Feb. 4, 1882; EPDH Jan. 28, 1883
Date & place of death: Feb. 2, 1882

PEREA, JOSE LEANDRO
Paper & date: LS Apr. 7, 1883
Date & place of death: Apr. 2, 1883 Bernalillo, N. M.

PEREZ, ____ - boy; mortally wounded in shootout between GUS KREMPKAU,
JOHN HALE, GEO. CAMPBELL & DALLAS STOUDENMIRE.
Paper & date: EPDH Dec. 28, 1881
Date & place of death: Apr. 17, 1881 El Paso, Texas

PEREZ, Dona BERNABE (BESARBE) - Mystery surrounding death; hus. deserted
her 3 years ago; she had belonged to a good native family.
Paper & date: LS Feb. 18, 1885; RGR Feb. 16, 1885
Date & place of death: Feb. 8, 1885 Las Cruces, N. M.

PEREZ, MANUEL - Beaten by JOSEPH WILSON & HARRY MORGAN in jail.
Paper & date: LS Dec. 29, 1883; LS Jan. 2, 1884
Date & place of death: Jan. 1, 1884 El Paso, Texas

PERKINS, FRANKLIN SHARON - age 4; par. surv.
Paper & date: EPT June 17, 1885; SH June 21, 1885
Date & place of death: June 16, 1885 El Paso, Texas

PETERS, P. H. (Mayor) - Consumption.
Paper & date: LS Oct. 6, 1883
Date & place of death: Sherman, Texas

PETERSON, F. M. (mail carrier)
Paper & date: EPT July 29, 1885
Date & place of death: few days ago near Harshaw, Ariz.

PETRIE, ____ - of Black Range Cattle Co.; killed by Indians.
Paper & date: EPT Sept. 29, 1885
Date & place of death: N. Mex.

PETRY, GEORGE of Wills Point, Texas; murdered by JOHN WHETSTONE, noted
    desperado.
    Paper & date: LS Jan. 21, 1882
    Date & place of death: 1862

PETRIKEN, Maj. _____ - Killed by savages.
    Paper & date: EPDH Nov. 8, 1882
    Date & place of death: ....

PETTY, M/M JOSEPH - Indians murdered them and carried off their 3 child-
    ren - 2 girls and a boy aged respectively 13, 11 and 8; children
    found butchered.
    Paper & date: LS Nov. 22, 1884; SH Nov. 23, 1884; EPT Nov. 24, 1884
    Date & place of death: near Pena Colorado, Presidio co., Texas

PFAHL, MARTIN - Became lost; body found; disappeared 15 days ago; well-
    to-do rancher near Sargesa, 50 mi. No. of Ft. Davis, Texas.
    Paper & date: EPT Feb. 24, 1885; EPDH July 13, 1884
    Date & place of death: June 1884 Eagle Mtns. near Sierra Blanca, Tex.

PFEIFFER, HENRY - Lynched.
    Paper & date: LS Jan. 2, 1884
    Date & place of death: Dec. 25, 1883 McDade, Texas

PFITZMAIER, GEORGE - Struck over head and robbed. MARQUES RAMIRES chg'd.
    Paper & date: LS Mar. 28, 1885; EPT Mar. 28, 1885
    Date & place of death: Mar. 26, 1885 El Paso, Texas

PHELAN, JAMES - Dead in bed.
    Paper & date: LS Nov. 12, 1884
    Date & place of death: Nov. 6, 1884 Virginia City, Nev.

PHILIBERT, Mrs. ANNIE - hus.: PAUL PHILIBERT formerly of N. Mex.
    Paper & date: BU May 1, 1883
    Date & place of death: Parsons, Kans.

PHILIPS, _____ family - butchered by GERONIMO's band.
    Paper & date: EPT June 4, 1885
    Date & place of death: near Silver City, N. M.

PHILLIPS, _____ 4 yr. old child - drowned; fa.: WARNER PHILLIPS.
    Paper & date: EPT Mar. 22, 1885
    Date & place of death: Ysleta, Texas

PHILLIPS, Mrs. JAMES (ELLA) - outraged and murdered; hus. and son.
    Paper & date: LS Dec. 30, 1885; EPT Dec. 27, 1885
    Date & place of death: Dec. 25, 1885 Austin, Tex.

PHILLIPS, JAMES - Murder - is dying; Mo.: Mrs. Phillips.
    Paper & date: EPT Dec. 27, 1885
    Date & place: Austin, Tex.

PHILLIPS, WENDELL
    Paper & date: RGR Feb. 9, 1884
    Date & place of death: recently

PHILLIPS, WM. - to die for murder in Indian Terr. (Okla.)
    Paper & date: EPT Feb. 1, 1885
    Date & place of death: Apr. 7, 1885 Ft. Smith, Ark.

PICKETT, Gov. E. B. - C. S. A. Col. in Texas politics; born in Tenn.
    Paper & date: LS Jan. 25, 1882
    Date & place of death: Jan. 20, 1882 Liberty, Tex.

PICKETT, NELLIE of Ft. Summer, N. M. - died naturally, apparently mis-
    tress of "Billy the Kid".
    Paper & date: LS Aug. 23, 1882
    Date & place of death: last week

PICKETT, ROBERT - Killed by PHILLIP GATES.
Paper & date: LS May 9, 1885
Date & place of death: last week Atascosa co., Texas

PICKETT, TOM (gambler) - Shot by FRANK TARBELL, recently of Silver City, N. M.
Paper & date: LS Feb. 14, 1885
Date & place of death: Camp Thomas, Ariz.

PIERCE, FRANK - Fell off train near Pearsall Station. Brakeman on International & Great Northern.
Paper & date: LS Jan. 4, 1882
Date & place of death: recently

PIERCE, Col. THOMAS W. of Boston - apoplexy. Pres. of Galveston, Harrisburg & San Antonio R. R. Property owner in El Paso, Texas. Bro.: ANDREW PIERCE of San Antonio, Texas. 2 children (minors); nephew: THOMAS W. PIERCE, JR. of El Paso, Texas. IVORY W. M. PIERCE claims to be son of JULIA WILLIAMSON who m. Col. PIERCE Jan. 1, 1839 in New Hampshire.
Paper & date: EPT Oct. 6, 23, 28, 1885; EPT Nov. 6, 28, 1885; EPT Dec. 31, 1885
Date & place of death: Oct. 1, 1885 Clifton Springs, N. Y.

PIERSON, Judge WM. M. - bur. Feb. 9 in El Paso, Texas. Poor health for some time. Niece (only relative), wife of Judge BEALL, of Los Angeles, Calif. and Columbus, Miss. BEALL, executor of estate (80,000 to 125,000). PIERSON had lived in El Paso since 1868. Native of Western Virginia. Age 61.
Paper & date: LS Feb. 7, 10, 1883; EPDH Feb. 11, 1883
Date & place of death: Feb. 5, 1883 Hot Springs, Ark.

PILKERSON, FRANK - Dragged to death by his horse.
Paper & date: LS July 21, 1883
Date & place of death: Mora co., N. M.

PINEDA, JESUS of Santa Tomas, N. M. - thrown from horse - badly lacerating hand - gangrene. Widow and several children.
Paper & date: RGR Nov. 24, 1883
Date & place of death: Nov. 20, 1883

PINER, JOHN - Suicide.
Paper & date: LS July 11, 1883
Date & place of death: Bonham, Texas

PIQUEMEL_, J. C. Wells Fargo Agent - typhus fever.
Paper & date: EPT June 10, 1885
Date & place of death: June 9, 1885 Guanajuato, Mex.

PITON, WILLIE - age 12; typhoid fever;died at home of B. F. HOSIER; par.: of San Antonio, Texas M/M P. L. PITON; younger bro.
Paper & date: LS Oct. 25, 1884; EPT Oct. 24 & 27, 1884
Date & place of death: Oct. 24, 1884 El Paso, Texas

PITTMAN, GEORGE (negro) - murder; arrested was DAVIS LIGHTFOOT.
Paper & date: LS Aug. 26, 1882
Date & place of death: Henderson co., Tex.

PITTS, BOB - Fight with bro. NAT PITTS.
Paper & date: LS Aug. 1, 1883
Date & place of death: Cason, Morris co., Tex.

PITTS, JAMES - Shot while escaping; wife; mo.-in-law Mrs. E. A. DRAWN.
Paper & date: LS Feb. 25, 1885; EPT Feb. 24, 1885
Date & place of death: Feb. 21, 1885 near New Braunsfel , Tex.

PITTS, NAT - Fight with bro. BOB PITTS.
Paper & date: LS Aug. 1, 1883
Date & place of death: Cason, Morris co., Tex.

PIZGODE, OTTO -slit his throat - ill health the cause.
 Paper & date: LS Aug. 18,1883
 Date & place of death: San Antonio, Texas

PLASBY, _____ _ killed in fight with _____ MAY.
 Paper & date: LS Aug. 1, 1883
 Date & place of death: near Denison, Texas

PLATT, Miss AMELIA aka AMY NELSON - prima dona; fever; par.: in San Fran-
 cisco, Calif.; fa. built Platt Opera House in San Francisco.
 Paper &' date: EPT Sept. 15 & 18, 1883
 Date & place of death: Sept. 11, 1883, Silver City, N. M.

POLK, JAMES K. - runaway team.
 Paper & date: LS Jan. 20, 1883
 Date & place of death: Jan. 16, 1883, Ft. Worth, Texas

POLLACK (POLLOCK), BRADY - killed on his ranch by Indians; ranch 12 mi.
 from Lake Valley, N. M.
 Paper & date: LS Sept. 12, 1885; RGR Sept. 19, 1885
 Date & place of death: Sept. 11, 1885, Lake Valley, N. M.

POLLING, _____ - 16 yr. old girl; cyclone hit school; fa.: J. POLLING.
 Paper & date: EPT Apr. 24, 1885
 Date & place of death: Apr. 22 or 23, 1885 Prairie Grove, Texas(near
 Mexia.)

POLLOCK, DANIEL - Given morphine instead of quinine.
 Paper & date: LS Oct. 21, 1885
 Date & place of death: Dallas, Texas

PORTER, _____ - actor; shot and killed by JAMES R. CURRIE (CURRY), city
 marshall of San Marcial, N. M.
 Paper & date: LS Aug. 16, 1882; LS Nov. 3, 1883; EPDH June 10, 1883
 Date & place ot death:........

PORTER, GEORGE - Shot and killed by mob of 25 men. He was supposed to
 have been a horse thief.
 Paper & date: LS Aug. 12, 1882
 Date & place of death: last week near Lampasas, Texas.

POSEY, JOHN T. & CARNOT - 2 bro. killed in a riot by negroes; bro.: G. G.
 POSEY of Silver City, N. M.
 Paper & date: LS Jan. 2, 1884
 Date & place of death: recently Yazoo City, Miss.

POSTER, BILLY - Stabbed by BILLY JOHNSON, both negroes.
 Paper & date: LS Dec. 28, 1881
 Date & place of death: Dec. 20, 1881 Crockett, Texas

POTTER, AL - Murdered. JASPER THOMASON, son of JOHN M. THOMASON of Den-
 nis, Kans. accused.
 Paper & date: BU Oct. 17, 1885; BU May 14, 1887
 Date & place of death: Cooney, N. M.

POTTER, Col. CHAS. of Las Vegas, N. M. - murdered by MARIANO LEYVA. Step-
 son of Gov. VANZANDT of Rhode Island.
 Paper & date: EPT Mar. 31, 1887; LS Apr. 1, 1882
 Date & place of death: 1881 near Golden, Colo.

POTTS, ARCHIE - Fell under moving train. Brakeman on T & P R. R.
 Paper & date: LS Feb. 4, 1882
 Date & place of death: Jan. 27, 1882 Dallas, Texas

POWELL, _____ - child - Bitten by mad dog; fa.: W. R. POWELL.
 Paper & date: LS July 25, 1883
 Date & place of death: Oville, Texas

POWELL, CLARENCE MURRAY - 3 mo. 13 da. elderst twin son; par.: CLARENCE
 M. & PATTIE FLOURNOY POWELL. P/D: EPT May 20 & 27,1883-D/P:May 19,1883
 El Paso, Texas

POWELL, FRANK - Thrown from buggy - may prove fatal.
Paper & date LS Aug. 18, 1883
Date & place: Waco, Texas

POWELL, Mrs. JOHN - Suicide - drowning; hus.: Rev. JOHN POWELL.
Paper & date: LS Dec. 26, 1885
Date & place of death: Jacksboro, Tex.

POWELL, LIONEL HERBERT - 3 mo. 21 da. younger twin; par.: CLARENCE M. &
PATTI FLOURNOY POWELL.
Paper & date: EPT May 27, 1883
Date & place of death: May 27, 1883 El Paso, Texas

POWERS, Judge of Brownsville, Texas; member of legislature.
Paper & date: LS Feb. 15, 1882
Date & place of death: Feb. 9, 1882

POWERS, WILLIAM or FRANK - shot by JOHN PRICE & JOHN WRIGHT.
Paper & date: LS Jan. 24 & 31, 1885; LS Feb. 7, 1885
Date & place of death: Feb. 1885 Ft. Worth, Tex.

PREAGER, CHARLES - Accidental discharge of gun.
Paper & date: LS Aug. 30, 1882
Date & place of death: last week, San Diego, Tex.

PRESCOTT, Capt. L. M. of Alma, N. M. - missing several months. Body
found near Savoya. Killed by white men.
Paper & date: BU May 1, 1884; BU Oct. 3, 1885; BU July 10, 1886
Date & place of death: Mogollon Mts., Ariz.

PRESCOTT, GEORGE T. - Typhoid fever. Formerly of San Antonio and Eagle
Pass, Tex.; bro.-in-law: _____ WARD of Eagle Pass, Tex.
Paper & date: EPDH July 19, 1882
Date & place of death: July 18, 1882 El Paso, Tex.

PRESTON, _____ - Overdose of morphine.
Paper & date: LS Sept. 17, 1884
Date & place of death: Sept. 12, 1884 Ft. Worth, Tex.

PRESTON, WALTER - Shot by E. H. WHEELER. Both were lawyers.
Paper & date: LS Aug. 5, 1882
Date & place of death: Seymour, Tex.

PRICE, _____ - Civil Engineer - train wreck.
Paper & date: EPT May 1, 1883
Date & place of death: on T & P R. R. near Ft. Worth, Tex.

PRIDAY, _____ bro s. - drowned in White Oaks Bayou.
Paper & date: LS Jan. 31, 1885
Date & place of death: Houston, Tex.

PRIOR or FRIER, _____ - Killed by Indians.
Paper & date: LS Dec. 16, 1885
Date & place of death: Mogollon Mts., N. M.

PRITCHARD, SIMON - Suicide by cutting throat with razor.
Paper & date: LS Nov. 23, 1881
Date & place of death: Nov. 13, 1881 - of Texarkana, Texas

PROCK, OLIVER - Waylaid and killed.
Paper & date: LS Aug. 22, 1885
Date & place of death: near Paris, Texas

PRYOR, FRANK D. - Young man; consumption; bur. in military cemetery; Mo.:
Mrs. F. D. PRYOR (FANNIE D.); sis. & bros.; bro.: JOHN D. PORTER(name
given as PAYWORTH 3/15)
Paper & date: LS Mar. 18, 1882; LS Mar. 15, 1882; EPDH Mar. 15, 1882;
EPDH Apr. 25, 1882
Date & place of death: Mar. 14, 1882 El Paso, Texas

PUGH, THOMAS K. - Young man; killed by Indians; uncle: _____ PUGH of Ohio.
Paper & date: EPDH Nov. 2 & 9, 1881; EPDH Dec. 28, 1881
Date & place of death: June 29-July 6, 1881 near Candelaria, Chih.,
Mexico.

PUGH, WILEY - Run over by train; widowed mother.
Paper & date: EPT Aug. 5, 1885
Date & place of death: Ranger, Texas

PURDY, _____ - Fight with Indians in Stein's Peak range near Lordsburg,
New Mexico.
Paper & date: LS Oct. 19, 1881
Date & place of death: Oct. 13, 1881

PUTEGNAT, WM. H.
Paper & date: LS Aug. 2, 1884
Date & place of death: last week - Brownsville, Texas

PUTNAM, JAMES - knife; fight 27 Feb. with THOMAS HAINEY - not expected
to live.
Paper & date: LS Feb. 28, 1885
Date & place: Gallup, N. M.

PUTNEY, ELLIS - Fall from horse.
Paper & date: EPT May 7, 1884
Date & place of death: May 4, 1884 Eagle Lake, Texas

PYE, HARRY - Killed by Indians.
Paper & date: BU Aug. 30, 1892
Date & place of death: ca. 1878 between Silver City and Chloride, N.
Mexico.

PYLE, M/M _____ - Murdered by ROGER NEUR, negro of Tahlequah, Okla. Another
man was convicted and hanged.
Paper & date: EPDH Jan. 31, 1890
Date & place of death: abt. 8 yrs. ago, Indian Terr. (Okla.)

QUARLES, GEORGE - Shot by HENRY BLUM in self defense.
Paper & date: LS Oct. 1, 1884
Date & place of death: Sept. 20, 1884 Fairview, Sierra co., N. M.

QUARTERMAN, W. H. - Smallpox
Paper & date: EPDH Jan. 20, 1884
Date & place of death: July 15, 1883 on Mex. Cen. R. R. - Mex.

QUE BOO - Deadly assault by CHUNG AU GONG. Affadavit by AH KING.
Paper & date: EPT Aug. 2, 1884
Date & place of death: on R. R. at Wilder, Tex.

QUIGLY, _____ R. R. Conductor; _____ MONTGOMERY convicted in Beckett,
Texas.
Paper & date: EPT Sept. 28, 1883
Date & place:..........

QUIGLEY, TOM - R. R. Conductor - train accident. Woman claims to be
widow.
Paper & date: LS Apr. 18, 1883
Date & place of death: year ago near Las Vegas, N. M.

QUINLAN, THOMAS - by GEORGE MATHEWS at Lordsburg (who is under arrest).
Not yet dead.
Paper & date: EPT Apr. 11, 1883
Date & place of death: N. M.

QUINN, MICHAEL (bartender) - shot by WM. H. LESSING a lawyer.
Paper & date: LS Dec. 23, 1885
Date & place of death: Big Springs, Tex.

QUINONES, FRANCISCO, JR. - Hung by outlaws; fa.: FRANCISCO QUINONES, SR.
Paper & date: EPMS Dec. 10, 1884
Date & place of death: June 1884 Huachucas, Ariz.

RABB, J. W. of La Grande, Tex. - Suicide.
Paper & date: LS Apr. 29, 1885
Date & place of death: Apr. 10, 1885 Nashville, Tenn.

RAFF, KATIE - age 4 - accidentally drank morphine.
Paper & date: LS July 18, 1883
Date & place of death: Denison, Texas

RAFFERTY, JAMES & family - murdered.
Paper & date: LS Oct. 18, 1884
Date & place of death: found Oct. 4, 1884, RAFFERTY Ranch, SW corner
Cochise co., Ariz.

RAGSDALE, _____ - Sher., Fannin co. - killed while arresting SAM & ELI
DYER.
Paper & date: LS May 16, 1885; EPT June 10, 1885
Date & place of death: Mar. 10, 1885, Dallas, Texas

RAHL, _____ - Suicide; surv. wife "attempted to cut her throat on Oct.20".
Paper & date: LS Oct. 25, 1882
Date & place of death: last week, Galveston, Texas

RASCOMB, PAZ of Silver City, N. M. - murdered by Apaches.
Paper & date: RGR June 27, 1885
Date & place: recently

RATHER, Mrs. Dr. H. M. - Suicide - strychnine.
Paper & date: LS Dec. 26, 1885
Date & place of death: Tyler, Texas

RAVEL, C. F. - young man; drowned.
Paper & date: LS May 6, 1885
Date & place of death: during late flood, White Rock Creek, Dallas co.
Texas

RAWLEY, Judge R. G.
Paper & date: LS July 11, 1884
Date & place of death: Houston, Texas

RAY, FRED - to die for murder in the Ind. Terr. (Okla.)
Paper & date: EPT Feb. 1, 1885
Date & place of death: Apr. 7, 1885 Ft. Smith, Ark.

RAY, KING - negro; shot by JOE GIST.
Paper & date: LS July 11, 1883
Date & place of death: Pilot Point, Texas

RAYMOND, CHARLES - Miner; at work in a mine - bad air.
Paper & date: LS July 22, 1885
Date & place of death: Gallop, N. M.

RAYMOND, JOSEPH & family - Murdered.
Paper & date: LS Oct. 18, 1884
Date & place of death: found Oct. 4, 1884, RAFFERTY Ranch, SW corner
Cochise co., Ariz.

RAYNER(RAYNOR), WM. P. - shot Apr. 14, 1884 by R. B. RENICK in self-de-
fense; surv. mo. and bro.
Paper & date: LS Apr. 15, 1885; LS June 10, 1885: EPT Apr. 15, 18,19
& June 9 & 27, 1885
Date & place of death: June 7, 1885 El Paso, Texas

RAYNOLDS, MADISON - son: JEFFERSON RAYNOLDS of El Paso, Texas
Paper & date: EPT Aug. 28, 1883
Date & place of death: Aug. 23, 1883 Canton, Ohio

READ, _____ baby; "b. last week & has since d. & been buried"; par.:M/M
D. M. READ
Paper & date: RGR Nov. 1, 1884
Date & place of death: ......

REAVES, J. L. - stabbed by a lunatic.
Paper & date: RGR Dec. 6, 1884
Date & place of death: Deming, N. M.

RECTOR, Mrs. MARTHA - suicide - jealous of hus; surv.: hus.
Paper & date: LS Jun. 9, 1883
Date & place of death: Galveston, Tex.

REDDISH, JAMES of Clifton, Ariz. - miner; shot - apparent suicide.
Paper & date: LS Oct. 11, 1884
Date & place of death: no. of Ascension, Mex.

"RED RIVER TOM" - shoot out with police; Sher. JESSE LEE, KIMBERLY, Mc-
CALL (McPHAUL) & HICKENBAUGH - held.
Paper & date: LS Mar. 18, 1885; EPT Mar. 19 & 20, 1885
Date & place of death: Mar. 16, 1885, Springer, N. M.

REED, JOSEPH M. of Las Cruces, N. M. - suicide - had been sick a long
time; surv.: wife, several small children.
Paper & date: LS Jan. 14, 1882
Date & place of death: Jan. 9, 1882, last Monday.

REED, R. R. - drowned.
Paper & date: LS Jun. 13, 1883
Date & place of death: Dallas, Texas

REEVES, ANDREW
Paper & date: TB Jul. 24, 1872
Date & place of death: Jul. 20, 1872, Silver City, N. M.

REEVES, GEORGE - suicide
Paper & date: LS Nov. 24, 1883
Date & place of death: Gatesville, Texas

REILLEY, _____ - gambler - killed by CHAS. SMITH
Paper & date: LS Aug. 26, 1885
Date & place of death: 3 yrs. ago, Laredo, Texas

REILLY, _____ - killed by McKEE SCOTT and AL COOK - justifiable verdict
in Prescott, Ariz., Jul. 19, 1884
Paper & date: EPT Jul. 21, 1884
Date & place of death: Arizona

REILLY, JAMES - rattlesnake bite - he was a snake charmer.
Paper & date: RGR Aug. 2, 1884
Date & place of death: recently

REINERS, ROBERT - fa.: H. REINERS, Brooklyn, N. Y.
Paper & date: LS Feb. 18, 1885
Date & place of death: Feb. 4, 1885, Socorro, N. M.

REISTER, FELIPE - bright's disease.
Paper & date: RGR Jun. 14, 1884
Date & place of death: Mon., Jun. 9, 1884, Las Cruces, N. M.

RENEAU, FRANK
Paper & date: LS Aug. 15, 1885
Date & place of death: hanging for 4 days near Elgin, Texas

RENFRO, Dr. _____ - fight with R. J. McDOWELL - received "mortal wounds".
Paper & date: LS Jun. 6, 1883
Date & place of death: Killeen, Texas

RENFRO, JOHN
Paper & date: BU May 1, 1883 D/P of death: San Accasio, N. M.

RENNARD, GEORGE W. - drowned; at one time was Sgt. in Co. I, 15th Inf.at
Ft. Selden; relatives at Wheeling, Va.
Paper & date: RGR Jun. 6, 1885
Date & place of death: May 29, 1885

RENNOLDS, W. L. - suicide
Paper & date: LS Aug. 27, 1884
Date & place of death: Houston, Texas

REVELIN, MARK aka Mr. BRIHAM - killed by Indians.
Paper & date: TB Apr. 27, 1871
Date & place of death: Apr. 15, 1871, between Ralston & Sulphur Spgs.

REYES, _____ 2 sons of Presidio Rio Grande - cattle thieves killed by
patrol under Dty. Sher. O'MEARA; fa.: RAFAEL REYES.
Paper & date: LS Feb. 11, 1885
Date & place of death: Feb. 5, 1885

REYNAND, _____ - murdered by two barkeeps - justifiable.
Paper & date: LS May 31, 1884
Date & place of death: Houston, Texas

REYNOLDS, _____ - killed by Indians.
Paper & date: EPDH Jan. 21, 1883
Date & place of death: recently, Dragoon Mtn., Arizona

REYNOLDS, JOHN - surgical operation; Grant co., N. M. blacksmith.
Paper & date: LS May 16, 1885
Date & place of death: New York

REYNOLDS, JOSEPH - murdered.
Paper & date: LS Jan. 23, 1884
Date & place of death: Jan. 17-21, 1884, Ojo Caliente, Mexico.

REYNOLDS, JOSEPH - suddenly at his home.
Paper & date: LS Jan. 13, 1883
Date & place of death: last Wed., Mesilla, N. M.

REYNOR, KENNETH, Jr. - sonsumption & typhoid fever; fa.: Hon. KENNETH
REYNOR, former solicitor of U. S. Treasury.
Paper & date: EPT Jul. 31, 1885
Date & place of death: Dallas, Texas

RHEINER, PETER - accidentally shot by bro. WILLIE RHEINER while hunting;
surv. bro. WILLIE RHEINER.
Paper & date: LS Dec. 19, 1885
Date & place of death: near Sabinal Sta., Texas

RHODES, Mrs. _____ - murdered by hus. - he to hand May 22 in Galveston,
Texas; hus.:JASPER RHODES
Paper & date: LS Apr. 1, 1885
Date & place of death: Texas

RHODES, JASPER - hanged for murdering his wife; fa.: JASPER RHODES.
Paper & date: LS Jun. 17, 1885
Date & place of death: May 22, 1885, Galveston, Texas

RHODES, JOSEPH - negro - hanged.
Paper & date: LS May 30, 1885
Date & place of death: May or Jun. 22, Galveston, Texas

RICE, FRITZ - 1 yr. old; par.: M/M JOHN RICE.
Paper & date: BU Dec. 19, 1885
Date & place of death: Dec. 11, 1885, Socorro, N. M.

RICE, 1st Lt. WM. F., 23 Reg., Inf. - walked off train in his sleep.
Paper & date: LS Jun. 18, 1884; EPT Jun. 12, 1884
Date & place of death: Jun. 4, 1884, Mexico, Mo.

RICH, Dr. A. C. (RICK) - killed by 3 men in his home; young man, only
   2_ yrs. old; surv.: wife; came from Ga. several yrs. ago.
   Paper & date: LS Apr. 28, 1883; EPT Apr. 26, 1883
   Date & place of death: Apr. 24, 1883, Lampasas, Texas

RICH, LEAH - young; bro. of El Paso, Texas; SI L. RICH
   Paper & date: EPT Aug. 4, 1884
   Date & place of death: Jul. 27, 1884, Arrowhead Springs, Ca.

RICHARDS, _____ - Conductor; yellow fever contracted in Guaymas, Mex.
   Paper & date: EPT Sept. 18, 1885
   Date & place of death: last week, Nogales, Ariz.

RICHARDS, E. W. - shot from ambush by GEORGE DICKEY, JAMES M. & EDWARD
   THOMAS BENNETT near Las Tabias.
   Paper & date: LS Aug. 27, 1884; EPT Aug. 20, 1884
   Date & place of death: Aug. 16, 1884, White Oaks, N. M.

RICHARDS, Capt. E. W. of Organ, N. M.; ill for some time; had joined his
   family in La.
   Paper & date: RGR Mar. 7, 1885
   Date & place of death: recently, Louisiana

RICHARDSON, Pvt. _____ of Ft. Craig, N. M. - a deserter, black, killed
   during recapture.
   Paper & date: LS Nov. 26, 1881
   Date & place of death: ....

RICHARDSON, J. - overcome by heat - will probably die.
   Paper & date: LS Aug. 11, 1883
   Date & place of death: Burnett, Texas

RICHARDSON, THOMAS - crushed by elevator in the Capitol Hotel.
   Paper & date: LS Nov. 17, 1883
   Date & place of death: Nov. 12, 1883, Houston, Texas

RICHEY, WM. - stabbed by J. H. CARROLL of Ellis co., Texas
   Paper & date: EPT Aug. 26, 1885
   Date & place of death:_ Abilene, Texas

RICKELSON, GEORGE B. of San Francisco, Ca. - yellow fever.
   Paper & date: EPT Sept. 20, 1883
   Date & place of death: Guaymas, Mexico.

RICO (?), Commandant & Mrs. _____ - killed by Mex. bandits.
   Paper & date: EPT Jan. 23, 1885
   Date & place of death: Yuma, Arizona

RIDGE, Maj. _____ age 64; Cherokee Indian; killed in feud.
   Paper & date: EPT Jun. 26, 1883
   Date & place of death: Jun. 23, 1838, near Boston Mtns, Ind. Terr.

RIDGE, JOHN - Cherokee Indian; killed in feud; fa.: Maj. RIDGE.
   Paper & date: EPT Jun. 26, 1883
   Date & place of death: Jun. 23, 1838, Honey Creek, Ind. Terr.

RIEHLE, ALFRED - age 13 days; only ch. of M/M E. A. RIEHLE.
   Paper & date: EPT Jun. 19 & 20, 1885
   Date & place of death: Jun. 18, 1885, El Paso, Texas

RILEA, JNO. S.
   Paper & date: LS Dec. 23, 1885
   Date & place of death: Dec. 20, 1885, Silver City, N. M.

RILEY, _____ - gambler; murder
   Paper & date: LS Mar. 8, 1882
   Date & place of death: other day, Laredo, Texas

RILEY, or ROCKFORD _____ of Ft. Worth, Tx. - small pox
   Paper & date: LS Apr. 7, 1883 D/P of death: Apr. 5,1883,San Augustin,
   N. M.

RILEY, Sgt. _____ - Texas Ranger - shot by _____ GONZALES, age 13, son
of PILANUS GONZALES.
Paper & date: EPT Jun. 4, 1885
Date & place of death: few days ago, near Laredo, Texas

RILEY, JNO. - effects of alcohol.
Paper & date: LS Aug. 1, 1885
Date & place of death: near Nacogdoches, Texas

RILEY, ROBERT - negro - shot and killed by mob while in jail accused of
attempted rape of the dau. of Co. Treas.
Paper & date: EPT Sept. 5, 1884
Date & place of death: Aug. 27, 1884, Refugio, Texas

RILEY, ROSIE - 9 mos. - interocolitis.
Paper & date: LS Jul. 28, 1883
Date & place of death: Jul. 27, 1883, El Paso, Texas

RILEY, TIM - fell from horse; bur. Paso del Norte, Mexico
Paper & date: EPT Jul. 18, 1884
Date & place of death: few days ago.

RIMAN, PETER - a Frenchman - murdered by FRANCISCO MONAL & FRANCISCO
LEON.
Paper & date: EPT Sept. 6, 1885; EPT Sept. 12, 1885
Date & place of death: May 10, 1885, Mexico City, Mexico

RING, WILLIAM M. - drowned
Paper & date: LS Nov. 7, 1883
Date & place of death: 3 weeks ago, Los Alamos, N. M.

RIOS, JULIAN - killed by Indians.
Paper & date: EPDH Oct. 5, 1881
Date & place of death: between Wilcox & San Carlos, Arizona

RIPSTEIN, LOUIS - age 20; blew his brains out; surv.: father
Paper & date: LS Apr. 18, 1885
Date & place of death: the other night, on Salado River near San
Antonio, Texas

RISQUE, JOHN P. - killed by Indians; bro.: F. W. RISQUE; came to Pinos
Altos, N. M. from St. Louis, Mo.
Paper & date: LS Mar. 31, 1883; BU Sept. 2, 1890; EPDH May 17, 1882
Date & place of death: Apr., 1882, Grant co., N. M., near Clifton,
Arizona.

RIVERA, CORNELIO - bullet in head.
Paper & date: LS Feb. 24, 1883
Date & place of death: found last week near Hudson's Hot Springs,N.M.

RIWELL, JACK
Paper & date: LS Sept. 27, 1884
Date & place of death: Cleburne, Texas

ROBERTS, Mrs. Gov. _____
Paper & date: LS Dec. 5, 1883
Date & place of death: Nov. 27, 1883, Austin, Texas

ROBERTS, ALBERT - d. in jail as result of wound rec'd earlier.
Paper & date: LS Mar. 22, 1882
Date & place of death: last week, Athens, Texas

ROBERTS, C. H. - shot by TOM LITTLE.
Paper & date: LS Sept. 19, 1885
Date & place of death: Sept. 14, 1885, Deming, N. M.

ROBERTS, Mrs. J. - yellow fever; hus.: Capt. J. ROBERTS of schooner "Sur-
prise".
Paper & date: EPT Nov. 25, 1885
Date & place of death: Guaymas, Mexico.

ROBERTS, Mrs. ROBERT - shot by robbers.
    Paper & date: LS Dec. 12, 1883
    Date & place of death: Dec. 10, 1883, Bisbee, Arizona

ROBERTS, S. M. of Albuquerque, N. M.
    Paper & date: EPT Apr. 13, 1883
    Date & place of death: Apr. 10, 1883, Copper City (N.M.?)

ROBERTS, W. M. att'y. of Lincoln co., N. M. - died suddenly.
    Paper & date: LS Mar. 28, 1883
    Date & place of death: Mar. 25, 1883, Denver, Colo.

ROBINETTE, _____ - suicide.
    Paper & date: LS Jul. 12, 1884
    Date & place of death: San Antonio, N. M. or Tx.?

RODERIQUES, _____ - shot - probably fatal; bro.: PEDRO RODERQUES.
    Paper & date: EPT Nov. 3, 1884
    Date & place of death: Paso del Norte, Mexico

RODREGUEZ, JUAN of San Antonio, Texas - age 82 - wandered away & found
    dead.
    Paper & date: LS Apr. 14, 1883
    Date & date of death: near Castroville, Texas

RODRIGUEZ, RAMON - shot by SANTIAGO MONTES.
    Paper & date: LS Nov. 10, 1883
    Date & place of death: Nov. 9, 1883, Paso del Norte, Mexico

ROE, MICHAEL - ca. 40 yrs.; suicide - shot himself; wife; native of
    Mich., had lived in Laramie, Wyo. to 1868 later Houston, Tx., Vallejo,
    Ca. to Sacramento, Benito, Yuma and Tucson; bur. Mar. 16.
    Paper & date: LS Mar. 18, 1885; EPT Mar. 17, 1885
    Date & place of death: Mar. 15, 1885, El Paso, Texas

ROESCHLER, _____ of San Antonio*- Indian massacre by COCHISE. See MILLS,
    _____ bro. of Maj. MILLS. (*Texas)
    Paper & date: EPT Jan. 20, 1887
    Date & place of death: June 1860, Cook's Peak, Grant co., N. M.

ROFF, ANDREW & JAMES of Cooke co., Texas killed while with a posse at-
    tempting to arrest stock thieves.
    Paper & date: LS May 9, 1885
    Date & place of death: LEE's Ranch, Ind. Terr., Ok.

ROGERS, _____ negro desperado - affray.
    Paper & date: EPT Apr. 9, 1885
    Date & place of death: Indian Terr., Ok.

ROGERS, Dty. Sher. _____ - shot through lungs by a negro, _____ JACKSON.
    Paper & date: LS Oct. 3 & 6, 1883
    Date & place of death: Sept. 29, 1883, Palestine, Texas

RODGERS, _____ - a teacher - killed in fight over management of school.
    Paper & date: LS Feb. 21, 1883
    Date & place of death: Feb. 15, 1883, Young co., Texas

ROGERS, _____ of Raton, N. M. - shoot out with police officers.
    Paper & date: LS Mar. 18, 1885
    Date & place of death: Springer, N. M.

ROGERS, DICK - killed; Sher. JESSE LEE, KIMBERLY & McCALL (McPHAUL),
    HICKENBAUGH (HIXENBAUGH) listed as killer
    Paper & date: RGR Mar. 21, 1885; EPT Mar. 17, 19, 20, 1885; LS May
    2, 1885
    Date & place of death: Mar. 16, 1885, Springer, N. M.

ROGERS, JIM - thrown from wagon while drunk.
    Paper & date: LS Sept. 24, 1884
    Date & place of death: Johnson co., Texas

141

ROGERS, JOHN - shot by _____ BENT; self-defense.
   Paper & date: LS Jul. 7, 1883
   Date & place of death: Ash Forks, N. M.

ROGERS, LENA - throat cut by PAT PENDERGRAFT of Corsicana, Texas
   Paper & date: LS Jun. 3, 1885
   Date & place of death: Jun. 1, 1885, MOLLY BROWN's House, Tyler, Tx.

ROHMAN, A. P. - one of oldest Americans in territory;   surv.: widow and
   family.
   Paper & date: TB Sept. 28, 1872
   Date & place of death: Sept. 25, 1872, Membres Hot Springs, N. M.

ROIVAL, _____ - shot and killed by FRANCISCO NOLAN at a baile in Sapello,
   San Miguel co., N. M.; NOLAN killed the two and then went home and
   cut off his wife's ears; fa.: MATIAS ROIVAL.
   Paper & date: LS Dec. 13, 1882
   Date & place of death: San Miguel co., N. M.

ROLLAND, CHARLES - killed by train.
   Paper & date: LS Jun. 9, 1883
   Date & place of death: near Corsicana, Texas

ROMERO, ANDREAS - drowned
   Paper & date: LS Jul. 8, 1885
   Date & place of death: San Juan River, Largo, N. M.

ROMERO, FERMIN - drowned in Rio Grande; surv.: wife and 2 children in
   Las Cruces, N. M.
   Paper & date: LS Jul. 25, 1885; RGR Jul. 18, 1885
   Date & place of death: Jul. 11, 1885, near San Diego, N. M.

ROMERO, FRANCISCA - age 2; par.: MARGARITO & JREWA ROMERO
   Paper & date: LS May 2, 1885
   Date & place of death: Las Vegas, N. M.

ROMERO, JUAN - shot by CANDIDO CASTILLO & JUAN CASTILLO
   Paper & date: LS Apr. 12, 1884
   Date & place of death: N. M.

ROMERO, JUAN - drowned
   Paper & date: LS Jul. 8, 1885
   Date & place of death: San Juan River, Largo, N. M.

ROMEROS, MARIA - age 13; shot in neck; fa.: and some bro.
   Paper & date: LS Jul. 18, 1883
   Date & place of death: Jul. 17, 1883, El Paso, Texas

ROMERO, Mrs. MIGUEL - killed by hus.
   Paper & date: LS Oct. 28, 1885
   Date & place of death: Penasco, Rio Lucelle co., N. M.

RONEY, THOMAS - driven out of Lincoln, N. M. by masked men; died of ex-
   posure.
   Paper & date: LS Aug. 12, 1885
   Date & place of death: Ft. Stanton, N. M.

RONQUILLO, JOSE IGNACIO (This is not the Lt. Col.)-bur. Paso Del Norte,
   Mex.; ch.: ESTANISLADO N. ROQUILLO, b. El Paso co., ca. 1825.
   Paper & date: EPDH Jan. 28, 1890; EPDH Jan. 30, 1890
   Date & place of death: between 1852 and 1860, San Elizario, Texas

RONQUILLO, Lt. Col. JOSE IGNACIO - surv.: wife and 2 dau.
   Paper & date: EPDH Jan. 28, 1890
   Date & place of death: 1835 at Hot Springs ca. 30 mi above Presidio
   del Norte, Chihuahua, Mexico

ROOKER, Dr. _____ of Lyon's Point, Texas - shot through window by unknown.
   Paper & date: LS Jan. 13, 1883
   Date & place of death: last week

ROONEY, JOHN an Irishman - suicide by morphine
    Paper & date: LS Nov. 22, 1882
    Date & place of death: Nov. 16, 1882, Austin, Texas

ROOS, LOUIS - shot and killed by ERNEST FROMONT, Jr.
    Paper & date: LS Sept. 23, 1882
    Date & place of death: Sept. 19, 1882, Houston, Texas

ROSAS, JOHN - killed by Ranger Sgt. DILLARD
    Paper & date: LS Sept. 17, 1884
    Date & place of death: Brownsville, Texas

ROSE, G. W.
    Paper & date: LS Aug. 25, 1883
    Date & place of death: Fleming Camp, New Mexico

ROSE, GRACIE - had a spasm and fell into the fire.
    Paper & date: EPMS Dec. 17, 1884
    Date & place of death: Bosque co., Texas

ROSE, THEODORE of Houston, Texas - for many years connected with Houston
    & Texas Central R. R.
    Paper & date: LS Dec. 10, 1881
    Date & place of death: ....

ROSECRANS, _____ infant girl; fa.: NEWTON ROSECRANS
    Paper & date: TB May 25, 1871
    Date & place of death: May 9, 1871, Mesilla, N. M.

ROSS, _____ - murdered; JOHN H. HOWARD charged
    Paper & date: LS Feb. 24, 1883
    Date & place of death: before the war, Brazos co., Texas

ROTHSCHILD, Mrs. CHARLES - sudden illness - peritonitis; bur. Concordia
    Hebrew Cem.; hus, ch. 9 mos. old and sis. of Chicago.
    Paper & date: LS Jul. 29, 1885; EPT Jul. 28, 1885; SH Aug. 2, 1885
    Date & place of death: Jul. 26, 1885, El Paso, Texas

ROUALT, AMELIA - infant; par.: TEODORE & MARGARITA C. ROUALT
    Paper & date: LS Jul. 21, 1883; RGR Jul. 21, 1883
    Date & place of death: Jul. 15, 1883, Las Cruces, N. M.

ROUILLER, VICTOR - shot & killed by JUAN JOSE LOPEZ who has now been ar-
    rested at San Francisco, Socorro co., N. M.; cousin: NUMA REYMOND:
    bro.: JOHN G. ROUILLER
    Paper & date: RGR Dec. 15, 1883
    Date & place of death: 4 yrs. ago

ROWE, W. P. of Grabail, Washington co., Texas - a farmer; shot
    Paper & date: LS Dec. 10, 1881
    Date & place of death: Dec. 1, 1881

ROWLAND, M. - thrown from buggy - will die
    Paper & date: LS Aug. 15, 1883
    Date & place of death: Ft. Worth, Texas

ROWLEY, SAM - hydrophobia
    Paper & date: BU Aug. 16, 1892
    Date & place of death: 1882, Prescott, Arizona

ROYAL, PERRY - suicide by drowning
    Paper & date: LS Aug. 4, 1883
    Date & place of death: San Antonio, Texas

ROZELL, R. A. - suicide - family trouble
    Paper & date: LS Jun. 16, 1883
    Date & place of death: Ft. Worth, Texas

RUDER, CHARLES H.[- unintentional suicide by laudanum
    P/D: LS Mar. 22, 1882 D/P: Mar. 16, 1882, San Rafael, N. M.

RUMPH, Mrs. WILLIAM - shot by hus. WILLIAM RUMPH - accident
    Paper & date: LS Sept. 12, 1883
    Date & place of death: Sept. 9, 1883, Pine Grove, Texas

RUNNELS, _____ of Ft. Worth, Texas aka "BOB RIDLEY" in FORREST's Command
    Paper & date: LS Nov. 30, 1881
    Date & place of death: Nov. 21, 1881

RUSS, Dr. _____ - lawyer
    Paper & date: LS Mar. 5, 1884
    Date & place of death: Mar. 2, 1884, St. Vincents Hosp., Santa Fe,NM

RUSSELL, CLARA - negro - shot in the calaboose - CLARK CLEVELAND, negro,
    suspected
    Paper & date: LS Nov. 8, 1884
    Date & place of death: Nov. 2, 1884, Temple, Texas

RUSSEL, JERRY - murdered by ANDREW JACKSON - sentenced to death at Bryan
    Paper & date: LS Apr. 8, 1885; LS Oct. 14, 1885
    Date & place of death: last year, Bryan, Texas

RUSSELL, WHIT - shot and killed by JAMES LASITER
    Paper & date: LS May 12, 1883
    Date & place of death: Mount Pleasant, Texas

RUSSELL, Judge WM. J. - widow: Mrs. ELEANOR RUSSELL
    Paper & date: LS Nov. 25, 1882; EPT Jun. 29, 1883; EPDH Mar. 25, 1890
    Date & place of death: Nov. 5, 1882, Laredo, Texas

RUSSELL, WILLIAM M. - shot in a bagnio by CLIFF COOK
    Paper & date: LS Dec. 23, 1885
    Date & place of death: San Antonio, Texas

"RUSSIAN BILL" - hanged; rustlers
    Paper & date: LS Nov. 16, 1881
    Date & place of death: last week

RUTLEDGE, WILLIAM - heirs bring suit for land in Ft. Worth, Texas
    Paper & date: LS Nov. 17, 1883
    Date & place:.................

RYAN, Pvt. _____ - killed by Pvt. _____ NOLAN
    Paper & date: LS Nov. 10, 1883
    Date & place of death: Nov. 3, 1883, Ft. Union, N. M.

RYAN, _____ - typhoid fever; RYAN had lived in Paso del Norte and said
    to be a physician; came over here with fever and ill; no known rela-
    tives.
    Paper & date: LS Nov. 18, 1882
    Date & place of death: El Paso, Texas

RYAN, Mrs. MAGGIE of Elgin, Ill. - age 23; consumption; bur. Elgin, Ill.;
    hus.: CHAS. RYAN of Elgin, Ill.; cousin: M. WALLACE of Water Canon,NM
    Paper & date: BU Jun. 2. 1885
    Date & place of death: May 27, 1885, Water Canon, N. M.

SAFFEL, Lt. _____ - murdered by WM. PENLAND
    Paper & date: LS Jul. 2, 1884
    Date & place of death: 1864

SAINZ(S), DOROTEO, of La Mesa, N. M. - rustler; shot by Maj. A. J. FOUN-
    TAIN of N. M. State Militia whiles escaping; age 30, 5'7", dark com-
    plexion; gang members: EUGENIO PEDRAZA, DIEGO GARCIA, CLEMENTE SAINS,
    PANCHO SAINS, FAUSTINO LOPEZ, REFUGIO PROVENCIO, RAFAEL SIERRA, MAR-
    GARITO SIERRA, JUAN CARABOJOL, TEVDORO SIERRA, PABLO CARABOJOL; bro.:
    PANCHO SAINZ.
    Paper & date: LS Mar. 3, 1883; EPDH Mar. 18, 1883
    Date & place of death: Mar. 2, 1883, near Concordia, Texas

SAIS, JUAN - jeweler - got drunk - slept out - froze to death
   Paper & date: LS Dec. 12, 1885
   Date & place of death: Santa Fe, N. M.

SALAMON, _____ - lightening; formerly lived on the Ocate
   Paper & date: LS Sept. 2, 1885
   Date & place of death: Aug. 15, 1885, near Liberty, N. M.

SALAZAR, _____ - mail carrier from Silver City, N. M. to Pinos Altos
   Paper & date: TB Jun. 12, 1872
   Date & place of death: ....

SALAZAR, JOSE - shot by S. SANDOVAL - justifiable
   Paper & date: LS Aug. 13, 1884
   Date & place of death: Aug. 4, 1884, Golden, Colo.(?)

SALAZAR, PILAR - murdered - AGAPITO CALLES charged
   Paper & date: LS Oct. 11, 1884
   Date & place of death: found Oct. 7, 1884, near Silver City, N. M.

SALEIDO, PLUTERIO of Santa Rita, N. M. - murder by CASERNERIO CORDOVA
   Paper & date: LS Dec. 30, 1882
   Date & place of death: Dec. 25, 1882

SALES(SALAS?), LUIS - killed by a train; surv.: fa.; a boy has turned up
   claiming to be LUIS but fa. says NO
   Paper & date: LS Apr. 25, 1883
   Date & place of death: some time ago, Deming, N. M.

SALS, MARCUS - murdered
   Paper & date: LS Aug. 1, 1883
   Date & place of death: Las Lunas, N. M.

SALSIVA, LOUIS - shot accidentally
   Paper & date: LS Aug. 29, 1883
   Date & place of death: Deming, N. M.

SALVADOR son of MANGAS COLORADO; killed in Maj. KELLY's recent fight with
   the Apaches
   Paper & date: TB Apr. 13, 1871
   Date & place of death:.........

SAMANIEGO, B. - killed by Indians; member of M. G. SAMANIEGO's freight
   train
   Paper & date: EPDH Oct. 5, 1881
   Date & place of death: between Wilcox and San Carlos, Arizona

SAMPLE, RED - to be hanged for murder - Bisbee, Ariz.
   Paper & date: LS Mar. 26, 1884
   Date & place of death: Mar. 28, 1884, Tombstone, Arizona

SAMPLES, B. A. - blown 30 feet by premature blast in a rock cut -thought
   to be fatal injuries
   Paper & date: LS Feb. 25, 1882
   Date & place of death: near Lampasas, Texas

SAMUELS, J. B. of Ft. Worth, Texas - drowned while attempting to drive a
   team across river
   Paper & date: LS Nov. 5, 1881
   Date & place of death: last week

SANCHES, _____ - murdered - murderers acquitted
   Paper & date: LS Dec. 2, 1882
   Date & place of death: San Miguel co., N. M.

SANCHEZ, _____ son; dragged to death; fa.: FELIPE SANCHEZ
   Paper & date: LS Oct. 24, 1885
   Date & place of death: near La Cinta, New Mexico

SANCHEZ, EULOGIO - TOMAS MAESTAs jailed and charged with murder at Las
Vegas, N. M.
Paper & date: LS Nov. 11, 1885
Date & place of death: near Canyon Largo, on Red River, New Mexico

SANCHEZ, FRANCISCO - shot by unknown
Paper & date: LS Aug. 4, 1883
Date & place of death: near Laredo, Texas

SANCHEZ, MANUEL - shot by MELCHOR LUNA cousin of Delegate LUNA
Paper & date: LS Feb. 28, 1883; LS Nov. 17, 1883
Date & place of death: last week, Belen, N. M.

SANCHEZ, PERFECTO - killed in a quarrel over a woman by another Mexican
Paper & date: LS Sept. 16, 1885
Date & place of death: Sept. 13, 1885, Laredo, Texas

SANDERS, Mrs. _____ - son: ADOLPH SANDERS, El Paso, Texas
Paper & date: EPT Oct. 4, 1884
Date & place of death: Columbus, Georgia

SANDER, THOMAS J. - 12 yrs. - drowned in Colorado River
Paper & date: LS Aug. 8, 1885
Date & place of death: Austin, Texas

SANDLE, J. P. - shot and killed by GEORGE CLAYTON at STEEL's Store in
Brazos Bottom
Paper & date: LS Dec. 31, 1881
Date & place of death: Dec. 21, 1881, near Bryan, Texas

SANDOVAL (Navajo Indian) - killed by _____ HERNANDEZ and others
Paper & date: LS Apr. 25, 1885
Date & place of death: few months ago, N. M.

SANDOVAL, JOSE - murdered - JUAN MOLINO charged
Paper & date: LS May 27, 1885
Date & place of death: New Mexico

SANDOVAL, JUAN of Las Vegas, N. M. - thrown from wagon
Paper & date: LS Jul. 4, 1883
Date & place of death: on way to San Jeronimo, N. M.

SANFORD, Mrs. C. E. - 14 yr. old son accused; surv.: hus. and son
Paper & date: LS Nov. 14, 1885
Date & place of death: Buffalo Springs, Tx.

SAN JUAN, JACK youngest son - named for Col. FOUNTAIN; fa.: SAN JUAN -
Mescalero chief
Paper & date: LS Sept. 2, 1885; RGR Aug. 29, 1885
Date & place of death: Aug. 25, 1885, N. M.

SAPP, PETER L. - heart disease
Paper & date: LS Jul. 8, 1885
Date & place of death: Jul. 5, 1885, Animas, N. M.

SATTERFIELD, W. G. - fell between cars of train
Paper & date: LS Aug. 27, 1884
Date & place of death: Tyler, Texas

SAULS, ABRAHAM - shootout - family feud with BASHAW family; surv.: GREEN
SAULS, HENRY HARRIS (?)
Paper & date: LS Dec. 5, 1884
Date & place of death: Dec. 5, 1884, Galesville, Texas

SAULS, Dr. T. J. - shootout - feud with BASHAW family; surv.: GREEN SAULS,
HENRY HARRIS (?)
Paper & date: LS Dec. 5, 1884
Date & place of death: Dec. 5, 1884, Galesville(Gatesville?), Tx.

SAUNDERS, _____ - killed by Indians
    Paper & date: EPDH Oct. 5, 1881
    Date & place of death: near Camp Apache, Arizona

SAUNDERS, GEORGE K. - killed by Indians; native of New York
    Paper & date: TB Jun. 8, 1871
    Date & place of death: Jun. 1, 1871, Calabasas

SAURIN, JOHN - shot; S. C. MILLER arrested on suspicion; name given as
    SAUN also
    Paper & date: BU Nov. 14 & 21, 1885
    Date & place of death: Nov. 7, 1885, San Marcial, N. M.

SAVAGE, Mrs. MARION - burned; died next day
    Paper & date: LS Feb. 28, 1885
    Date & place of death: Marysville, Texas

SAWYER, _____ - disappeared from Rincom, N. M.; Mexican arrested
    Paper & date: LS Mar. 3, 1883
    Date & place of death: 2 or 3 mos. ago.

SAWYER, E. T. - should have come directly from Ohio instead of lingering
    in Colo. - to Mesilla, N. M.
    Paper & date: RGR Jan. 5, 1884
    Date & place of death: recently

SCATES, J. M. of Orange, Texas - snow slide
    Paper & date: EPT Dec. 24, 1885
    Date & place of death: Dec. 22, 1885, San Juan co., Colo.

SCHAEFER, AUGUST & wife - AUGUST apparently shot his wife and then com-
    mitted suicide; surv.: son
    Paper & date: LS Mar. 11, 1885
    Date & place of death: Boerne, Texas

SCHAFFNER, _____ - bro.: JACOB
    Paper & date: LS Jan. 23, 1884
    Date & place of death: Las Vegas, N. M.

SCHAFFNER, JACOB - deranged over death of his brother
    Paper & date: LS Jan. 23, 1884
    Date & place of death: near Springer, N. M.

SCHAVOIR, LEON - typhoid probably contracted at Ft. Craig; he was a re-
    cruit of Troop H
    Paper & date: RGR Oct. 25, 1884
    Date & place of death: Oct. 3, 1884

SCHENK, Mrs. KATHARINA - son: AUGUSTUS SCHENK of Las Cruces, N.M.:dau.of
    Germany
    Paper & date: RGR Sept. 13, 1884
    Date & place of death: Aug. 21, 1884, Baden, Germany

SCHERNERB,HERMAN - suicide by morphine
    Paper & date: LS Jul. 25, 1883
    Date & place of death: Austin, Texas

SCHIEF, ERNEST of Giddings, Texas - suicide
    Paper & date: LS Jan. 14, 1882
    Date & place of death: Jan. 6, 1882

SCHIEFFELIN, ALBERT E. - age 35 - he and his brother EDWARD well-known
    in El Paso and southwest
    Paper & date: EPT Oct. 16, 1885
    Date & place of death: Oct. 13, 1885, Los Angeles, Ca.

SCHIENER, PETER - old citizen
    Paper & date: EPDH Nov. 9, 1881
    Date & place of death: San Antonio, Texas

147

SCHIER, CHARLES in Galveston, Texas - sign post fell on him; he was old.
Paper & date: LS Aug. 12, 1882
Date & place of death: Aug. 7, 1882

SCHILDKNECHT, Mrs. ISABELLE (nee ISABELLE BLANCHARD of El Paso co.) -
typhoid fever; hus.: A. SCHILDKNECHT
Paper & date: EPT Nov. 29, 1885
Date & place of death: Ysleta, Texas

SCHILLER, - his wife and child 3 yrs. - man and woman shot, child's skull
crushed; an old Bohemian
Paper & date: LS Nov. 12, 1884; EPT Nov. 10, 1884
Date & place of death: Nov. 8, 1884, Bryant Sta., Texas

SCHLEYER, EMIL of Las Vegas, N. M. - disappeared and friends think he has
been murdered.
Paper & date: LS Dec. 13, 1882
Date & place of death:.........

SCHNEIDER, "DOC" - dropped dead; he was a gambler
Paper & date: LS Feb. 14, 1883
Date & place of death: last week, Santa Fe, N. M.

SCHNEIDER, HAROLD infant and only child - lingering illness; par.: M/M
A. F. SCHNEIDER
Paper & date: BU Jan. 1, 1885
Date & place of death: Dec. 23, 1884, Socorro, N. M.

SCHONDEMANTEL, Mrs. ____ - lightening; hus. in Galveston, Texas
Paper & date: LS Aug. 12, 1882
Date & place of death: a few days ago

SCHRINER, JACOB - eating diseased pork; JACOB and his 8 children - does
not state they died
Paper & date: LS Jan. 20, 1883
Date & place of death: near Fredricksburg, Texas

SCHROEDER, HENRY - suicide
Paper & date: LS Mar. 15, 1882
Date & place of death: last week, Palestine, Texas

SCHUTZ, Mrs. AARON of Las Cruces, N. M. - age 28; hus.: AARON SCHUTZ, 2
children; Mr. SCHUTZ is returning to Germany
Paper & date: LS Dec. 23 & 27, 1882
Date & place of death: childbirth

SCHUTZ, CONRAD - disappeared - feared murdered
Paper & date: LS Aug. 18, 1883
Date & place of death: San Antonio, Texas

SCHWARTZ, ALONZO - bro.: EDWARD SCHWARTZ of Santa Fe, N. M.
Paper & date: LS Jan. 9, 1884
Date & place of death: recently, Elizabeth, N. J.

SCHWARTZ, B. - believed killed by a Mexican
Paper & date: LS Aug. 4, 1883
Date & place of death: couple of years ago, San Antonio, Texas

SCHWARTZ, LOUIS - age 18 - consumption; clerk at L. FREUDENTHAL & Co. for
ca 3 weeks; became ill and died
Paper & date: RGR May 10, 1884
Date & place of death: May 6, 1884

SCHWOB, FRANK - a German - pneumonia; bur. El Paso, Texas Apr. 14, 1885;
formerly of Denver, Colo.
Paper & date: EPT Apr. 14, 1885
Date & place of death: El Paso, Texas

SCIOTTE, LOUIS - A. D. MOORE struck him on the head with a scantling -
(cont'd next page)

Sciotte, Louis cont'd: - he will die.
    Paper & date: LS May 9, 1885
    Date & place of death: Malone, N. M.

SCOTT, _____ ca 30 yrs. old - murdered by Dty. Sher. FRANK P. NICHOLS;
    fa. - wealthy rancher of Pennsylvania
    Paper & date: LS Sept. 27, 1884; EPT Sept. 24, 1884; LS Feb. 2, 1884
    Date & place of death: Jul. 1883, Springer, N. M.

SCOTT, _____ hack driver - shot by Policeman AMONET resisting arrest.
    Paper & date: LS Oct. 11, 1884
    Date & place of death: Oct. 4, 1884, Waco, Texas

SCOTT, ISAM - to hand for murder in Palestine, Texas
    Paper & date: LS Nov. 29, 1882
    Date & place of death: Jan. 5, 1883

SCOTT, J. B. - train accident; wife: Mrs. ANN SCOTT
    Paper & date: LS Mar.12, 1884
    Date & place of death: some time ago, near Longview, Texas

SCOTT, Dr. ROY B. - broken neck - thrown from horse
    Paper & date: LS Oct. 11, 1884
    Date & place of death: Oct. 4, 1884, Trinity Mills, Texas

SCOTT, SAM - killed by JO IRWIN
    Paper & date: LS Dec. 31, 1881
    Date & place of death: Dec. 25, 1881, near Richmond, N. M.

SCOTT, Mrs. W. W. - burned during epileptic fit; surv.: hus. who is blind
    Paper & date: LS Feb. 28, 1885
    Date & place of death: Marshall, Texas

SCOTT, WM. "GOVERNOR" - age 85
    Paper & date: LS Oct. 14, 1885
    Date & place of death: Louisville, Brazoria co., Texas

SCOTTON (SCOTTEN), EDWARD H. - age 24 - shot on street by CLEM BAREFOOT;
    bur. Sept. 6 in Concordia Cem., El Paso, Texas; surv.: mo. Mrs. SCOT-
    TEN, El Paso, Texas; bro. FRANK SCOTTEN, El Paso, Texas; fa. of Lou-
    isiana, Mo.; b. Dec. 19, 1850 in Louisiana, Mo., came to Texas 1875,
    to El Paso 1880;mo. and bros. following
    Paper & date: LS Sept. 3, 1884; LS Sept. 6, 1884; EPT Sept. 3,5, & 9,
    1884
    Date & place of death: Sept. 2, 1884, Hunnewell, Kansas

SCRUGGS family - poisoned by servant girl; Mrs. SCRUGGS will recover
    Paper & date: LS Mar. 1, 1884
    Date & place of death: Kerens, Texas

SEALES, Miss _____ - fell in fire and burned to death
    Paper & date: LS Sept. 20, 1884
    Date & place of death: Burleson co., Texas

SEALS, SAM - negro - killed by W____ HUDSON, negro
    Paper & date: LS Aug. 25, 1883
    Date & place of death: Phoenix Park, Texas

SEALY, JOHN - age 63 - suddenly; ex-pres. of G. C. & S. F. R. R.
    Paper & date: LS Sept. 3, 1884; EPT Sept. 1, 1884
    Date & place of death: Aug. 30, 1884, Galveston, Texas

SEAMAN, _____ - shot by HITTSON's gang of cattle thieves; served in
    KIT CARSON Reg.; Postmaster Loma Parda; Chief of Police
    Paper & date: TB Sept. 28, 1872
    Date & place of death:.........

SEBES, _____ inf. dau. of Guadalajara, Mexico - cholera infantum; par:
    M/M HENRY SEBES and family; family was enroute to Europe
    (cont'd next page)

149

Sebes cont'd:
    Paper & date: LS Jun. 10, 1885; EPT Jun. 9, 1885
    Date & place of death: Jun. 8, 1885, Grand Central Hotel, El Paso,Tx.

SEELER, Maj. JOHN - insurance agent - in dying condition
    Paper & date: EPT Aug. 5, 1884
    Date & place of death: San Antonio, Texas

SEELEY, T. J. - Gen. Mgr. of Sonora R. R.
    Paper & date: LS Oct. 6, 1883
    Date & place of death: Oct. 3, 1883, on special car of A. T. & S. F.
    R. R., between Atchison & Valley Fall, Kansas

SEIKER, Lt. _____ Texas Ranger - shot by _____ GONZALES, age 13,
    son of PILANUS GONZALES
    Paper & date: EPT Jun. 4, 1885
    Date & place of death: few days ago, near Laredo, Texas

SELIGMAN, ABRAHAM of Ca.; bros.: JESSE & JAMES of Santa Fe, N. M.
    Paper & date: LS Feb. 18, 1885
    Date & place of death: Jan. 26, 1885, Frankfort, Germany

SELLERS, Mrs. _____ of Sacramento, Ca. - possible foul play; agent: A. A.
    STRAUSS (STRAWS); also listed as ELLERS & SHELLAS
    Paper & date: LS Jul. 16, 1884; EPT Jul. 14 & 17, 1884; EPDH Jul. 13,
    1884
    Date & place of death: Jul. 7, 1884, El Paso, Texas

SENA y BACA, Capt. JESUS MARIA - frozen to death while under the influ-
    ence of liquor; age 50; wife is daughter of ANTONIO M. ORTIZ;he was
    veteran of Battle of Valverde.
    Paper & date: LS Jan. 21, 1885; EPT Jan. 18, 1885
    Date & place of death: Jan. 15, 1885, Santa Fe, N. M.

SERNA, Mrs. PEDRO - chronic affliction; hus.: PEDRO SERNA
    Paper & date: RGR Aug. 22, 1885
    Date & place of death: Aug. 19, 1885

"SEVEN UP JOE" - beaten by JOHN CHENOWORTH - will probably die
    Paper & date: LS Dec. 19, 1883
    Date & place of death: Mangus Springs, New Mexico

SEVILLE, FREDDIE - song and dance girl - suicide
    Paper & date: LS Mar. 17, 1883
    Date & place of death: Mar. 13, 1883, Ft. Worth, Texas

SEYMOUR - negro - shot by policeman TOM SAMS
    Paper & date: LS Jul. 18, 1885
    Date & place of death: Hearne, Texas

SEYMOUR, THOMAS - shot and killed by W. L. MORRISON, a lunatic in the
    wards of St. Mary's Infirmary
    Paper & date: LS Jan. 17, 1883
    Date & place of death: recently, Galveston, Texas

SHAHAN, JOHN - accidentally shot himself; Red River, N. M. Cattle Co.
    Paper & date: LS Apr. 16, 1884
    Date & place of death: last week

SHANKS, HENRY - stabbed by ADAM WEIMAR during a religious discussion
    Paper & date: LS Oct. 10, 1883
    Date & place of death: Dallas, Texas

SHANNON, HENRY W. - pneumonia; also of Leadville, Colo.; formerly of Sil-
    ver City, New Mexico where he deserted his wife and family
    Paper & date: LS May 26, 1883; EPT May 22, 1883
    Date & place of death: May 21, 1883, Kingman, Arizona

SHANNON, JOHN - shot while escaping; son: J. T. SHANNON
    (cont'd next page)

150

Shannon, John cont'd:
    Paper & date: LS Mar. 28, 1883; LS May 9, 1883
    Date & place of death: Mar. 22, 1883, Lake Valley, New Mexico

SHARP, _____ - sentenced to death for rape of AMANDA CLARK in Gainesville,
    Texas
    Paper & date: EPT Sept. 9, 1883
    Date & place of death: Texas

SHARPE, H. M. - to be hanged for murder of E. KNESECK
    Paper & date: LS Jun. 3, 1885
    Date & place of death: Jun. 26, 1885

SHARP, THOMAS - shoot-out; resisting arrest
    Paper & date: LS Mar. 25, 1885
    Date & place of death: Mar. 20, 1885, Malone, Grant co., N. M.

SHAW, _____ - old man; killed by Indians; info. letter dated Jun. 19,
    1885
    Paper & date: BU Jun. 27, 1885
    Date & place of death: few days ago, near Lake Valley, N. M.

SHAW, SAMUEL WARNER ca. 45 yrs.- suicide; b. Newcastle, Lawrence co.,Pa.
    in 1838; had discharge papers
    Paper & date: LS Jun. 30, 1883; EPT Jun. 26, 1883
    Date & place of death: Jun. 24, 1883, Deming, New Mexico

SHEA, CHARLES
    Paper & date: LS Feb. 14, 1885
    Date & place of death: Laredo, Texas

SHEAN (SHEON), JOHN C. - age 32 - knifed by DAVID "DUTCH DAVE" OPPENHEIM-
    ER; bur. Athol, Mass.; highly connected in Vermont; young widow in
    Syracuse, N. Y.; m. Jan. 1, 1884 MAGGIE HARRINGTON of Athol, Mass.;
    child recently born; mother in Millers Falls; bro. and sis. in Otter
    River.
    Paper & date: EPT Sept. 5 & 23, 1885; LS Sept. 5 & 9, 1885
    Date & place of death: Sept. 4, 1885, Paso del Norte, Mexico

SHEARER, THOMAS C. of Marfa, Texas - suicide
    Paper & date: LS Feb. 8, 1882
    Date & place of death: Feb. 2, 1882

SHELBY, Capt. _____ - rumored killed by marauding Mexican nationals.
    Paper & date: EPT Feb. 12, 1885
    Date & place of death: Dimmitt co., Texas

SHELDON, Judge _____ of Tucson, Arizona; bus. closed Feb. 1, 1884 in mem-
    ory.
    Paper & date: LS Feb. 6, 1884
    Date & place of death:........

SHELTON, BURNETT - fell from pecan tree; "a young man"
    Paper & date: LS Oct. 25, 1882
    Date & place of death: Oct. 13-20, 1882, Harrison Sta., Texas

SHELDON, SIM - killed by P. R. RANDOLPH(?) (bad film)
    Paper & date: LS May 5, 1883
    Date & place of death: near Tyler, Texas

SHEPARD, GEO. B. from Arizona; yellow fever; bur. El Paso, Texas; cus-
    toms insp. at Nogales, Ariz.; surv. family; also listed as J. D. SHEP-
    HERD.
    Paper & date: EPT Jul. 23, 1884
    Date & place of death: Jul. 22, 1884, El Paso, Texas

SHEPHERD, JONES - killed by Mexicans; he was mail carrier on Mex.Cen.R.R.
    Paper & date: LS Mar. 28, 1883
    Date & place of death: in Mexico

SHEPHERD, TOM of Ft. Worth, Texas; shot by H. M. ST. CYR of Texas in
self-defense.
Paper & date: EPT Oct. 20, 1884
Date & place of death: Oct. 11, 1884, Chiquito Jaquino Mining Camp,
Mexico.

SHERFEY, J. W. - eminent physician; bro. at Champaign, Illinois
Paper & date: RGR Mar. 8, 1884
Date & place of death: recently

SHERMAN, R. M.[- fell down mine shaft (120 ft.) in the Jarillas; - Mr.
McMANUS also fell about 90 ft., but was able to crawl into camp for
assistance; bro. at Lake Valley, N. M.
Paper & date: RGR Jan. 12 & 19, 1884
Date & place of death: Jan. 9, 1884

SHERMAN, Dr. SILAS - negro - stabbed by JACK THOMPSON, a mulatto
Paper & date: LS Aug. 1, 1885; EPT Jul. 23, 1885
Date & place of death: last week, Longview, Texas

SHERRY, W. H. of Silver City, N. M. - pneumonia; pioneer newspaper man
Paper & date: LS Nov. 25, 1882
Date & place of death: last week

SHIELDS, EDWARD - frozen to death
Paper & date: LS Jan. 12, 1884
Date & place of death: Jan. 5, 1884, Chickasaw Nation (Okla.)

SHIELDS, HENRY - frozen to death
Paper &.date: LS Jan. 12, 1884
Date & place of death: Jan. 5, 1884, Chickasaw Nation (Okla.)

SHIPLEY, _____ wife and ch.; dau.-LULU; son-HARRY N.
Paper & date: EPDH Feb. 25, 1896; EPDH Dec. 3, 1896
Date & place of death: 14 yrs. ago

SHIRBY, GEO. of WILLIAM's Ranch, Texas - struck on head with a rock by
BILL WILLIAMS
Paper &.date: LS Dec. 14, 1881
Date & place of death: several days ago

SHOEMAKER, JEROME - shot by JAMES SAVAGE
Paper &.date: LS Mar. 17, 1883
Date & place of death: Mar. 10, 1883, Burlington, Montague co., Tex.

SHORT, R. A. - shot by S. H. WHEELER
Paper & date: LS May 16, 1883
Date & place of death: 11 mi. west of Gilmer, Texas

SHOUT, Dr. J. H. - oldest physician in Las Vegas, New Mexico
Paper & date: RGR Jan. 26, 1884
Date & place of death:.........

SHULTZ, Judge JULIUS of Austin, Texas; killed by HERMAN ZEAK
Paper & date: LS Aug. 5, 1882
Date & place of death: Jul. 30, 1882, Fayetteville, Texas(?)

SIEBENBORN, CHAS. of Ft. Davis, Texas; bro.-in-law: JOSEPH SCHUTZ of El
Paso, Texas
Paper & date: LS Oct. 29, 1881
Date & place of death: Oct. 24, 1881

SIEMERING, Judge. A.
Paper & date: EPT Oct. 5, 1883
Date & place of death: San Antonio, Texas

SILVA, MANUEL - MA. MIGUELA de SILVA & JULIAN SILVA, adm. of Estate; MA.
MIGUELA - guardian of her minor ch. ROSAURO & PEDRO.
Paper & date: BU May 12, 1885
Date & place of death: Socorro co., N. M.

SIMMONDS, _____ - shot by LOUIS EBERHART for abusing his wife.
Paper & date: LS Mar. 18, 1885
Date & place of death: Albuquerque, New Mexico

SIMMONS, _____ - negro - stabbed in throat by _____ REICKERTZ, negro;
he will die
Paper & date: LS Aug. 11, 1883
Date & place of death: San Antonio, Texas

SIMMONS, K. - shot by 3 masked men.
Paper & date: LS Oct. 8, 1884
Date & place of death: Sept. 30, 1884, near Coleman, Texas

SIMMONDS, T. A. - train accident
Paper & date: EPT May 1, 1883
Date & place of death: on T & P R. R. near Ft. Worth, Texas

SIMPSON, _____ - killed by COCHISE's band
Paper & date: TB May 18, 1871
Date & place of death: May 5, 1871, Whetstone Mtns.

SIMPSON, _____ - killed by ISKBIA(?)
Paper & date: EPT Jun. 2, 1883
Date & place of death: on Mescalero Ind. Res., N. M.

SIMPSON, Judge GEO. S. - bur. Sept. 7, 1885; sons: P. A. & R. SIMPSON
of Socorro, N. M.; dau: RAFAELITA of Trinidad, Colo.
Paper & date: BU Sept. 12 & 26, 1885
Date & place of death: Trinidad, Colo.

SIMPSON, L. V. - shot by Dr. CALHOUN LAWRENCE in argument
Paper & date: EPMS Dec. 4, 1884
Date & place of death: Dec. 2, 1884, Nechesville, Texas

SIMS, HENRY - shot by W. W. DILLARD - self defense
Paper & date: LS May 12, 1883
Date & place of death: DeKalb, Texas

SINCLAIR, A. - boat overturned while fishing; sur.: wife and 2 children
Paper & date: LS Aug. 8, 1885
Date & place of death: 12 mi. from Palestine, Texas

SINCLAIR, GEORGE- cut in two by saw in his sawmill
Paper & date: LS Nov. 17, 1883
Date & place of death: Dublin, Texas

SING LEE - Chinaman - dropped dead; left El Paso for California
Paper & date: LS Dec. 22, 1883
Date & place of death: Dec. 19, 1883, Deming, N. M.

SING WING - Chinaman; LEE TAI & SAM LING took body to China
Paper & date: EPT Aug. 1, 1884
Date & place of death: Jul. 31, 1884, Ft. Worth, Texas

SINGER, JOHN - German - shot by Col. GEORGE W. STONEROAD during drunken
fracas
Paper & date: LS Mar. 11, 1885
Date & place of death: Mar. 6, 1885, Las Vegas, N. M.

SISMONDI, CAMILO - apoplexy; Prof. of English at University
Paper & date: EPT Jul. 10, 1883
Date & place of death: Jul. 7, 1883, Chihuahua, Mexico

SITTON, DREW - murdered
Paper & date: LS Jan. 24, 1885
Date & place of death: near Tyler, Texas

SLAUGHTER, TOM - old and respected; dead in bed
Paper & date: EPT Aug. 1, 1884
Date & place of death: Jul. 31, 1884, near Corsicana, Texas

SLAWSON, Capt. _____ of Santa Rita Iron & Copper Co., Arizona; killed
    by Indians; nephew: WILLIAM SLAWSON
    Paper & date: EPT Apr. 13, 1883
    Date & place of death: last spring

SLEDD, JOSE T. - an old resident of Mesilla, New Mexico
    Paper & date: RGR Dec. 13, 1884
    Date & place of death: Dec. 4, 1884

SLEEPING or SLEEPY RABBIT - killed while trying to escape arrest; Creek
    Indian, leader of recent Indian revolt
    Paper & date: LS Mar. 17, 1883; EPDH May 20, 1883
    Date & place of death: last week, Okmulgee, Ind. Terr., Okla.

"SLIM JIM" - lynched
    Paper & date: LS Nov. 19, 1881
    Date & place of death: ca 2 weeks ago, Tierro Amarilla, N. M.

SLOAN, ANDREW C. - typhoid pneumonia; lawyer of Silver City, N. M.;"A.C.
    SLOAN, whose headquarters are at Kansas City, but whose destination
    is Hades, left for home today."
    Paper & date: LS Sept. 26, 1883; RGR Sept. 8 & 23, 1883
    Date & place of death: Sept. 3, 1883, Silver City, N. M.

SMALL, SOLOMON of Houston, Texas
    Paper & date: LS Dec. 14, 1881
    Date & place of death: Dec. 2, 1881

SMART, ANDREW - killed by bro.-in-law ASA BROWN
    Paper & date: LS Aug. 4, 1883
    Date & place of death: San Saba, Texas

SMART, DALLAS - murdered by 2nd Lt. J. W. HEARD, 3rd Cav. - arrested at
    Big Sandy, Texas and taken to Pittsburg, (Pa.? Tex.?)
    Paper & date: LS Jul. 29, 1885
    Date & place of death: last winter

SMART, J. L. of Waco, Texas - suicide by morphine
    Paper & date: LS Nov. 18, 1882
    Date & place of death: recently

SMITH, Lt. _____ 9th Cav. - killed by Indians
    Paper & date: EPDH Dec. 28, 1881
    Date & place of death: Aug. 1881, Dona Ana co.(?), N. M.

SMITH, _____ horse thief - killed in fight with GEORGE THOMPSON & 12
    others
    Paper & date: EPT Sept. 25, 1883
    Date & place of death: near Bloomfield, N. M.

SMITH, _____ baby b. Oct. 19, 1885; par.: M/M _____ SMITH (SMITH &
    THOMPSON Firm)
    Paper & date: EPT Oct. 23, 1885
    Date & place of death: El Paso, Texas

SMITH, _____ - killed by Indians
    Paper & date: TB Jul. 11, 1874
    Date & place of death: between Ft. Davis and El Paso, Texas

SMITH, _____ child; fa.: ROBERT SMITH murdered his own child.
    Paper & date: LS Sept. 24, 1884
    Date & place of death: Kildare, Texas

SMITH, Mrs. _____ - son: E. W. SMITH of El Paso, Texas
    Paper & date: EPMS Dec. 14, 1884
    Date & place of death: at home, Sanford, Texas

SMITH, ALFRED - negro - shot by BILL MARSHALL
    Paper & date: LS Apr. 12, 1884
    Date & place: shot Sat. night, Beaumont, Tx.;d. Apr. 9, 1884

SMITH, CHARLES of Colorado City, Texas - fell in well & drowned
    Paper & date: LS May 12, 1883
    Date & place of death: Seven Wells, Texas

SMITH, CHARLIE - a faro man; small pox
    Paper & date: LS Dec. 2, 1882
    Date & place of death: Nov. 29, 1882, El Paso, Texas

SMITH, D. T. - rancher on San Pedro - shot by robbers
    Paper & date: LS Dec. 12, 1883
    Date & place of death: Dec. 10, 1883, Bisbee, Arizona

SMITH, FRED - will die - stabbed by Mexicans MANUEL _____ & DALZIO
    Paper & date: EPT Jan. 27, 1885
    Date & place of death: near San Angelo, Texas

SMITH, GEORGE - killed in wind and hail storm
    Paper & date: EPT Nov. 25, 1883
    Date & place of death: Nov. 23, 1883, Marshall, Texas

SMITH, GEORGE F. - killed by JOHN SHINN
    Paper & date: LS Jun. 23, 1883
    Date & place of death: Ross Sta., Central R. R., Texas

SMITH, GUSTAV A. - general
    Paper & date: LS Dec. 16, 1885
    Date & place of death: Dec. 11, 1885, Santa Fe, N. M.

SMITH, J. D. - run over by train; surv.: widowed mother
    Paper & date: EPT Aug. 5, 1885
    Date & place of death: Ranger, Texas

SMITH, JACK - shot by Dty. Sher. LONG in self-defense
    Paper & date: LS Dec. 26, 1885
    Date & place of death: Dec. 19, 1885, Lamy, N. M.

SMITH, JOHN - native of Grand Rapids, Michigan
    Paper & date: LS Apr. 22, 1885
    Date & place of death: Albuquerque, N. M.

SMITH, L. H. - old and respected citizen
    Paper & date: LS Apr. 22, 1885
    Date & place of death: Bryan, Texas

SMITH, Gen. LARKIN - age 71 - vet. of Mex. War; Confederate general
    Paper & date: EPMS Dec. 5, 1884
    Date & place of death: Dec. 3, 1884, San Antonio, Texas

SMITH, PETER R. - killed by DALLAS LOGAN
    Paper & date: LS Apr. 8, 1882
    Date & place of death: 1873, Mansfield, Texas

SMITH, R. L. - killed by lightening while mowing hay
    Paper & date: LS Aug. 22, 1885
    Date & place of death: Animas, New Mexico

SMITH, ROBERT of Little Blue, Arizona - murdered by Apaches
    Paper & date: RGR Jun. 27, 1885
    Date & place of death: recently

SMITH, Mrs. ROBERT & 2 children - murdered by mulatto named JOHNSON
    Paper & date: LS Dec. 16, 1885
    Date & place of death: Minn's Prairie, Montgomery co., Texas

SMITH, TOM Capt., Clerk of Court - train accident - suit filed
    Paper & date: LS Jan. 16, 1884
    Date & place of death: Tyler, Texas

SMYTHE, WM. A. - age 28 (31?) - poor health; formerly of El Paso, Texas
    Paper & date: LS Sept. 2, 1885; EPT Aug. 29, 1885; SH Aug. 30, 1885

SMYTHE, WM. A. (cont'd):
Date & place of death: Aug. 28, 1885, Hot Springs, N. M. (or Las Vegas?)

SMITHER, Mrs. HATTIE - age 25 - native of Pa.
Paper & date: EPT Nov. 11, 1885
Date & place of death: Nov. 9, 1885, El Paso, Texas

SMITHSON, FANNY of Woodbury, Tenn. - enticed away from Tenn. by _____
TUCKER and abandoned in Texas
Paper & date: LS Nov. 30, 1881
Date & place of death: few days ago, Dallas, Texas

SNEED, H. S. - telegrapher of El Paso; heart disease; native of Lynchburg,
Va.; bro. in Lynchburg
Paper & date: LS Aug. 18, 1883; EPT Aug. 18, 1883
Date & place of death: Aug. 17, 1883, El Paso, Texas

SNOW(?), _____ - policeman - murdered by HENRY CAMPBELL, negro
Paper & date: EPT Jun. 25, 1884
Date & place of death: year ago, Houston, Texas(?)

SOLOMON, FRANCISCO - killed by Indians; well-known in Silver City, N. M.
Paper & date: EPDH May 3, 1882
Date & place of death: other day, near Clifton, Arizona

SOTO, AMBROSE - killed by M. ANDRO
Paper & date: LS Mar. 31, 1883
Date & place of death: Mar. 23, 1883, Bracketsville, Texas

SOTO, M/M DEMETRIO - aged - stabbed by 4 people - 1 was a woman
Paper & date: LS Nov. 21, 1883; EPT Nov. 25, 1883
Date & place of death: Nov. 18, 1883, Paso del Norte, Mexico

SOTO, PABLO - murdered
Paper & date: EPT Jul. 2, 1885
Date & place of death: Mar. 1885, 60 mi. SW of Tucson, Arizona

SOTOMAYOR, _____ - shot by PEDRO GARZA who also killed a companion of
_____ SOTOMAYOR
Paper & date: LS Jul. 9, 1884
Date & place of death: Mexico City, Mexico

SOUR, Miss _____ of Marshalltown, Iowa - consumption; on Spiegelberg ex-
cursion; bro. in Los Angeles, California
Paper & date: LS Nov. 28, 1883; EPT Dec. 2, 1883
Date & place of death: Nov. 24, 1883, near Deming, N. M.

SPANERSALL, FRITZ - drowned - supposed suicide
Paper & date: LS Nov. 25, 1885
Date & place of death: San Antonio, Texas

SPARKS, J. C. - shot from ambush; surv.: wife and 5 children (one is a
12 year old son)
Paper & date: LS Sept. 26, 1885; EPT Sept. 25, 1885
Date & place of death: near Big Springs, Texas

SPARKS, Capt. JOHN of Rangers - by a cattle thief
Paper & date: LS Apr. 18, 1883
Date & place of death: few days ago, Navarre co., Texas

SPAULDING, _____ - engienner, G.H. & S.A. R. R. - train accident
Paper & date: EPT Sept. 11, 1884
Date & place of death: Sept. 10, 1884, near Sanderson, Texas

SPEERS, JOE - murder by ISOM SCOTT; SCOTT sentenced to hang on Jan. 5,1883
Paper & date: LS Nov. 29, 1882
Date & place of death: Jan. 1, 1882, Palestine, Texas

SPELLMAN, BESSIE - infant; par.: M/M C. H. SPELLMAN

SPELLMAN, BESSIE (cont'd.):
Paper & date: LS Oct. 13, 1883
Date & place of death: Oct. 11, 1883, El Paso, Texas

SPENCER, Dr. _____ - pulmonary complaint - recent; surveyor general of
the territory; a general
Paper & date: TB May 10, 1872
Date & place of death:........

SPENCER, ALDEN G. - nephews: JOHN W. & DAVID WALTON, who left Dallas, Tx.
for N. M. 4 yrs. ago.
Paper & date: BU May 21, 1887
Date & place of death: 1885, LeSeuer, Minn.

SPENCER, CHARLES - "horse thief & murderer"; killed by a posse after a
jail-break at Silver City, N. M.
Paper & date: RGR Mar. 15, 1884
Date & place of death: Mar. 10, 1884

SPENCER, M. M. - proprietor of Spencer House; argument about a debt with
GEORGE BAHNEY which resulted in shooting and death
Paper & date: RGR Jul. 14, 1883; LS Jul. 7, 1883
Date & place of death: San Marcial, N. M.

SPLAINE, HERBERT - stabbed in back by _____ MORALES
Paper & date: EPT Aug. 11, 1884
Date & place of death: Aug. 10, 1884, near Straus, N. M.

SPRUNBERGER, Capt. T. W. - age 51 years
Paper & date: LS Mar. 22, 1882
Date & place of death: Mar. 17, 1882, Brenham, Texas

SPURLOCK, JAMES - shot by FRED ROTH; SPURLOCK was insane
Paper & date: LS May 16, 1885
Date & place of death: CHISUM Ranch, Lincoln co., N. M.

STAAB, ZADOC
Paper & date: LS Aug. 2, 1884
Date & place of death: Santa Fe, N. M.

STANDEFER, MART - killed by frightened team
Paper & date: LS Dec. 16, 1882
Date & place of death: Dec. 11, 1882, Waco, Texas

STANDERLING, _____ (family) - murdered - supposed by JNO. M. CARROTHERS,
arrested in Denver Hosp., Nov. 16
Paper & date: LS Nov. 22, 1884
Date & place of death: ....

STANDIFORD, JACK - suicide after killing his mistress
Paper & date: EPT Oct. 7, 1883
Date & place of death: Oct. 3, 1883, Tombstone, Arizona

STANIFORTH, _____ - young - killed
Paper & date: LS Jul. 22, 1885
Date & place of death: San Antonio, Texas (?)

STANLAND, _____ young man - shot by CHAS. WILLIAMS
Paper & date: EPT Jul. 22, 1884
Date & place of death: Jul. 16, 1884, Duck Creek near Franklin, Tx.

STANTON, Capt. _____ - killed by CHATTO (CHATO)'s Indians
Paper & date: EPDH Sept. 9, 1883
Date & place of death: Spring 1855, near San Miguel, N. M.

STAPLETON, PAUBLA BACA de - anniversary service; hus.: R. H. STAPLETON of
Socorro, N. M.
Paper & date: BU Mar. 13, 1886
Date & place of death: Mar. 11, ____

STEADMAN, J. H. - age 28 yrs., 13 days - Bright's disease; left Las Cruc-
es for better climate; surv.: wife; also spelled STEEDMAN
Paper & date: LS Oct. 10, 1883; RGR Oct. 6, 1883
Date & place of death: Sept. 26, 1883, Colorado City, Texas

STEELE, _____ - murder by step-father, GREEN; mother: Mrs. GREEN; bro.:
_____ STEELE
Paper & date: LS Aug. 16, 1882
Date & place of death: last week, Denton, Texas

STEFFIAN, PETER L.
Paper & date: LS Apr. 1, 1885
Date & place of death: Laredo, Texas

STEIN (STERN), JOSEPH - German - murdered with an axe
Paper & date: LS Jan. 10, 1885
Date & place of death: dead several days, near Uvalde, Texas

STEINMER(STEMMER), JOHN - brewer - burned in home; surv.: wife and 1 ch.
Paper & date: LS Nov. 26, 1884; EPT Nov. 24, 1884
Date & place of death: Nov. 20, 1884, Flagstaff, Arizona

STEPHENS, Dr. JNO. H. of Dallas, Texas - had been chief surgeon for
STONEWALL JACKSON of C.S.A.
Paper & date: LS Jan. 4, 1882
Date & place of death: recently

STEPPI, JOSEPH - shot himself
Paper & date: LS Dec. 22, 1883
Date & place of death: Dallas, Texas

STERLING, CHAS. M. - hanged for murder of ELIZA GRUMBACHER
Paper & date: BU Jun. 11, 1887
Date & place of death: Apr. 22, 1877, N. M.

STEVENS, CHAS. or HENRY - shot in back while plowing; Uncle AMOS STEVENS
and EDWARD BEAN arrested; BEAN confessed to getting gun and giving it
to AMOS STEVENS; surv. by wife
Paper & date: LS May 23, 1883; LS Jun. 9, 1883; EPT Jun. 25, 1885
Date & place of death: Gladewater, Texas

STEVENS, GEORGE - yellow fever
Paper & date: EPT Sept. 9, 1885
Date & place of death: Guaymas, Mexico

STEVENS, JAMES T. - native of Danbury, Conn.- murdered by H. H. HALL of
Corpus Christi and FRED DELANEY; fa.: EZRA STEVENS, Brookfield, Conn.,
nearly 70 years old
Paper & date: LS Sept. 6, 1884; EPT Sept. 8 & 29, 1884; SH Feb. 15,
1885
Date & place of death: Sept. 1, 1884, above El Paso, Texas

STEVENS, W. of Decatur, Ill. - suicide by drowning
Paper & date: LS Jun. 30, 1883
Date & place of death: San Antonio, Texas

STEVENSON, BILL - killed by a Mexican; deserter from Col. BAYLOR's Co.
Paper & date: LS Nov. 14, 1883
Date & place of death: few days ago, near Chihuahua, Mexico

STEVENSON, CHARLES - killed by Indians
Paper & date: EPT May 27, 1885
Date & place of death: May 23, 1885, near Grafton, N. M.

STEVENSON, Rev. J. P. - oldest Methodist preacher in Texas - preached 1st
Meth. sermon in Texas
Paper & date: LS Aug. 5, 1885
Date & place of death: last week, Breckenridge, Texas

STEWART, TOM - ex-sher. of Wilbarger co., Texas; killed - L. SHANKIN of
    Wichita Falls tried and acquitted
    Paper & date: LS Apr. 29, 1885
    Date & place of death: ....

STEWART, WM. "COONSKIN" - shot by son-in-law ROBERT FOSTER of Choctaw
    Nation, Okla., in self-defense
    Paper & date: EPT Jan. 23, 1885
    Date & place of death: Jan. 21(?), 1885, near Ft. Smith, Arkansas

STIFF, JAMES E. - body found murdered; started from Galiana for Guadalupe
    y Calvo 1 Dec. with money and gold bullion; well-known in El Paso, Tx
    and Chihuahua, Mex.
    Paper & date: LS Dec. 29, 1883; LS Jan. 2, 1884
    Date & place of death: Mexico

STODDARD, H. W. of Ca.- drowned in Rio Grande
    Paper & date: EPDH Dec. 28, 1881
    Date & place of death: Aug. 1881

STOKES, M/M _____ - killed by neighbor AL LOCKIE
    Paper & date: LS Aug. 29, 1885
    Date & place of death: Aug. 24, 1885, Blanco co., Texas

STONE CALF - Cheyenne Chief
    Paper & date: EPT Nov. 14, 1885
    Date & place of death: from Canton

STONE, DEWITT C. - Col.; former mayor of Galveston
    Paper & date: LS Aug. 9, 1884
    Date & place of death: Aug. 5, 1884, Wichita Falls, Texas

STOPE, G. W. - did not reveal where he buried $5,000 in gold
    Paper & date: LS Aug. 8, 1883
    Date & place of death: few days ago, Troupe, Texas

STOUDENMIRE, DALLAS - shot by MANNING Bro's - JAMES, FRANK, JOHN & Dr. G.
    F.; bur. at Columbus, Texas; ex-U.S. Marshall; Dty. U.S. Marshall;
    young bride; b. Dec. 11, 1845, Abafoil, Macon co., Alabama; to Texas
    1867 Columbus
    Paper & date: LS Sept. 20, 1882; EPDH Apr. 22, 1882; EPDH Sept. 20,
    1882
    Date & place of death: Sept. 18, 1882

STOVALL, Dr. J. - shot by assassinators few nights ago - has since died;
    BOB PEARSON charged, TOM PEARSON convicted
    Paper & date: LS Mar. 25, 1885; LS Apr. 22, 1885; LS Nov. 18, 1885
    Date & place of death: near Austin, Texas

STRACHAN, DOC _____ of Albuquerque, N. M. - probably fatally sick at
    Jemez Hot Springs
    Paper & date: LS Jul. 15, 1885
    Date & place of death:.........

STRANGE, J. - shot by friend W. H. BEAL
    Paper & date: EPT Jul. 17, 1884
    Date & place of death: Jul. 13, 1884, Dallas, Texas

STRAUSS, DAVID - 14 mos. - par.: M/M A. L. STRAUSS; other ch.
    Paper & date: BU Dec. 19, 1885
    Date & place of death: Socorro, N. M.

STREETER, L. N. - ca 50, b. Ca.; will probably be killed; white man with
    GERONIMO & JU - captured by Mex. soldiers; fa. was English merchant-
    man captain; mo. a native of Ca.; oldest son of GERONIMO was named for
    him.
    Paper & date: EPT May 11, 1883; EPT Jun. 12, 1883
    Date & place of death:......

STRICKLAND, ROBERT - murder by JIM STANLEY
    Paper & date: LS Dec. 13, 1882
    Date & place of death: Nov. 27, 1882, Eagle Lake, Texas

STRINGSON, JULIUS - murdered
    Paper & date: EPDH Nov. 25, 1883; EPDH Apr. 12, 1882
    Date & place of death: Apr. 8, 1882, Paso del Norte, Mexico

STROZZI, BENJAMIN - fell under his wagon
    Paper & date: LS Jul. 18, 1883
    Date & place of death: Socorro co., N. M.

STUART, _____ bro.: C. B. STUART of Waco, Texas; suit against Western Un-
    ion
    Paper & date: EPT Apr. 22, 1883
    Date & place of death: Feb. 3-5, 1883, Marshall, Texas

STUART, ARCHIE - shot by HANK PARRISH, self-defense; wife and ch.
    Paper & date: EPT Jul. 24, 1884
    Date & place of death: Jul. 12, 1884, Vegas Ranch on Ariz.-Nev. line

STUART, J. H. - bro. E. A. STUART of El Paso
    Paper & date: LS Dec. 16, 1885
    Date & place of death: Dec. 15, 1885, El Paso, Texas

STUART, Mrs. MAY of Marshall, Texas; hus. C. B. STUART, JR.: fa.: JAMES
    TURNER
    Paper & date: LS Nov. 26, 1881
    Date & place of death: Nov. 18, 1881

STURENBERG, FRANK (FRANCIS) an old German - complicated diseases ending
    in paralysis; wife: EMILY, insurance rec'd
    Paper & date: LS Jul. 28, 1883; EPDH Jul. 29, 1883 (Biography); EPDH
    Dec. 9, 1883
    Date & place of death: Jul. 28, 1883, El Paso, Texas

STURTEVANT, HARRY - negro - shot
    Paper & date: EPMS Nov. 27, 1884
    Date & place of death: Nov. 20, 1884, near Palestine, Texas

SULLIVAN, _____ - a Congregational minister, on way East from California;
    d. on train; wife and a little daughter
    Paper & date: LS Feb. 22, 1882
    Date & place of death: Feb. 15, 1882, near Albuquerque, N. M.

SULLIVAN, C. J. - former baggage master El Paso branch A.T. & S.F. R. R.
    Paper & date: LS Feb. 24, 1883
    Date & place of death: Feb. 18, 1883, Las Vegas Hot Springs, N. M.

SULLIVAN, O. M. - murdered by ALLEN GREGG
    Paper & date: LS Sept. 27, 1884
    Date & place of death: Kildare, Texas

SUMNER, IRIS A. of Arkansas - consumption
    Paper & date: LS Jan. 31, 1885
    Date & place of death: Albuquerque, N. M.

SUTHERLAND, _____ - murdered by Indians
    Paper & date: TB Mar. 16, 1871
    Date & place of death: between Casas Grandes and Gavilan on way to
    Silver City, New Mexico

SUTHERLAND, HENRY ca 19 yrs. - shot by Mexicans
    Paper & date: EPDH Sept. 7, 1881; EPDH Oct. 12, 1881
    Date & place of death: Sept. 3, 1881, Pittsburg, near El Paso, Texas

SUTTER, _____ 2 bros. - GERONIMO & his Apaches
    Paper & date: LS May 27, 1885
    Date & place of death: Alma, N. M. vicinity

SUTTLE, Mrs. ____ of Corsicana, Texas - clothing caught fire
    Paper & date: LS Jan. 27, 1883
    Date & place of death: Jan. 22, 1883

SUTTON, JOHN - killed by citizens for eloping with the wife of JOHN JAMES
    Paper & date: LS Jul. 30, 1884; RGR Jul. 26, 1884
    Date & place of death: Jul. 16, 1884, Lincoln co., New Mexico

SWAN, PAT - dynamite blast
    Paper & date: LS Mar. 28, 1885
    Date & place of death: 9 mi-Wichita Falls, Texas

SWEENEY, ____ - jail guard - mortally wounded by negro mob
    Paper & date: EPT Sept. 5, 1884
    Date & place of death: Refugio, Texas

SWEENY, DICK or SWANY, DAN - lynched by mob
    Paper & date: EPT Apr. 16, 1883; LS Mar. 15, 1882; LS Apr. 18, 1883
    Date & place of death: Feb. 1883, Rodgers' Bend, Bernalillo co.,N.M.

SWEENEY, JAMES - suicide by strychnine in coffee - too much liquor
    Paper & date: LS Jan. 31, 1885; EPT Jan. 30, 1885
    Date & place of death: Jan. 29, 1885, Houston, Texas

SWEENEY, LOUIS SARSFIELD - 2 or 3 yrs old; fa.: JOSEPH SWEENEY; bur, in
    San Antonio, Texas; whooping cough
    Paper & date: LS Jan. 24, 1885; EPT Dec. 24, 1884; EPDH Dec. 28, 1884
    Date & place of death: Dec. 22, 1884, El Paso, Texas

SWEENEY, PAT - gambler - shot by yard man of Mex. Cen. R. R.
    Paper & date: EPT Jun. 5, 1883
    Date & place of death: Jun. 2, 1883, Chihuahua, Mex.

SWIM, Mrs. LIZZIE of Ft. Worth, Texas - burns when firecrackers in her
    store were lighted deliberately and exploded by CLARENCE VEIGHT; he
    fled unhurt.
    Paper & date: LS Jan. 3, 1883
    Date & place of death: Dec. 1882

SWISS, CHARLES - burned alive in his house - fire set at 4 A.M. by Indians
    Paper & date: TB Feb. 14, 1872
    Date & place of death:.........

TABLER (TABLOR), RICHARD - R.R. conductor; murdered by DOC CAIN or DOC
    KANE; orig. from Shelbine, Mo.; bro.: W. R. TABLER of Los Angeles, Ca.
    Paper & date: LS May 26, 1883; LS Dec. 17, 1883; EPT May 19, 1883
    Date & place of death: May 17, 1883, Deming, New Mexico

TAGGERT, FRANK - hung by mob after jail break
    Paper & date: LS Mar. 12, 1884
    Date & place of death: Mar. 10, 1884, near Silver City, N. M.

TALAMANTES, KUSEVLO of Silver City, N. M.; fight with MANUEL GONZALES near
    Ascension, Mexico
    Paper & date: LS Jan. 3, 1883
    Date & place of death: a few days ago

TALBOT, ____ - 10 mo. old - burned; fa.: W. S. TALBOT
    Paper & date: LS Nov. 21, 1885
    Date & place of death: Patrick, Texas

TANTON, R. J. of McGregor, Texas - "gone to see his ancestors via the
    poison route"
    Paper & date: LS Dec. 9, 1882
    Date & place of death: recently

TAPIA, TEOFILA - one of the original settlers of Mesilla, N.M.
    Paper & date: RGR Aug. 16, 1884
    Date & place of death:.........

TAPIE, CONCEPCION - Sgt. of Co. B. (Mesilla) Territorial Militia
    Paper & date: RGR Mar. 8, 1884
    Date & place of death: Mar. 1, 1884

TAPPEINER, J. C. of the Copper Queen - shot by robbers
    Paper & date: LS Dec. 12, 1883
    Date & place of death: Dec. 10, 1883, Bisbee, Arizona

TARDY, Rev. Mr. _____ - pastor of Socorro, N. M. Baptist Church
    Paper & date: RGR Aug. 11, 1883
    Date & place of death: Aug. 5, 1883

TARDY, R. S. - between 25 and 30 yrs of age; resided in Ft. Worth, Texas;
    member of Col. BAYLOR's Rangers
    Paper & date: LS Feb. 17, 1883
    Date & place of death: Feb. 15, 1883, Ysleta, Texas

TARPY, Sgt. JAMES - killed by WILLEY & CLIFFORD; murderers were caught &
    hung on a telegraph pole
    Paper & date: TB Nov. 23, 1872
    Date & place of death: Nov. 13, 1872, Ft. Union

TATE, FRED - killed by JOHN ARTO, hus. of TATE's step-daughter
    Paper & date: LS Aug. 18, 1883
    Date & place of death: Galveston, Texas

TATE, JAMES of Chicago, Ill. - probably by Apaches
    Paper & date: EPT Sept. 29, 1884
    Date & place of death: recently, mtns. 300 mi. beyond Chihuahua, Mex.

TATE, W. M. of Missouri - shot by JAMES J. CROW
    Paper & date: LS Apr. 11, 1883
    Date & place of death: Apr. 6, 1883, Wills Point, Texas

TAYLOR, _____ - horse fell
    Paper & date: EPMS Dec. 17, 1884
    Date & place of death: Dec. 6, 1884, Whitesboro, Texas

TAYLOR, _____ - executed for murder; the last of the TAYLOR Brothers
    Paper & date: LS Nov. 28, 1883
    Date & place of death: Nov. 23, 1883, Londen, Texas

TAYLOR, BOB - negro - accidentally shot by APUELLO(?) - not expected to
    live
    Paper & date: LS Jul. 18, 1883
    Date & place of death: Sherman, Texas

TAYLOR, CHAS. - negro - shot by unknown
    Paper & date: LS May 24, 1884
    Date & place of death:........

TAYLOR, GEORGE - of Houston, Texas; run over by train
    Paper & date: LS Dec. 10, 1881
    Date & place of death: Nov. 30, 1881

TAYLOR, GEORGE - shot by Prof. BOB NEWLAND
    Paper & date: LS Sept. 24, 1884; EPT Sept. 19, 1884
    Date & place of death: Sept. 16, 1884, Gatesville, Texas

TAYLOR, JAMES - negro - hanged for murder
    Paper & date: LS Dec. 29, 1883; EPT Nov. 18, 1883
    Date & place of death: Dec. 22, 1883, Galveston, Texas

TAYLOR, LOUIS - negro - shot by THOMAS GRAY, a white man
    Paper & date: LS Aug. 4, 1883
    Date & place of death: Gallup, New Mexico

TAYLOR, Mrs. MATTIE, nee P___MAN - burned
    Paper & date: LS Mar. 1, 1884
    Date & place of death: Mineral Wells, Texas

162

TAYLOR, TOM aka COAL OIL JIMMY - shot by confederates in a robbery
Paper & date: TB Nov. 15, 1871
Date & place of death: ca Oct. 31, 1871

TAYS, Rev. JOSEPH (or JOHN) WILKINS - brief illness; b. Nova Scotia, Dec.
15, 1827; sons: JAMES A. TAYS, EUGENE ALEXANDER H. TAYS; wife: Mrs.
VIOLA R. TAYS; Mrs. TAYS leaves for her mother's home in Napa, Calif.;
of Scotch-Irish descent; educated in Penn.; taught in Penn. and West
Point, N. Y.; came to El Paso March 1881.
Paper & date: LS Nov. 22, 1884; LS Apr. 13, 1896; EPT Mar. 18, 1885;
EPT Nov. 18, 1883; EPT Nov. 29, 1883; EPDH Nov. 23, 1884; EPT Sept.
20, 1885; EPT Jan. 13, 1885
Date & place of death: Nov. 21, 1884 at 4:15 P.M. at home, El Paso,Tx

TEAGUE, M. D. - knifed in fight with M. FRIER
Paper & date: EPT Sept. 19, 1884
Date & place of death: Sept. 16, 1884, Abbott Sta., near Hillsboro,Tx

TELFUIN, "RUSSIAN BILL" - hanged by citizens; fa.: Count TELFUIN
Paper & date: LS Oct. 16, 1883
Date & place of death: few yrs. ago, Shakespeare, N. M.

TELLES, EVANGELISTO - pneumonia
Paper & date: RGR Jun. 21, 1884
Date & place of death: Jun. 14, 1884

TERRAZAS, TERESA - said to be relative of Gov. TERRAZAS of Chihuahua, Mex.
or N. M.?
Paper & date: LS Oct. 6, 1883
Date & place of death: Oct. 1, 1883, Silver City, N. M.

TERRELL, ____ young man; shot by JACK COCHRAN who later confessed; WILLIAM
GRIMMETT convicted and hanged, but was innocent
Paper & date: EPDH Jan. 31, 1890
Date & place of death: 1858-9, Indian Terr.

TERRY, ____ - hanged; two men hanged by mob for stealing cattle of a poor
widow
Paper & date: LS Dec. 6, 1882
Date & place of death: a few nights ago, Hazel Dell, Texas

TERRY, ____ - Sher. of Llano co., Texas - killed by EMMETT BUTLER
Paper & date: LS Dec. 30, 1884; EPT Dec. 30, 1884
Date & place of death: Dec. 28, 1884, Galveston, Texas

TERRY, Col. FRANK - killed in cavalry charge; bro.: DAVID S. TERRY of Ca.;
sons: KYLE & DAVID S.(b. FRANK and name changed later)
Paper & date: EPDH Jan. 24, 1890
Date & place of death: Dec. 16, 1861, Mumfordsville, Kentucky

TERRY, JOHN - accidentally shot by ALFRED BOLTON - will probably die
Paper & date: LS May 23, 1883
Date & place of death: near Houston, Texas

TERRY, STEVE - suicide
Paper & date: LS Dec. 2, 1885
Date & place of death: Waskom, Texas

"TEXAS FRANK" - killed by Indians in reprisal for killing one of them
without reason - townspeople refused protection for him
Paper & date: EPDH Nov. 9, 1881
Date & place of death: last week, Socorro, N. M.

"TEXAS JOE" a sporting man
Paper & date: LS Sept. 29, 1883
Date & place of death: few days ago, Greenville, Texas

THATCHER, Capt. J. M. - well known in El Paso
Paper & date: EPT Dec. 16, 1885
Date & place of death: Nashville, Tenn.

THOMAS, ____ baby; fa.: B. H. THOMAS
    Paper & date: LS Jun. 17, 1885
    Date & place of death: Albuquerque, N. M.

THOMAS, ____ - brief illness; family in Florida
    Paper & date: LS Dec. 16, 1882
    Date & place of death: Dec. 15, 1882, El Paso, Texas

THOMAS, ____ - freighter; killed by ____ HUGHES; another man named ____
    THOMAS involved
    Paper & date: LS Jun. 20, 1883
    Date & place of death: Abilene, Texas

THOMAS, Dr. A. L. - accidentally shot with "unloaded pistol" by J. CAL
    MATHEWS
    Paper & date: LS Sept. 20, 1884
    Date & place of death: Sept. 18, 1884, Spring Hill, Texas

THOMAS, ADA LORENA - 7 mos. and 12 days; mother deserted by worthless hus-
    band; several small children; mo.: Mrs. MARY or LORENA THOMAS; name
    also given as THOMA
    Paper & date: EPT Jun. 24 & 25, 1885; SH Jun. 28, 1885
    Date & place of death: Jun. 23, 1885, El Paso, Texas

THOMAS, ED - train wreck caused by EMANUEL CORTEZ, JERRY MARTIN & JESSE
    HENDERSON
    Paper & date: LS Apr. 8, 1885
    Date & place of death: Nov. 14, 1885, Waller co., Texas

THOMAS, FRED - Indian massacre by COCHISE. See MILLS, ____ bro. of Maj.
    MILLS.
    Paper & date: EPT Jan. 20, 1887
    Date & place of death: June, 1860, Cook's Peak, Grant co., N. M.

THOMAS, GHESS - hanged; he had killed another negro last winter; he met
    his fate bravely
    Paper & date: LS Aug. 16, 1882
    Date & place of death: Aug. 11(?), 1882, Palestine, Texas

THOMAS, R. L. - peddler - found in house; left Raton, N. M. about 3 weeks
    ago with C. THURMAN
    Paper & date: LS Dec. 2, 1885
    Date & place of death: near Liberty, N. M.

THOMPSON, A. H. - cartridge exploded in his hand
    Paper & date: LS Jun. 6, 1883
    Date & place of death: Gasa Grande, N. M. or Ariz. or Mex.

THOMPSON, ALICE a cyren (siren?) - shot by WILLIAM HEFFNER
    Paper & date: LS Sept. 13, 1884
    Date & place of death: Sept. 6, 1884, Ft. Worth, Texas

THOMPSON, BEN - shot down in self-defense by JOE C. FOSTER & JACOB S.COY;
    diamonds sold for wife's benefit and ch. of Austin; bro.: BILL
    Paper & date: LS Mar. 22, 1884; LS Apr. 15, 1885; LS Mar. 26, 1884;
    EPDH Mar. 16, 1884
    Date & place of death: Mar. 11, 1884, Austin, Texas

THOMPSON, DAN - shot by JOB GUNTER; surv. wife
    Paper & date: LS Sept. 20, 1884
    Date & place of death: Sept. 14, 1884, Sherman, Texas

THOMPSON, J. D. - killed by Indians
    Paper & date: EPT Nov. 11, 1885
    Date & place of death: near Rincon, New Mexico

THOMPSON, Dr. JAMES - dentist; consumption
    Paper & date: LS Dec. 12, 1885
    Date & place of death: Dec. 8, 1885, Las Vegas, New Mexico

THOMPSON, NED - negro; shot by JIM COOPER, negro, not expected to live
    Paper & date: LS Sept. 26, 1883
    Date & place of death: Dallas, Texas

THOMPSON, R. T. - former Maj. in KIT CARSON's Reg't.
    Paper & date: EPDH Apr. 5, 1882
    Date & place of death: last week, Laredo, Texas

THOMPSON, ROBERT - shot himself
    Paper & date: LS May 30, 1883
    Date & place of death: Ranger, Texas

THOMPSON, WILLIAM C. - shot by ALECK CALVIN, negro
    Paper & date: EPT Sept. 3, 1885
    Date & place of death: Aug. 24, 1885, Greer co., Texas

THORNTON, Judge J. J.
    Paper & date: LS Mar. 5, 1884
    Date & place of death: K-----bury, Texas

THORP, JAMES - consumption
    Paper & date: LS Jun. 27, 1885
    Date & place of death: Springer, N. M.

THURMOND, J. M. - justifiable homicide by ROBERT E. COWART; COWART re-
    leased by Coroner's inquest; indicted by Grand Jury Mar. 22, 1882;
    former Mayor of Dallas
    Paper & date: LS Mar. 18, 1882
    Date & place of death: Mar. 14, 1882, Dallas, Texas

TIBBS, SAMUEL - negro - shot by WM. BROOKWATER
    Paper & date: EPT Oct. 4, 1885
    Date & place of death: Oct. 2, 1885, Circleville, Texas(?)

TICKLE, HENRY - shot by county officers
    Paper & date: LS Nov. 28, 1885
    Date & place of death: Coleman co., Texas

TIELMAN, CHARLES - murdered by Apaches
    Paper & date: RGR Jun. 27, 1885
    Date & place of death: recently, Arizona

TIGHE, Mrs. _____ - stabbed by bro-in-law S. P. HOLMES; sis.: Mrs. HOLMES
    Paper & date: EPT May 21, 1885
    Date & place of death: Paris, Texas

TITE, FRED - negro; shot; son-in-law JOHN HART charged; wife and daughter
    Paper & date: EPT Aug. 15, 1883
    Date & place of death: Aug. 14, 1883, Galveston, Texas

TITTSWORTH, NORA
    Paper & date: LS Aug. 8, 1885
    Date & place of death: Lake Valley, N. M.

TITUS, Mrs. KATIE - age 28(?) yrs.; sudden - convulsions; bur. Oakland,
    California, her home, Sept. 1, 1884; hus.: W. B. TITUS; par. of Oak-
    land, Ca; here about 1 year
    Paper & date: EPT Sept. 4, 1884; SH Aug. 31, 1884
    Date & place of death: Aug. 29, 1884, El Paso, Texas

TOLBERT, TOM - fell dead while plowing
    Paper & date: LS May 30, 1885
    Date & place of death: May 22, 1885, near Greenville, Texas

TOLEY, PAT of Joplin, Missouri - accidentally shot by friend - probably
    fatal
    Paper & date: LS Apr. 28, 1883
    Date & place of death: Socorro, N. M.

TOMASA - Indian woman age 105
    Paper & date: LS Feb. 23, 1884
    Date & place of death: Feb. 18, 1884, Pueblo of Naurbe(?)`, N. M.

TOME, JUAN - killed by Indians
    Paper & date: TB May 4, 1871
    Date & place of death: Apr. 27, 1871, near BREMAN's saw mill, Silver
    City, New Mexico

TOME, PASCUALA of Las Cruces, New Mexico - shot during assault by "SCOTTY"
    McNEIL
    Paper & date: LS Nov. 19, 1881
    Date & place of death: Nov. 9-16, 1881

TONSALO, A. - Italian - accidentally shot by a Chinaman - probably fatal
    Paper & date: EPT Apr. 16, 1883
    Date & place of death: Tucson, Arizona

TOOEY, JAMES JR. - pneumonia; age 28 years; moved to Brookfield, Missouri
    -1867; bur. Brookfield, Missouri May 2, 1884, Catholic Church; bro.:-
    HENRY of Brookfield, Mo.; Mrs. JOHN DOUGHER (sister?); uncle: JULIUS
    TOOEY; uncle: JAMES TOOEY; Mrs. GUS TOOEY
    Paper & date: LS Apr. 26, 1884; EPT May 8, 1884
    Date & place of death: Apr. 24, 1884, Central Hotel, El Paso, Texas

TORRES, ISABELLA - little daughter - fa.: Don JUAN TORRES
    Paper & date: BU May 1, 1883
    Date & place of death: last month, Socorro, New Mexico

TOWNSEND, IRA - attacked by bear - will probably die
    Paper & date: LS Aug. 4, 1883
    Date & place of death: Grant co., New Mexico

TOWNSEND, JOSHUA - Texas veteran
    Paper & date: EPT Oct. 14, 1884
    Date & place of death: Oct. 10, 1884, Limestone co., Texas

TOWNSLY, Mrs. ___ -son: Dr. L. M. TOWNSLY of El Paso, Texas; son & sis.
    Paper & date: EPT Sept. 7, 1883
    Date & place of death: Sept. 6, 1883, Albany, Texas

TRAINER, JAMES of Albuquerque, New Mexico - "well-known character" whose
    mother-in-law and wife last spring near Wingate met tragic ends
    Paper & date: LS Oct. 29, 1881
    Date & place of death: last week

TREGIDO, TROLIVO - shot by TRINIDAD SALAZAR
    Paper & date: LS Aug. 8, 1885
    Date & place of death: Albuquerque, New Mexico

TREMBLE, ELMORE - will die - stabbed by Mexicans MANUEL ___ & DALZIO;
    name also given as TREBBLE
    Paper & date: EPT Jan. 27, 1885; LS Jan. 31, 1885
    Date & place of death: near San Angelo, Texas

TRESCOTT, B. L. - ambushed; formerly of San Antonio, Texas
    Paper & date: EPDH May 3, 1882
    Date & place of death: Apr. 21, 1882, near Clifton, Arizona

TREVINO, ___ - shot himself over death of his father, LOUIS TREVINO
    Paper & date: EPT Aug. 7, 1884
    Date & place of death: Aug. 5, 1884, near Matamoros, Mexico

TREVINO, Mrs. Gen. BERTHE ORD - dau. of Gen. ORD of San Antonio, Texas;
    hus.: Gen. GERONIMO TREVINO & son of near Monterrey, Mex.; step-dau.:
    (dau. of Gen.'s first wife)
    Paper & date: EPDH Mar. 9, 1884; EPDH Apr. 27, 1884
    Date & place of death: few days ago, Old Point Comfort

TREVINO, LOUIS - dragged by horse; son   (cont'd next page):

TREVINO, LOUIS (cont'd):
    Paper & date: EPT Aug. 7, 1884
    Date & place of death: Aug. 5, 1884, near Matamoros, Mexico

TRIGG, NORA - shot accidentally by little bro.; Dr. TRIGG, fa.; bro.
    Paper & date: EPT Jul. 11, 1884
    Date & place of death: Jul. 8 or 9, 1884, Lockhart, Texas

TRUBY, C. - small pox; asthma, came west for health; watchmaker; formerly
    in Illinois & Kansas; wife in Sumner co., Kansas; 3 children
    Paper & date: LS[Dec. 9, 1882; EPDH Dec. 6, 1882
    Date & place of death: Dec. 5, 1882, El Paso, Texas

TRUESDALE, Miss ____ of Giddings, Texas; suddenly while at breakfast table
    Paper & date: LS Jan. 7, 1882
    Date & place of death: Dec. 28, 1881

TRUJILLO, ____ - son; accidentally shot; fa.: NERIO TRUJILLO
    Paper & date: LS Jul. 4, 1883
    Date & place of death: Wagon Mound, New Mexico

TRUJILLO, EULALIO - 12 yrs.; thrown from a horse; fa.: JOSE ABUNCIO TRU-
    JILLO
    Paper & date: LS Oct. 31, 1885; RGR Oct. 31, 1885
    Date & place of death: Oct. 28, 1885, Las Cruces, N. M.

TUCKER, SCOTTY - remains found - believed murdered
    Paper & date: BU Jun. 25, 1887
    Date & place of death: 2 yrs. ago, near Flagstaff, Arizona

TUCKER, W. H. - suddenly
    Paper & date: LS Jun. 23, 1883
    Date & place of death: Albany, Texas

TUMEY, A. C. (TWOMEY) - shot by Col. L. F. CAMPBELL; both of Austin, Tx.;
    route agent for Tx. Central R. R.
    Paper & date: LS Feb. 28, 1883
    Date & place of death: Feb. 23, 1883, near Hempstead, Texas

TURNER, ____ - shot to death in his bro.'s saloon; formerly kept the Gem
    Saloon of El Paso, Texas; bro.
    Paper & date: LS Jan. 10, 1883
    Date & place of death: ....

TURNER, Mrs. ____ of Belton, Texas; effects of Wizard Oil
    Paper & date: LS Feb. 15, 1882
    Date & place of death: recently

ULIBARRI, TIODOSO - shot by rustlers on a drunken spree; rustlers - BILLY
    WILSON, TOM PICKETT, YANK BEALE, PONEY WILLIAMS
    Paper & date: RGR Jan. 19, 1883
    Date & place of death: Jan. 15, 1884, Seven Rivers, near Tularosa,New
    Mexico

UNRUH, FRANK - killed by ____ BAKER, jealousy
    Paper & date: LS Dec. 19, 1885
    Date & place of death: northern New Mexico

UNTER, ____ - murdered by Indians
    Paper & date: TB May 4, 1871
    Date & place of death: Apr. 13, 1871, San Pedro Valley

URISATE, LUIS - struck by lightening
    Paper & date: LS Jul. 25, 1885
    Date & place of death: Jul. 18, 1885, Santa Fe, N. M.

UTTER, CHARLIE - killed; a gambler
    Paper & date: EPDH Sept. 20, 1882
    Date & place of death: Chihuahua, Mexico

VALDEZ, _____ - accidentally shot
   Paper & date: LS Aug. 13, 1884
   Date & place of death: other day, San Antonio, Texas

VALDEZ, JUAN - killed by JUAN BACA - arrested in Tecolote (Colo. or N.M.?)
   Paper & date: EPT Apr. 14, 1885
   Date & place of death: in camp in N. M.

VALDEZ, MARTIN - age 35 yrs., 6 mos.; bro.: MARCIAL VALDEZ, editor of El
   Tiempo
   Paper & date: RGR May 26, 1883
   Date & place of death: May 21, 1883

VALDEZ, PEDRO of San Miguel co., N. M.
   Paper & date: RGR Dec. 6, 1884
   Date & place of death: recent

VALDEZ, Col. PEDRO of Mexican Army; wounds; lived near San Antonio, Texas
   as a boy; called WINKER; lived at Eagle Pass, Texas as well as Mexico
   Paper & date: EPDH Aug. 9, 1882
   Date & place of death: Zaragoza, Coah., Mex.

VALENCIA, ANTONIO - froze after missing a foot bridge - too much tangle-
   foot (drink)
   Paper & date: LS Feb. 7, 1885
   Date & place of death: Watrous, N. M.

VALENTINE, TOM - shot by "ranch jumpers"
   Paper & date: RGR Mar. 1, 1884
   Date & place of death: Feb. 20, 1884, Penasco, N. M. SE corner of Mes-
   calero

VAN ALSTEIN, _____ - shot by Constable JOHN HATTON - claims self-defense;
   wife shot 2 times
   Paper & date: LS Jul. 21, 1883
   Date & place of death: Brownsboro, Texas

VANATAN, _____ infant; name also given as VANSTAN; par.: M/M WM. VANATAN
   Paper & date: LS Feb. 11, 1885; EPT Feb. 11, 1885
   Date & place of death: Feb. 9, 1885, El Paso, Texas

VANDA, FELIPA - run over by JESSE BELL
   Paper & date: LS Aug. 18, 1883
   Date & place of death: San Antonio, Texas

VAN DYKE, H. of Toyah, Texas; small pox
   Paper & date: LS Feb. 18, 1882
   Date & place of death: Feb. 12, 1882

VANHORENBECK, FRANCIS - exhaustion while stacking hay
   Paper & date: LS Sept. 24, 1884
   Date & place of death: Sept. 19, 1884, near San Antonio, Texas

VAN OSTEN, _____ - run over by locomotive; engineer on Palmer & Sullivan
   R. R.; resident of Laredo, Texas
   Paper & date: LS Mar. 11, 1882
   Date & place of death: recently, near Huc Huc Foca, Mexico

VAN VLECKBURG, J. J. of Chicago - suddenly
   Paper & date: LS Aug. 27, 1884
   Date & place of death: Aug. 22, 1884, Dallas, Texas

VAN WINKLE, _____ - shot by _____ LYNCH
   Paper & date: BU Aug. 21, 1886
   Date & place of death: Aug. 14, 1886, Magdalena, N. M.

VARGAS, IGNACIO - drunken brawl-shot by _____ GUTIERREZ in Paso del Norte,
   Mex.; name given also as IGNATIOUS VHORGES; wife & several small ch.
   Paper & date: LS Jun. 27, 1883; EPT Jun. 26, 1883
   Date & place of death: Jun. 24, 1883, El Paso, Texas

VASQUEZ, Gen. _____ - shot by soldiers; article dateline - Monterrey,Mx.
   July 31
   Paper & date: EPT Aug. 1, 1884
   Date & place of death: near Satuta, Mexico

VAU, WILLIAM - 30 years in Albuquerque
   Paper & date: LS Jun. 3, 1885
   Date & place of death: Albuquerque, New Mexico

VAUGHN, CLEVELAND - fa.: Prof. S. A. VAUGHN
   Paper & date: LS Oct. 1, 1884
   Date & place of death: Sept. 28, 1884, El Paso, Texas

VAUGHN, Mrs. S. A. - hus.: Prof. S. A. VAUGHN; ch.; one recently burned
   Paper & date: LS Sept. 10, 1884
   Date & place of death: Sept. 6, 1884, El Paso, Texas

VELA, Mrs. JOSEFA RIVAS
   Paper & date: LS Nov. 19, 1884
   Date & place of death: Nov. 14, 1884, San Antonio, Texas

VELARDE, MARGARITA - age 100; 11 grand children; 50 great-grandchildren;
   20 great-great-grandchildren
   Paper & date: LS Dec. 26, 1885
   Date & place of death: Abiqui, New Mexico

VERNON, SAM -
   Paper & date: BU Jul. 11, 1885
   Date & place of death: Jul. 8, 1885, Santa Fe, New Mexico

VERNON, STACY - young son; par.: SAMUEL & JESSIE VERNON
   Paper & date: BU Jun. 1, 1883
   Date & place of death: May 29, 1883, Socorro, New Mexico

VICTORIO - Indian Chief; battle with Mexican troops; at least 2 daughters
   Paper & date: EPT Sept. 15, 1883; LS Jun. 16, 1883; EPT Oct. 6, 1883;
   EPDH Dec. 20, 1882
   Date & place of death: 1881, Tres Castillas, Mexico

VIDAURI, ALEJANDRO - assassinated
   Paper & date: LS Aug. 26, 1885
   Date & place of death: few days ago, Zapata co., Texas

VIGIL, Mrs. _____ - murdered; hus.: FRANCISCO VIGIL; son
   Paper & date: LS Sept. 13, 1884
   Date & place of death: near Chimayo, New Mexico

VIGIL, JUAN - murdered by JOSE PEDRO SANDOVAL
   Paper & date: LS Aug. 19, 1885
   Date & place of death: Puerto de Luna, New Mexico

VOGEL, CLARA BEATRICE - 4 mo's.; par.: JOSEPH & EMMA VOGEL
   Paper & date: EPT Oct. 17, 1885
   Date & place of death: Oct. 16, 1885, El Paso, Texas

WADDELL, _____ - hung by mob- charged with hiring CHAS. MITCHELL, a neg-
   ro, to ravish and kill his wife
   Paper & date: LS Nov. 8, 1884
   Date & place of death: Nov. 3, 1884, Little Rock, Arkansas

WADDELL, Mrs. _____ - of Texarkana, Texas; murdered by negro who ravished
   her than split her head with hatchet
   Paper & date: LS Nov. 5 & 8, 1884
   Date & place of death: near Richmond, Arkansas

WADE, MANFORD - 11 yrs. old; killed by stray bullet from shooting gallery
   Paper & date: LS May 23, 1883
   Date & place of death: Raton, N. M.

WAGGONER, DANIEL - a German; cold & neglect in prison (cont'd next page)

169

WAGGONER, DANIEL (con'td):
Paper & date: LS Jan. 9, 1884
Date & place of death: recently, Dallas, Texas

WAGNER, HENRY - same complaint his wife died of - (she died of child-
birth). (Item from San Antonio, Texas "Times", copied from "Express")
Paper & date: EPDH Sept. 16, 1881
Date & place of death: ....

WAGNER, HERMAN - runaway team
Paper & date: LS Jan. 6, 1883
Date & place of death: Dec. 31, 1882, Bastrop, Texas

WAHL, _____ infant; par.: Dr. & Mrs. G. W. WAHL
Paper & date: EPDH May 13, 1883
Date & place of death: few days ago, Ysleta, Texas

WAILER, CARL - German shoemaker; shot himself
Paper & date: LS July 25, 1883
Date & place of death: Ft. Worth, Texas

WAITE, FRED E. - hanged for killing a jailor in 1882
Paper & date: LS Mar. 28, 1883
Date & place of death: Mar. 23, 1883, Franklin, Milano co., Texas

WALDO, WM. O. - killed by Indians; younger bro.: Judge WALDO of Santa Fe,
New Mexico
Paper & date: LS Nov. 28, 1885; RGR Nov. 28, 1885
Date & place of death: Nov. 24, 1885 near Ft. Apache, Arizona

WALKER, ED - killed by JAMES PITTS
Paper & date: LS Oct. 15, 1884
Date & place of death: Oct. 7, 1884, Richmond, Texas

WALKER, TOM of Dallas, Texas; probably murdered - last wrote family June
20, 1885
Paper & date: EPT Aug. 12, 1885
Date & place of death: Arizona

WALKER, WM. - age 20; consumption; mo. & fa.; gen'l solicitor for Chica-
go & Milwaukee R. R .
Paper & date: LS Jan. 16, 1884
Date & place of death: Jan. 12, 1884, El Paso, Texas

WALLACE, _____ - shot by _____ ALVIS in self defense
Paper & date: LS Feb. 11, 1885
Date & place of death: few days ago - near Gainesville, Texas

WALLACE, _____[- murdered by QUIRINO LUCERO & EPIMINTO APOLARIO
Paper & date: LS Nov. 5, 1884
Date & place of death: New Mexico

WALLACE, _____ - shot by _____ STEVENS, a young man; trial in Ft. Worth
Paper & date: EPT June 20, 1885
Date & place of death: Mansfield, Texas

WALLACE, Col. _____ of Anderson co., Texas; late county collector
Paper & date: LS Nov. 26, 1881
Date & place of death:.........

WALLACE, "BIG FOOT" - found dead in his cabin
Paper & date: EPDH Jan. 20, 1884
Date & place of death: last week, Atascosa co., Texas

WALLACE, C. O. of St. Louis; suicide in Houston, Texas
Paper & date: LS Nov. 1, 1882
Date & place of death: Oct. 26(?), 1882

WALLACE, G. W. - shot by W. W. LITTLEFIELD
Paper &‗date: LS Nov. 7, 1883 D & P: Leesville, Gonzales co., Texas

WALLACE, ROBERT - mine cave-in
    Paper & date: EPT May 19, 1884
    Date & place of death: May 18, 1884, Grass Valley (N. M. or Calif.?)

WALLACE, WILLIE R. - heart disease
    Paper & date: LS Nov. 19, 1884
    Date & place of death: Nov. 14, 1884, San Antonio, Texas

WALLER, JOHN R. of New York City; thrown from his carriage Apr. 21, 1883,
    has since died of injuries; (Name given as WALTER also.) Wife & rel.;
    GEORGE A. WALLER (middle initial shown also as R. or W.)
    Paper & date: LS Apr. 28, 1883; EPT Apr. 27, 1883; BU May 1, 1883
    Date & place of death: Apr. 24, 1883 near Silver City, New Mexico

WALLER, Mrs. JOHN R. formerly of Socorro, New Mexico
    Paper & date: BU Aug. 15, 1885
    Date & place of death: latter part of July, New York

WALSH, JOHN (or WELCH) - hung by mob for murder
    Paper & date: LS May 2, 1883; EPT May 3, 1883
    Date & place of death: Apr. 29, 1883, Lordsburg, New Mexico

WALTERS, MITCHELL - drowned in Trinity River
    Paper & date: LS July 7, 1883
    Date & place of death: near Dallas, Texas

WARD, _____ child; shot accidently by playmate; 10 yr. old son of Capt.
    WARD
    Paper & date: LS Nov. 25, 1882
    Date & place of death: Nov. 20, 1882, Ft. Worth, Texas

WARD - a Chickasaw Indian - fight with cowboys
    Paper & date: EPT Jul. 22, 1885
    Date & place of death: Jul. 18, 1885, Indian Terr. (Okla.)

WARD, CHARLES - executed for outraging person of DORA ELLENMAN; he denied
    his guilt to the last; age 35, from Athens, Alabama
    Paper & date: LS Aug. 26, 1882
    Date & place of death: Aug. 21, 1882, San Antonio, Texas

WARD, JOE from New Mexico; shot while attempting escape from penitentiary;
    confessed to murder of JACK HARRIS in Leavenworth, Kansas in 1880
    Paper & date: EPT Feb. 19 & 20, 1885
    Date & place of death: Feb. 18, 1885, Canon City, Colorado

WARD, Mrs. JOHN G. - sis.: Mrs. ALFRED J. BUCHOZ of Las Cruces, N. M.
    Paper & date: RGR Aug. 30, 1884
    Date & place of death: Aug. 14, 1884, Clifton, A. T.

WARD, Mrs. LOUISE P. - dau.: Mrs. G. W. LANE, Sec'y of Territory-N. M.
    Paper & date: BU Nov. 28, 1885
    Date & place of death: Nov. 25, 1885, Santa Fe, N. M.

WARD, WM. L. - heart disease; a young ex-Ranger, age 28
    Paper & date: LS Mar. 8, 1882; EPDH Mar. 8, 1882
    Date & place of death: Mar. 6, 1882

WARREN, B. J. - murdered by W. J. WOOD & NEIL BARNETT
    Paper & date: LS Feb. 28, 1885
    Date & place of death: Feb. 10, 1885, Sweetwater, Texas

WASHBURN, D. W. - Chief Eng. - Gould R. R.; train collision
    Paper & date: EPDH Feb. 8, 1882
    Date & place of death: Feb. 7, 1882 near Waco, Texas

WASHINGTON, BUTTON - peddler; murdered by WALTER BRADY, negro, for money
    Paper & date: LS Apr. 25, 1885
    Date & place of death: few days ago, near Victoria, Texas

WASHINGTON, Dr. LAWRENCE A. of Denison, Texas; grand-nephew of GEORGE

WASHINGTON, Dr. (cont'd):
WASHINGTON and nearest living relative of GEORGE WASHINGTON
Paper & date: LS Aug. 16, 1882
Date & place of death: last week

WATKINS, GEORGE - negro; acute mania?
Paper & date: LS June 13, 1883
Date & place of death: Houston, Texas

WATKINS, O. B. - an American; bur. in Chihuahua; services by Rev. Mr.EAT-
ON of Boston
Paper & date: EPDH Apr. 26, 1882
Date & place of death: few days ago, Chihuahua, Mexico

WATLINGTON, Miss BESSIE, age 26; ill for many weeks; died unexpectedly in
arms of her bro.: Lt. O. D. WADLINGTON of Las Cruces; no other surv.
relatives.
Paper & date: RGR Aug. 11, 1883
Date & place of death: Aug. 6, 1883, Rincon, New Mexico

WATROUS, S. B., Jr. of Watrous, New Mexico; suicide; fa.: S. B. WATROUS
Paper & date: LS May 2, 1885; BU May 27, 1886
Date & place of death: Colorado

WATSON, JOHN - shot by JOHN SWILLEY
Paper & date: LS Nov. 25, 1885
Date & place of death: Liberty, Texas

WATTS, JOHN - shot by New Mexico Militia
Paper & date: LS Mar. 28, 1883
Date & place of death: Lake Valley, New Mexico

WATTS, ELI - killed by train
Paper & date: LS Oct. 1, 1884
Date & place of death: Sept. 25, 1884, Van Alstyne, Texas

WATTS, WILLIAM[- Administrator of Estate, A. KUHNE, Dona Ana co., N. M.
Paper & date: MT June 30, 1861
Date & place of death: before May 18, 1861

WEAVER, J. O. (Weaver Organ Co., York, Penn.) - lost his mind and commit-
ted suicide
Paper & date: LS Dec. 26, 1885
Date & place of death: Dec. 19, 1885, Dallas, Texas

WEBB, _____ - shot in a fight at Cimarron; he was a desparado
Paper & date: TB Feb. 14, 1872
Date & place of death:........

WEBB, Mrs. _____ - killed by lightening
Paper & date: LS Jul. 18, 1885
Date & place of death: Jul. 13, 1885, La Grange, Texas

WEBB, JNO. - old settler; stabbed himself - suicide over money problems;
former pilot at Brazos Santiago; large family
Paper & date: EPT Aug. 7, 1884
Date & place of death: Aug. 6, 1884, Brownsville, Texas

WEBB, MATT - 10 yrs. old; accidentally shot by WILLIAM RASMUS
Paper & date: LS Jul. 11, 1883
Date & place of.death: Silver City, New Mexico

WEBER, JUAN - shot & killed by LUTE WARDER; bro.: HENRY, also wounded by
WARDER
Paper & date: LS Oct. 29, 1881
Date & place of death: Oct. 22, 1881 - of Las Golondrinas, N. M.

WEBSTER, EUGENE (Train Conductor) - killed while resisting a robbery; KIT
JOY tried in Sierra co., N. M.
P/D: LS Nov. 5, 1884 D/P: Gage Sta., N. M.

WEBSTER, T. C. - R. R. Engineer - shot by train robbers; train robbers:
    MITCH LEE, who killed WEBSTER, GEORGE WASHINGTON CLEVELAND, "KID" JOY
    & FRANK TAGGART; surv.: wife
    Paper & date: LS Nov. 28 & 29, 1883; LS Jan. 5, 1884
    Date & place of death: Nov. 24, 1883, Gage Sta., N. M.

WELDING, E. E. - shoot out with Judge TERRELL & bro. FRANK TERRELL
    Paper & date: LS Feb. 13, 1884
    Date & place of death: near Ft. Stanton, N. M.

WELLINGTON, Mrs. R. H. of Bullard's Peak, Grant co., N. M. - poor health
    Paper & date: LS May 23, 1885
    Date & place of death: St. Paul, Minn.

WELLS, CLINTON G. - suicide - morphine
    Paper & date: LS Jan. 31, 1885; EPT Jan. 27, 1885
    Date & place of death: Jan. 25, 1885, Galveston, Texas

WELLS, Mrs. MARY - age 80; paralysis; dau.: Mrs. DANIEL TAYLOR
    Paper & date: LS May 20, 1885
    Date & place of death: Albuquerque, N. M.

WELNANZ, J. - shot by JOE FOUNTAIN
    Paper & date:_ EPT May 8, 1883
    Date & place of death: May 6, 1883, Benson, Arizona

WERNER, Hon. MELCHIOR of Albuquerque, N. M.
    Paper & date: RGR Sept. 8, 1883
    Date & place of death: Sept. 3, 1883

WEST, Mrs. ____ of Austin, Texas
    Paper & date: LS Dec. 3, 1881
    Date & place of death: Nov. 22, 1881

WEST, Judge CHAS. S.
    Paper & date: LS Oct. 28, 1885
    Date & place of death: Oct. 23, 1885, Austin, Texas

WEST, FRANK - came from Pueblo, Colo.; accidentally shot himself; about
    25 years old; par.: live in Ohio
    Paper & date: EPT Oct. 9, 1884
    Date & place of death: Oct. 8, 1884, El Paso, Texas

WEST, NELLIE - a Cyprian - suicide by morphine
    Paper & date: LS June 20, 1883
    Date & place of death: Corsicana, Texas

WESTSELL, HOMER - R. R. Conductor; slipped and fell under the train
    Paper & date: LS June 13, 1883
    Date & place of death: Marshall, Texas

WETMER, JOHN W. of Sondesburg, Penn.- consumption; died on train; Masons
    conducted the service
    Paper & date: EPMS Jan. 3, 1885
    Date & place of death: between Wagon Mound and Las Vegas, N. M.

WHALEN, WILLIE - age 8; drowned
    Paper & date: LS Jun. 16, 1883
    Date & place of death: Houston, Texas

WHEAT, J. B. - shot in home
    Paper & date: LS Nov. 7, 1885
    Date & place of death: near Richmond, Texas

WHEATINGTON, TOM (aka "RED RIVER TOM") - shot; LEE, KIMBERLY & McCALL(or
    McPHAUL) & HIXENBAUGH (or HICKENBAUGH) tried
    Paper & date: LS May 9, 1885; RGR Mar. 21, 1885
    Date & place of death: Springer, N. M.

WHEELER, WILLIE - aged 12 - accidentally shot (cont'd. next page)

WHEELER, WILLIE (cont'd):
Paper & date: LS June 27, 1883
Date & place of death: Wichita Falls, Texas

WHIPPLE, WILLIAM of Deming, N. M.; killed by the (R.R.) cars·
Paper & date: LS Nov. 5, 1884
Date & place of death: Oct. 23, 1884, Tucson, Arizona

WHITBURN, RICHARD - murdered; bur.: Temosachic, Mexico
Paper & date: EPDH Feb. 8, 1882
Date & place of death: last week, near Dolores, Mexico

WHITE, Capt. A. B. (Mayor)
Paper & date: LS Dec. 23, 1885
Date & place of death: Dec. 17, 1885, Whitesboro, Texas

WHITE, ALLEN - sinking an axe into his head up to the eye by PETE BUCKNER.
Both negroes
Paper & date: LS Feb. 22, 1882
Date & place of death: last week near Crockett, Texas

WHITE, C. S. (Mail agent T & P R. R.) typhoid malaria
Paper & date: EPMS Dec. 2, 1884; LS Dec. 2, 1884
Date & place of death: Nov. 27, 1884, Dallas, Texas

WHITE, D. C. - publicly executed; in 1867 pardoned in Louisiana for mur-
der
Paper & date: LS Feb. 8, 1882
Date & place of death: Feb. 3 (?), 1882, Canton, Texas

WHITE, H. L. - 6 Mexican men and 2 women arrested for his murder; info
letter dated 19 June - says one day last week body found; killed by
MADELINO GARCIA
Paper & date: LS June 20, 1885; BU June 27, 1885
Date & place of death: early June 1885, near Hillsboro, N. M.

WHITE, JACK (policeman) - killed while quelling some negro revelers;Hero
of the Confederacy
Paper & date: LS Mar. 24, 1883
Date & place of death: Mar. 17, 1883, Houston, Texas

WHITE, JAMES C. - son: JAMES H. WHITE of El Paso, Texas
Paper & date: LS Sept. 9, 1882
Date & place of death: Aug. 31, 1882, of Eastville, Virginia

WHITE, JENNIE - negro; age 122; b. in eastern Ga. - at 20 moved to Tenn.
for 96 yrs.; last 10 in St. Joseph; cook for Capt. WATERFALL of GEO.
WASHINGTON's staff during War of Revolution
Paper & date: EPT Aug. 11, 1885
Date & place of death: Aug. 3, 1885, St. Joseph, Missouri

WHITE, JIM (horse thief) - shot by officers
Paper & date: LS Dec. 23, 1885
Date & place of death: Dec. 18, 1885 on Mimbres River, New Mexico

WHITE, JOHN - suicide by morphine
Paper & date: LS Aug. 15, 1885
Date & place of death:Ft. Worth, Texas

WHITE, PHIL - wagon overturned on him and choked him; he is from England
and unmarried
Paper & date:˷ EPT Aug. 13, 1884
Date & place of death: Aug. 11, 1884 near Coolidge, N. M.

WHITE, WM. - fell through R. R. bridge and killed while drunk
Paper & date: LS Jan. 3, 1883
Date & place of death: last week - of Bryan, Texas

WHITE, WILLIE - age 5 yrs; burned to death (cont'd next page)

WHITE, WILLIE (cont'd):
Paper & date: LS Apr. 21, 1883
Date & place of death: Ft. Worth, Texas

WHITESIDE, JAMES - fell from cab of engine
Paper & date: LS Sept. 27, 1884
Date & place of death: Longview, Texas

WHITMAN, WILLIAM - murdered by FRANK FUNDERBURG, Tyler, Texas court
Paper & date: LS Aug. 13, 1884
Date & place of death: 1866

WHITMORE, S. S. - formerly of Galveston, Texas
Paper & date: LS Dec. 24, 1881
Date & place of death: Dec. 13, 1881 - of Calvert, Texas

WHITNEY, FRED - congestive chill; left Las Cruces after marriage to care
for his father's farm at Rochester, New York; wife, daughter of J. H.
RYNERSON, will return home with her uncle Col. W. L. RYNERSON, on his
return from the East.
Paper & date: RGR Fall of 1884
Date & place of death: two weeks ago

WHITNEY, J. - killed by posse after he murdered PETER McLAUGHLIN in Palo
Pinto co., Texas
Paper & date: LS Sept. 16, 1882
Date & place of death: Sept. 11, 1882

WHITNEY, ROBERT H. - killed by COCHISE' men at Horse Shoe Canon in Chiri-
cawas
Paper & date: TB Nov. 8, 1871
Date & place of death: Oct. 24, 1871

WHITNEY, WEST - shot and killed by saloon keeper, FRANK D. ALLEN
Paper & date: LS Mar. 18, 1882
Date & place of death: last week, Paschal, Burro Mts., N. M.

WHITTIN, Deacon _____ - wealthy Mass. man left $5000 to University of New
Mexico
Paper & date: LS Sept. 20, 1882
Date & place of death: recently

WICKES, Capt. _____ -schooner "Lilly Ida:; drowned; news rec'd from Cor-
pus Christi, Texas
Paper & date: LS Jan. 2, 1884
Date & place of death:........

WIGGINS, WILLIAM - hanged by 4 murderers to his own house beam after he
had appeared in court against their side; rumor states that citizens
hanged the 4 murderers; PATRICK CARMODY tried
Paper & date: BU Dec. 3, 1887; LS Sept. 27, 1882
Date & place of death: Sept. 1882, San Marcial, New Mexico

WILCOX,_____ - killed by VICTORIO's Apaches
Paper & date: BU Nov. 1, 1884
Date & place of death: Apr. 1880, Wilcox district of Mogollon Mtns.,
Ariz.-N. M.

WILKERSON, LEWIS - shot while resisting arrest
Paper & date: LS June 10, 1885
Date & place of death: Trinity bottom, Texas

WILKERSON, W. M. - shot by D. H. CAIN
Paper & date: LS June 20, 1883
Date & place of death: Ft. Worth, Texas

WILKES, Rev. Dr. _____ - illness of several weeks; Chaplain of Senate of
Texas
Paper & date: LS Dec. 17, 1881
Date & place of death: Dec. 7, 1881, Lampasas, Texas

WILKINSON, Miss ____ - suicide
    Paper & date: LS Feb. 18, 1882
    Date & place of death: Feb. 13, 1882 - of Whitesboro, Texas

WILKINSON, W. F. S.
    Paper & date: LS Oct. 4, 1884
    Date & place of death: Sept. 27, 1884, Longview, Texas

WILLEY, CHARLES (also WILLIE) - malaria; remains shipped to bro. in Kansas City; Mr. WILLIE had been a fireman on El Paso to Rincon route
    Paper & date: LS Oct. 12, 1881; EPDH Oct. 12, 1881
    Date & place of death: Oct. 9, 1881

WILLIAMS, ____ - (negro); murder by son, 16 yr. old who said his stepmother instigated him to it; wife & son by former marriage surv.
    Paper & date: LS Jan. 31, 1883
    Date & place of death: Jan. 15, 1883, Brenham, Texas

WILLIAMS, ____ - killed some time ago; law-partner of Judge W. M. PIERSON
    Paper & date: EPDH Feb. 11, 1883
    Date & place of death: El Paso, Texas

WILLIAMS, ____ - estate settlement - El Paso county, Texas; WM. WILLIAMS, Mrs. OLDS & Mrs. ST. JOHN
    Paper & date: SH Aug. 10, 1884
    Date & place of death:.........

WILLIAMS, ____ - shot; old settler here
    Paper & date: EPT Nov. 27, 1887
    Date & place of death: Dec. 1869, El Paso, Texas

WILLIAMS, ____ .- shot by THOMAS SHARP
    Paper & date: LS Mar. 25, 1885
    Date & place of death: Mar. 20, 1885, Malone, Grant co., N. M.

WILLIAMS, Mrs. ____ of Warm Springs, N. M. - age 43; hus. & 12 ch.
    Paper & date: LS July 8, 1885
    Date & place of death: Silver City, N. M.

WILLIAMS, ALFONSO or ALONZO - negro; shot by JOHN HENRY ANDERSON, negro
    Paper & date: BU June 27, 1885; BU July 4, 1885; BU May 7, 1887
    Date & place of death: June 22, 1885, Socorro, N. M.

WILLIAMS, B. F. - tragic
    Paper & date: EPDH Apr. 13, 1896
    Date & place of death: Dec. 7, 1870, El Paso, Texas

WILLIAMS, BILL - killed by BILL JACKSON
    Paper & date: LS Jan. 24, 1885
    Date & place of death: Marshall, Texas

WILLIAMS, CHAS. - young man; shot by ____ STANLAND
    Paper & date: EPT July 22, 1884
    Date & place of death: July 19, 1884 on Duck Creek near Franklin, Tx.

WILLIAMS, CHAS. - beaten with lantern and chair by M/M TOM BOLES; whiskey row
    Paper & date: LS Apr. 25, 1885
    Date & place of death: Apr. 24, 1885, Greenville, Texas

WILLIAMS, CURLEY - murdered
    Paper & date: LS May 16, 1883
    Date & place of death: Jefferson, Texas

WILLIAMS, Mrs. DAVID - strychnine
    Paper & date: LS Apr. 14, 1883
    Date & place of death: few days ago, San Saba, Texas

WILLIAMS, DICK - negro waiter; murdered by ALLEN SMITH, negro - shot
    P/D: EPT May 23, 1884   D/P: May 22, 1884, Albuquerque, N. M.

WILLIAMS, DOC - murdered by Indians led by Chief NANE
    Paper & date: RGR Dec. 15, 1883
    Date & place of death: ca 1880, Lake Valley, New Mexico

WILLIAMS, GILL - lynched; family
    Paper & date: EPT June 30, 1885
    Date & place of death: a week ago near Headtown, Texas

WILLIAMS, JACK - "A butcher" - killed at Apache Pass by Indians
    Paper & date: TB Mar. 7, 1872
    Date & place of death: "one day last week"

WILLIAMS, JAMES from Leadville, Colo. - prospector; rel. in Cleveland,
    Ohio; shot by JIM JACKSON
    Paper & date: EPT May 14, 1884
    Date & place of death: May 12, 1884, Lake Valley, New Mexico

WILLIAMS, JOHN "Happy Jack" - foul play; body found; an Irishman; driver
    on water wagon for Mexican Central
    Paper & date: LS Nov. 9, 1881; EPDH Nov. 9, 1881
    Date & place of death: Nov. 5, 1881, Paso del Norte, Mexico

WILLIAMS (or WILLIS), JNO. G. - heart disease; formerly of St. Joseph,Mo.
    Paper & date: NTF June 18, 1881; EPDH Dec. 28, 1881
    Date & place of death: June 8, 1881, El Paso, Texas

WILLIAMS, MILAM - murdered by a group of negroes - one was JERRY SCOTT
    Paper & date: EPT Apr. 22, 1883
    Date & place of death: Houston (?), Texas

WILLIAMSON, Dr. _____ of Moreles, Mex. - murdered by unknown; native of
    Lousiana; bro. of Gen. GEORGE WILLIAMSON; had lived in Eagle Pass and
    Medina county; fought duel with Dr. DEVEREAU
    Paper & date: EPDH Jan. 17, 1883
    Date & place of death: ....

WILLIAMSON, BILL - lynched
    Paper & date: EPT June 18, 1885
    Date & place of death: June 16, 1885, Indian Terr. (Okla.)

WILLIAMSON, Judge S. C. of Akron, Ohio
    Paper & date: LS Mar. 31, 1883
    Date & place of death: Mar. 27, 1883, Las Vegas, New Mexico

WILLIAMSON, WILLIE - cannon exploded prematurely
    Paper & date: EPT Nov. 15, 1884
    Date & place of death: Nov. 8, 1884, Bryant, Texas

WILLIS, JAMES A. - drowned; neck broken and skull fractured; money miss-
    ing; murdered
    Paper & date: LS Apr. 25, 1885
    Date & place of death: Apr. 17, 1885 Leon River, Belton, Texas

WILSON, _____ - 3 yr. old boy; par.: _____ & KITTY WILSON (bad film)
    Paper & date: LS June 23, 1883
    Date & place of death: few days ago, Tombstone, Arizona

WILSON, _____ - negro woman; shot while in jail
    Paper & date: EPT Nov. 5, 1884
    Date & place of death: Nov. 2, 1884, Temple, Texas

WILSON, _____ - Indian massacre by COCHISE; see MILLS, ___ bro. of Maj.
    MILLS
    Paper & date: EPT Jan. 20, 1887
    Date & place of death: June 1860, Cook's Peak, Grant co., N. M.

WILSON, _____ - mad dog bit the negro child
    Paper & date: LS Dec. 13, 1882
    Date & place of death: last week near Rice, Texas

WILSON, Mrs. GEORGE - negro - murder by hus. GEORGE WILSON, negro
    Paper & date: LS Aug. 23, 1882
    Date & place of death: last week, Georgetown, New Mexico

WILSON, Mrs. _____ - accidentally shot herself; wife of Sher. WILSON
    Paper & date: LS Oct. 24, 1885
    Date & place of death: Terrell, Texas

WILSON, CHARLES B. - killed by JACK CROW, BENTON, an Indian and seven
    other Choctaws
    Paper & date: EPT Oct. 30, 1887
    Date & place of death: Aug. 7, 1884, Choctaw Nation, Ind. Terr.(Okla.)

WILSON, CUNNY - age 11; dragged to death by ADAMS, 12 yr. old negro boy
    Paper & date: EPT Apr. 26, 1883
    Date & place of death: near Houston, Texas

WILSON, GEO. - shot and killed by his cousin JIM IVY for making remarks
    about his wife
    Paper & date: LS Nov. 2, 1881
    Date & place of death: Oct. 24, 1881 near Baird, Texas

WILSON, GEORGE - fell in a mine; fa.: J. M. WILSON, Dty. Coll. of Customs
    Deming, New Mexico
    Paper & date: LS Sept. 2, 1885
    Date & place of death: mine near Chihuahua, Mexico

WILSON, HARRY of Dallas, Texas
    Paper & date: LS Jan. 11, 1882
    Date & place of death: Jan. 4, 1882

WILSON, HARRY - Engineer; train accident at Algodones, N. M.- broken
    neck; bur.: Butler, Missouri, his old home; wife
    Paper & date: LS July 22, 1885; EPT July 21, 1885
    Date & place of death: July 19, 1885 near Wallace, New Mexico

WILSON, Mrs. HARRY - sudden
    Paper & date: LS Sept. 23, 1885
    Date & place of death: Sept. 18, 1885, Gallup, New Mexico

WILSON, HENRY - engineer on train - wrecked by a wash-out, 9 mi. east of
    Bernalillo, New Mexico
    Paper & date: RGR July 25, 1885
    Date & place of death: July 18, 1885

WILSON, JAMES - Scotchman ; shot and killed at Frio Water Hole, 60 miles
    West of San Antonio, Texas by bro. ADAM
    Paper & date: LS Oct. 7, 1882
    Date & place of death: Oct. 3, 1882

WILSON, L. C. - accidental discharge of gun, near Knobb's School.
    Paper & date: LS Dec. 21, 1881
    Date & place of death: Dec. 9, 1881, Lee co., Texas

WILSON, MONROE - killed by FRANK HAYES
    Paper & date: LS June 16, 1883
    Date & place of death: Ft. Worth, Texas

WILSON, SAM (Sher.) - suicide - shot himself
    Paper & date: LS Sept. 3, 1884
    Date & place of death: Aug. 30, 1884 Uvalde co., Texas

WILSON, STEPHEN F. - guillotined - decapitated
    Paper & date: RGR June 27, 1885
    Date & place of death: June 27, 1885

WIMS, ISOM - negro - jumped from train
    Paper & date: LS Aug. 8, 1885
    Date & place of death: near West Sta., Texas

WINCHESTER, _____ - killed by MITCHELL ANDERSON, a Choctaw Indian - prob-
ably Marhala Tubbee Dist.
Paper & date: EPT May 8, 1885
Date & place of death: last summer, Indian Terr. (Okla.)

WINDOM, _____ of Colorado City, Texas; killed by Indians; older bro. of
Colorado City, Texas
Paper & date: EPT Dec. 30, 1885; LS Dec. 30, 1885
Date & place of death: near Duncan, Arizona

WINDSOR, ISAAC - result of being struck by lightening - six weeks ago
Paper & date: LS Aug. 9, 1882
Date & place of death: Aug. 5, 1882 Glorietto, New Mexico

WINDY, _____ - lynched
Paper & date: LS June 30, 1883
Date & place of death: Springer, New Mexico

WINFIELD, M/M JOSEPH - JAMES RAFFERTY's Ranch in Huachuca Mtns, Arizona;
found murdered, possibly in revenge by Mexicans from Sonora, Mexico
Paper & date: EPT Oct. 8, 1884
Date & place of death: Oct. 3, 1884

WINKLER, JIMMIE age 13 mos.; only ch. of AUGUST & EMMA(?) WINKLER
Paper & date: BU Oct. 10, 1885
Date & place of death: Oct. 4, 1885, Socorro, N. M.

WINKLER, NEAL age 1 yr. 23 days; only son of AUGUST & ELLA(?) WINKLER
Paper & date: BU Aug. 1, 1884
Date & place of death: July 13, 1884 Socorro, N. M.

WINSON, THOMAS
Paper & date: LS Feb. 14, 1885
Date & place of death: Lordsburg, N. M.

WINSTON, BILL of Ft. Worth, Texas; shot by H. M. ST. CYR of Texas in
self defense
Paper & date: EPT Oct. 20, 1884
Date & place of death: Oct. 11, 1884 Chiquito Jaquino Mining Camp,
Mexico

WISE, _____ Dty. City Marshal of Ft. Worth, Texas - waylaid and murdered
while trailing 2 murderers.
Paper & date: LS Oct. 11, 1884
Date & place of death: near Oxford, Mississippi

WISE or (WISER) ADDISON - killed by WYATT BANKS, negro, and FRED E. WAITE
& DANIEL COMPTON
Paper & date: LS Apr. 25, 1883; EPT Apr. 25, 1883
Date & place of death: May 28, 1882 Robertson co., Texas

WISHART or WISHERT, AL - killed by J. MILTON FLY, son of Maj. FLY, Gon-
zales co., Texas; bur.: Del Rio, Texas
Paper & date: LS Nov. 14, 1883; EPDH Oct. 28, 1883; EPDH Nov. 4, 1883;
EPDH Dec. 28, 1884
Date & place of death: Oct. 23, 1883 Murphysville, Texas

WITHERLY, _____ fireman on G.H. & S.A. R. R. - train accident
Paper & date: EPT Sept. 11, 1884
Date & place of death: Sept. 10, 1884 near Sanderson Tex.

WITHROW, JENNIE L. - age 20 - youngest dau. of Dr. WITHROW of Organ, N.M.
Paper & date: RGR May 30, 1885
Date & place of death: not given - Dennison, Texas

WITTE(?), Dr. of German birth, naturalized American; son age 13
Paper & date: EPT Dec. 18, 1885
Date & place of death: Dec. 16, 1885 Paso del Norte, Mexico

WOESSNER, JOHN - suicide (cont'd next page)

WOESSNER (cont'd):
    Paper & date: LS Sept. 17, 1884
    Date & place of death: Sept. 10, 1884 Corpus Christi, Texas

WOMACK, JESSE - Texas veteran
    Paper & date: EPT Oct. 14, 1884
    Date & place of death: Oct. 10, 1884 Grimes co., Texas

WONG TAI - shot by WONG TI, WONG CHUNG & WONG AKUK
    Paper & date: EPT Sept. 24, 1885
    Date & place of death: Phoenix, Arizona

WOOD, BESSIE - bur. Oct. 9, 1881
    Paper & date: EPDH Oct. 12, 1881
    Date & place of death: last week, El Paso, Texas

WOOD, GEORGE - age 23; pneumonia; came here from Albuquerque, January 4,
    1884; alias WILLIAM WHITE; fa.: in Mellville, Missouri
    Paper & date: LS Jan. 9, 1884
    Date & place of death: Jan. 7, 1884 El Paso, Texas

WOOD, LEE - shot by JOE BARBER, old feud
    Paper & date: EPT Sept. 19, 1883
    Date & place of death: near Mexia, Texas

WOODALL Bros. (2) - fight with HENRY ALLEN & SAMUEL FAULKNER; the bros.
    will die; all came from Arkansas
    Paper & date: LS Aug. 9, 1884; EPT Aug. 12, 1884
    Date & place of death: Fredonia, Texas

WOODLIEF, Mrs. ____ of McKinney, Texas; her physician, Dr. C. N. ABBOTT
    arrested for murder; crime of malpractice in treating her
    Paper & date: LS Jan. 31, 1883
    Date & place of death: two weeks ago

WOODRUFF, Dr. A. M.
    Paper & date: LS Nov. 21, 1883
    Date & place of death: Nov. 19, 1883 Las Vegas, N. M.

WOODS, ____ - killed by Indians
    Paper & date: EPT June 6, 1885
    Date & place of death: June 4, 1885 near Duncan Sta., N. M.

WOODS, ____ - quarrel and shooting affray with ____ LANG
    Paper & date: LS Jan. 20, 1883
    Date & place of death: recently at Georgetown, N. M.

WOODS, BEN - brief illness
    Paper & date: EPDH May 31, 1882
    Date & place of death: May 30, 1882 El Paso, Texas

WOODS, LORENZO - suicide - cut throat; fa.: Judge WOODS of Dixon, Ill.
    Paper & date: EPT Nov. 25, 1883
    Date & place of death: Nov. 24, 1883 Albuquerque, N. M.

WOODS, SIM (or JIM) - negro; shot by officers - not expected to recover
    Paper & date: LS July 25, 1885
    Date & place of death: Waco, Texas

WOODSON, J. C. of Abilene, Texas - typhoid fever
    Paper & date: LS Oct. 25, 1882
    Date & place of death: a few days ago

WOOSTER, L. B. - Papagos sacked the Tubac Valley and killed WOOSTER some
    three weeks ago
    Paper & date: TB May 4, 1871
    Date & place of death:.......

WORMINGTON, ___ of Santa Fe, N. M. - killed by Utes
    Paper/date: EPT Sept. 6, 1884 Date/place: Southern Utah

WORSF, ___ - fell from scaffolding;not expected to live
    Paper & date: LS Feb. 11, 1885
    Date & place of death: Paris, Texas

WORSLEY, ALEXANDER - shot by father-in-law _____ CLEMENT; self defense
    Paper & date: EPT Sept. 11, 1883
    Date & place of death: Sept. 10, 1883 near Bonham, Texas

WREN, _____ - stabbed by THOMAS OGDEN
    Paper & date: LS June 23, 1883
    Date & place of death: Winona, Texas

WRIGHT, _____ 10 yr. old daughter; clothes caught fire; par.
    Paper & date: LS May 2, 1885
    Date & place of death: last week near Alleytown, Texas

WRIGHT, _____ - killed by Indians
    Paper & date: LS Dec. 26, 1885
    Date & place of death: Gatlin, New Mexico

WRIGHT Bros. - killed by Indians
    Paper & date: EPT Dec. 4, 1885
    Date & place of death: Dec. 2, 1885 near Solomonville, Arizona

WRIGHT, BUCK (Dty. U. S. Marshal) anvil burst and piece flew into saloon
    killing him
    Paper & date: LS Nov. 15, 1884
    Date & place of death: Nov. 8, 1884, Luling, Texas

WRIGHT, DANIEL
    Paper & date: LS Sept. 3, 1884
    Date & place of death: Aug. 29, 1884 Quitman, Wood co., Texas

WRYNSEABER, WILLIAM - killed by Mexicans - NICHOLAS OLGUIN and 10 others
    Paper & date: LS Dec. 29, 1883
    Date & place of death: Dec. 10, 1883 near Clifton, Arizona

WYCKLAND, CHARLES - contractor on Mex. Nat'l R. R.; murdered by PAUCLEY
    or PAUST and NUDD or MUDD
    Paper & date: EPT May 16 & 17, 1883
    Date & place of death: May 12, 1883 near Monterrey, Mexico

YARBERRY, MILTON - hanged for killing _____ CAMPBELL; YARBERRY aka JOHN
    ARMSTRONG in Arkansas in 1879; killed a man in Sharp co., Arkansas;
    trouble in Decatur, Texas
    Paper & date: LS Feb. 7, 1883
    Date & place of death: Feb. 9, 1883 New Mexico

YARBROUGH, KENNETH - shot by W. A. BROOKS
    Paper & date: LS June 24, 1885
    Date & place of death: New Boston, Bowie co., Texas

YATES, THOMAS - pneumonia - ill 8 hours; from Missouri; was one of Gen.
    LEE's veterans of all Virginia campaigns
    Paper & date: RGR Jan. 17, 1885
    Date & place of death: Jan. 13, 1885

YEATER, M/M A. JOHN - killed by Apaches; from Sedalia, Missouri; related
    to J. K. YEATER, pres. of 1st Nat'l Bank of Sedalia
    Paper & date: LS Nov. 11, 1885; EPT Nov. 11, 1885; RGR Nov. 14, 1885
    Date & place of death: Nov. 7, 1885, near Deming, New Mexico

YEATMAN, CHARLES E. - consumption; d. at residence of THOS. J. BULL
    Paper & date: TB Mar. 23, 1871
    Date & place of death: Mar. 13, 1871, Mesilla, New Mexico

YELLOW BEAR - blew out gas in hotel and suffocated; son-in-law: QUANAH
    PARKER, also dangerously ill
    Paper/Date: LS Dec. 26, 1885   Date/Place: Fort Worth, Texas

YERGES, HENRY - shooting scrape Mar. 23 with a cowboy - mortally wounded;
cowboy BILL WEAR; bro.: in El Paso - L. YERGES
Paper & date: LS Mar. 25, 1885; SH Mar. 29, 1885; SH Apr. 8, 1885
Date & place of death: Mar. 25, 1885, Toyah, Texas

YHARBO, LOUIS - shot by bartender
Paper & date: EPDH Oct. 12, 1881
Date & place of death: other day, San Antonio, Texas

YORK, _____ - fight with Indians in Stein's Peak range near Lordsburg,
New Mexico
Paper & date: LS Oct. 19, 1881
Date & place of death: Oct. 13, 1881

YOUMANA, Prof. _____ from Canada; music teacher; stabbed by S. P. HOLMES
Paper & date: EPT May 21, 1885
Date & place of death: May 4, 1885, Paris, Texas

YOUNG, _____ boy, 4 yrs. old; fell in ditch and drowned; par.: M/M ROB-
ERT YOUNG
Paper & date: LS Apr. 4, 1883; EPDH Apr. 1, 1883
Date & place of death: Mar. 31, 1883, Paso del Norte, Mexico

YOUNG, _____ - knifed by _____ ANGLIN
Paper & date: LS July 7, 1883
Date & place of death: near Weatherford, Texas

YOUNG, ANNIE - shot herself- suicide
Paper & date: LS Oct. 15, 1884
Date & place of death: early last week, Sandy Point, Texas

YOUNG, CHARLES - 13 yr. old negro - murdered
Paper & date: LS Dec. 23, 1885
Date & place of death: Pittsburg, Texas

YOUNG, DOCK - killed by H. CONUTESON, dty. sher.
Paper & date: LS Mar. 26, 1884
Date & place of death: near Cleburne, Texas

YOUNG, ROBERT - pneumonia; age ca 40 yrs.; native of Dubuque, Iowa or
more recently of California; musician; wife, who will leave tomorrow
for California
Paper & date: LS Jan. 20, 1883
Date & place of death: Jan. 19, 1883, El Paso, Texas

ZABER. _____ - dau.; killed by street car; fa.: WILLIAM ZABER
Paper & date: LS Apr. 21, 1883
Date & place of death: May 1882, Galveston, Texas

ZILLARD, WILLIAM - shot by N. M. militia
Paper & date: LS Mar. 28, 1883
Date & place of death: Lake Valley, New Mexico

ZIMPLEMAN, Mrs. C.(?) R. - hus.: Maj. C(?) R. ZIMPLEMAN
Paper & date: EPT Nov. 15, 1885
Date & place of death: Nov. 12, 1885, Austin, Texas

ZOLLARS, Mrs. JNO. W. - 6 mo. lingering illness; hus.- 1st Nat'l Bank of
El Paso, Tx; relatives in Canton, Ohio
Paper & date: LS Sept. 5, 1885
Date & place of death: Sept. 4, 1885, Canton, Ohio

ZORK, LOUIS - father-in-law of A. KRAKAUER of El Paso, Texas
Paper & date: SH May 17, 1885
Date & place of death: past week at home, San Antonio, Texas

PARENTS	CHILD	PAPER and DATE

AMADOR,   JUAN   RGR May 14, 1887
on May 14, 1866; celebrated 21st birthday

BENNETT,   LOLA JENNETT   RGR July 17, 1886
on July 13, 1877; celebrated 9th birthday

BOWMAN,   Mrs. SARAH   EPDH Feb. 11, 1890
on Feb. 11, 1800; widow of Galveston, Texas; celebrated birthday

CALDWELL, Judge and Mrs. W. M.-JULIA   EPT June 23, 1894
on June 22, 1885; 9th birthday

CAMPECA,   JESUS   EPT May 3, 1892
Spain in 1738; celebrated his birthday May 2, 1892; aged 154, now
lives in Mexico City

CATLIN, Clerk   LUCILE   EPDH Mar. 16, 1898
on Mar. 15, 1885; celebrated 13th birthday

CLARK,   C. C.   BU Jan. 21, 1888
of Kelly, New Mexico - on Jan. 17, 1834; 54th birthday

CLARK,   F. P.   EPT Apr. 9, 1887
on Apr. 8, 1852; celebrated his 35th birthday

COLES,   OTIS   EPDH Mar. 3, 1898
on Mar. 1, 1877 ; 21st birthday; bro. A. P. COLES, FRANK COLES, all
of El Paso, Texas

CRAWFORD, JACK   EVA   RGR July 9, 1887
born 1870 - celebrated 17th birthday

DE REIMER,   E. G.   EPT Sept. 21, 1894
born Sept. 20, 1871 ; 22nd birthday

ECKER,   Maj. SAM   EPDH May 2, 1889
born May 2, 1847 ; birthday party age 42

HANNA, L. K. & MAGGIE A.   CLARA ALICE   BU June 26, 1886
on Feb. 14, 1885; died

HENSLEY, M/M   OLIVE   BU Oct. 23, 1886
on Oct. 18, 1879; 7th birthday

HOLLAND, T. J. & EDNA POOR   girl   EPT Jun. 2, 1888
about 7 years ago (1881) in Hillsboro, Texas; grand parents M/M HENRY
POOR, Hillsboro, Texas; mother of unsound mind, committed 2 years ago;
father of El Paso, Texas now

KRAKAUER,   ADOLFO   EPDH May 24, 1890
on May 23, 1846 ; his 44th birthday

LANE,   FLORIN   EPT Sept. 30, 1894
on Sept. 30, 1878 ; 16th birthday

LEICHAM,   ESSIE   BU Mar. 10, 1888
on Mar. 10, 1874 ; 14th birthday

LONGUEMARE, ___   CHARLES J.   BU Mar. 20, 1886;
     BU Mar. 27, 1886
on Mar. 17, 1840; Editor of "The Bullion" of Socorro, New Mexico

LOPEZ,   PEDRO ANTONIO   EPDH Jun. 16, 1890
In 1776; lives at La Puebla, N. M.; found by census enumerator; total-
ly blind; age verified by documents

PARENTS	CHILD	PAPER and DATE

McCHESNEY,   DAVID   EPT May 19, 1894
on May 18, 1874; 20th birthday

McKINNEY, Dr. & Mrs.   ALMA LEE   EPT Jan. 26, 1887
on Jan. 26, 1880 ; 7th birthday - entertained 30 friends

MEISEL,   AUGUST   EPDH Mar. 12, 1896
on Mar. 9, 1846 ; 50th birthday

MERRICK, CHARLES   OSCAR   EPT Apr. 7, 1888
on Apr. 6, 1867 ; 21st birthday - FRED MERRICK, WALLIE MERRICK, OSCAR
MERRICK, attended party

MONTFORT,   Mrs. C. C.   EPT Mar. 1, 1896
on Feb. 29, 1844; 13th birthday - son CHARLES age 14; her next birthday 1904

OETLING,   ADOLPH   EPT June 17, 1894
on June 16, 1870 ; 24th birthday

PAYNE, Chief of Police   REBECCA   EPDH June 5, 1894
on June 4, 1880 ; 14th birthday

PIONTKOWSKY,   FRED   RGR Oct. 29, 1887
on Oct. 28, 1836 ; celebrated his 50th birthday

READ, Rev. & Mrs. H. W.   MARY   EPT Nov. 6, 1886
in 1873; party for their adopted daughter's 13th birthday (adopted
at age 11)

RECKHART,   D. W.   EPT July 24, 1897
on July 23, 1864

SCHAUBLIN,   JAKE   RGR May 21, 1887
on May 17, 1827; celebrated 60th birthday

SECTON, M/M O. G.   BRUCE   EPT June 28, 1892
on June 27, 1882 at home on Magoffin Ave.; celebrated 10th birthday
on June 27, 1892

SISNEROS,   JULIAN   BU Nov. 13, 1886
in 1776 - 110 years old

SPERLING,   FRANK   BU Jan. 23, 1886
on Jan. 18, 1856 ; 30th birthday

STETTHEIMER,   J. J.   EPT May 9, 1894
on May 8, 1856 ; 38th birthday

TILTON,   MILDRED   EPDH May 22, 1890
pm May 19, 1884 ; 6th birthday party

WALES,   ED   EPT Nov. 23, 1897
on Nov. 21, 1851 ; 46th birthday - of El Paso, Texas

WESTON,   ISAIAH   EPDH Apr. 9, 1896
on Apr. 9, 1826 ; 70 years old - of El Paso, Texas

WOODYARD, M/M   MARION   BU Jan. 9, 1886
on Jan. 7, 1870 ; 16th birthday

BIRTHS

PARENTS	CHILD	PAPER and DATE

ABEYTA y MONTOYA, M/M ABRAN   boy   BU July 18, 1885
   on July 13, 1885 in Socorro, New Mexico

ABRAHAM, M/M ABE   LS May 2, 1885
   on April 30, 1885 in Silver City, New Mexico

ADELMAN, M/M CHARLES   second born   BU Feb. 1, 1884
   in Socorro, New Mexico

ALDERMAN, J. W.   boy   LS Dec. 15, 1883
   on Dec. 9/10, 1883 in Fort Worth, Texas; baby boy 12 hours old left
   on porch on Dec. 10 - adopted

ALLEN, M/M H. F.   girl   LS Mar. 22, 1884
   in El Paso, Texas

ALVEY, M/M J. M.   boy   LS May 23, 1885
   in Taos, New Mexico

AMADOR, M/M MARTIN   girl   RGR Jan. 17, 1885
   on Jan. 13, 1885

AMES, M/M SENECA   girl   RGR Dec. 27, 1884

ANDREAS, M/M AUGUST   boy   RGR Sept. 26, 1885
   on Sept. 23, 1885 in Las Cruces, New Mexico

ASCARATE, GUADALUPE   girl   RGR Sept. 1, 1883
   on Aug. 30, 1883 in Las Cruces, New Mexico. "She was immediately ap-
   pointed Deputy Sheriff".

ASCARATE, Dty. Sher. & Mrs. JAMES girl   RGR Oct. 10, 1885

AUSTIN, M/M SYDNEY   girl   RGR July 12, 1884
   on July 7, 1884 in Las Cruces, New Mexico

BACA, M/M CONRAD A.   ----   BU Aug. 1, 1885
   on July 9, 1885 in Socorro, New Mexico. Grandfather: Judge J. M.SHAW

BAIL, Judge & Mrs.   girl   RGR June 23, 1883
   recently in Silver City, New Mexico

BAINES, Rev. & Mrs. GEORGE W.   boy   LS Oct. 28, 1885
   on Oct. 24, 1885 in El Paso, Texas

BEAUMONT, M/M FRANK   boy   LS Feb. 17, 1883
   on Feb. 15, 1883 in El Paso, Texas

BEEBE, M/M A. M.   girl   RGR Jan. 5, 1884
   in Rincon, New Mexico

BEELER, M/M DAN T.   girl   BU Sept. 26, 1885
   on Aug. 15, 1885 in Kelly, New Mexico

BELL, M/M J. B.   boy   BU June 27, 1885
   on June 21, 1885 in Socorro, New Mexico

BENNETT, Col. & Mrs. J. F.   boy   LS Oct. 18, 1882
   of Silver City, New Mexico; on Oct. 15, 1882 in Paso del Norte, Mexico. A nine pound Democrat.

BERLINER, M/M GEORGE   girl   EPDH May 13, 1883
   over 2 weeks ago in El Paso, Texas

PARENTS	CHILD	PAPER and DATE

BERRIEN, M/M E. V.   boy   EPDH Feb. 3, 1884
   in El Paso, Texas

BIAS, M/M R. B.   boy   EPT May 9, 1883
   at 2 a.m. on May 8, 1883 in El Paso, Texas

BLACKWELL, M/M C. N.   CHARLES LAWRENCE   BU Jan. 1, 1884
   in Socorro, New Mexico

BLANCHARD, CHARLES   boy   BU Nov. 14, 1885
   on Nov. 13, 1885 in Socorro, New Mexico

BLANCHARD, M/M WARD   girl   EPDH July 19, 1882
   several days ago in El Paso, Texas. Another girl.

BLUM, M/M S. (Alderman)   boy   LS June 6, 1883
   on June 4, 1883 in El Paso, Texas

BOOTH, M/M G. C.   boy   RGR Oct. 31, 1885
   on Oct. 21, 1885 in Las Cruces, New Mexico. Father is agent for Singer Sewing Machines.

BOOTH, Dr. & Mrs.   ----   RGR Jan. 24, 1885
   last week Jan. 18, 1885 in Las Cruces, New Mexico

BOSS, M/M J. E.   boy   BU July 1, 1884
   latter part of June 1884 in Socorro, New Mexico

BRAHAM, M/M BEN   girl   LS Jan. 30, 1884
   on Jan. 29, 1884 in El Paso, Texas

BRAY, M/M A.   girl   BU Apr. 1, 1884
   on Mar. 31, 1884 in Socorro, New Mexico

BRINCK, M/M W. C.   boy   LS Aug. 11, 1883
   on Aug. 7, 1883 in El Paso, Texas

BRINKER, M/M JOHN B.   WILLIAM HUGH   BU Apr. 28, 1885
   on Dec. 23, 1851 in Crawford county, Missouri. Lives in Socorro, New
   Mexico - life history.

BROOKS, M/M BELL   BELL, JR.   EPT Oct. 20, 1884
                                 SH Mar. 29, 1885
   on Oct. 19, 1884 in El Paso, Texas. He is Manager of Western Union.

BROWN, M/M HENRY   boy   LS July 11, 1885
   in Albuquerque, New Mexico

BROWN, M/M M. W.   boy   BU Apr. 1, 1884
   on Mar. 11, 1884 in Socorro, New Mexico

BRYAN, M/M J. D.   DOMINICK SHERIDAN   RGR Sept. 12, 1885
                                   RGR Sept. 26, 1885
   in Las Cruces, New Mexico. Baptized last Sunday, Sept. 20, 1885

BUCHOZ, M/M ___   girl   RGR Dec. 6, 1884
   on Dec. 1, 1884. First and only girl in a family of ten.

BULL, M/M ALEX   CHARLES   RGR Feb. 9, 1884
   recently in Mesilla, New Mexico. Names for Uncle CHARLES. Will be
   called "CHARLEY".

BURNHAM, M/M PARKER   boy   EPT Sept. 15, 1883
   in Silver City, New Mexico

BURT, M/M ___   WINNIE   RGR Feb. 14, 1885
   on Feb. 6, 1866. Celebrated 19th birthday.

PARENTS	CHILD	PAPER and DATE

CAMPBELL, M/M _____   boy   EPT Nov. 22, 1885
in El Paso, Texas. Father: mechanic and bricklayer

CAMPBELL, M/M EUGENE   BLAINE CLEVELAND   SH July 20, 1884
few days ago in El Paso, Texas

CARPENTER, M/M A. F.   boy   BU Apr. 28, 1885
on Apr. 22, 1885 in Socorro, New Mexico

CHAVEZ, M/M DEMETRIO   _____   RGR June 23, 1883
recently in Mesilla, New Mexico. Married 2 years - 2 children.

CLARKE, M/M F. P.   boy   LS Sept. 27, 1882
on Sept. 24, 1882 in El Paso, Texas. Ass't Dty. Co. Clerk.

COFFIN, M/M C. C.   girl   LS Jan. 2, 1884
on Dec. 31, 1883 in El Paso, Texas

CONANT, M/M WILLIAM   JOSSIE   EPT Oct. 11, 1884
on Oct. 10, 1879. Fifth birthday party.

CONNORS, M/M AL   girl   LS July 11, 1885
in Albuquerque, New Mexico

COON, M/M H. K.   boy   BU Feb. 1, 1885
on Jan. 26, 1885 in Socorro, New Mexico. Christened Jan. 27, 1885 by
Father LESTRA. THOMAS LEESON and Mrs. MA. LUZ CHAVEZ, sponsors.

COONEY, Hon. & Mrs. M.   boy   BU June 2, 1885
on May 24, 1885 in Cooney Camp (near Socorro, New Mexico)

CORTESY, M/M A.[boy   BU Nov. 7, 1885
on Nov. 1, 1885 in Socorro, New Mexico

COTTINGHAM, M/M ___   boy   EPDH Feb. 8, 1882
     EPDH Jan. 3, 1883
on Feb. 1, 1882 in El Paso, Texas. Grandpa: _____ PIPKEN

COURTRIGHT, M/M JAMES   girl   EPT Oct. 23, 1885
about 4 months ago up on the Canadian line. Well known in New Mexico
and Texas.

COWAN, _____   J. V., (Dr.)   RGR Dec. 12, 1885
On Dec. 7, 1842. His 43rd birthday = surprise party.

CROSS, GEORGE H.   girl   BU Oct. 31, 1885
in Santa Fe, New Mexico. He is with "Santa Fe New Mexican".

CUNNINGHAM, _____   MAMIE   BU May 12, 1885
on May 8, 1871. 14th birthday.

CURREN, M/M P. E.   girl   LS Aug. 13, 1884
in Deming, New Mexico

DANTIN, M/M LOUIS   boy   EPT Apr. 13, 1883
on Apr. 10, 1883 in Chihuahua, Mexico. Another heir.

DARBYSHIRE, M/M ED   girl   LS July 11, 1885
in Silver City, New Mexico

DAVIS, M/M W. M.   girl   EPMS Dec. 16, 1884
on Dec. 14, 1884 in El Paso, Texas

DECKER, M/M J. F.   girl   LS Oct. 1, 1884
on Sept. 28, 1884 in El Paso, Texas

DE LOS ANGELES, Don MANUEL & Sra. JOSEFA   ARGUELLES DE TREVINO (cont'd):

PARENTS	CHILD	PAPER and DATE

(cont'd from page 187)   ABELARDO   EPDH Jan. 10, 1883
    on Oct. 12, 1882 in Matamoros, Mexico. Youngest son. Godparents:
    JAMES M. & ROSA TREVINO BELDEN. Christened Jan. 4, 1883.

DE LOS SANTOSCOY, Sr. ROMAN & Sra.
GUADALUPE ARGUELLES DE LOS SANTOSCOY
                FRANCISCO JOSE   EPDH Jan. 10, 1883
    in Matamoros, Mexico. Christened Jan. 4, 1883. Godparents: JAMES M.
    & ROSA TREVINO BELDEN.

DUBEL, M/M ___   girl   LS Mar. 14, 1885
    in El Paso, Texas

DUNNE, M/M PAT C.   EDDIE   SH Aug. 24, 1884
    about 6 years ago.

EASLEY, M/M C. F.   boy   LS May 2, 1885
    in Santa Fe, New Mexico

EGGER, M/M JOHN   boy   BU Feb. 1, 1884
    in Socorro, New Mexico

EMERSON, M/M GEORGE WASHINGTON   ----   EPDH Mar. 11, 1883
                                        EPDH Apr. 29, 1883
    two weeks ago in El Paso, Texas

EMERSON, M/M GEORGE WASHINGTON   girl   SH Feb. 15, 1885
    on Feb. 10, 1885 in El Paso, Texas

EMMERSON, M/M J. D.   girl   BU July 25, 1885
    on July 19, 1885 in Socorro, New Mexico

ERRICHSON, M/M JOHN   boy   LS Apr. 25, 1885
    in Albuquerque, New Mexico

EVANS, M/M D. M.   girl   RGR Nov. 1, 1884
    on Oct. 25, 1884 in Las Cruces, New Mexico

FARLEY, M/M TOM   boy   BU Aug. 22, 1885
    on Aug. 19, 1885 in Socorro, New Mexico. (Merrit Mine Camp)

FEWELL, M/M WILL J.   girl   SH Mar. 1, 1885
    past week in El Paso, Texas

FOUNTAIN, M/M A. J.   twins(one died)   NTF June 18, 1881
    on June 17, 1881 in Las Cruces, New Mexico

FOUNTAIN, Col. & Mrs. A. J.   girl   RGR Sept. 13, 1884
    on Sept. 5, 1884 in Las Cruces, New Mexico

FOX, M/M P. P.   girl   LS May 2, 1885
    in Albuquerque, New Mexico

FREUDENTHAL, M/M MORRIS   girl   RGR Jan. 17, 1885
    on Jan. 13, 1885 in Mesilla, New Mexico

FUGATT, M/M ___   boy   EPDH Dec. 21, 1881
    in El Paso, Texas

GANDARA, M/M ESPETACION   girl   LS Feb. 20, 1884
    in Mesilla, New Mexico

GARCIA, M/M JESUS C.   boy   RGR Jan. 26, 1884
    on Wednesday, Jan. 23, 1884 in Las Cruces, New Mexico

PARENTS	CHILD	PAPER and DATE

GIER, _____   THEODORE   BU June 2, 1885
  on May 30, 1862. Last Saturday was 23rd birthday.

GILLESPIE, M/M   girl   EPT Aug. 28, 1883
  on Aug. 27, 1883 in El Paso, Texas. He's a conductor.

GILLETT, Marshal & Mrs. JAMES B.-boy   LS Sept. 27, 1882
  on Sunday Sept. 24, 1882 in Ysleta, Texas

GILLETT, M/M JAMES B.   boy   LS Sept. 6, 1884
  on Sept. 5, 1884 in Ysleta, Texas

GREY, M/M G. W.   girl   BU July 25, 1885
  on July 20, 1885 in Socorro, New Mexico

HAAS, M/M ISAAC   ISAAC, JR.   EPT Feb. 17, 1885
  of El Paso, Texas. On Feb. 15, 1885 in New York City at grandpar.

HAGUE, M/M J. P.   boy   SH Dec. 21, 1884
  past week in El Paso, Texas

HARRELL, M/M WILLIAM   girl   LS July 21, 1883
  on July 19, 1883 in El Paso, Texas

HARRELL, M/M WILLIAM   ----   EPT Sept. 24, 1885
  on Sept. 22, 1885 in El Paso, Texas. 3rd child.

HARTMAN, M/M G. W.   boy   SH Oct. 19, 1884
  on Oct. 18, 1884 in El Paso, Texas

HAWES, M/M D. A.   boy   EPT Sept. 25, 1883
  on Sept. 23, 1883 in Deming, New Mexico

HILZINGER, M/M JOSEPH T. & ALLIE   LS Nov. 15, 1884
                       GROVER CLEVELAND
  on Nov. 12, 1884 in El Paso, Texas. Mother and child later died.

HING, M/M SAM   SAM, JR.   EPT Oct. 15, 1885
                                   EPT Sept. 16, 1885
                                   LS Oct. 14, 1885
  (New Orleans Creole wife). On Oct. 14, 1885 in El Paso, Texas. First
  Chino-Americano baby born in Texas

HIRSCH, M/M WILLIAM   boy   RGR June 28, 1884
  on June 7, 1884 in Tularosa, New Mexico

HOAG, M/M _____   boy   EPT Oct. 20, 1885
  on Oct. 18, 1885 in El Paso, Texas. (Firm of HOAG & WARD)

HOY, M/M J. M.   boy   RGR Jan. 5, 1884
  in Rincon, New Mexico

HULT, M/M E. G.   HALO ANDY   BU Nov. 1, 1884
  on Oct. 11, 1884 in Socorro, New Mexico

HURGZ, M/M JIM   boy   RGR Dec. 26, 1885
  in Tularosa, New Mexico

HUTCHASON, M/M JOHN J.   boy   LS Nov. 1, 1882
  on Oct. 30, 1882 in El Paso, Texas. Roadmaster for A. T. & S. F. R.R.

HUTCHINSON, M/M G. H. (J. G.)   boy   RGR Feb. 2, 1884

HUTFORD, M/M JOHN F.   boy   RGR July 25, 1885
  on July 22, 1885 in Las Cruces, New Mexico

PARENTS	CHILD	PAPER and DATE
JACKSON, M/M C. T.	girl	SH Oct. 26, 1884
on Oct. 18, 1884 in El Paso, Texas		
JACKSON, M/M FLETCHER	WILLIAM CLARK	RGR Oct. 13, 1883
		RGR Nov. 24, 1883
		RGR Jan. 6, 1884
in Las Cruces, New Mexico. Bapt. Nov. 18, 1883		
JACOBS, M/M W. W.	boy	LS May 9, 1885
last week in Springer, New Mexico		
JERRELL, M/M W. L.	girl	LS Feb. 11, 1882
in Las Cruces, New Mexico. Grandmother - DUPER		
JERRELL, Sher. W. L.	WILLIAM CHRISTIAN	LS Jan. 2, 1884
		RGR Feb. 9, 1884
		RGR Jan. 19, 1884
on Dec. 30, 1883 in Las Cruces, New Mexico. Names for grandfather-		
CHRISTIAN DUPER		
JOHNSON, M/M J. B.	----	LS Dec. 30, 1884
		SH Jan. 4, 1885
on Dec. 25, 1884 in El Paso, Texas		
JUDIA, _____[	boy	RGR May 17, 1884
on May 15, 1884 in Organ, New Mexico		
KELLER, M/M ___	girl	EPDH June 29, 1884
in El Paso, Texas		
KENNEDY, M/M NICK	boy	LS Oct. 10, 1885
		RGR Oct. 10, 1885
of South Fork, New Mexico. On Oct. 7, 1885 in Las Cruces, N. M.		
KINNE, M/M J. M.	girl	LS June 24, 1885
on June 21, 1885 in El Paso, Texas		
KOHLBERG, M/M ERNEST	boy	EPT Aug. 30, 1885
		SH Aug. 30, 1885
on Aug. 29, 1885 (Aug. 28, 1885) in El Paso, Texas		
KRATER, M/M JOHN	----	SH July 5, 1885
in El Paso, Texas		
KRAUSE, M/M ERNEST	girl	EPDH Feb. 10, 1884
in El Paso, Texas		
LAPOINT, _____	ALICE	RGR Feb. 2, 1884
on Jan. 25, 1874. 10th birthday party.		
LAPOINT, _____	LAWRENCE	RGR Nov. 22, 1884
on Nov. 19, 1838. Birthday party. Aged 46		
LAPOINT, M/M LAWRENCE	WILLIAM	RGR Apr. 4, 1885
		RGR Aug. 8, 1885
on Apr. 1, 1885 in Las Cruces, New Mexico. Bapt. Aug. 10, 1885		
LATZKE, M/M PAUL	girl	RGR Sept. 12, 1885
in Las Cruces, New Mexico. First child.		
LIEBERT, M/M A.	girl	LS May 23, 1885
in Taos, New Mexico		
LLEWELLYN, Maj. & Mrs. ___	girl	RGR Apr. 19, 1884
last week		

PARENTS	CHILD	PAPER and DATE
LLEWELLYN, Maj. & Mrs. W. H.	twins	RGR Oct. 17, 1885

on Mescalero Reservation, New Mexico

LOEWENSTEIN, M/M ___   boy   EPT May 13, 1884
  May 13, 1884 in Ysleta, Texas

LOHMAN, M/M J. FRED   boy   RGR Mar. 21, 1885
  week of Mar. 21, 1885 in Las Cruces, New Mexico

LONGSTREET, M/M A.   girl   EPDH Sept. 21, 1881
  on Sept. 19, 1881 in El Paso, Texas

LONGUEMARE, M/M CHARLES J.   MARIE CLEMENTINE   BU Feb. 1, 1885
  Christened Dec. 29, 1884 in Socorro, New Mexico. Sponsors: THOMAS
  DORSEY & Mrs. P. DORSEY

LOOK, M.M JAMES   boy   EPDH Nov. 4, 1883
  on Nov. 2, 1883 in El Paso, Texas

McDADE, M/M CHARLES   girl   RGR Aug. 9, 1884
  on Aug. 5, 1884 in Organ, New Mexico

McLACHLEN, M/M W. B.   girl   EPDH Mar. 9, 1884
  past week in El Paso, Texas

McNAMARA, M/M F. K.   girl   EPT Aug. 14, 1883
  of Deming, New Mexico. About 3 mo's ago in Columbus, Nebraska

MACKAY, M/M W. G.   boy   EPT Sept. 22, 1883
  in El Paso, Texas

MANZANAREZ, Hon. & Mrs. FRANK A. ----   LS Jan. 30, 1884
  on Jan. 27, 1884

MERRILL, Rev. & Mrs. J. A.   girl   EPDH Dec. 28, 1881
  on May 3 - 11, 1881 in El Paso, Texas

MEYERS, M/M A.   girl(too fat to   LS Mar. 7, 1883
  on Mar. 4, 1883 in El   mention)
  Paso, Texas

MITCHELL, M/M J. J. (SUSAN)   girl   LS Feb. 21, 1885
                EPT Feb. 21, 1885
  on Feb. 18, 1885 in El Paso, Texas

MOODY, M/M HENRY   girl   RGR May 2, 1885
  on Apr. 28, 1885 in Organ, New Mexico

MOORE, M/M J. H.   boy   LS Aug. 19, 1885
  on Aug. 17, 1885 in El Paso, Texas

NASH, M/M ROBERT   girl   RGR Oct. 3, 1885
  on Sept. 27, 1885 in Las Cruces, New Mexico

NEAL, Maj. & Mrs. J. H.   girl   BU Feb. 1, 1884
  on Jan. 4, 1884 in Marshall, Missouri. Socorro, New Mexico citizens.

NEFF, M/M ___   boy   LS July 11, 1885
  in Silver City, New Mexico

NEILL, M/M G. G. (or G. F.)   girl   EPT July 14, 1885
  on July 12, 1885 in Ysleta, Texas

NEWMAN, M/M G. T.   boy   LS Apr. 4, 1883
  on Mar. 28, 1883 in El Paso, Texas

PARENTS	CHILD	PAPER and DATE
NEWMAN, S. H. & JESSIE on Tuesday, Jan. 16, 1883 in St. Louis, Missouri	girl	LS Jan. 24, 1883
NEWMAN, S. H. & JESSIE on June 17, 1884 in El Paso, Texas	boy	LS June 18, 1884
NEWMAN, S. H. & JESSIE on Dec. 3, 1885 in El Paso, Texas	girl	LS Dec. 5, 1885
NICHOLS, M/M FOSTER on June 12, 1884 in El Paso, Texas	boy	EPT June 14, 1884
NICHOLS, M/M FOSTER on July 24, 1885 in Mexico City, Mexico	girl	SH Aug. 2, 1885
OAKFORD, M/M J. D. on Sept. 23, 1885 in Las Cruces, New Mexico	girl	RGR Oct. 3, 1885
O'CONNOR, M/M P. T. on May 12, 1885 in Organ, New Mexico	girl	RGR May 16, 1885
OLIVE, M/M FRANK in Raton, New Mexico	----	LS Apr. 18, 1885
OWEN, M/M O'DARWIN on Mar. 28, 1885 in El Paso, Texas	girl	LS Apr. 8, 1885
OXENDINE, M/M G. in Albuquerque, New Mexico	----	LS May 16, 1885
PARKER, M/M GEORGE on Apr. 5, 1884 in El Paso, Texas	twins (boy & girl)	EPDH Apr. 6, 1884
PATRICK, M/M GEORGE F. in Silver City, New Mexico	twins	LS June 20, 1885
PATTERSON, M/M ___ on Dec. 21, 1885 in El Paso, Texas	boy	EPT Dec. 23, 1885
PATTON, M/M JOHNNY on June 6, 1884 in Las Cruces, New Mexico	boy	RGR June 7, 1884
PHILLIPS, M/M W. H. in El Paso, Texas	girl	LS Feb. 25, 1882
PIONTKOWSKY, M/M H. D. Baptized, Aug. 2, 1885. Sponsors: JOHN L. MAY & Miss CRESCLIUS	ERNEST MAY	RGR Aug. 8, 1885
PITTS, M/M J. D. on Feb. 10, 1885 in El Paso, Texas	girl	LS Feb. 18, 1885
POWELL, CLARENCE M. & PATTI FLOURNOY on Feb. 6, 1883 in El Paso, Texas	twins-CLARENCE MURRAY & LIONEL HERBERT	EPT May 27, 1883
PRATT, M/M F. T. in Albuquerque, New Mexico	----	LS Apr. 22, 1885
PRATT, M/M W. S. on July 8, 1885 in Socorro, New Mexico	boy	BU July 18, 1885
READ, M/M D. M. on Oct. 20, 1884 in Las Cruces, New Mexico	boy	RGR Oct. 25, 1884

PARENTS	CHILD	PAPER and DATE

READ, M/M D. M.   boy   RGR Dec. 5, 1885
  on Dec. 2, 1885 in Las Cruces, New Mexico

RICHARDS, Capt. & Mrs. _____   girl   RGR May 26, 1883
  recently in Organ, New Mexico

RILEY, M/M JOHN H.   JOHN DOLAN   RGR Sept. 12, 1885
                                                 RGR Oct. 3, 1885
  In Las Cruces, New Mexico. Baptism by Rev. Father LASAIGNE. Sponsors
  were grandparents M/M H. J. CUNIFFE

ROBBINS, M/M A. O.   twins   LS Mar. 21, 1883
  in El Paso, Texas

ROBERTS, M/M WILLIAM   boy   SH Aug. 17, 1884
  a few nights ago in El Paso, Texas

ROTHSCHILD, M/M CHARLES   girl   SH Dec. 21, 1884
  past week in El Paso, Texas

ROUAULT, M/M TEODORO   girl   RGR July 14, 1883
  on Sunday, July 8, 1883 in Las Cruces, New Mexico

ROUALT, M/M THEODORE   boy   RGR July 19, 1884
  on July 13, 1884 in Las Cruces, New Mexico

ROUILLER, M/M A. E.   boy   RGR June 16, 1883
  On June 13, 1883 in Parajo, New Mexico

RUSSELL, M/M E. E.   boy   EPT Mar. 24, 1885
                                                 SH Mar. 29, 1885
  Telegram to father announcing birth. Baby a week old on Mar. 29,1885

RUSSELL, Col. & Mrs. F.   girl   SH Feb. 22, 1885
  in Ysleta, Texas

SALADY, M/M P.   girl   BU Aug. 1, 1885
  on July 29, 1885 in Socorro, New Mexico

SANCHES, M/M PABLO   MARGERITA   BU June 9, 1885
  of Limiter, New Mexico. Christened last week in Socorro, New Mexico

SANDOVAL, M/M JUAN   triplets   LS Oct. 1, 1884
  last week in Mora county, New Mexico

SANDOVAL, PANTELEON   RGR Feb. 28, 1885
  Announces that although he has lived in his step-father's home and
  used his name (Hon. JOSE M. GALLEGOS) many years, he wishes to be
  called by his own name - SANDOVAL - Tularosa, New Mexico Feb. 21,1885

SCHENCK, M/M A.   JAMES JOSEPH   RGR May 24, 1884
  of City Bakery; on May 17, 1884 in Las Cruces, New Mexico

SCHENK, M/M A.   AUGUST   RGR July 25, 1885
                                                 RGR Aug. 8, 1885
  on July 21, 1885 in Las Cruces, New Mexico. Sponsors at baptism, Don
  and Mrs. JACINTO ARMIJO

SCHUSTER, M/M BEN   boy   EPDH Sept. 30, 1883
  in El Paso, Texas

SCHUSTER, M/M BERNARD   boy   EPDH Jan. 20, 1884
  in El Paso, Texas

SCHUTZ, M/M SAMUEL   FANNIE   SH July 5, 1885
  about 12 years ago. Bro.: ADOLPH, age 14; Sis.: HELEN, older. All
  being educated in New York City.

PARENTS	CHILD	PAPER and DATE

SCHUTZ, M/M SOL   boy (7 lbs.)   EPDH Mar. 15, 1882
   in El Paso, Texas

SIMPSON, P. A.   MAMIE C.   BU Aug. 22, 1885
                                               BU Aug. 29, 1885
   on Aug. 25, 1871. 14th birthday party to be given.

SLADE, M/M S. C.   GERTRUDE E.   EPT Oct. 29, 1885
   on Oct. 28, 1878 in El Paso, Texas

SMITH, M/M ___   boy   EPT Oct. 20, 1885
   on Oct. 19, 1885 in El Paso, Texas. (Firm of SMITH & THOMPSON)

SMITH, Mrs. CAROLINE   triplets   LS Feb. 17, 1883
   on Feb. 7, 1883 in Dallas, Texas

SORENSON, M/M ___   girl   EPT Sept. 24, 1885
   in El Paso, Texas

SPEARE, M/M F. M.   girl   BU July 1, 1884
   latter part of June 1884 in Los Lunas, New Mexico

SPINTZ, (SPRINTZ), M/M ___ boy   SH Dec. 21, 1884
   past week in El Paso, Texas

STANTON, M/M C. Q.   boy   LS May 23, 1885
                                               EPT May 23, 1885
   in El Paso, Texas

STANTON, LOUIS K. & ___ TOWNSEND boy   EPDH Feb. 8, 1882
   on Jan. 27, 1882 in Morris, Minn. Grandparents: GIDEON & MARY AHSLEY
   TOWNSEND of New Orleans, Las. & Pres. LINCOLN's Sec'y. of War. Aunt:
   Miss CORA TOWNSEND.

STEINEMANN, JOHN   girl   BU Dec. 5, 1885
   in Kelly, New Mexico

STEWART, M/M LEVINS M.   girl   LS Aug. 5, 1885
   in White Oaks, New Mexico

STRAUSS, M/M A. L.   boy   BU Oct. 1, 1884
   on Sept. 22, 1884 in Socorro, New Mexico. Bro.-in-law: PHILIP LEVI
   of Paris, France and L. LEVI of Socorro, New Mexico

SULLIVAN, M/M ___   boy   RGR Apr. 19, 1884
   "The Slugger". (He was arrested a short time ago for beating his wife)

SULLIVAN, M/M ___   girl   LS Mar. 18, 1885
                                               EPT Mar. 17, 1885
   Fa.: Conductor on Mexican Central R. R. This is seventh daughter.

SWEENEY, M/M JOE   boy   EPDH June 14, 1882
                                               EPDH Jan. 3, 1883
   in El Paso, Texas

TAYS, M/M ALEXANDER   girl   EPT Nov. 15, 1885
   in El Paso, Texas

TERRELL, M/M ED.   girl   RGR July 25, 1885
   on July 5, 1885 in Ruidoso, New Mexico

THOMAS, M/M BEVERLY G.   girl   LS Nov. 22, 1884
                                               EPT Nov. 20, 1884
   on Nov. 19, 1884 in El Paso, Texas. Grandfather: RAND

TIERNEY, M/M ___   girl   LS May 23, 1885
   in Albuquerque, New Mexico

PARENTS	CHILD	PAPER and DATE

TOENNIGES, M/M LOUIE   boy   EPT Sept. 17, 1885
   in El Paso, Texas

TONKIN, M/M W. C.   girl   BU July 18, 1885
   on July 14, 1885 in Socorro, New Mexico

TREVINO, Gen. & Mrs. ___   boy   EPDH Feb. 3, 1884
   some months ago near Monterrey, Mexico. Mother is daughter of Gen.
   ORD of San Antonio, Texas, BERTHE. Gen. DIAZ of Mexico - godfather.
   Mother has consumption - baby may have.

VALDEZ, M/M FELIPE   boy   LS May 27, 1885
   on May 25, 1885 in El Prado, New Mexico

VALDEZ, M/M MARCIAL   girl   RGR Sept. 8, 1883
   in Las Cruces, New Mexico. Father is editor of "El Tiempo"

VALLEJOS, Mrs. MARIA   triplet girls   BU Feb. 1, 1885
   on Jan. 14, 1885 in Santa Rita, New Mexico

VANATAN, W. F. & CELZA   ----   EPT Feb. 11, 1885
   on Feb. 9, 1885 in El Paso, Texas. Lived but a short time

WADE, M/M SAM   girl   LS July 30, 1884
   in El Paso, Texas

WAGNER, M/M PAUL F.   girl   RGR Sept. 19, 1885
   in Las Cruces, New Mexico

WAHL, Dr. & Mrs. G. W.   girl   EPDH July 8, 1884
                                     SH Jan. 11, 1885
   on July 5, 1884 in Ysleta, Texas

WEAVER, M/M___   boy   RGR May 17, 1884
   on May 15, 1884 in Organ, New Mexico

WHITE, Capt. & Mrs. J. H. boy   EPT June 23, 1885
                                     RGR June 27, 1885
   (Sher.) - in the past week in El Paso, Texas. Mrs. WHITE dau. of Sra.
   DOLORES DUPER

WHITE, M/M Z. T.   boy   EPT May 24, 1885
   on May 23, 1885 in El Paso, Texas

WHITEHILL, M/M HARRY   girl   EPT Sept. 15, 1883
   few days ago in Silver City, New Mexico

WILLIAM, M/M TOM   TOM, JR.   RGR May 17, 1884
                                     RGR May 31, 1884
   on May 15, 1884 in Organ, New Mexico

WILLIAMS, M/M TOM C.   GRACIE   RGR Nov. 28, 1885
                                     RGR Jan. 9, 1886
                                     LS Nov. 25, 1885
   on Nov. 22, 1885 in Las Cruces, New Mexico. Baptized - Catholic Church
   Sponsors: M/M A. M. DAGUERRE

WILSON, Dr. & Mrs. GEORGE M. girl   RGR July 21, 1883
   on July 16, 1883 in Rincon, New Mexico

WINFIELD, M/M ___   ----   EPT June 5, 1883
   in Texarkana, Texas. Mr. WINFIELD of T & P. R. R. summoned home last
   night - mother doing well.

WING, M/M ___   boy   LS Nov. 25, 1882
   the other night in El Paso, Tex. Fa.: R. R. Engineer

PARENTS	CHILD	PAPER and DATE
WINGFIELD, M/M C. W. on July 18, 1885 in Ruidoso, New Mexico	girl	RGR July 25, 1885
WINSOR, M/M ___ past week in El Paso, Texas	girl	SH Nov. 9, 1884
WOOD, M/M DAVID in Las Cruces, New Mexico	boy	RGR Sept. 8, 1883
WOOTEN, DICK & 4th wife in Raton Pass, New Mexico. 25th child of father.	boy	LS Aug. 26, 1885
YOUNG, M/M ___ on Sept. 20, 1884 in Socorro, New Mexico	girl	BU Oct. 1, 1884
YOUNG, M/M ROBERT on Jan. 29, 1884 in El Paso, Texas	boy	LS Jan. 30, 1884
YOUNG, M/M BENJAMIN on Sept. 3, 1885 in Alamillo, Socorro county, New Mexico	LUCIUS DUNCAN	BU Sept. 5, 1885

MARRIAGES

GROOM	BRIDE	PAPER and DATE

———, ———   CLARK, ———   SH Sept. 28, 1884
last week, Galveston, Texas.;bro. Maj. J. MASTELLA CLARK, owner and
publisher "Two Republics" of Mexico City.

AARID, LOUIS F.   STEVENS, INEZ   LS Jan. 14, 1885
  in Santa Fe, New Mexico

ABBOTT, FRANK H.   SMITH, MAGGIE G.   LS July 11, 1883
  of El Paso   of Corning, N. Y.   EPT July 10, 1883
  on June 23, 1883, ISAAC P. FERGUSON home, Dryden, N. Y.

ABEYTA y MONTOYA, RICARDO   CHAVEZ, LEONIDAS   BU June 20, 1885
  of Socorro, N. M.   of Polvadero, N.M. BU July 4, 1885
  on July 10, 1885 by Father LESTRA   BU July 18, 1885
  Parents: Don and Mrs. LUCIANO CHAVEZ, bride about 17 years old.

ACTON, JOHN   ——————————   LS Apr. 15, 1885
  in Los Lunas, New Mexico

AGUILAR, JULIAN   RAMIREZ, MARGARITA EPT Jan. 18, 1884
  in El Paso by Justice DAVIS at home of bride's parents on W. Overland
  Street

AH GIT (a Chinaman)   SNUGGLES, Mrs. DINAH LS Jan. 28, 1885
  in Belton, Texas   (negro)

ALARCON, MARTIN   SAMANIEGO, LORETA   LS Feb. 1, 1882
  license issued in January, El Paso, Texas

ALBERS, Dr.   ——————————   EPT Jan. 22, 1884
  in New Orleans, La.

ALBILLOR, EVARISTO   FLORES, NICOLOZA   SH Feb. 22, 1885
  past week, El Paso, Texas by Father DE PALMA

ALLEN, CHARLES F.   ANGELL, EVA M.   LS Jan. 11, 1882
  this evening in Las Vegas, New Mexico

ALLEY, ——————   JOHNSTON, ——————   EPT Dec. 23, 1884
  of Alabama. License issued Dec. 17, 1884 in Albuquerque, N. M.

ANDERSON, R.   HOPKINS, LILA F.   LS Aug. 13, 1884
  of Chihuahua, Mex.   of Easton, Md.   EPT Aug. 14, 1884
  on Aug. 12, 1884 in El Paso, Texas by Parson J. W. TAYS. Relative:
  Mr. J. R. HOPKINS of New York City.

APODACA, LAURO   APODACA, MARIA PRESCA BU Sept. 26, 1885
  on Sept. 21, 1885 in Socorro, N. M. by Father LESTRA

ARLING, ELBAR   Waco, Tex.   IVEY, CARRIE   EPT Nov. 21, 1895
  Native of china   of Calvert, Tx.
  14 years ago in Austin, Texas. Several children - one named ALICE,
  age 6.

ARTO, JOHN   ——————————   LS Dec. 5, 1883
                                   FRED TATE's step-dau.
  on Dec. 3, 1883 in Galveston, Texas jail

ASCARATE, JAMES   VAN PATTEN, EMILIA LS Feb. 18, 1885
  Groom's bro. GUADALUPE; bride's par.: EUGENE VAN PATTEN
  on Feb. 16, 1885 in Las Cruces, N. M. by Father LASSAIGN

ASHENFELTER, SINGLETON M.   BENNETT, NELLIE A. TB Dec. 21, 1872
  on Nov. 21, 1872 in Silver City, N. M. by U. S. Dist. Judge WARREN
  BRISTOL.

GROOM	BRIDE	PAPER and DATE

ATKINSON, Gen.   SHERWIN, ADA J.   LS Dec. 17, 1881
on Nov. 30, 1881 in Lincoln, Neb. He was Surveyor General of N. M.

AUGUR, FERD   HALL, Miss ___   EPT Sept. 16, 1883
groom's parents: Gen. C. C. AUGUR. on Sept. 20, 1883 in San Antonio,
Texas

BABB, T. C.   RIVERS, LENA   EPT July 17, 1884
license issued July 16, 1884 in El Paso, Texas

BACA, GENARO   REED, ILVERSA   BU Sept. 26, 1885
on Sept. 21, 1885 in Socorro, N. M. by Father LESTRA

BACA, JUAN   CASTILLO, BONIFACIA BU Sept. 26, 1885
on Sept. 21, 1885 in Socorro, N. M. by Father LESTRA

BACA, NICANOR   DOMINGUES, MA. VENCESLADOS
                                                   RGR May 10, 1884
on Tuesday in Las Cruces, N. M.

BANEGA, ESTEVAN   ERRERA, CATALINA   RGR Apr. 25, 1885
on Apr. 22, 1885 at her father's residence in Dona Ana, N. M. by
Father LASSAIGNE

BARELA, ELISEO   LOBATO, PELEGRINA   LS June 13, 1885
in Pajarito, Bernalillo co., N. M.

BARNABY, A.   WHITE, MARY C.   LS June 13, 1885
in Kingston, Arizona

BARR,____   WILEY, ____   EPDH Aug. 19, 1883
married in surf in Ocean City (from Galveston, Texas "News")

BARRON, JOSE M.   NUNEZ, FERNANDA   LS Feb. 1, 1882
license issued in January in El Paso, Texas

BARTOW, Col.J. L.   LONG, FLORENCE C.   LS Nov. 15, 1884
of Waco, Texas   of San Antonio, Texas
on Nov. 12, 1884

BASS, E. A.   GURNEY, ROSA   BU Nov. 1, 1883
of Socorro, N. M.
on Oct. 1, 1883 in South Abington, Mass.

BATES, J. W.   TAGGART, MARTHA   LS Feb. 1, 1882
on Jan. 30, 1882 in Ysleta, Texas by Judge FALVEY

BAULIN(BOULIN), CHRISTIAN F. OCHSCHNAR, MARIA   RGR Sept. 8, 1883
on Sept. 2, 1883 in Belen, N. M. by Rev. M. MATTHISON at residence of
JOHN BECKER. Both are residents of Valencia county.

BAYLESS, SAMUEL   MURTH, ANNIE   LS Nov. 25, 1885
license issued in El Paso, Texas

BEAL, CHARLES F.   BIGLOW, MAY   EPT Oct. 30, 1883
on Oct. 28, 1885 in El Paso, Texas by Rev. GEORGE W. BAINES

BEARDSLEY, ARLEN E.   WHITE, MATTIE   LS July 1, 1885
of Detroit, Mich.   of Nashville, Tenn.
in Deming, New Mexico

BEAUMONT, FRANK   _____   EPDH Mar. 15, 1882

BEEBE, ALBERT M.   MILLER, NANNIE E.   LS Mar. 28, 1883
of Rincon, N. M.
on Mar. 25, 1883 in El Paso, Texas by Bishop H. W. READ

GROOM	BRIDE	PAPER and DATE

BELDEN, JAMES M.   TREVINA, ROSA   EPDH Jan. 10, 1883
   of Matamoros, Mex.
   on Jan. 4, 1883 in Matamoros, Mexico

BELLHOUSE, JACK "HAPPY JACK"   LUNA, JUNNA   LS May 23, 1885
   in Pinos Altos, New Mexico

BENJAMIN, D.   ____, ____   BU Aug. 22, 1885
   in Kansas City. Guests in San Marcial, New Mexico

BENNETT, J. B.   DUNLAP, GRACE E.   LS Oct. 8, 1884
   of Whitesboro, Tex.   of El Paso, Tex.   SH Oct. 12, 1884
   on Oct. 7, 1884 in El Paso, Texas by Rev. J. K. FOWLER. Bride's parents: B. H. DUNLAP. She is only daughter and will live in Whitesboro.

BERLINER, GEORGE   NUNN, MARY   EPDH May 10, 1882
   of El Paso, Texas   of California
   on May 3, 1882 in El Paso, Texas by Rev. J. W. TAYS at home of mother

BERLITH, GEORGE C.   BAIN, Mrs. CARRIE A. LS May 23, 1885
   of McKenzie's Sta.,N.M. of Texas
   on May 20, 1885 in Santa Fe, New Mexico by Rev. Dr. JONES

BERRIEN, E. V.   GUGERTY, ELIZA   EPDH Jan. 28, 1883
   of El Paso, Texas   of St. Louis, Mo.
   few days ago in St. Louis, Missouri

BETTERTON, CHARLES H.   CAHILL, MAUD   LS Apr. 29, 1885
   on Apr. 30, 1885 in Deming, New Mexico

BIGGER, J. C.   THURMOND, Mrs. AMANDA
                            widow of Judge J.M. EPMS Dec. 10, 1884
                            THURMOND
   on Dec. 3, 1884 in Dallas, Texas

BLACKINGTON, CHARLES F.   MARTIN, RHONDA   LS Jan. 7, 1882
   on Jan. 1, 1882 in Socorro, New Mexico

BLANCHARD, BENJAMIN H.   BRYANT, MARY   LS Feb. 1, 1882
   on Feb. 1, 1882 in Ysleta, Texas. Groom's par.: W. B. BLANCHARD, Esq.

BLANCHARD, HERMAS   TINGUELY, LILLIE   BU Feb. 1, 1884
                            of Polvadero, N. M.
   last week on Jan. 27, 1884 in Socorro, New Mexico by Father LESTRA.
   Groom's bro.: CHARLES BLANCHARD was in for wedding.

BLAZER, Dr. J. H.   McWADE, JULIA   RGR Jan. 26, 1884
   of New Mexico   of Wisconsin
   will live on the reservation; married in Monroe, Wisconsin

BLUENER, HERMAN F.   SPINNER, SOPHIE   LS Oct. 18, 1884
   early this week in Albuquerque, New Mexico

BOERBECK, JOHN   ELRENSTEIN, Mrs. MAGDALENA
                                                 LS Apr. 18, 1885
                                                 EPT Apr. 17, 1885
   on Apr. 16, 1885 in El Paso, Texas by Judge LOU DAVIS

BOVIER, ARTHUR A.   BORCHERDING, LULU   EPDH June 22, 1884
   (R. R. man)
   on June 19, 1884 in El Paso, Texas by Rev. J. W. TAYS

BRASO, GEORGE   GAVOLY, COALARAN   LS Nov. 28, 1885
   license issued in El Paso, Texas

BRINKER, WILLIAM HUGH   HUTCHINSON, LILLIE L.
   in 1874. Par. of groom M/M JOHN B. BRINKER
                                                 BU Apr. 28, 1885

GROOM	BRIDE	PAPER and DATE

BROOKS, _____   HARSH, _____   SH Sept. 5, 1885
   bride's par.: M/M _____ HARSH of El Paso, Texas; lives in Memphis,
   Tenn.

BROOK, Judge J. D.   HARRISON, Mrs. H. M. BU Nov. 7, 1885
   on Nov. 1, 1885 in Socorro, New Mexico by Bishop DUNLAP; bride is
   sister of W. M. CHEWNING.

BROWN, L. M.   O'DELL, Miss L. C.   BU Nov. 7, 1885
   on Oct. 15, 1885 in Kelly, New Mexico; bride's par.: Col. J. O'DELL.

BRYANT, CHARLIE   BROWN, JOSEPHINE(Mrs.)
   of Kelly, N. M.   of Kelly, N. M.   LS July 18, 1885
                                                   BU July 11, 1885
   on July 5, 1885 in Socorro, New Mexico by Dr. ROBINSON

BUCHANAN, CHRISTOPHER H.   LE ROY, MINNIE   EPT May 17, 1884
   on May 17, 1884 in El Paso, Texas; he is porter at ASHBRIDGE's Bath
   House.

BUCHOZ, LOUIS R.   (not given)   RGR June 6, 1885
   last week in Detroit, Michigan; groom's par.: A. J. BUCHOZ of Las
   Cruces, New Mexico.

BURKE, C.   MADDEN, FLORA   BU Dec. 19, 1885
   of Engle, N. M.
   on Dec. 23, 1885 in Socorro, New Mexico by Justice CURTIN.

BURKE, C. H.   PIERCE, IDA M.   LS Mar. 15, 1882
   of Chicago   EPH Mar. 15, 1882
   ca. Mar. 5 to 15, 1882 in San Antonio, Texas; bride's father, Rev.
   J. N. PIERCE of Clinton, Missouri; bride came out and married him a
   couple of days before he died.

BUSH, Rev. J. D.   NEAL, NANNIE   BU Apr. 28, 1885
   on Apr. 12, 1885 in Socorro, New Mexico by Rev. Mr. PACKARD of Albuquerque.

BUSHYHEAD, D. W. (Hon.)   BUTLER, ELOISE   EPDH Nov. 4, 1883
   (Chief of Cherokee Indians) of Tallequah, Ind. Terr.
   on Nov. 1, 1883 in Indian Territory

CAHOON, ALBERT E.   McCUISTION, ELOISA   BU May 12, 1885
                                                  BU May 19, 1885
                                                  LS May 20, 1885
   on May 13, 1885 in Socorro, New Mexico by Rev. CHASE; bride's par.:
   Alderman McCUISTION

CAMPBELL, M. D.   CROGER, MARGARET   EPT Mar. 3, 1885
   license issued in El Paso, Texas

CARR, C. E.   HERBERT, Miss ___   LS Nov. 5, 1881
   in Fort Worth, Texas; members of theatrical troupe.

CARRICO, M. W.   SIMMS, MARY   LS Oct. 29, 1881
   owner of E. P. Times   of Ft. Worth, Tex.
   on Oct. 25, 1881

CARSON, TOM P.   ___, _____   EPT Aug. 14, 1883
   of Silver City, N. M.   EPT Aug. 31, 1883
   on Aug. 8, 1883 in Pennsylvania; returning with bride.

CARTER, E.   BREEDING, _____   EPDH Oct. 26, 1881
   of Ft. Stockton, Tex.   of Ft. Stockton, Tex.
   last evening Oct. 19, 1881 in Ft. Stockton, Texas by Hon. F. W. YOUNG,
   County Judge.

GROOM	BRIDE	PAPER and DATE

CARUTHERS, L. B.   VAN HORN, LINA   EPDH Sept. 16, 1883
    of Ft. Davis, Texas   of Carizo, Texas
    on Sept. 11, 1883 in Carizo Pass, Texas by Rev. GEORGE BAINES

CEREFINO, EMANUEL   HERNANDEZ, TRINIDAD LS Nov. 7, 1885
    license issued in El Paso, Texas

CHAPMAN, G. W.   DAY, MINNIE   LS June 13, 1885
    of Sacramento, Calif.   of Silver City, N. M.

CHAVEZ, Don BLAS   SALAZAR, CANDELARIA RGR Feb. 2, 1884
    of Hillsboro, N. M.
    bride's par.: Don CRISTOBAL SALAZAR of Peralta, New Mexico

CHAVEZ, ESTANISLAO   MARTIN, FANNIE V.   BU Nov. 1, 1883
    of Socorro, N. M.
    on Nov. 25, 1883 at her mother's home, Marshall, Texas

CHAVEZ, FELIZ   MENDOZA, FELICITA   LS Aug. 5, 1882
    of Mesilla, N. M.
    on Aug. 3, 1882 at Concordia by Rev. Father J. MONTENARELLI; bride's
    par.: MAURICIO MENDOZA of Concordia, Texas

CHAVEZ, FRANCISCO P.   ORTIZ, TERESA   LS Aug. 29, 1885
    in Abiquiu, Rio Arriba co., New Mexico

CHAVEZ, JACOBO   ROMERO, RAFACIA   LS Jan. 11, 1882
    on Jan. 7, 1882 in Valencia, New Mexico

CHAVEZ, MELITON   BACA, FRANCISCA   LS July 25, 1885
    on Sept. 18, 1885 in Albuquerque, New Mexico

CHEWNING, W.   BALDWIN, MAY   BU Dec. 1, 1883
    last Tuesday in Socorro, New Mexico home of bride's par.: by Rev. Mr.
    CAASON.

CLARK, GEORGE M.   RUIZ, CANDIDA   EPDH Oct. 7, 1883
    last week in El Paso, Texas by Judge LOOMIS

CLEGHORN, W. M.   MILLER, M. L.   LS Aug. 9, 1882
                                (or M. D.)   EPDH Aug. 9, 1882
    on Aug. 8, 1882 in El Paso, Texas, home of par.: by Bishop H. W. READ,
    assisted by Elder BAINES

COLDWELL, W. M.(WILLIAM M.)   BRINCK(BRINK), STELLA M.
                                                    LS Nov. 12, 1884
                                                    EPT Nov. 11, 1884
    on Nov. 9, 1884 in El Paso, Texas residence of bride's mother by Rev.
    J. W. TAYS; bride's mother: Mrs. C. E. BRINK

COLE, Dr. J. A.   MONTOYA, CARRIE   LS Apr. 25, 1883
    of San Elizario, Texas   of Collinsville, Tx. EPT Apr. 24, 1883
                                                    EPT Apr. 25, 1883
                                                    EPDH Apr. 22, 1883
    on Apr. 21, 1883 in Ysleta, Texas or San Elizario, Texas by Judge
    ROGERS or Judge FALVEY; bride adopted daughter of T. M. COLLINS, Col-
    linsville, Texas; bridesmaid: Mrs. BLACK of San Elizario; groomsman:
    MANUEL E. FLORES of Ysleta, Texas

COLLINS, GEORGE H. Sgt.   COX, MATTIE (MARGARET)
                                                    LS Feb. 18, 1885
                                                    EPT Feb. 19, 1885
    on Feb. 17, 1885 in El Paso, Texas; (SH Feb. 22, 1885, bride given as
    MATTIE WILCOX)

CONTRERAS, FRANCISCO   MARQUES, PRUDENCIA   LS Feb. 1, 1882
    license issued during January in El Paso, Texas

GROOM	BRIDE	PAPER and DATE

COOPE, FREDERICK   BILLING, BERTHA   BU Oct. 1, 1884
(English)
on Sept. 15, 1884 in Salt Lake City, Utah; bride's par.: M/M F. W.
BILLING of Salt Lake City, Utah; uncle: GUSTAV BILLING of Socorro,N.M.

COSGROVE, JOSEPH   MARQUEZ, ANGELITA   SH Feb. 22, 1885
past week in El Paso, Texas by Father DE PALMA

COWLES, C. C.   WHITE, LILY   BU July 18, 1885
of Socorro, N. M.
on July 7, 1885 in Zanesville, Ohio; bride's par.: HOMER WHITE

COXE, ROBERT E. Lt.   BACON, HELEN   TB Feb. 14, 1872
of Ft. Selden, N. M.
on Feb. 1, 1872 at Germantown

CRAIG, A. W.   ANDREA, LOUISA   SH Jan. 25, 1885
day or two ago in Ysleta, Texas by Justice LEW DAVIS in his office.

CRAIN, M. S.   SHERROD, JESSIE V. LS Dec. 31, 1881
Dist. Atty. of Shreveport, La.
on Dec. 21, 1881; bride's par.: Dr. L. L. SHERROD of Marshall, Texas

CRAWFORD, HARRY   WILSON, Miss ___   LS Nov. 5, 1881
in Fort Worth, Texas; members of theatrical troupe

CREWELL, ALFRED   BUSTARDO, ___   EPT July 14, 1885
on July 13, 1885 in El Paso, Texas by Father DE PALMA

CROW, E. F.   BYRN, MINNIE   RGR Nov. 28, 1885
Rincon telegrapher
on Tuesday Nov. 24, 1885 in Socorro, New Mexico; Indiana gentleman
arrived 24 hours too late (expecting to be the groom)

DANIEL, W. A.   ALLEN, LEONA   LS Mar. 31, 1883
of Organ, N. M.   of White Oaks, N. M.
on Mar. 29, 1883 in Montezuma Hotel, Las Cruces, New Mexico by Justice
MARCIAL VALDEZ

DANIELS, W. A.   McDADE, _____   RGR June 23, 1883
(Wild Texas Boy)
some months ago; in a small quarrel, DANIELS drew knife on brother of
bride who then hit DANIELS over head with a chair - DANIELS fired at
McDADE with a shotgun but missed.

DANNEMILLER, DAN   PETERS, LIZZIE   BU Dec. 5, 1885
on Nov. 22, 1885 in Kelly, New Mexico

DARROW, Prof. L. R.   MUNGER, MINNIE M. RGR May 31, 1884
                                         LS June 5,6,& 7,
                                         1884
on May 22, 1884 in bride's home, Lake Valley, New Mexico; bride's par.
Dr. MUNGER

DAVIDSON, J.   SCOTT, JENNIE   LS May 30, 1885
of Pinos Altos, N. M.   of Elmdale, Nova Scotia
in Pinos Altos, New Mexico

DAVIS, _____   RUDD, _____   BU Sept. 5, 1885
on Aug. 27, 1885 in Kelly, New Mexico; both strangers in town but
settled in to live there.

DAVIS, H. B.   PLATT, FRANKIE E. EPT Oct. 15, 1885
of Chihuahua, Mex.   of Jackson, Mich.
on Oct. 13, 1885 in El Paso, Texas by Rev. GEORGE W. BAINES

GROOM	BRIDE	PAPER and DATE

DAVIS, O. L.   DENAHAN, Mrs.   BU May 19, 1885
   on May 12, 1885 in Lake Valley, New Mexico

DAY, MATHIAS W.   _____, EMELIE   EPT Apr. 4, 1885
   on Nov. 27, 1879; groom 1st Lt. Troop "I", Cavalry U. S. Army;divorce
   action.

DEAL, B. F.   HORSLEY, TINA (Mrs.) LS Dec. 5, 1883
                                                     EPDH Dec. 9, 1883
   on Dec. 4, 1883 in El Paso, Texas by Rev. J. A. MERRILL

DEANE, C. F.   GARNETT, MAUDE   EPT Dec. 13, 1885
   with Mex. Central R.R.   of Denver, Colo.
   Mexico City
   on Dec. 12, 1885 in El Paso, Texas by Rev. GEORGE W. BAINES

DEDRICK, J. M.   FOSTER, JENNIE   EPDH May 31, 1882
   of Paso del Norte, Mex.   of Ysleta, Texas
   on May 23, 1882 in Ysleta, Texas by Rev. RICHARD WALSH

DE GUERRO, ALEX N.   OCHOA, DELFINA   EPDH Dec. 28, 1881
   on Aug. 3-10, 1881 (in Paso del Norte, Mex.?) by Father ORTIZ

DELGADO, J.   OTERO, BEATRICE   LS Nov. 22, 1884
   on Nov. 17, 1884 in Las Vegas, New Mexico

DOLAN, Maj. FD   PRESCOTT, BELLA   LS Aug. 16, 1884
                                of Wallace, N. M.
   on Aug. 11, 1884 in Pino Blanco, New Mexico

DONALDSON, J. M.   EAGAN, LIBBIE   SH Aug. 17, 1884
   on Aug. 16, 1884 in El Paso, Texas by Judge LOOMIS

DOUGHTY, H. H.(HOWARD H.)   HURLEY, Mrs. MARCIA E.
                                nee MARBURG of Detroit, Mich.
                                                     LS July 23, 1884
                                                     EPT July 22, 1884
   on last Tuesday, July 15, 1884 in Ft. Davis, Texas by Post Chaplain
   F. H. WEAVER

DRYER, DAVID P.   YOUNG, JENNIE   LS Jan. 26, 1884
   on Jan. 25, 1884 in El Paso, Texas by Rev. J. R. CARTER

DUBOSE, Rev. H. M.   LS Dec. 28, 1881
   Pastor of St. James Methodist Episcopal Church south of Galveston,Tx.;
   has returned with his bride.

DUDLEY, BOYD   BU Feb. 1, 1885
   formerly of Socorro, New Mexico; in Gallatin, Missouri

DUDLEY, E. G.   GILLETTE, MARY C.   BU Oct. 1, 1884
   on Sept. 10, 1884 in Kansas City; well known in Socorro, N. M. and
   mine owner in area

DUFUR, WILLIAM T.   HARRIS, PHEBE   LS Apr. 11, 1885
   of Lincoln, N. M.; in Roswell, N. M.

DUNBAR, S. C.   LOCKERSMITH, LAVINA LS Nov. 18, 1882
   (Conductor on Mexican Central R.R.)
   on Nov. 14, 1882 in El Paso, Texas by Rev. J. W. TAYS

DUNNE, JOHN C.   PURCELLE, LAURA   EPT July 14, 1883
   of Houston, Texas   of Oakland, Calif.
   on June 18, 1883 in El Paso, Texas by Rev. J. W. TAYS

DURGIN, Prof. HENRY C.   DAILEY, KATE   LS Apr. 29, 1885
   on Apr. 23, 1885 in Santa Fe, New Mexico

GROOM	BRIDE	PAPER and DATE

DURRELL, LOUIS W.   FRAYER, CALLIE   EPDH Dec. 30, 1883
   of Ft. Stockton, Tex.
   on Dec. 21, 1883 in Ysleta, Texas; par.: of bride, Hon. Judge and Mrs.
   _____ FRAYER of Ft. Stockton, Texas; W. G. DURRELL, best man.

EARL, _____   MUNDY,_____   EPDH July 12, 1882
   of Colo.   of Colo.
   on July 12, 1882 in El Paso, Texas, by Rev. J. W. TAYS

EASTON, D. M.   ANDREWS, LIZZIE R.   RGR Aug. 23, 1884
   of South Fork, N. M.   of Atlanta, Ga.
   on Aug. 14, 1884 in residence of EZRA ANDREWS, Atlanta, Georgia

EISEMAN, ALBERT   GRUNSFELD, LILLIE   LS Mar. 1, 1884
   on Feb. 26, 1884 in Albuquerque, New Mexico

ELBERT, HENRY   _____, EMMA   EPT Apr. 11, 1883
   on May 20, 1878 in Tarrant co., Texas; suit for divorce El Paso co.Tx.

ELDERTON, W.   BURTON, Mrs. ALICE   BU Dec. 5, 1885
   on Nov. 26, 1885 in Kelly, New Mexico

ELLIOTT, STEPHEN   CONNELLY, DELLA(DELIA)
                                  EPT Mar. 15, 1885
   on Mar. 10, 1885 in El Paso, Texas by Bishop H. W. READ

ELLIS, Col. A. A.   KELLEY, CLARA J.   EPT Nov. 25, 1883
   of El Paso, Texas   of Lewiston, Maine
   in Lewiston, Maine; he is an engineer on S. P. R. R.

EPPERSON, Sher._____   SHOTWELL, FANNIE   LS Oct. 1, 1884
   Polk co., Texas   of Livingston, Texas
   on Sept. 25, 1884

ERRETT, Sgt. S. S.   CHAMBERLAIN, EVA   EPT June 10, 1883
   in Santa Fe, New Mexico; niece of Gen. and Mrs. LOGAN

ESTRADA, JESUS   GONZALLES, FRANCISCA RGR Feb. 7, 1885
   on Jan. 31, 1885 in Las Cruces, New Mexico by Judge VALDEZ

EVANS, JOB M.   ROBISON (ROBESON), CLARA J.
   Cashier of Dona Ana Bank,   RGR June 20, 1885
   Las Cruces, N. M.   BU June 27, 1885
   on Saturday, June 13, 1885 at bride's home in Mankato, Minn.

FAUDOA, Sr. FRANCISCO   OCHOA, JUANITA   LS Jan. 7, 1882
   of Chihuahua, Mex.
   on Jan. 4, 1882 in El Paso, Texas

FAY, LOU   SHOEMAKER, Miss   LS May 23, 1885
   in the Mogollons, New Mexico

FERNANDEZ, SAMUEL C.   SCHOOLER, Mrs. GEORGIA
                                LS June 13, 1885
   on June 10, 1885 in El Paso, Texas by Rev. W. P. McCORKLE

FIELD, E. J.   LEESON, ISADORA E.   BU Nov. 7, 1885
   on Nov. 1, 1885 in Socorro, New Mexico

FINK, E. M.   DICKEY, RUTH   LS June 27, 1883
   of El Paso, Texas   of Hartford City,   EPT June 25, 1883
                       Indiana
   on June 14, 1883 in Hartford City, Indiana; the ranch is at Antelope
   Springs near Toyah, Texas

GROOM	BRIDE	PAPER and DATE

FINK, W. W.   DOANE, CLARA   LS Oct. 20, 1884
 of El Paso, Texas   of El Paso, Texas EPT Oct. 20, 1884
 on Oct. 19, 1884 in El Paso, Texas by Rev. GEORGE W. BAINES; bride's
 par.: (D. E.?) DOANE

FISHER, WILLIAM E.   ESTEL, Miss   EPT July 13, 1883
 of Trinidad, Colo.   of El Paso, Texas
 on July 11, 1883 in El Paso, Texas by Rev. G. W. BAINES

FLEMING, JOHN   PRITCHET, HETTIE EPT Oct. 25, 1885
 of Anthony, N. M.   of Anthony, N. M.
 on Oct. 24, 1885 in El Paso, Texas by Rev. G. W. BAINES

FONNER, JOHN C.   McMICHAEL, ELLA LS Dec. 10, 1881
 last week in Raton, New Mexico

FORSYTHE, Gen.   BEAUMONT, Miss LS May 6, 1885
 on May 1, 1885 in Ft. Bowie, Arizona; bride's par.: Col. BEAUMONT

FOUNTAIN, Lt. ALBERT J.(JR.) _____ EPT May 13, 1883
 to be married; groom's par.: Maj. and Mrs. A. J. FOUNTAIN, SR. of Las
 Cruces and Mesilla, N. M.; sis.: MARIANITA FOUNTAIN

FROST, MAX   WRAY, VIOLA M. LS
 of Santa Fe, N. M.
 in Troy, Missouri

FUFF, Hon. F. J.   TERRY, Miss CLINTON EPMS Dec. 4, 1884
 on Nov. 29, 1884 in Columbia, Texas

FUHRMANN, AUGUST   MOST, CLARA EPT Aug. 18, 1884
 on Aug. 17, 1884 in El Paso, Texas by Rev. RICHARD WALSH

FULTON, JAMES   HAZEL, Mrs. M. L. LS May 13, 1885
                 EPT May 11, 1885
 on May 10, 1885 in El Paso, Texas by Justice DAVIS

GAINES, THOMAS (negro) THOMPSON, THULA(negro)
                 EPDH May 27, 1883
 on May 23, 1883 in El Paso, Texas by Rev. GEORGE W. BAINES

GALE, Lt. _____   WILSON, MAGGIE LS June 18, 1884
                 RGR Mar. 15, 1884
 at Ft. Stanton, New Mexico; bride's par.: Post Chaplain; bride is a
 sis.(?) of Major VAN HORN.

GALLEGOS, ALBINO   GALLEGOS, ANASTASIA LS Sept. 20, 1884
 on Sept. 15, 1884 at Los Alamos, New Mexico; double wedding

GALLEGOS, LUCIANO B. GALLEGOS, PETRIETIA LS Sept. 20, 1884
 on Sept. 15, 1884 in Los Alamos, New Mexico; double wedding

GARCIA, JESUS   AMADOR, EMILIA LS Dec. 7, 1881
 on Dec. 1, 1881 in Las Cruces, N. M.; bride's par.: Don MARTIN AMADOR
 of Las Cruces, N. M.

GARDENER, Cpl.___   WELLWOOD, Miss ___ EPT Feb. 11, 1885
 in Ft. Bayard, New Mexico

GASSOWAY, J. B.   SMITH, FLORENCE EPT July 17, 1884
 license issued July 17, 1884 in El Paso, Texas

GILDEA, ED BEAUREGARD THOMPSON, JENNIE A. EPT Dec. 7, 1884
 of San Antonio, Texas of El Paso, Texas SH Nov. 30, 1884
 on Nov. 30, 1884 in El Paso, Texas; bro.: C. A. GILDEA of Kinney co.,
 Texas; bro.: A. M. GILDEA of Pecos co., Texas

GROOM	BRIDE	PAPER and DATE

GILLOCK, BRAXTON W.   GILLOCK, MARY ELIZABETH
                                             EPT Feb. 8, 1887
She was born in Versailles co., Kentucky 1815 and came to El Paso co.
1857. He was first mayor of El Paso. Member of Constitutional Con-
vention of 1866 - became ill on way home and died 5 days later. "One
of the oldest citizens of Ysleta".

GOLD, ABE   ____, ___   EPDH Apr. 4, 1895
celebrated 28th anniversary of their marriage yesterday.

GONZALES, ADRIAN   APODACA, NESTORIA   RGR June 23, 1883
of Las Cruces, N. M.   of San Antonio, N.M. RGR June 9, 1883
on June 12, 1883 in San Antonio, New Mexico; groom's par.: Don TOMAS
GONZALES of San Antonio, New Mexico; bride's par.: live in San Antonio, New Mexico.

GONZALES, NAVIDAD   PENA, FELICIANA   EPT Feb. 5, 1885
on Feb. 3, 1885 in El Paso by Rev. R. V. POLIMARES

GOODPASTURE, MORGAN   SCOTT, PEARL   EPT Apr. 3, 1885
                             of Sherbourne, Fleming
                             co., Kentucky
on Mar. 26, 1885 in Owingsville, Kentucky; formerly of El Paso, Texas;
firm ROBERTS & GOODPASTURE.

GRANT, Dr. J. B.   BUCHANAN, MATTIE   LS Dec. 28, 1881
of Austin, Texas   of Bastrop, Texas
on Dec. 20, 1881 in Bastrop, Texas

GRAVES, J. W.   IRELAND, MARY   LS Dec. 6, 1882
of Seguin, Texas
to be Dec. 12, 1882; bride is daughter of Gov. IRELAND.

GRIESINGER, A.   AGETHEN(?), A.   LS June 3, 1885
in Las Vegas, New Mexico

GRIGSBY, THOMAS   ____,____   EPDH Mar. 3, 1890
on Mar. 4, 1865; celebrated 25th anniversary

GROSSTET, A. C.   POURADE, CLEMENCE   BU May 1, 1883
last Friday, in Socorro, New Mexico in father's residence by Judge
SHAW; HERMAS BLANCHARD and SILVIO POURADE assisted in the ceremony.

GUERRA, SABINO   BORREGO, LUCIA   LS Feb. 1, 1882
license issued in January in El Paso, Texas

GUITEAU, F. R.   RICHARDSON, EVA A. EPDH Sept. 28, 1881
of Denison, Texas   of Denison, Texas
other day in Denison, Texas; he is cousin of Pres. GARFIELD's assassin, CHARLES GUITEAU.

GUITIERREZ, Col. FELIX   FLORES, HERMINIA   EPT Apr. 18, 1883
of Mexican Army
on Apr. 14, 1883 in Cathedral in San Antonio, Texas

GUITTARD, ALPHONSE   GROSSTETE, Mrs. CLEMENCE
of White Oaks, N. M.   of Socorro, N. M.   BU Dec. 5, 1885
                                                 BU Dec. 19, 1885
                                                 BU Jan. 2, 1886
on Dec. 24, 1885 in Socorro, New Mexico by Judge WILLIAM E. KELLEY at
home of parents; groom's par. in Canada; bride's sister: GILBERTE &
SYLVIA POURADE and a brother.

HAAS, ISAAC   HAHN, CARRIE   EPDH Nov. 4, 1883
of El Paso, Texas   EPDH Jan. 13, 1884
on Jan. 22, 1884 in New York City, 204 E. 79th St.;EPDH Jan. 27, 1884
bride's par.: M. HAHN.

GROOM	BRIDE	PAPER and DATE

HADLEY, WALTER C.   PAXON, ALICE C.   RGR Oct. 13, 1883
   of Las Vegas, N. M.   of Philadelphia
   on Oct. 18, 1883 in Philadelphia, Penn.; wedding invitation, HADLEY
   is of the Las Vegas, N. M. Gazette.

HAILE, J. T.   LOWRY, Miss   EPMS Nov. 30, 1884
   in San Antonio, Texas

HAING, A. W.   IVEY, CAROLINE   LS Nov. 23, 1881
   Chinaman, recently naturalized
   last week in Austin, Texas by Dr. PHILPOTT

HANSON, HOWARD B.   HAYES, IDA B.   EPT Apr. 15, 1885
                                     of Chihuahua, Mex.
   on Apr. 14, 1885 in El Paso, Texas by Rev. J. K. FOWLER.

HARDY, WILLIAM   SHIELDS, FRANCES   EPDH Apr. 5, 1882
   (of French origin)   (negro)
   in 1882 in Bexar co., Texas

HARRIS, WILL J.   SCHULTZ, EMILIE   LS May 9, 1885
   of El Paso, Texas   (SCHUTZ, AMELIA nee   SH May 3, 1885
                                     Mrs. DAY -(sic)   SH May 10, 1885
   on May 7, 1885 in Ysleta, Texas; he is nephew of ex-gov. and U. S.
   Senator ISHAM G. HARRIS of Tennessee.

HARRISON, JOHN   LITTLE, MARY A.   LS Nov. 30, 1881
                                     of Marshall, Texas
   on Nov. 21, 1881

HART, FRANK   RAND, FLORENCE   LS Aug. 8, 1883
   "Tarantula Bill"   LS Aug. 25, 1883
   on Aug. 5, 1883 in Episcopal Church, El Paso, Texas; bride's par.:
   GEORGE RAND

HEDRICK, JOHN I.   LISENBEE, ANNIE   LS Mar. 25, 1885
   in Las Vegas, New Mexico

HENRY, EDWARD A.   RUSSELL, Mrs. INEZ L.
   of Silver City, N. M.   of New Orleans, La.   EPT Sept. 20, 1883
   on Sept. 17, 1883 in Silver City, N. M. by Judge JAMES CORBIN; She is
   an actress using name Miss CARLYLE.

HERNANDEZ, JESUS   GOMEZ, DOLORES   LS Feb. 1, 1882
   license issued in January in El Paso, Texas

HICKOX, FRANK E.   STEDMAN, WILLIE   RGR Nov. 24, 1883
   of Las Cruces, N. M.   of Texas
   on Nov. 20, 1883 in Las Cruces, N. M. by Rev. Mr. MATTHIESON

HIGLEY, S. W.   HENSON, SALLY   BU Dec. 12, 1885
   on Dec. 9, 1885 in Socorro, N. M. by Rev. J. D. BUSH; bride's bros.:
   ED & HENRY & ARTHUR HENSON; fa.: Col. L. HENSON.

HILL, E. C.   CUTBIRTH, IDA   LS Nov. 15, 1884
   on Nov. 12, 1884 in Belle Plain, Texas

HILL, FRANK   WILSON, SARAH   BU Nov. 7, 1885
   in Socorro, New Mexico; Mrs. ROBERT BENN, sister of bride.

HOECK, FRED P.   VAUGHN, JESSIE P.   EPDH May 31, 1882
   on May 30, 1882 in El Paso, Texas; groom's par. J. F. HOECK of Appenade, Germany.

HOLLING, BERNARD D.   WALLENHAULT, ELISE E. L.
   license issued in El Paso, Texas   LS Nov. 14, 1885

GROOM	BRIDE	PAPER and DATE

HOPEWELL, W. S.   FULLER, DAISY   BU July 25, 1885
   of Vega Blanca & Palomas,   of Hillsboro, N. M.
   N. M. or Mex.
   par.: of bride - G. M. FULLER

HOPF, CHARLES   SYDNER, KATE   LS Nov. 21, 1885
   of Ysleta, Texas   of Ysleta, Texas   EPT Dec. 23. 1885
                 (or SYDNOR)   EPT Dec. 25,1885
   on Dec. 22, 1885 in Ysleta, Texas by Rev. RICHARD WALSH; married at
   home of Col. G. H. BAYLOR, husband of bride's sister.

HORSLEY, LOUIS L.   , TINA   EPDH Mar. 4, 1883
   in 1867 in Morgan co., Missouri; suit for divorce; ch.: ELLA L., age
   14; CLARA M., age 6.

HOSTETTER, LOUIS   SCHLESINGER, FANNIE RGR Oct. 4, 1884
   of Albuquerque, N. M.   of Omaha, Neb.   LS Jan. 10, 1885
   on Jan. 6, 1885 in Omaha, Neb. (one paper gives date as Sept. 20,1884)

HOUGHTON, E. C.   WINRAM, GEORGIE   BU Nov. 28, 1885
   recently in San Marcial, N. M.; bride's par.: JOHN A. WINRAM of Clo-
   ride, N. M.; eldest daughter.

HOWARD, A. A.   LYNAN (or TYNAN), ANNA
   of El Paso, Texas   of El Paso, Texas   LS Nov. 8, 1884
                                  EPT Nov. 6, 1884
   on Nov. 2, 1884 in El Paso, Texas Catholic Church by Rev. Father
   DE PALMA.

HUBBS, O.   DANFORD, MARY   LS Nov. 19, 1881
   of Las Vegas, N. M.   of Michigan
   on Nov. 12, 1881 in Trinidad, Colorado

HUDSON, J. M.   LEVI, Mrs. WILLIE   EPDH May 4, 1884
   last Tuesday (22 or 29 Apr. 1884) in Weatherford, Texas by Judge TAY-
   LOR of Colorado City, Texas; married by telephone.

HUDSON, Hon. RICHARD   STEVENS, MARY E.   TB Oct. 4, 1871
   of Silver City, N. M.   of Silver City, N. M.
   on Sept. 24, 1871 in Silver City, New Mexico

HURGZ, JAMES H.   PITTS, Mrs.   RGR Sept. 27, 1884
   of Organ, Las Cruces &   of Tularosa, N. M.
   Lincoln, New Mexico
   Mrs. PITTS is the mother of BILLY.

HUTCHINSON, CHARLES G.   KNAPP, JENNIE (or CAMP)
   on May 13, 1885 in El Paso, Texas by Judge LOU DAVIS
                              EPT May 14, 1885
                              SH May 17, 1885

HUTCHINSON, IKE C.   LS Oct. 4, 1884
   on Sept. 24, 1884 in Waco, Texas

IRLAND, F. D.   EPT Nov. 1, 1885
                 of Houston, Texas
   returned with bride.

JACKSON, CHARLES T.   HOGAN, CLARA A.   LS Nov. 10, 1883
   on Nov. 8, 1883 at home.in El Paso, Texas by Rev. J. R. CARTER; brides
   par.: Capt. T. V. HOGAN.

JAMES, W. M.   FLINT, JESSIE   LS Feb. 21, 1883
   of El Paso, Texas
   on Feb. 12, 1883 in Ottumwa, Iowa.

GROOM	BRIDE	PAPER and DATE

JOHNSON, J. W.   SMITH, J. A.   LS Nov. 4, 1885
  (policeman)   EPT Nov. 6, 1885
  on Nov. 3, 1885 in El Paso, Texas by Rev. GEORGE W. BAINES

JOHNSON, L. H.   ETHRIDGE, MAGGIE K.   LS Dec. 10, 1881
  on Dec. 1, 1881 in Hallville, Harrison co., Texas; groom is Train
  Dispatcher for Texas & Pacific R. R.

JONES, _____   ENNIS, JENNIE   EPDH Nov. 18, 1883
  at Ft. Bliss, Texas

JONES, JESSE   BERRY, SARAH   BU Nov. 7, 1885
  of Las Vegas, N. M.   of Newcastle, Eng.   BU Nov. 14, 1885
  on Nov. 10, 1885 in Socorro, New Mexico by Rev. J. W. FORBES

JONES, LEE H.   DAVIDSON, FLORENCE   LS Oct. 4, 1884
  on Oct. 2, 1884, eloped; bride's par.: Ret. English Gen. of San Antonio, Texas

JONES, PAUL   CUNNINGHAM, KATE   LS July 15, 1885
  on July 19, 1885 in Las Vegas, New Mexico

JONES, TONEY   HINCHMAN, BELLE   LS May 16, 1885
  other day in Waco, Texas

JUDA, M.   ROSENFIELD, TILLIE   LS Mar. 4, 1882
  formerly with STAAB & Co., Santa Fe, N. M.
  last week in Socorro, New Mexico

JURADO, EUJENIO   ARIAS, SOLEDAD   LS Feb. 1, 1882
  license issued in January in El Paso, Texas

KELLER, J. M.   BURNS, Mrs. CATHERINE
  of El Paso, Texas   of Monteluma, Mex.   EPT July 14, 1883
  by Squire LOOMIS, J. P.   EPDH July 15, 1883

KELLEY, EUGENE, JR.   MILMO, SARITA   LS Feb. 21, 1885
  on Apr. 12, 1885. Groom's par. - New York Banker; bride's par.:
  PATRICIO MILMO, banker, Monterrey, Mexico. bro.: J. HUGHES KELLEY,
  best man.

KELLY, JOHN T.   O'HARA, CATHERINE   LS July 7, 1883
  on July 7, 1883 in El Paso, Texas by J. P.

KENNEDY, N. J.   LEMON, CARLITA   LS Sept. 17 & 20,
  of Organ, N. M.   of Las Cruces, N.M.   1884
  on Sept. 24, 1884 in Las Cruces, N. M.   LS Sept. 24, 1884
                                          RGR Sept. 27, 1884

KENNION, LOUIS C.   JENNISON, Miss   EPT May 13, 1883
  of Las Cruces, N. M.   of Hillsboro, N. M.
  few days ago in Lake Valley, New Mexico

KEPHART, JAMES H.   CRARY, Mrs. LOTTIE A.LS Dec. 26, 1885
                                         EPT Dec. 25, 1885
  Dec. 24, 1885 in El Paso, Texas by Rev. GEORGE W. BAINES

KERL, CHARLES   STOUDENMIRE, Mrs. BELLE
  longtime R. R.   (widow of DALLAS STOUDENMIRE)
  conductor in Texas   EPDH Dec. 16, 1883
  in Galveston, Texas. Left for San Antonio, Texas.

KLAUSER, A. E.   _____   BU Dec. 1, 1884
  formerly of Socorro, N. M.
  recently; in business in East Saginaw, Michigan

GROOM	BRIDE	PAPER and DATE

KLEINWORTH, W. H.   COTES, MOLLIE   LS Dec. 12, 1885
   eloped from Fort Worth, Texas

KOEHLER, JOHN   RECKTER,FLORENCE LS Nov. 26, 1881
   on Nov. 23, 1881; bride's par.: Capt. RECKTER of Ft. Bliss, Texas

KOHLBERG, ERNEST   EPT Aug. 30, 1884
   of El Paso, Texas   from Germany   SH July 20, 1884
   in Germany

KOOYGLER, W. G.   HOUSE, Miss   LS Nov. 5, 1881
   of Las Vegas "Gazette" of Richmond, Iowa
   N. M.
   on Oct. 25, 1881

KRATER, JOHN A. (R.?)   SH July 13, 1884
   last week in El Paso, Texas

KRAUSE, A.   BEACH, FLORA   EPDH Jan. 17, 1883
   of El Paso, Texas   of Gonzalez, Texas
   on Dec. 23, 1882 in Gonzalez, Texas

LABADIE, TRANQUILINO   ROMERO, FLORENTINA LS Mar. 12, 1884
   on Mar. 8, 1884 in Las Vegas, New Mexico; bride's par.: ex-Mayor
   ROMERO

LAND, JAMES   McSWAIN, CORA   EPMS Nov. 27, 1884
   of Buffalo, N. Y.   of Corsicana, Tex.
   on Nov. 20, 1884

LANE, NATHAN DELMER   CASAD, JENNIE   LS Mar. 12, 1884
   of Prescott, Ariz.   RGR Mar. 8, 1884
   formerly of Mesilla, N. M.
   on Mar. 5, 1884 in Mesilla, N. M. by Rev. M. MATTHIESON; bride's par.:
   THOMAS CASAD

LANG, JOHN   RUSSELL, SOPHIA   BU June 9, 1885
   of Carthage, N. M.   of Wishaw, Lanarkshire,
                    Scotland - age 17

   on June 6, 1885 in Socorro, N. M. by Rev. M. D. A. STEEN; LANG left
   Scotland 4 years ago - she was about 13 years at that time. Groom's
   sis. - bridesmaid.

LARQUE, EDWARDO   DUCHENE, LUISA   LS Jan. 14, 1882
                                  EPDH Jan. 11, 1882
   on Jan. 7, 1882 in Paso del Norte, Mexico at home by Father ORTIZ;
   bride's par.: EMILIO DUCHENE

LAW, E.   COOK, IDA   BU Dec. 12, 1885
   on Dec. 6, 1885 in Socorro, N. M. by Rev. J. M. ROBINSON

LAWRENCE, JOHN B.   , MAUD M.   BU Sept. 29, 1891
   in 1873 in Nevada; divorce action - lived in Texas together till 1887
   he deserted - 1 child

LEDDY, P.   BU July 25, 1885
   of Socorro, N. M.
   in Amboy, Illinois

LEGRAND, B. V.   CLARKE, DIXIE   LS Sept. 27, 1884
   of Santa Fe Railroad
   in Hempstead, Texas; bride is sister of editor of "Two Republics",
   Mexico City.

LEGHTON, JAMES W.   CHADWICK, ELIZABETH BU July 18, 1885
   of Kelly, N. M.   of Leeds, England (cont'd next page)

LEGHTON cont'd:
on July 16, 1885 in Socorro, New Mexico by Rev. N. W. CHASE.

LEONARD, W. E.   McCULLOUGH, NETTIE   BU Jan. 1, 1885
on Jan. 1, 1885 in home of bride's parents in Socorro, New Mexico by
Rev. W. C. BARKLEY

LITTELL, Lt. ISAAC WILLIAM   BARRETT, JULIA MAY   LS Jan. 24, 1885
of Ft. Lyon, Colo.   EPT Jan. 23, 1885
on Jan. 22, 1885 in Ft. Bliss, Texas by Rev. J. K. FOWLER. Bride's
parents, Capt. and Mrs. GREGORY BARRETT, Ft. Bliss, Texas

LOHMAN, J. FRED   MEYER, JULIA   RGR Apr. 26, 1884
on Apr. 29, 1884 in St. Louis, Missouri. Bride's par. M/M JOHN MEYER

LOHMAN, MARTIN   SCHAUBLIN, AMANDA   LS Sept. 8, 1883
                                             LS Sept. 15, 1883
                                           RGR Sept. 15, 1883
on Sept. 13, 1883 in Las Cruces, New Mexico by Rev. MATHIESON, Pres-
byterian; bride's par.: JACOB SCHAUBLIN. AMANDA eldest daughter; sis.
AMELIA SCHAUBLIN; bro. of groom J. FRED LOHMAN and fa. of St. Louis,
Missouri

LORING, G. A.   MARSH, MAGGIE   EPT Apr. 16, 1883
of Oakland, Ca.   of Oakland, Ca.
on Apr. 15, 1883 in El Paso, Texas by Rev. R. TAYLOR

LOWRY, ALVA C.   PARISH, HATTIE L.   LS Mar. 1, 1884
of Kingston, N. M.
on Feb. 18, 1884 in Providence, Rhode Island

LUCERO, EVORISTO   SENA, Miss.....   LS May 2, 1885
today in Santa Fe, New Mexico; par. of bride: JOSE D. SENA

LUGO VINA, Col. NICALIS de   HANDY, TILLIE   SH Aug. 2, 1885
of Mexico City, Mex.
on July 26, 1885 in Ocean City, Md.; HANDY, youngest dau. of Judge
ALEXANDER A. HANDY of Miss.; sis. of bride: Mrs. OTTO SUTRO of Baltimore and Mrs. MARY HANDY

LURKINS, FRED   BAILEY, JACQUETTE   EPDH Jan. 6, 1884
of El Paso, Texas   of Clarksville, Tex.
on Dec. 19, 1883 in Clarksville, Texas

LYNCH, JAMES H.   HURLBURT, JENNIE C. LS Dec. 16, 1885
of Kansas   of Kansas   EPT Dec. 16, 1885
License issued m. Dec. 15, 1885 in El Paso, Tex; by Rev. Dr. KEYES

LYON, Dr. WILLIAM B.   BOWMAN, CARRIE   LS Sept. 16, 1882
of Albuquerque, N.M.   of Mesilla, N. M.
on Thursday - Sept. 14, 1882 in Mesilla, N. M. by Rev. HENRY FORRES-
TER of Episcopal Church Albuquerque. Will live in Albuquerque.

McALISTER, H.   YOUNG, MABEL   LS Aug. 15, 1883
of Socorro, N. M.   age 16 when ma.
newly married; she was m. previously; bride's par.: BRIGHAM YOUNG and
3rd wife.

McGAILLARD, H. D.   _____, _____   BU Dec. 25, 1886
on Dec. 20, 1861; 25th anniversary

McGUIRE, F. E.   FREY, MILLIE   EPT Oct. 31, 1885
                             of Oshkosh, Wisc.
arrived in El Paso Oct. 30, 1885 with "prize"

McKAY, D. W.   CUMMINGS, Mrs. VIRGINIA M.
of El Paso, Texas   EPDH Apr. 6, 1884
on Apr. 2, 1884 in Kansas City, Missouri

GROOM	BRIDE	PAPER and DATE

MACMANUS, FRANCISCO   ASUNCELO de JAZUEZ, MARIA
  of Chihuahua, Mex.   EPT Aug. 12, 1884
  on Aug. 12, 1884 in Chihuahua, Mex.; banking firm F. MACMANUS & SONS

MACMANUS, IGNACIO   OLIVARES, SILVERIA LS Nov. 28, 1883
  of Chihuahua, Mex.   EPT Dec. 2, 1883
  on Nov. 25, 1883 in El Paso, Texas(?); groom's par.: F. MACMANUS,
  banker; bride's par.: Don PEDRO OLIVARES

McMURRAY, JOHN N. (or A.)   DONELLY, ANNIE   LS July 1, 1885
                                         BU June 27, 1885
  on June 28, 1885 in San Marcial, New Mexico by Father HAYES

MACK, M. J.   CRIUCKSHANK, GRACE RGR July 21, 1883
  of Albuquerque, N. M.
  on Saturday, July 14, 1883 in Santa Fe, New Mexico; quietly married

MADDOX, E. T.   WEGLEY, IODA   EPDH Feb. 4, 1883
  in January 1883 in Hillsboro, Texas by Rev. G. W. SWOFFORD; bride appears to be only 10 or 12 years old, though father swore she would be
  15 next month.

MADRID, FRANCISCO   CANO, PILAR   LS Feb. 1, 1882
  license issued in January in El Paso, Texas

MADRID, LUZ   WOOD, CATHERINE   LS Oct. 3, 1885(1)
  age 19   LS Nov. 7, 1885(2)
  (1) eloped and married Sept. 29, 1885 in Dona Ana, New Mexico by Judge
  BUTSCHOFSKY; (2) married Nov. 4, 1885 in Catholic Church; she was educated at Vassar - he is illiterate and can't speak English; bride's
  parents: Col. G. W. WOOD, Mesilla, New Mexico

MANDELL, _____   _____   BU June 20, 1885
  recently; home in Albuquerque, New Mexico; cousin: D. WEILER of Socorro, New Mexico

MARENGO, AMBROSIO   GIRON, TOMASITA   LS Nov. 11, 1885
  license issued in El Paso, Texas

MARSH, WILLIAM D.   HART, PAULINE S.   LS Dec. 5, 1885
  license issued in El Paso, Texas

MARTIN, FRED   WILEY, ANNIE   LS Oct. 8, 1884
  on Oct. 7, 1884 in Las Vegas, New Mexico

MARTINEZ, ANTONIO   MEDINA, CRUZ   LS May 23, 1885
  of Ponil, New Mexico   of Ponil, New Mexico
  in Springer, New Mexico by Father ACCORSINI

MASTIN, PATRICK P.   PERKINS, Mrs. SARAH J.
                                           TB Apr. 3, 1872
  on March 25, 1872 at Fort Bayard, New Mexico by Esq. HARSHBERGER

MATTHEWS, J. B.   BATES, DORA M.   RGR July 21, 1883
  of Lincoln, New Mexico
  in Rio Penasco, New Mexico; par. of bride: J. T. BATES

MAY, J. A.(Mr. and Mrs.)   RGR May 2, 1885
  trip to El Paso yesterday to celebrate first anniversary

MEADER, AL   GOODRICH, ANNIE   BU Dec. 12, 1885
  on Dec. 10, 1885 in Socorro, New Mexico by Justice CURTIN

MERRICK, FRED W.   FRISBIE, GRACE   EPT June 17, 1883
  of El Paso, Texas   of Kankakee, Ill. LS June 17, 1883
  on June 21, 1883 in Kankakee, Illinois; bride, niece of M/M J. S.
  BRIGGS, Kankakee, Ill.; bro.: CHARLES M. MERRICK

GROOM	BRIDE	PAPER and DATE

MERRILL, ISAAC A.   CODE, MARY E.   EPDH Sept. 3, 1890
   in Oct. 1882 in El Paso, Texas; found that her marriage to MERRILL was
   bigamous since she was still married to H. C. CODE

METCALF, CHARLIE   BOWMAN, SADIE M.   RGR Aug. 22, 1885
   of "Rio Grande Republican"   LS Aug. 15, 1885
                                      EPT Aug. 18, 1885
                                      BU Aug. 8, 1885
   on Aug. 15, 1885 in Las Cruces, New Mexico by Rev. Mr. MATTHIESON;
   bride s par.: Dr. _____ BOWMAN

MEYER, JAMES   CASEY, MOLLIE   LS June 13, 1885
   of Deming, N. M.   of Cawker City, Kans.
                       && Las Vegas, N. M.
   in Deming, New Mexico

MILLER, ADAM   KESSLER, ANNIE   LS Oct. 13, 1883
   on Oct. 10, 1883 in El Paso, Texas; both employed at the Central Hotel

MILLER, N. J.   McDANIEL, Mrs. FANNIE
                                          LS May 23, 1885
   on May 20, 1885 in El Paso, Texas at home of JOHN LORENSON by Rev. Dr.
   KEYES

MINER, C. E.(CHARLES E.)   BURROUGHS, CLARA   LS Feb. 4, 1885
   of El Paso, Texas   of Illinois   EPT Feb. 4, 1885
                                        EPT Apr. 21, 1885
   on Jan. 29, 1885 in New Orleans, La. by Dr. B. M. PALMER

MINER, J. A. C.   MILLER, Mrs. MARY C. LS Sept. 20, 1884
   on Sept. 15, 1884 in Las Vegas, New Mexico

MODIE, Mr. ___   TRAVIS, Mrs. ____   LS Feb. 22, 1882
   of Socorro, N. M.
   on Feb. 15, 1882 in Ft. Union, New Mexico

MONTANO, SALOMON   MONTANO, FLORA   LS June 20, 1885
   on June 13, 1885 in Lincoln, New Mexico

MONTOVA, ENTEMIO   PEREZ, SALLIE A.   BU Feb. 1, 1885
   of San Antonio, N. M.   of Las Vegas, N. M.
   on Jan. 15, 1885 in Las Vegas, N. M.; bride's par.: M/M _____ PEREZ

MONTOYA, JUAN   BARELA, MANUELA   RGR Aug. 4, 1883
   on July 29, 1883; bride's par.: Rev. MARCUS BARELA

MOORE, F. H.   MADDEN, Mrs. FANNIE EPDH Feb. 17, 1884
   on Feb. 14, 1884 in El Paso, Texas by Rev. J. W. TAYS

MOORE, JOHN H. (negro)   PAYNE, ESTELLE (negro)
                                          EPDH July 15, 1883
   this week in El Paso, Texas by Rev. TAYS

MOORE, JUNE J.   ROACH, LUCY   LS Oct. 8, 1884
   on Oct. 4, 1884 in El Paso, Texas, home of JAMES HOPE

MORALES, HILARIO   AGUIRRE, SABINITA   TB Nov. 23, 1872
   on Nov. 16, 1872 in Las Cruces, N. M. by Rev. AUGUSTIN BERNARD

MOREHEAD, O.   MAESE, REGINA   SH Dec. 28, 1884
   on Dec. 25, 1884 in El Paso, Texas by Rev. Mr. MacDONELL

MOREHOUSE, C. H.   BROWNE, JESSIE   BU Oct. 3, 1885
   of Evansville, Wisc.   of Brodhead, Wisc.
   on Sept. 23, 1885 in Brodhead, Wis.; works for R. R. in Socorro, New
   Mexico

MORGA, MANUEL   PACHECO, GUADALUPE LS June 20, 1885

MORGA cont'd:
 in Lincoln, New Mexico

MORGAN, HUGH F.   BOLON, CATHARINE EPT Oct. 25, 1885
 license issued Oct. 24, 1885 in El Paso, Texas

MORRISSEY(MORRISY), D. B. MITCHEL, MAGGIE E. EPT Sept. 3, 1884
 of Memphis, Tenn.   of Algiers, La. EPT Sept. 4, 1884
 on Sept. 3, 1884 in El Paso, Texas by Rev. Father Se. PALMER

MULGRAVES, JOHN   ROURK, Mrs. JOSIE LS Apr. 15, 1885
 in Socorro, New Mexico

MULL, CHARLES   _____   BU Oct. 10, 1885
 he and bride arrived in Socorro, New Mexico from the East

MULLALLY, CHARLES B.   BENNETT, MAGGIE LS Nov. 26, 1884
                   EPMS Nov. 28, 1884
 on Dec. 1, 1884 in San Antonio, Texas

MULLINS, _____   _____   EPDH June 11, 1890
 on June 5, 1840; 50th anniversary celebrated in Aubrey, Texas; three
 (3) sons, two (2) daus., nineteen (19) grand children and two (2) gr.
 grand children present

MURRAY, M.   HENDERSON, MARY LS May 30, 1885
 in Albuquerque, New Mexico

MURRELL, ROBERT E.   GILLETTE, VIRGINIA E.
                   LS Jan. 7, 1882
 on Dec. 20, 1881 in Houston, Texas

NEBAKER, (NEBEKER), B. A. DOWING, SARAH EPDH July 1, 1883
 of El Paso, Texas   of Indianapolis, Ind.
 in Indianapolis, Indiana

NEPPLE, CARL   WRIGHT, CARRIE LS Apr. 15, 1885
 on April 8, 1885 in Santa Fe, New Mexico

NEVILL, Capt. C. L.   CROSSON, SARAH E. EPDH Jan. 10, 1883
 of Ft. Davis, Texas
 on Jan. 4, 1883 in Ft. Davis, Texas; bride's par.: GEORGE CROSSON of
 Ft. Davis, formerly of San Antonio, Texas

NEWCOMB, Judge S. B.   READ, ABBIE J. RGR Dec. 6, 1884
 of Las Cruces, N. M.   EPT Nov. 30, 1884
 on Nov. 29, 1884 in Las Cruces, New Mexico by Rev. M. MATHIESON; bride's
 par.: JOHN READ, Esq. of Pugwash, Nova Scotia; his cousin READ or REED;
 bride is younger daughter

NEWMAN, S. H.   GECK, JESSIE   LS Mar. 8, 1882
 on Mar. 6, 1882 in Las Cruces, New Mexico by Rev. Father LASSAIGNE

NICCOLLS, Dr. A. L.   JENNESS, EDITH EPDH May 10, 1882
 of El Paso, Texas   of Bloomington, Ill.
 on May 7, 1882 in El Paso, Texas by Rev. J. W. TAYS; bride's par.:Hon.
 R. E. JENNESS of Kansas

NICHOLS, FOSTER   BRINK, _____ EPT Sept. 4, 1883
 of El Paso, Texas   EPT Oct. 15, 1885
 returns from honeymoon

NICHOLS, J. E.   CLIFFORD, ANNIE LS July 1, 1885
 last week in San Marcial, New Mexico

NITSCHMANN, REINHARD   REMINDER, KATHERINA EPT Apr. 24, 1885
 on Apr. 23, 1885 in El Paso, Tex. by Judge LOU H. DAVIS

GROOM	BRIDE	PAPER and DATE

NOVAREZ, PEDRO   OLGUIN, REFUGIO   LS Feb. 1, 1882
    license issued in January in El Paso, Texas

OCHOA, FRANCISCO   VILLA, GUADALUPE   EPT Feb. 5, 1885
    on Feb. 3, 1885 in El Paso, Texas by Rev. R. V. POLIMARES

O'CONNOR, TOM   RGR June 14, 1884
    of Memphis Mine   from East
    came from Rincon, N. M. on a hand car because of flooding

O'NEIL, BIGE   CHAVEZ, FELICITOS   LS Apr. 11, 1885
    of White Oaks, N. M.
    in Las Tablas, Lincoln county, New Mexico

OPPENHEIMER, B.   EPDH Sept. 7, 1881
    of San Antonio, Texas   of New York
    soon; bride is an actress

OSBORN, ROWLAND   MARTIN, ANNIE   LS Nov. 14, 1885
    license issued at El Paso, Texas

PACHECO, VENTURO   LUCERO, RAMONA   LS Feb. 1, 1882
    license issued in January at El Paso, Texas

PALMER, JOHN W.   HARRIS, MATTIE   LS June 17, 1885
    in Albuquerque, New Mexico by Rev. KISTLER

PAPIN, LEWIS (LOUIS PAPPIN)   SCOTT, MARY C.   EPT Sept. 4, 1885
    of Chihuahua, Mex.   of St. Louis, Mo. SH Aug. 30, 1885
    formerly of St. Louis, Mo. and
    San Marcial, Mex.
    on Sept. 3, 1885 in Catholic Church in El Paso, Texas by Rev. RICHARD
    DI PALMA; bride is sister of S. H. SCOTT, American Consul in Chihuahua,
    Mexico

PARKE, J. D."OLD BLACK JOE"   LS May 23, 1885
                           new wife
    in Philadelphia, Penn.

PARKER, CHARLES F.   SWINDELL, A.   LS Jan. 7, 1882
    on Dec. 20, 1881 in Houston, Texas

PATTISON, CHARLES E.   TERRY, SUDIE L.   LS Feb. 28, 1885
                                       EPT Feb. 27, 1885
    on Feb. 26, 1885 in El Paso, Texas by Rev. ROBERT W. McDONELL;bride's
    par.: M/M TERRY of El Paso, Texas

PAULSON, HENRY C.   YOUNG, IRENE   LS Sept. 30, 1885
    on Sept. 29, 1885 in El Paso, Texas by Rev. W. S. KEYES

PEREZ, ANTONIO   ORTEGA, JOHANA   EPT Mar. 25, 1885
                                       SH Mar. 29, 1885
    on Mar. 24, 1885 in El Paso, Texas by Justice of Peace LOU DAVIS

PHISTER, Lt. N. P.   FIFIELD, K.   EPDH Jan. 25, 1882
    on Jan. 18, 1882 in Ft. Stockton, Texas by Rev. B. L. BALDRIDGE

PIERCE, R. T.   McBRITNEY, HATTIE EPDH Jan. 13, 1884
    of El Paso, Texas   of Paso del Norte
    on Jan. 1, 1884 in El Paso, Texas by Rev. RICHARD WALSH

PIEZZER, J. G.   ROACH, BEATRICE   SH Feb. 22, 1885
    past week in El Paso, Texas by Father DE PALMA

PILSBY, A. H.   MONTES, JUANA   EPT June 12, 1883
    of Mex.-Cen. R. R.   of Chihuahua, Mex. (cont'd)

PILSBY cont'd:
  at San Jose Sta., Mexico.
  on June 10,11, 1883 in Ysleta, Texas by County Clerk

PIONTKOWSKY, H. V.   FISHER, MATTIE   RGR Sept. 13, 1884
  of Las Cruces, N. M.   of Ontario, Ca
  met bride in Deming before returning to Las Cruces

POE, Sher. J. W.   ALBERDING, SOPHIE A.
  of White Oaks, N. M.   EPT May 24, 1883
  on May 5, 1883 in Roswell, New Mexico

POLATAKIS, CHARLES   ROEHM, SOPHIE   EPT May 19, 1885
  license issued in El Paso, Texas; he is in Army

PONCE, JESUS   GARCIA, MANUELITA   EPT Sept. 3, 1885
  on Sept. 3, 1885 in Ysleta, Texas by Rev. A. ECHALLIER; both of
  Ysleta, Texas

PORTER, GAY E.   STUBENRAUCH, CAMILLE RGR Mar. 29, 1884
  on Mar. 27, 1884 in residence of Col. J. H. WATTS of Silver City,N.M.

POSEY, G. G.   FOOTE, JESSIE   BU May 5, 1885
  of Silver City, N.M.   of Paris, Ill.
  few days ago in Indianapolis, Ind.; takes bride to his former home in
  Mississippi

POVER, G. F.   BELL, ADDIE   LS Feb. 16, 1884
  R.R. Conductor of Big Spring,   formerly of El Paso,
  Texas   Texas
  on Feb. 8, 1884 in Colorado, Texas

PRESLEY, JOHN   McCANLEY, WINNIE   RGR Sept. 26, 1885
  formerly of Lake Valley,   of Lake Valley, N.M.
  now of Quizote, Ariz.
  on Wed., Sept. 23, 1885 in Catholic Church in Lake Valley, by Rev.
  Father LASSAIGNE

PRICE, MORRIS   PRAGER, ANNIE   BU Sept. 5, 1885
  on Sept. 2, 1885 in Socorro, N. M. by Rabbi GLUCK; bride's bro.: PHIL-
  LIP PRAGER; groom's bro.: JULIUS PRICE of Denver, Colo.

PRINCE, Judge BRADFORD   BEARDSLEY, MARY C.   LS Nov. 23, 1881
  of N. M.   of New York City
  on Nov. 17, 1881 in Trinity Church, New York City

PROVENCIO, FELIX   FRESQUES, LEONOR   LS Nov. 11, 1885
  license issued in El Paso, Texas

PRYOR, JOHN   SH Nov. 2, 1884
  has returned to El Paso bringing blushing supplement

PULVER, GEORGE A.   KNIGHT, SALLIE   LS Sept. 27, 1884
  on Sept. 20, 1884 in Marshall, Texas

QUAST, ALFRED   JOHNSON, ALICE   EPT July 8, 1884
  (age about 50)   (age 15)
  on July 7, 1884 in El Paso, Texas by Rev. G. W. BAINES; bride's fa.:
  is El Paso policeman; fa. indignant - claims license secured illegally

QUEBEDAUX, J. W.   BURNHAM, EMMA   BU Nov. 21, 1885
  (French)
  recently in Flato, Fayette county, Texas; bride's uncle Maj. C. T.
  RUSSELL of Water Canon, New Mexico

RADCLIFF, A.   DALTON, LUCY   BU Sept. 1, 1883
  on Aug. 7, 1883 in Socorro, New Mexico

GROOM	BRIDE	PAPER and DATE

RATON, G. W.   McALLISTER, MAUDE   LS Jan. 7, 1882
  of Santa Fe, N. M.   of Elizabethtown, N. M.
  on Jan. 1, 1882 in Las Vegas, New Mexico

READ, Capt. JOHN F.   FROST, MAY E.   BU May 19, 1885
  of Socorro, N. M.   of Chicago, Ill.   BU May 26, 1885
  and New Orleans   BU June 2, 1885
  on Apr. 22, 1885 in New Orleans, La.; bride's bro.: CLARK FROST of
  Las Vegas, New Mexico

REILEY, JAMES M.   MASSIE, CATARINA   EPDH Oct. 12, 1881
  on Oct. 5, 1881 in Ysleta, Texas

RHEA, GEORGE   _____   EPDH Aug. 26, 1883
  of El Paso, Texas
  spending honeymoon in Chihuahua, Mexico

RHODES, Dr. _____   ENGLISH, Mrs. MAGGIE LS July 1, 1885
  in Albuquerque, New Mexico

RICHARDSON, _____   BUGBY, _____   EPT Dec. 23, 1884
  license issued Dec. 18, 1884 in Albuquerque, N. M.

RILEY, J. H.   CUNIFFE, Miss ANNE   LS Nov. 11, 1882
  on Nov. 9, 1882 in Las Cruces, N. M. at home of bride's parents by
  Rev. Father _____

ROBINSON, E. P. M.   HUBBARD, Miss LIZZIE LS Oct. 25, 1882
  of Round Rock, Texas
  on Oct. 18, 1882 in Hill's Prairie, Texas

ROGERS, Dr. W. S.   WYNNE, NETTIE E.   LS Nov. 19, 1884
  on Nov. 12, 1884 in Lampasas, Texas

ROMERO, ANTONIO   JURADO, NARCISA   LS Feb. 1, 1882
  license issued in January in El Paso, Texas

ROMERO, FARRON   ROMERO, FRANCISCO   EPT July 28, 1884
  on July 28, 1884 in El Paso, Texas by Judge A. M. LOOMIS

ROSE, DUDLEY C.   MELLEN, SHARLEY   EPDH Jan. 6, 1884
                                                     RGR Dec. 22, 1883
  on Dec. 27, 1883 in San Augustine, New Mexico by Rev. Dr. TAYS of El
  Paso, Texas; bride's sister: Mrs. H. M. FORSTER

ROSE, SOLON E.   MASON, Miss BOOKER   LS June 3, 1885
  of Albuquerque, N. M.   of Prospect, Tenn.

RUSSELL, Col. F.   CAMPBELL, EVA   LS Jan. 30, 1884
  on Jan. 26, 1884 (or 28) in Ysleta, Texas by Justice JOSE APODACA

RUSSELL, H. WAYNE   McCLELLAND, ADA M.   BU Sept. 19, 1885
                                                     BU Nov. 7, 1885
  on Sept. 16, 1885 in Magdalena, N. M. by Rev. N. W. CHASE

RUSSELL, HAMLIN   _____   EPT Sept. 4, 1883
  in St. Louis, Mo.; to be married (was married)

RUSSELL, HORACE J.   COLES, MAGGIE MAY   BU Nov. 14, 1885
  on Nov. 13, 1885 in Socorro, N. M. by Rev. N. W. CHASE; both of Magdalena, N. M.

RYNERSON, Col. W. L.   LEMON, Mrs. LUCIANA TB Dec. 28, 1872
  on Dec. 22, 1872 at Mesilla, N. M. by Rev. Father MORIN

SAAVEDRA, GREGORIO   MORENO, IRENE   SH Sept. 7, 1884
  in Guadalajara, Mexico in Civil Marriage

GROOM	BRIDE	PAPER and DATE

SANBORN, WILLIAM   DEAL, MARY B.   EPDH July 5, 1882
    Prof. of State Normal   of Cass co., Mo.
    School, Warrensburg, Mo.
    on June 21, 1882 in Raymore Twp., Cass co., Missouri by Rev. A. T.
    ROBERTSON at home of bride's uncle: W. H. BARRON, Esq.; bro.: B. F.
    DEAL, El Paso, Texas

SANCHEZ, JOSE   CADENA, CLARA   EPT Oct. 25, 1885
    license issued Oct. 19, 1885 at San Elizario, Texas

SAN JUAN   _____   RGR July 21, 1883
    Chief of Mescaleros   a squaw of Santa Fe, N. M.
    "Groom dressed in a fig-leaf, and the costume of the bride was entire-
    ly too previous"

SARGENT, Mr. _____   KENNETT, IDA   LS June 13, 1885
    in Santa Fe, N. M.

SAUNDERS, JAMES T.   MOORE, HELEN F.   LS Sept. 29, 1883
    on Sept. 25, 1883 in Albuquerque, N. M. by Judge C. C. McCOMAS

SCHENK, AUGUST   ADELMAN, ROSA   RGR June 16, 1883
    on June 6, 1883 in Catholic Church, Socorro, New Mexico by Rev. Fr.
    LESTRA; bride's bro's.: CHARLES & JOSEPH ADELMAN; couple will reside
    in Las Cruces, New Mexico

SCHILDKNECHT, ADOLPH, Jr.   BLANCHARD, ISABEL   LS Oct. 13, 1883
                            (BELLE M.)   LS Sept. 3, 1884
                                                 EPT Sept. 2, 1884
                                                 SH Aug. 31, 1884
    on Sept. 1, 1884 in Ysleta, Texas; bride's par.: WARD B. & ISABEL
    BLANCHARD

SCHUSTER, BERNHARD   ANGERSTEIN, EMILIE   LS Feb. 28, 1883
    on Feb. 24, 1883 in Paso del Norte, Mexico at bride's home, by Judge
    ESCOBAR; bride's par.: Mrs. SENOBIA ANGERSTEIN

SCHUTZ, Dr. H.   _____   EPT Dec. 10, 1884
    of Durango, Mex.
    bride's par.: Gov. of Durango, Mexico

SCHUTZ, MAX   SMITH, LOUISE   EPT Mar. 3, 1885
                                                 SH Mar. 8, 1885
    on Mar. 7, 1885 at El Paso, Texas

SCOTT, JOHN H.   BALLARD, ETTIE   EPT July 2, 1885
    last week in Abilene, Texas by Rev. BENNETT HATCHER; bride's father
    objected to marriage; all from Phantom Hill, Texas

SCOTT, SA VAMY   HENRY, LIZZIE   LS July 28, 1883
                                                 EPT July 26, 1883
    on July 25, 1883 in Windsor Hotel, El Paso, Texas by Rev. J. R. CARTER

SCUDDER, GILBERT   RITCH, NELLIE   LS June 6, 1883
    on June 21, 1883 in Church of Holy Faith, Santa Fe, New Mexico;bride's
    par.: M/M W. G. RITCH

SEAY, J. H.   CUTBIRTH, LENNIE   LS Nov. 15, 1884
    on Nov. 12, 1884 in Belle Plain, Texas

SENNA, GEORGE   CARRILLO, TERESITA   LS July 8, 1885
    on June 25, 1885 in Lincoln, New Mexico

SEWARD, EDWIN B.   DAVIS, EMMA   LS June 10, 1885
    of Santa Fe, N. M.   of Espanola, N. M.

SHAFTOE, ROBERT S.   DICKEY, BESSIE   LS Apr. 11, 1885
    of Belmont, Ohio/ in Albuquerque, N. M.

GROOM	BRIDE	PAPER and DATE

SHANNON, C. M.   RAY, Miss   LS July 8, 1885
   of Silver City, N. M.   of San Antonio, N. M.

SHANNON, CHARLEY   _____   BU June 27, 1885
   of Silver City, N. M.
   in San Antonio, Texas

SHANNON, CHARLES M.   BETTERTON, MOLLIE   LS Oct. 3, 1885
   of Silver City, N. M.   of Dallas, Texas
   on Oct. 13, 1885 in Dallas, Texas

SHAW, FLOYD P.   FROST, HARRIET E.   BU Sept. 12, 1885
   of Socorro, N. M.   of N. Evans, N. Y.
   on Sept. 10, 1885 in Socorro, New Mexico by Rev. N. W. CHASE

SHEERS, JOHN H.   _____, MARIA L.   BU Dec. 8, 1891
   in 1865; divorce petition

SHERIDAN, CHARLES B.   PALMER, ELIZABETH   EPT Oct. 25, 1885
   license issued Oct. 22, 1885 in El Paso, Texas

SHERIDAN, JOE   BARNEY, Mrs. J. G.   BU Jan. 1, 1885
                                  (widow)
   in Socorro, New Mexico; live at Cooney, N. M.

SHIELDS, BENJAMIN (negro)   ADAMS, JOSIE (white)   EPDH Apr. 5, 1882
                                  age 17
   in 1882 at Bexar county, Texas; bride's par.: J. C. ADAMS formerly of
   Highland, New York

SHIELDS, E. GARNER   _____   LS Jan. 11, 1882
                                  widow with 5 ch.
   in Chicago, Illinois; Chief engineer of Socorro R. R.

SHOWALTER, Prof. A. J.   WATZER, CALLY   LS Nov. 23, 1881
   on Nov. 13, 1881 in Giddings, Texas; music writer and publisher of
   Virginia

SHRYOCK, JOHN A.   _____   RGR Nov. 1, 1884
   of Organ, N. M.
   on Oct. 29, 1884; not yet learnt the name of the happy bride

SIEBOLD, F. H.   MASTERSON, PEARLE   LS Aug. 29, 1885
   on Aug. 25, 1885 in Deming, N. M.; bride's par.: Judge MURAT MASTER-
   SON

SILSBY, A. H.   MONTES, Miss   LS June 9, 1883
   Telegraph operator on Mex.
   Cent. R. R. at San Jose, Mex.
   on June 8, 1883 in Ysleta, Texas; bride's par.: Mrs. MONTES

SILVIA, FERDINAND   _____   LS May 6, 1885
   of Albuquerque, N. M.
   in Italy

SIMPSON, G. B.   BEAN, ANNA   EPT Sept. 6, 1883
                                  Castillian
   on Sept. 3, 1883 in Silver City, New Mexico

SMITH, JOHN   REED, ELLA   LS Dec. 12, 1885
                                  age 15
   eloped from Kopperl, Texas

SMITH, RANDOLPH W.   _____, LURA   BU Dec. 1, 1891
   on Jan. 25, 1880 in Michigan; divorce action, - 1 son NICHOLAS, age 10

SMITH, W. E.   COOB, CARRIE   LS Aug. 20, 1884
   on Aug. 18, 1884 in Silver City, New Mexico

GROOM	BRIDE	PAPER and DATE

SMITH, WILLIAM A.   WILLIAMS, Mrs. LOTTA EPT Apr. 19, 1885
 on Apr. 16, 1885 at residence of J. W. LOUDON, El Paso, Texas by Rev.
 GEORGE W. BAINES

SOLEY, W. B.   PANNELL, Mrs.   EPT Dec. 23, 1884
 license Dec. 17, 1884 in Albuquerque, New Mexico

SORENSON, JOHN   SMITH, ALICE C. LS Jan. 30, 1884
 of El Paso, Texas   of New Orleans, La.
 on Jan. 28, 1884 in El Paso, Texas by Rev. G. W. BAINES

SPEIGL, FRANK   GENTREY, LOTTIE LS Nov. 21, 1883
 on Nov. 19, 1883 in El Paso, Texas by Judge LOOMIS

SPENCER, A. W.   _____   EPT July 17, 1892
 celebrated 30th wedding anniversary - 1862

SPRINZ, RUDOLPH   KAMACK, SARAH   LS Sept. 19, 1883
 of El Paso, Texas   of New York City
 on Sept. 23, 1883 in New York City

SPRUNK, JOSEPH   LEE, Mrs. JENNIE LS Jan. 16, 1884
 of Organ, N. M.   of Organ, N. M. RGR Jan. 19, 1884
 on Jan. 16, 1884 in El Paso, Texas by JOSEPH MAGOFFIN, Mayor; par. of
 bride: W. S. LEE

STANTON, C. Q.   DOBSON, IDA   LS May 31, 1884
 (CHAPEL Q.?)   SH Jan. 11, 1885
 (CURTIS QUINTON?)
 on June 3, 1884 in San Antonio, Texas

STEEDMAN, J. H.   _____   LS Aug. 2, 1882
 Soda pop man of Las Cruces, N. M., will commit matrimony with a
 school marm lately of Las Cruces, New Mexico

STEIZER, FRANK   KODPRA, FANNIE LS Jan. 23, 1884
            of Raton, N. M.
 on Jan. 17, 1884 in Raton, New Mexico

STONE, JOHN A.   BARBER, WILLIE LS Dec. 28, 1881
 of Chapel Hill, Texas
 on Dec. 20, 1881 in Brenham, Texas

STOUDENMIRE, DALLAS   SHERRINGTON, BELLE EPDH Mar. 15, 1882
 on Feb. 22, 1882 in Columbus, Texas by Judge CHARLES RILEY

STUART, E. A.   HORNER, Miss   LS Nov. 19, 1884
 of El Paso, Texas
 on Nov. 13, 1884 in Rutland, Vermont

STUART, J. H.   _____   EPDH Sept. 30, 1883

STRATTON, GEORGE W.   THOMPSON, MINERVA E. RGR Oct. 4, 1884
 in Roswell, Lincoln county, New Mexico

SULLIVAN, GERALD   GEARY, ANNIE E. EPDH Nov. 1, 1882
            of Tiffin, Ohio
 in Tiffin, Ohio; he was formerly reporter in El Paso, Texas

SULLIVAN, JOHN   GONZALES, FRANCISCA EPT July 26, 1884
 license issued July 26, 1884 in El Paso, Texas

SUTHERLAND, S. H.   FINDLEY, CARRIE EPDH Aug. 5, 1883
 of El Paso, Texas
 last week in Greenville, Pa.

TABOR, Sen. H. A. W.   CLARK, _____ LS Mar. 3, 1883

GROOM	BRIDE	PAPER and DATE

TABOR cont'd: LS Mar. 10, 1883
                                                 LS Mar. 14, 1883
                          (she is of Denver, Colo.)
   to be married in Washington, D. C.; she was mistress - they visited
   Las Vegas, New Mexico; - aliases: DOE, DAVE & McCOURT. This marriage
   mentioned previously as Mrs. DOE. Both married previously and divorced.

TAFT, J. C.   DUFFY, NELLIE E.   LS Mar. 25, 1885'
                         of San Antonio, N. M.
   in Socorro, New Mexico

TARRIN, PASQUAL   VIRGIL, LUCE   EPDH Oct. 12, 1881
   on Oct. 5, 1881 in Ysleta, Texas

TAYLOR, JOSEPH (negro)   GOWENS, JOSEPHINE (white)
                                             EPDH Apr. 5, 1882
   in January 1882 in Bexar county, Texas

TAYS, Rev. JOSEPH W.   KIMBALL, VIOLA   EPDH Nov. 26, 1881
                         of Vallejo, Calif.
   on Nov. 22, 1881 in Vallejo, California

TAYS, L. (J.?) A.   SMITH, MINNIE SYDNEY EPT May 30, 1885
   of Ontario, Calif.   of Maitland, Hants SH May 31, 1885
                         co., Nova Scotia
   on May 28, 1885 in St. Clements Church, El Paso, Texas by Rev. JAMES
   HULME

TERRAZAS, E____ ELLO   WELCH, HELEN   EPT Sept. 29, 1883
                         Irish
   day or two ago in Paso del Norte, Mexico; he is nephew of Governor
   of Chihuahua.

THOMAS, BEVERLY G.   RAND, ELLIE   EPT Oct. 28, 1883
   on Oct. 26, 1883 in El Paso, Texas by Rev. Dr. TAYS; groom's par.:
   M/M GEORGE W. THOMAS; bride's par.: Maj. and Mrs. NOYES RAND; sister
   of bride: FLORRIE RAND; groom's sister: LILLIAN; many friends and
   relatives listed.

TIFFANY, ISAAC S.   POSEY, Miss ELIZA DIXON
                                             BU Apr. 28, 1885
                                             BU May 5, 1885
   on Apr. 29, 1885 in Socorro, N. M. by Rev. Dr. ROBINSON; bride's par.:
   Judge R. T. POSEY; groom's par.: M/M TIFFANY; groom's sis.: Mrs. W.
   O. GIBBS.

TINSLEY, R. I.   CUMMINGS, DAISY   LS Dec. 12, 1885
   eloped from Fort Worth, Texas

TOENNINGES, LOUIS   LUX, MARY   LS Sept. 10, 1884
                                             EPT Sept. 8, 1884
   on Sept. 7, 1884 in El Paso, Texas by Mayor JOSEPH MAGOFFIN; bride's
   par.: Mrs. ____ LUX

TOLLS, TOMMY   COFFEE, BERA   LS Oct. 15, 1884
   age 16   age 12
   eloped from Daingerfield, Texas; married in Indian Territory

TORREZ, ADOLFO   TORREZ, LUZ   BU Aug. 1, 1885
   on July 31, 1885 in Socorro, New Mexico

VAUGHN, ____   SPEED,____   EPT Dec. 23, 1884
   license issued Dec. 16, 1884 in Albuquerque, N. M.

VIGIL, VICENTE   CHAVEZ, TERESITA   BU July 25, 1885
   of Socorro, N. M.   of San Acacia, N. M. BU Aug. 1, 1885

VIGIL cont'd:
  on July 27, 1885 in San Acacia, New Mexico by Rev. P. H. MARTIN;groom's
  par.: ESQUIPULA VIGIL & wife; bride's par.: Mrs. MIGUELITA CHAVEZ;
  she is sis. of Mrs. GABRIEL PINO; he is nephew of MANUEL VIGIL.

VINCENT, WILLIAM A.   LS Nov. 21, 1885
  of N. M. (Judge)   of Springfield, Ill. BU Nov. 21, 1885
  on Nov. 17, 1885 in Springfield, Illinois

WADE, SAM H.   WITT, BLANCHE   LS Sept. 5, 1883
                                of Ysleta, Tex.   LS Oct. 6, 1883
  on Oct. 6, 1883 in Ysleta, Tex. by Rev. J. R. CARTER of El Paso, Tex.

WAGNER, BOB   EPDH June 22, 1884
                                widow of N. M.
  next week

WAGNER, HERBERT   MILLER, ELLA   LS Dec. 24, 1881
  on Dec. 15, 1881 in Crockett, Texas; bride's par.: Judge S. A. MILLER;
  groom's bro.: HAL WAGNER is foreman of E. P. Times office

WAGNER, ROBERT   _____   SH Jan. 18, 1885
  in San Francisco, California

WARD, JOHN W.   JOYCE, JANE   EPT Apr. 11, 1883
  on July 1, 1873 in Boston, Mass.; suit for divorce, El Paso Co., Tex.

WARREN, ALBERT J.   STEGER, CLARA M.   EPT Aug. 18, 1885
                                                   SH Aug. 23, 1885
  on Aug. 2, 1885 in El Paso, Texas by Rev. W. P. McCORKLE

WAUGH, Dr. J. C.   STONE, Mrs.   LS Nov. 30, 1881
  of Kentucky   widow of WARREN B.
                                STONE
  on Nov. 21, 1881 in Dallas, Texas

WELLS, FRANK   CANDELARIA, TRINIDAD LS June 10, 1885
  in Albuquerque, New Mexico

WELLS, LUTHER   WILLIAMS, MAGGIE   RGR Mar. 15, 1884
  of Lake Valley, N. M.   of Cambridge, Vt.

WHITE, GEORGE   FURGERSON, Miss ___ LS Feb. 25, 1882
  age 60, of Collins, Tex.   age 28
  few days ago

WHITE, JAMES H.   DUPER, BARBARA   LS Mar. 4, 1882
  on Mar. 2, 1882 in Las Cruces, N. M. home of Rev. Father LASSAIGNE

WHITE, THOMAS, Capt.   WOOD, NELLIE   LS Feb. 25, 1885
                                                   EPT Feb. 25, 1885
  on Feb. 24, 1885 in El Paso, Texas by Rev. MacDONELL; reception in
  home of bride's mother

WHITE, Z. T.   MATHIAS, MAGGIE   LS Nov. 22, 1882
  of El Paso, Texas   EPDH Nov. 22, 1882
  on Nov. 7, 1882 in Lynchburg, Va.

WILLIAMS, ED   _____   LS Oct. 15, 1884
  of Corpus Christi, Texas
  on Oct. 8, 1884

WILLIAMS, T. J.   OCHOA, Miss MAGDALENA
                                                   LS Feb. 10, 1883
  on Feb. 5, 1883 at Las Cruces, New Mexico at home of bride's parents
  by Rev. Father LASSAIGNE

GROOM	BRIDE	PAPER and DATE

WILLIAMSON, C.   CARROWAY, KATE   LS Sept. 3, 1884
  of Angus, Texas   age 15, of Corsi-
                          cana, Texas
  eloped last week for ceremony in Indian Territory

WILLIS, W. H.   KELLEY, ELINER   LS Oct. 7, 1885
                          age 14
  bride's par.: E. F. KELLEY, Bartlett, Texas

WILSON, H. H.   ADAMS, LUCINDA   LS May 2, 1885
  on Apr. 25, 1885 in Springer, New Mexico

WINN, CALVIN (negro)   PETTY, ANNIE (white) EPDH Apr. 5, 1882
  age 50   age 13
  in 1882 in Bexar county, Texas

WOODS, JOHN B.   FOSTER, ABBIE B.   LS Jan. 25, 1882
  of Washington, Mo.
  on Jan. 18, 1882 in San Antonio, Texas

WOODSIDES, ____   SMITH, ____   EPDH Mar. 9, 1884
  of Paso del Norte, Mex. of Paso del Norte, Mex.
  past week in El Paso, Texas by Rev. J. W. TAYS

WOODY, Dr. SAM   McIVER, EMMA   LS May 30, 1885
  of Louisville, Ky.   of Caldwell, Texas
  on May 9, 1885

WOOTON, DAN V.   BUTTROS, LILLIE   EPT May 19, 1885
  Engineer on Mex.-Cen. R.R.
  on May 11, 1885 in El Paso, Texas by Bishop H. W. READ

WUENSCH, A. F.   MAINEY, MARY E.   EPT Mar. 3, 1885
  license issued in El Paso, Texas

WULFF, HENRY   _____   EPDH Aug. 5, 1883
  formerly of El Paso, Texas
  just got married in San Antonio, Texas; has moved to Monterrey, Mex.

YATES, ENOCH   PEARMAN, Mrs. F. M. LS Oct. 10, 1883
  on Oct. 7, 1883 in Ysleta, Texas by Bishop H. W. READ

YOUNG, BENJAMIN   LORD, ELLA   BU Oct. 1, 1884
  on Sept. 29, 1884 in Socorro, New Mexico

YRISARRI, EUGENIO   PEREA, BARBARA   LS June 3, 1885
  in Santa Fe, New Mexico

ZOLLARS, Capt. J. W.   _____   EPDH May 10, 1882
  of El Paso, Texas   EPDH May 17, 1882
  in Ohio

Lone Star, Saturday, Aug. 2, 1882:
   ...mentioned among fines of drunks and fighting was "one busy house-
wife who was fined $2.00 for emptying a slop bucket into the streets".

Lone Star, Saturday, Sept. 9, 1882:
   Serious complaints re new cemetery established by city, on hill west
of the Sylvester Watts Water Works. Soil is loose gravel and next to im-
possible to dig a decent grave. Several burials have been delayed, after
the corpse and funeral procession had reached the cemetery, by the caving
in of the walls of the grave and the covering up of the box provided in
the bottom of the grave to receive the coffin, it being necessary to keep
the mourners waiting until the grave could be cleared out. Such inter-
ruptions at funerals are more than annoying - they are disgusting. If
the case is as bad as represented to us (i.e..editor), this cemetery
should be abandoned and a better site selected.

Lone Star, Saturday, Oct. 21, 1882:
   Three cents for 1,000 gallons of water in Buffalo (apparently N. Y.)
and 81.25 a thousand in El Paso! No wonder the people of this city drink
so much whiskey!

Lone Star, Saturday, Nov. 25, 1882:
   "Kingston, N. M. is not furnishing many sensational items in the way
of killings. This is a lack of enterprise for a new mining camp."

Lone Star, Saturday, Dec. 16, 1882:
   "When a letter is mailed in New Mexico there is a delightful uncertain-
ty about its ever reaching its destination."

Lone Star, Feb., 21, 1883:
   A teacher expelled a pupil at White Oaks, N. M. because he refused to
kindle a fire.

Lone Star, Apr. 7, 1883:
   Postal service by canoe has been established between Japan and Haines,
Alaska.

Lone Star, May 12, 1883:
   It would seem that Darwin's theories are to be confirmed from a total-
ly unexpected source and one that will convince many people. An exchange
says that the gentlemen now engaged in revising the Old Testament have
decided the word rib -- should be rendered tail, as the word originally
used had that signification.

Lone Star, May 23, 1883:
   The word dudine is being used by papers to signify the feminine of
dude.
   The name "Thirty Four" was given S. H. Newman's 1st paper in Las
Cruces, N. M. to memorialize the N. M. Shift from Republican to Demo-
cratic state by 34 vote win of Baca over Otero.

Lone Star, Oct. 10, 1883:
   Houston "Age" protests against exclusion of girls from State Agricul-
ture and Mechanic College.

Lone Star, Nov. 3, 1883:
   In Texarkana, the town lying partly in Texas and partly in Arkansas,
the Marshal for Texas and the Marshal for Arkansas were sent out to arrest a drunken man. It appears he was lying across the State line with
his head in Texas and his feet in Arkansas. Each Marshal argued for jur-
isdiction and finally the Texan won on the ground that the head was the
offending party as the legs did not intend to get drunk and had no part
in what superinduced intoxication.

EPH, Feb. 1, 1885:
   It is said that Burns' famous song, "Comin'Through the Rye", did not
have reference to a rye-field but to the samll river Rye, in Ayrshire,
which could be forded. In wading over, however, the lassies had to hold
up their petticoats, and it was a favorite pastime for Bobbie Burns and

mischievous companions to lie in wait for the lassies "comin' thro' the Rye". When they got midstream the 'laddies' would wade out and snatch a kiss from the 'lassies', who were unable to resist without dropping their clothes in the water.

Lone Star, Wed., Dec. 20, 1882:
  King of Omora in Western Coast of Africa leaves 700 widows.

EPDT, Aug. 28, 1884 - Stopping Street Cars
  In stopping street cars, an Omaha woman runs across the street and says "High"; a Council Bluffs woman shakes her Mother Hubbard; a Lincoln woman gives the Good Templar sign; a Boston woman shakes her book; a New York woman throws her parasol at the driver's head; a Brooklyn woman whistles; a Chicago woman puts her foot on the track; a St. Louis girl winks at the conductor; a Cincinnati woman says "Huba! Huba!, and the Pittsburg woman paralyzes the horses with a smile.

EPDT, Aug. 16, 1885:
  Kyle, Texas has no jail and prisoners are chained to a post. If they behave themselves, they are allowed the laon of an umbrella.

EPDT, Oct. 10, 1885:
  An old R. R. engineer writes --- "I can remember when a passenger train was almost as troublesome to manage as an ox cart on a hilly road. I was one of the first engineers that took a train over the State road. The engine was about the size of an ordinary stationary farm engine, and the cars were almost as small as those used on narrow-gauge roads. There were no brakes in those days. When the train drew near a station, speed was gradually reduced, and when the station was reached, railroad hands, armed with blocks of wood, would jump off and chock the wheels.

EPDT, Oct. 21, 1885:
  A singular accident caused the death of an inspector of trucks on the Mexican Central R. R., named LLAXAULPAS GUANAJUANIXZILIXIHUAPAN at MEGOWTUALXICOTPTIZLATANA. He was keying a CUERPZTZOPILOTEHUAHUAHUA under the TLALPAMJALAPACUAC when the spring hanger broke and cut off the in-spector's neck. His remains were taken by the coroner of HUEHUETOCA to TLALASPANTIA for interment. The LIFEZIXTL of a RAILROADTLAHANACANER in Mexico is ENVIRONEDIEPUCATAN with PERILDUACUARO.

www.ingramcontent.com/pod-product-compliance
Lightning Source LLC
Chambersburg PA
CBHW021859020426
42334CB00013B/406